BASIC PROCESSES IN READING:
Perception and Comprehension

Summer Institute on Perception and Comprehension

BASIC PROCESSES IN READING:
Perception and Comprehension

EDITED BY

DAVID LABERGE
S. JAY SAMUELS
University of Minnesota

 LAWRENCE ERLBAUM ASSOCIATES, PUBLISHERS
1977   Hillsdale, New Jersey

DISTRIBUTED BY THE HALSTED PRESS DIVISION OF

JOHN WILEY & SONS

New York   Toronto   London   Sydney

Lawrence Erlbaum Associates, Inc., Publishers
62 Maria Drive
Hillsdale, New Jersey 07642

Distributed solely by Halsted Press Division
John Wiley & Sons, Inc., New York

Library of Congress Cataloging in Publication Data

Summer Institute on Perception and Comprehension,
    University of Minnesota, 1975.
    Basic processes in reading.

    Lectures of an institute held in June 1975 and
sponsored by the Center for Research in Human Learning,
University of Minnesota.
    Includes bibliographical references and index.
    1. Reading––Congresses.   2. Perceptual Learning––
Congresses.   3. Reading Comprehension––Congresses.
4. Reading––Physiological aspects––Congresses.
I. Laberge, David L.   II. Samuels, S. Jay.
III. Minnesota. University. Center for Research in
Human Learning.   IV. Title.

LB1049.95.s897 1975   428'.4   77-17135
ISBN 0-470-99354-5

Printed in the United States of America

Contents

Preface

The purpose of this volume is to present the most recent theoretical views and experimental findings by prominent psychologists working in areas they consider to be most basic to the reading process. The chapters contain material that should be of value not only to persons interested in the applied and basic aspects of reading but also to those interested in language processing and information processing in general. The reason for the breadth of implications of a book of this kind is that the reading process involves an amazingly wide range of cognitive functions.

The book divides conveniently into two areas, perception and comprehension. The initial chapters are concerned with the perceptual processing involved in reading. In the first chapter, Estes sets the pace by describing the problems that reading research will have to deal with before we can understand how graphemic material is processed through the perceptual systems. James Anderson's chapter then gives us a glimpse into the neurophysiological substrata of the perceptual and comprehension process. Fortunately, this chapter does not lead the reader into a forest of physiological structures and terms, but emphasizes the relationship between a few basic neurological functions and psychological counterparts as exemplified by current research by Sternberg and Posner.

Neal Johnson's chapter is a frontal attack on the question of how small orthographic units are organized in perception. Johnson's concern, like that of Estes, strikes at the heart of a currently active question in reading. The problem is whether a perceptual unit is built up solely from its components or whether it comes about from emergent properties of the graphemic configuration.

The chapter by Schneider and Shiffrin treats the problem of attention in visual information processing. At early stages in learning to read, a good deal of attention is required for processing, especially at perceptual levels. Presumably, as fluency is attained, larger units come into play, and what previously required attention, now becomes automatic.

As a stimulating contrast to the information-processing approach of the previous authors, E. J. Gibson presents her framework for reading. Her basic differences concern the amount of processing intervening between sensory input and meaning and the possible ways that feedback mechanisms permit cognitive operations later in the system to influence operations such as visual processing, which occurs earlier in the system.

Next, Baron takes up problems related to those discussed by Gibson, because he is also interested in the ways vision, phonology, and meaning are interrelated in reading. In particular he explores the possibility that pronouncing words is involved in reading for meaning, even when the reader is fluent. This would seem to rule out theories that assume a single direct link between visual processing and meaning.

With the chapter by Carpenter and Just, the book proceeds into the area of comprehension. Comprehension is viewed by Carpenter and Just as an integrative process in which textual information from words and clauses is related to other information already in memory. Also, Carpenter and Just's model of information processing is extended to the writing of prose.

Closely related to the Carpenter-Just view of comprehension is the paper by Clark in which the role of inference in comprehension is examined in considerable detail. There is a contract between the writer and the reader and between the speaker and listener called the given–new contract, which is necessary if the reader or listener is to make the appropriate inferences based upon the information he receives.

If the previous two chapters could be characterized by dealing with the comprehension of words, clauses, and sentences, then the chapter by Rumelhart may be described as comprehension at the more global level of complete stories. Starting with a general model of story comprehension, Rumelhart accounts for details of structure typically found in many stories and shows how the gist of a story can be characterized by the model. Furthermore, the gist of a story is related to the way people recall simple stories by way of summarizations. This work could provide valuable guides for the continuing search for better measures of reading comprehension.

The final chapter by John Anderson is concerned with language acquisition from the point of view of an induction process. His immediate goal is to develop a computer program capable of learning language. In the process of developing the program of language acquisition, insights into how humans acquire language are produced. At first glance this problem might seem to be inappropriate for a book of this kind. However, in some ways the acquisition of reading could be considered the acquisition of a new language, especially if reading acquisition is considered from the beginning as a linguistic process. One model of the reading-acquisition process posits that skill acquisition is a hierarchical process in which small units are integrated into larger units in a bottom-up fashion until whole sentences are picked up by the child. On the other hand, one could take the position that the learning of even the smallest orthographic units takes place within a larger linguistic context. Furthermore, this linguistic context may not be completely parasitic on speech, but may have linguistic structures of its own which must be acquired. If this is the case, then the kind of problem that Anderson addresses may turn out to be of critical importance to the development of fluent reading skill.

This book is the outgrowth of a Summer Institute on Perception and Comprehension sponsored by the Center for Research in Human Learning at the University of Minnesota as part of the Center's training program. The conference, held in June, 1975, was organized by Dr. David LaBerge of the Psychology Department and Dr. S. Jay Samuels of the Psychological Foundations of Education Department. Ten scholars were invited to address the faculty and students of the Center on topics related to the processes underlying reading. These lectures have been brought together in this volume.

The editors gratefully acknowledge the invaluable assistance of Kathleen Casey, Helen Murphy, Penelope Pinson, and the staff of the Center for Research in Human Learning at the University of Minnesota, who managed to make the complicated arrangements of a two-week conference run very smoothly and who gave invaluable help in all phases of the preparation of this book. We also wish to acknowledge the assistance of Chris Bremer and Lee Brownston in the construction of the Index.

Finally, we wish to thank the National Institute of Child Health and Human Development whose grant (HD-00098) to the Center for Research in Human Learning supported the conference and made this volume a reality.

David LaBerge
S. Jay Samuels

BASIC PROCESSES IN READING:
Perception and Comprehension

1

On the Interaction of Perception and Memory in Reading

W. K. Estes

Rockefeller University

The recent surge of interest in reading on the part of experimental psychologists doubtless has at least two sources of motivation. One of these has to do with the urgent social problems of dealing with literacy and reading disabilities, the other with the fact that reading embodies a number of aspects of perception and memory that are of much current interest in their own right. The psychology of reading had a flying start during the first few years of this century with the pioneering work of Cattell (1886) and Huey (1908), using ingenious experimental techniques and instrumentation for the measurement of eye movements in reading and the analysis of perception during single fixations – work that has been improved upon but little down to the present. The slow development of the psychology of reading as a specialty within cognitive psychology, following that auspicious beginning, must be attributed, I think, to the fact that for many decades the state of theory lagged behind the advance of experimental methodology, and as a consequence concepts and models were not available to interpret the findings that laboratory techniques were capable of delivering.

Perhaps the first important accomplishment of experimental psychology in this area was to clarify the nature of the problem that the task of reading presents to an individual's cognitive processing system. The problem turned out to be quite different, and distinctly more complex, than might have been anticipated on the basis of impressions gained from everyday experience. If the reader of this chapter allows his eyes to run along the line of type at the top of Fig. 1, he may have the impression that his eyes move smoothly along the line, allowing him to see all of the letters, and that once he has seen the letters, he recognizes familiar words, then remembers their meanings and as a consequence comprehends the message conveyed by the passage of text. But the facts are quite different. In actuality, as every psychologist now knows, the eyes do not

1

move continuously and the letters are seen with varying degrees of distinctness (to the point where some may be missed altogether). Further, no discrete successive stages of sensation, perception, and comprehension can be marked off; rather, processes of perception and memory interact in complex ways throughout the succession of stages of visual processing that lead from the original sensory experience to comprehension of the text.

If, rather than allowing his eyes to move along the top line in Fig. 1, the reader fixates his gaze for a few moments at each of the points marked by an arrow, he can satisfy himself that what he is able to make out during each of these fixations has much the character of the illustrative displays on the lines below, these having been constructed, on the basis of tachistoscopic research, to represent approximately what we would expect a person to be able to report from each fixation. Only a few letters on either side of a fixation point can be distinguished at all: those at the center in general clearly, and sometimes also those more remote if they come at the end of a word. The arrows in the figure represent the points at which fixations actually occurred in the case of an experimental subject whose eye movements were photographed in a study cited by Woodworth (1938). It can be assumed that the eyes moved from one of these fixation points to the next so rapidly that nothing could be seen during the movements. The first task of the processing system during reading, then, must be to accept this typically fragmented and irregular stimulus input, clean it up, fill in gaps in a reasonable way, and generate a representation of the letter sequence that gave rise to the input at a level more abstract than that of the physical stimulus pattern. The second task entails an interaction between this representation and other informational inputs either from the background context or from the long-term memory system to enable the recognition of words and their meanings.

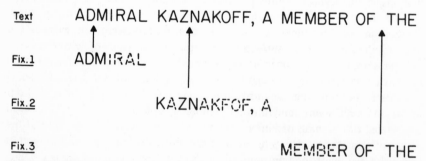

FIG. 1 Illustration of the sequence of fixations (indicated by vertical arrows) made by an individual while reading the line of text at the top. Below each fixation point is shown a hypothetical reconstruction of effective stimulus input during the fixation, letters near the fixation point being seen clearly and those further away less clearly, but always with an advantage for letters adjacent to spaces.

PROVISIONAL CHARACTERIZATION OF THE INTERACTION
OF PERCEPTION AND MEMORY: THE HIERARCHICAL FILTER MODEL

At a very general level, the way in which memory must enter into reading may seem almost obvious. Visual processing of text gives rise to representations of stimulus patterns, which are then compared with representations in memory of patterns previously experienced. Familiar patterns constituting syllables, words, or even larger units are recognized and by way of associative processes activate components of the semantic memory system that constitute or generate the meaning of the material perceived. The fundamental problem for a theory of reading is to prescribe more specifically just how this process of comparisons between sensory input and memory is accomplished.

Consider, say, the word "Admiral" in the top line of Fig. 1. Presumably, there exists in the memory system of each reader a representation of this word with which the sensory input could in some sense be compared—perhaps several representations, since the word may have been encountered in different type styles. But this word is only one among many thousands represented in the mental lexicon. Although it would be possible for each incoming sensory pattern to be compared successively with all of the word patterns in memory in search of a match (and just this procedure is followed in some primitive computer programs for pattern recognition), such a process seems exceedingly cumbersome in the light of the relatively slow rates of transmission of messages in the nervous system. It is conceivable that words are classified and encoded primarily in terms of a limited number of attributes or features having to do with overall shape and the like, but although this suggestion has been put forward many times, it has not yet adduced any substantial empirical support. Some specific relevant evidence will be presented in connection with an experiment to be described in a later section. In the meantime, I shall proceed on the assumption that global attributes of words play only a subsidiary role in word recognition.

A more promising approach arises from the observation that the word "Admiral," like any other, is not simply an arbitrary pattern of contours but, rather, is generated by a system of alphabetic elements. A recognition system that makes use of the properties of the alphabet can capitalize on the very large differences in frequency of occurrence of elements at different levels. The word "Admiral" occurs rather seldom in ordinary English text, but the constituent letter "A" occurs very much more often, and the horizontal bar in the A more frequently still. Cognizance of this important property of the alphabetic system led psychologists to the observation that the letters of the alphabet can be generated by combining in appropriate ways a smaller set of frequently occurring constituents, or "critical features," just as the large number of words in the lexicon can be generated by combining in appropriate ways the very much smaller number of letters (Geyer & DeWald, 1973; Gibson, 1969; Lindsay & Norman, 1972; Rumelhart, 1971).

The next step toward a model was the hypothesis that to these elementary constituents of letters there correspond organized subsystems in memory, "feature detectors," whose function is to sift the sensory input and transmit messages to higher levels of the system whenever their critical features are recognized.

In the current work of Estes (1975a, b) and LaBerge and Samuels (1974), it may be seen that a model incorporating a hierarchical arrangement of detectors can efficiently take advantage of the frequency properties of the alphabetic system and begin to provide a plausible account of some properties of letter and word recognition.

In this model, as illustrated in Fig. 2, it is assumed that detectors with similar properties are organized at the levels of critical features (F), letters (L), and

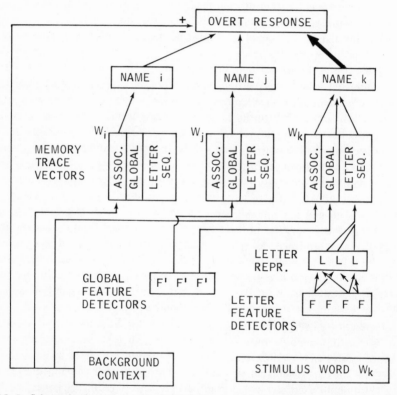

FIG. 2 Schematization of the hierarchical filter model for letter and word recognition. Visual input from a stimulus word is filtered initially through global feature detectors (F') and letter feature detectors (F). Output of F-combinations activate representations of letters (L); these in turn transmit to letter-sequence components of the memory trace vectors of words (W), through which are filtered all sources of information (including background context) contributing to activation of a letter-name response.

letter groups such as syllables and words (W). A detector at any level may be regarded as a memory trace or engram built up as a consequence of the individual's past experience with a particular frequently recurring subpattern. This trace structure functions as an interactive filter (Anderson, 1973), or logical gate, in the communication channel from the peripheral sensory mechanisms to higher cognitive centers. It is activated by an incoming pattern of information from the photoreceptors only if the input pattern matches the one that gave rise to the trace structure: When a match occurs, the detector is activated and transmits a pattern of excitation to the next higher level in the system; but when no match occurs, transmission through the given channel is blocked.

Efficiency is obtained at the first stage of processing in that the sensory input pattern need be directed only to a small number of feature detector units rather than to a very large number of detectors for letters or words. The process of comparison and selective transmission is assumed to continue through the higher levels of the system. If the combination of features corresponding to a particular letter is activated by the input on a given occasion, then the excitation transmitted from these in turn activates the representation of the corresponding letter.

One might ask whether efficiency is not lost as the system passes from the letter to the word level in that the pattern of excitation from a group of simultaneously activated letter detectors would have to be transmitted to all of the word patterns at the next level in order not to miss the possibility of a match. The answer, I suggest, is twofold. First, it is likely that the representations of the letter sequences of words are not accessed randomly but, rather, are so organized that excitation from the letter detectors is directed to subsets of word representations that have attributes in common, as, for example, the initial letter.[1] Second, and perhaps more important, the representation of a word in long-term memory must be assumed to incorporate more information than a particular letter sequence. Rather, as illustrated in Fig. 2, the memory trace vector for a word includes several components: (1) traces of verbal contexts in which it has frequently occurred (in effect, associations with other words); (2) global attributes of the printed word (outline shape, relative length, etc.); and (3) the letter sequence.

The sources of sensory and associative input to the components of a word trace vector in memory must be assumed to operate independently, often asynchronously, and with differing degrees of specificity. Input via associative paths from the background context provided by other words or letters perceived prior to or simultaneously with a given stimulus word will in general lead to partial activation both of the stimulus word and of many other words that share

---

[1] Since this passage was written, a study by Smith and Jones (1975) has appeared, presenting some empirical evidence for the hypothesis that verbal memory is organized in terms of the initial phonemes of words.

semantic attributes with it. Similarly, input from the global feature detectors excited by a stimulus word will partially activate the trace vectors of that word and others with similar visual patterns. Only the representation of the letter sequence of a stimulus word, activated by way of the critical feature system, generates input solely to the trace vector of that word. As a consequence of the convergence of inputs from the several sources on the trace vector of the stimulus word, its naming response will be more strongly and quickly activated than those of other words that share its associative or global attributes. Whether or not an overt response will occur on a given occasion depends also on nonspecific input from the background context (including the general task environment and instructions) to the response system.

If the stimulus displayed were a nonword letter string, or an isolated letter, processing through the critical feature system to the level of letter representations would proceed similarly. The output of the letter level would find no match at the word level, but would be transmitted to letter name and overt response mechanisms (by paths not shown in Fig. 2). Again, the actual occurrence of an overt response would depend on concurrent excitatory input from the background context to the response system. An important difference between word stimuli and random letter strings is that for the latter the naming response would not receive concurrent input from associative paths and global feature detectors. Consequently, if, say, a word and a random string were simultaneously displayed for a brief interval, a likely outcome is that input from the word would capture the naming response system and gain access to short-term memory while that from the random string would be lost.

EVIDENCE BEARING ON THE MODEL

The critical question demanding consideration at this point is the state of evidence for the type of model envisaged here. It is easy to imagine elaborate mechanisms that might account for the reading process, much more difficult to provide evidence that sharply distinguishes one possible interpretive schema from another. I shall try to address this problem in the remainder of this chapter by considering in turn a number of principal aspects of letter and word recognition as they are presumed to occur in reading, and presenting illustrations of what at present seems to me the most cogent evidence in each case bearing on the adequacy of the hierarchical, interactive filter model.

Sensory Channel Interactions

Although in the study of reading one's concern is primarily with the recognition of meaningful units such as words, an orderly account of the process must begin with consideration of factors that influence the perception of letters per se, whether or not they occur in meaningful contexts. As we have already noted, the eye, when registering the contents of a segment of text, does not act at all like a camera but, rather, transmits to the central processing mechanisms an uneven and often fragmented representation of the stimulus pattern that falls on the retina.

A typical result, from the standpoint of the observer, of viewing a string of letters for a brief interval is portrayed in the serial position functions in Fig. 3. These data are taken from a study by Estes, Allmeyer, and Reder (1976) in which subjects were presented with random strings of four consonant letters displayed in horizontal arrays in locations either near the fixation point (Positions 1–4) or further toward the periphery (Positions 4–7) of the visual field. The observer's task was to report as many letters as possible from each display, and the plotted points represent proportions of correct reports from each letter position. In the experiment, letter strings occurred also in corresponding positions to the left of the fixation point, but for convenience the serial position

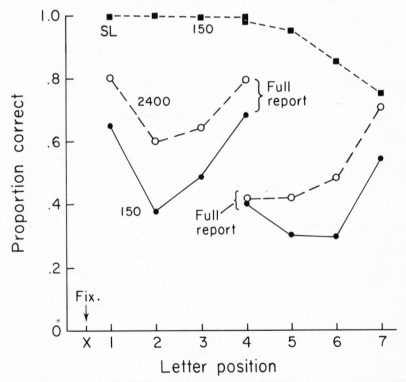

FIG. 3 Serial position functions for report of single letters (SL) or elements of multiletter arrays displayed at different distances from the fixation point (data from Estes, Allmeyer, & Reder, 1976).

functions have been "folded" so as to extend only to the right of the fixation point. If we consider first the functions for 150-msec exposures and the full-report procedure, we see just the picture that would be expected on the basis of the hypothetical illustration in Fig. 1. On the whole, correctness of report falls off from the center toward the periphery of the visual field, but even more conspicuously, perceptibility is poor in the interior positions of a string and much better at the ends.

The proper interpretation of these effects is, however, not immediately obvious. In fact, in the literature running back over many decades, explanations of two alternative types have been in continuing competition (Woodworth, 1938; Coltheart, 1972). One recurring hypothesis is that the apparent variations in perceptibility are actually due to limitations of memory; the observer actually sees the entire display of letters clearly for a brief instance, but is unable to hold all of the items in short-term memory long enough to report them. On this hypothesis, the form of the serial position function would have to be accounted for on the basis of the individual's strategy in tending to report the end items before the middle items. The alternative mode of explanation refers instead to properties of the visual system such as acuity and lateral inhibition.

At the time of Woodworth's (1938) review, it was difficult to choose between these interpretations, but a substantial body of data now available seems to point quite clearly to the conclusion that the serial position effects primarily represent degradations of input owing to properties of the visual system. This point can be illustrated by two other sets of curves from the Estes, Allmeyer, and Reder study, also included in Fig. 3. At the top of the figure are seen the results of a variation in which letters were presented at the same locations and for the same duration but singly rather than as components of multielement strings. Here memory limitations could scarcely have been a factor, but, as might have been expected on the basis of what is known concerning acuity at central and peripheral regions of the retina, the serial position function falls off smoothly with the distance from the fixation point to the periphery. However, the decrease is small compared to that observed in the 150-msec multielement displays.

To pin down the role of viewing time per se, four-letter displays were presented with the full-report procedure for very long exposures of 2,400 msec, but with the observer's eyes monitored so that they could not stray from the fixation point during stimulus exposure. Under this condition, limitations of memory should again have been negligible, since four letters is well within the memory span and 2,400 msec is adequate time to permit pronunciation of four letters. Nonetheless, the level of report is far below that of single letters and the forms of the serial position curves are very similar to those obtained with full report at the shorter exposure.

It is difficult to escape the conclusion that in the case of the multielement display, input is degraded at some early point in visual processing as a consequence of interactions between the processes initiated by adjacent letters. I have suggested elsewhere (Estes, 1972) that the entire pattern of results can be conveniently conceptualized in terms of the notion of input channels from the periphery to central feature detector mechanisms, the density of these channels being greatest near the fovea and decreasing toward the periphery, and with the magnitude of the lateral inhibitory interactions between concurrently activated channels varying inversely with the distance between them.

A question that comes to mind in connection with these results on serial position effects is why a reader under ordinary conditions is not normally aware of these patterns of degradation of input. One part of the answer, no doubt, is that the severely degraded inputs from segments of text remote from the fixation point simply are habitually ignored, but can readily be perceived if one's attention is directed to them. A more interesting question concerns the basis of the practiced reader's ability to recognize words that fall within a few degrees of the fixation point even though there must often be imperfect information available to higher processing centers concerning some of the interior letters. The answer suggested within the framework of the hierarchical model is based on the properties of the interactive filter mechanism. As illustrated for a particular example in Table 1, it is assumed that earlier occurrences of a clearly perceived stimulus pattern, the word *HAT* in the table, have established a trace structure, $[W_H]$, in the long-term memory system. On later occasions, stimulus inputs from a newly presented instance of the word (Occasion 2 in the table) are transmitted to the location of this trace structure, and if a match of the input pattern to the trace pattern occurs, then the trace structure activates continuing pathways responsible for the conscious experience of having seen the given word and also activation of the response mechanism responsible for its pronunciation. A partially degraded stimulus input (Occasion 3 in the table), as might arise from a brief exposure or a presentation in peripheral vision, would activate the response mechanism less strongly, whereas an incompatible input (Occasion 1) would not be transmitted beyond the level of memory vectors at all. The output of the comparison process is assumed to be all or none, in the sense that an input closely matching the memory trace leads to activation of the output pathways

TABLE 1

Possible Response Outcomes Resulting from Comparisons
between Various Stimulus Inputs and the Memorial
Representation (W_H) of the Word *Hat*

Occasion	Stimulus	Memory vector	Response
1	HAX	$[W_H]$	—
2	HAT	$[W_H]$	"HAT"
3	H\T	$[W_H]$	"HAT"

with probability near unity, a slightly degraded input has a slightly lower probability of activating the output pathways, and so on, but operation of the response mechanism is the same whether it is activated by a closely matching or an imperfectly matching input.

Interactions between Perceptual and Linguistic Factors

The Word Advantage

One of the bodies of data that gave rise to the filter model, at least the version I have presented, has been generated by the many studies showing advantages for the perception of a letter embedded in a word as compared to a letter embedded in a nonword display of letters (for reviews, see Baron, 1977; Estes, 1975a; Massaro, 1975; Smith & Spoehr, 1974). According to the model, the extent of the "word advantage" should be expected to depend on the way task parameters of a particular experiment constrain the level of processing of display information that provides the basis for the subject's response.

If the subject's response depends solely on a difference at the level of critical features between the target included in a display and the alternative target that might have been present, then the linguistic properties of other letters present in the display should have no effect. This condition is most closely realized in forced-choice detection studies in which the subject knows in advance of a block of trials the set of target letters (usually exactly two alternatives) that may be presented (e.g., Bjork & Estes, 1973; Thompson & Massaro, 1973). These studies have indeed yielded no trace whatsoever of an advantage for word over nonword contexts.

The results just cited presuppose the use of the WW–NN control introduced by Reicher (1969). The control refers to the construction of the displays used in the series according to a plan such that a subject who perceives some of the context letters but not the target in a display and chooses his response so as to complete a word will be unable to improve his likelihood of a correct response. The WW strings include a target letter embedded in a word with the property that substitution of the alternative target letter will also complete a word. If, for example, targets L and R were used equally often during a series of tasks, an acceptable WW string would be RENT, in which the target letter is R but in which another acceptable word would be produced by replacing R with L. Analogously, NN strings have the property that a target letter is embedded in a nonword string that remains a nonword if the alternative target letter replaces the one presented.

The WW–NN condition is negatively oriented in that it is sufficient only to rule out certain effects. One can, however, make progress toward distinguishing and monitoring the facilitating effects of context at different levels of processing when they do occur by combining the WW–NN with a WN–NW condition, as done by Bjork and Estes (1973). In this design, which might be termed W–N factorial, half of the trials conform to the WW—NN constraint. Of the remaining trials, half employ WN strings, the target letter being embedded in a word such that substitution of the alternative target letter would convert the word into a nonword; the other half employ NW strings, the target being embedded in a nonword so composed that substitution of the alternative target would convert the string into a word. On the trials on which the WN—NW condition is in effect, a subject who perceives some of the letters of a display but misses the target and responds on the basis of a bias for forming words will always be correct on WN displays and never on NW displays.

With this design we can expect to ascertain whether a word context facilitates detection of a target letter, and, if there is an effect, whether it should be attributed to a perceptual interaction, which would be revealed by a difference between WW and NN trials, or to an effect of redundancy, which would be revealed by a difference between WN and NW trials.

To show how these potentialities can be exploited, I shall develop some specific implications of the filter model for both detection and identification of letters in experiments conducted with the W—N factorial design. It will be convenient to continue to use the example in Table 1 for illustrative purposes. Suppose, first, that we are dealing with a forced-choice detection experiment with the WW—NN control, A and I being the alternative targets and HAT the display on a given trial. If the H and T are clearly perceived, but only some features of the A, it is likely that a representation of HAT at the word level in the memory system will be activated, since, of the word representations partially activated by the H_T, (HIT, HAT, HOT, HUT), HAT is favored by the partial feature information from the A in middle letter position. However, this event will confer no advantage on correct detection of the A embedded in HAT as compared to an A embedded in an NN string, say XAG; for the same partial feature information would in the latter case, as well as in the former, lead directly to a choice of A, rather than I, from the set of possible targets.

If, however, the displays were of the type WN (e.g., HAT displayed with A and D as alternative targets) versus NW (e.g., HDT displayed with the same alternative targets), the result would be quite different. If, again, all of the features of the first and third letters were detected, then even if no features of the middle letter were detected, a subject would necessarily be correct on the WN but incorrect on the NW display if he followed the strategy of selecting from the word representations partially activated the only one compatible with one of the target alternatives and responding accordingly.

The key point in terms of the model is that the partial feature information obtained from a stimulus letter may suffice to bias the individual's choice between known alternative targets or between partially activated memorial representations of words in the direction of a correct detection response, but at the same time may be insufficient to evoke a letter name response. Further, an advantage for a word context is expected to appear only on trials when context letters are better perceived than the target letter. Under ordinary circumstances, this state of affairs obtains on some unknown fraction of the trials of an experimental series, thus rendering predictions of context effects somewhat indeterminate. However, by appropriate experimental manipulations, it is possible to bring the relationship between perceptibility of target and context under experimental control.

Experimental Manipulations of Stimulus Asynchrony between Target Letter and Context

A procedure that achieves the desired objective was used by Estes (1975b) in a W—N factorial experiment in which the exposure duration of target and context letters of a display were varied independently, as illustrated in Fig. 4. Four-letter displays were presented on an oscilloscope screen controlled by means of a computer with programming that enabled the exposure durations of the target and the context letters of a display to be varied independently. The subject knew in advance the two possible targets, L and R, that would be used throughout a block of trials. On each trial, following a warning signal, a four-letter display including one or the other of the target letters was exposed for an interval of 15—25 msec, followed by a row of mask characters resembling dollar signs that remained in view until the subject made his response. In making up the display strings, the targets L and R were used equally often, and each was embedded equally often in word (WW or WN) and nonword (NW or NN) strings.

Previous studies (e.g., Bjork & Estes, 1973; Estes, Bjork, & Skaar, 1974) had used only the standard condition, shown at the top, in which both the target

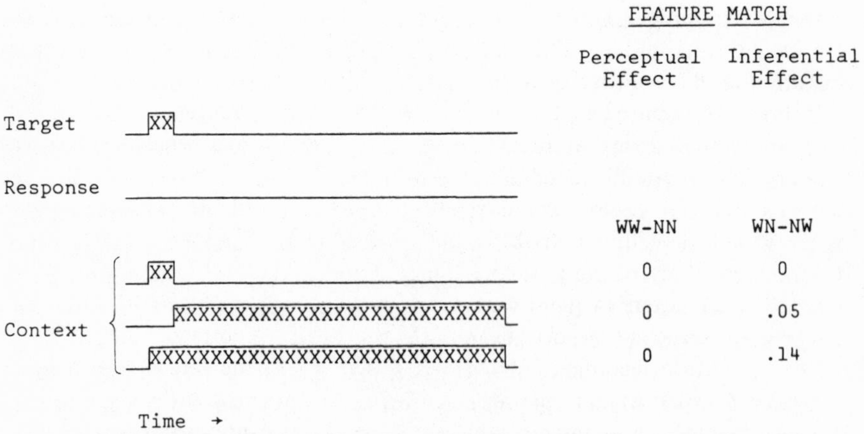

	FEATURE MATCH	
	Perceptual Effect	Inferential Effect
Target		
Response		
	WW-NN	WN-NW
Context	0	0
	0	.05
	0	.14

Time →

FIG. 4 Schematization (at left) of temporal relationships between onsets and offsets of target and context letters within a trial, together with summary data (from Estes, 1975b) for differences in detection probabilities between word and nonword displays under two control conditions.

letter and the context letters making up the word or nonword string all appear together; under this condition, no difference had been reported in percentage of correct detections between word and nonword strings. In the second and third conditions illustrated in Fig. 4, the target letter appears for the usual brief exposure, but the context letters of the display are available for a much longer interval, their onset being simultaneous with either the onset or the offset of the target letter, and in either case continuing until the subject makes his response, typically an interval of 1,000–2,000 msec. Thus, in the second and third arrangements, we can be sure that the subject perceives all of the context letters and the question is what the effect will be upon detectability of the target.

Under these circumstances, as anticipated on the basis of the preceding analysis, there were no differences in accuracy of detection between WW and NN displays under any condition, but in both of the conditions involving prolonged display of context letters, an advantage appeared for WN over NW strings.

The large difference in effectiveness between the Following and Continuing conditions fits well with an account in terms of the matching process of the filter model, but would not seem easily interpretable in terms of the principal alternative explanation – some form of sophisticated guessing. It should be noted in this connection that the diagrams at the left of Fig. 4 illustrating the temporal conditions of contextual display are not drawn to scale and that the difference in duration of the display of context between the Following and Continuing conditions is extremely small (10–25 msec where the overall duration is on the order of 1,000–2,000 msec). Thus, the opportunities for deliberate guessing on the basis of redundant information are essentially equal. Evidently, the critical difference is the simultaneous onset of target and contextual letters in the Continuing condition as compared to the asynchrony in the Following condition. This variable would be expected to be important only on the matching hypothesis. The pattern of on-effects in the visual pathways at the beginning of a word display would be more similar to those the individual had previously experienced in the case of the Continuing arrangement than in the case of the Following arrangement, and thus the former would tend more strongly to facilitate the matching process.

It is of interest also to examine the time course of the development of the word advantage within a trial. To this end, I have presented in Table 2 an additional analysis of the portion of the Estes (1975b) data representing detection of target letters in word versus nonword displays with the Following and Continuing contexts. Proportions of correct detections (corrected for guessing) are categorized in accordance with the reaction times of the detection responses. It will be seen that when responses occurred within 500 msec there is no trace of a word advantage. A difference between the W and N contexts begins to emerge for responses taking from 500 to 1,000 msec, and becomes very large for responses occurring at still longer reaction times. There would seem to be no support here for the perennially recurring suggestion that the word advantage

TABLE 2
Proportion of Detections[a] of Target Letters in
Word and Nonword Displays as a Function of
Reaction Time and Context

Reaction time (MSEC)	Context			
	Following		Continuing	
	W	N	W	N
0–500	.71	.85	.65	.64
500–1000	.74	.66	.71	.63
1000–1500	.63	.50	.48	.25
1500–2000	.23	.10	.42	.15

[a]Corrected for guessing.

depends on the perception of global features prior to the perception of individual letters. But on the other hand, the data follow just the pattern expected on the assumption that the faster responses are based on matches between input and memory at the level of individual features of the target letter whereas the slower responses represent cases when such matches did not occur and responses were based on decisions between partially activated letter groups at a later stage of processing.

Levels of Processing in Relation to Pre- and Postcue Conditions

In summary, all available evidence indicates that when recognition can be accomplished on the basis of a feature difference between familiar targets known in advance, a word context influences performance only by contributing redundant information. When conditions permit, this information enters into the decision process; otherwise it exerts no effect on recognition of a target letter. But although feature extraction evidently proceeds independently of linguistic context, we should expect, within the framework of the filter model, that the same would not be true of full identification. If a task requires the encoding of a target letter to the point of evocation of a naming response, then there are several avenues through which context may influence the process. First, properties of the context may alter the individual's criterion for generating a naming response on the basis of incomplete feature information. Second, regularities in the context may reduce the amount of positional information that must be encoded in order to synthesize a representation of a letter in its proper spatial relationship to other elements of a display (in particular, other letters and indicators used for response cueing). Third, the context determines whether or not the target letter is a constituent of a familiar letter group that is readily accessible from long-term memory and maintainable in short-term memory by rehearsal.

The first of these modes of influence seems to have been quite clearly implicated in the advantage sometimes observed for letters of words as compared to the same letters displayed alone in tachistoscopic studies (Estes, 1975b). The second and third should presumably be more important in comparisons between word and nonword letter strings as context for a target letter. In the remainder of this chapter, I should like to illustrate experimental paradigms that may permit detailed evaluation of our analyses both of the role of task requirements and of the process whereby context influences identification.

For the first of these examples, I shall present some data from an exploratory study conducted in my laboratory.[2] The apparatus and general procedures were the same as those used in the experiment on detection and context previously cited (Estes, 1975b). Subjects viewed 50-msec exposures of 4-letter displays preceded and followed by pattern masks and were cued either before or after the display with a probe letter that was the basis for their response decision.

Groups of 12 subjects were assigned to each of three conditions:

1. *Precue—Item:* On each trial, a single letter was presented on the oscillo-scope screen prior to the target display and the subject's task was to decide whether or not the probe letter appeared anywhere in the display.

2. *Postcue—Item:* The task was the same except that the probe letter was presented immediately after the target display.

3. *Postcue—Position:* This condition differed from the Postcue—Item condition only in that the probe letter was displayed directly below one of the four letter positions of the target display, and the subject's task was to decide whether the probe letter had appeared in that position of the display.

One-third of the trials involved single-letter displays, which will not be considered here. Each of the remaining displays comprised four letters, half being common words and half strings of unrelated letters. On 48 of the 4-letter trials, the target letter was either an L or an R (equally frequently and exactly one per display), and these displays were constructed in accordance with the WW—NN constraint. On the remaining trials, other letters were probed, but without the WW—NN control, and those will be treated simply as filler trials. Immediately following each display, the subject indicated on a scale of 1—4 his confidence that the probe letter had been in the display (Precue—Item and Postcue—Item) or had been in the indicated position (Postcue—Position).

The data from the L- or R-cued trials were treated in two ways. First, with a correct response defined as a rating of 3 or 4 if the probe letter was in the display and 1 or 2 if it was not, the proportion of correct recognitions was computed for each condition. Second, the d' measure of signal detectability theory was obtained in the usual way (see, e.g., Murdock, 1974) to provide an

[2] Edith Skaar assisted with this study.

index of recognition that might be relatively free of criterion effects. Both measures are included in Table 3.

In terms of the model, we expect the Precue–Item condition to permit correct recognition at the lowest processing level, for to the extent that subjects become aware of the frequent recurrence of the L, R target pair, they can respond on the basis of feature differences on L- or R-probed trials. The virtual equality of both recognition measures for WW versus NN displays in this condition bears out the analysis. In contrast, both of the other conditions were assumed to require full identification of the target letter and hence to reflect an advantage for a word context. Here again, the statistics shown in Table 3 are confirmatory, small advantages in proportion correct and more substantial advantages in the d' measure appearing for the WW displays. This result is of interest in demonstrating within a single experiment the pattern that has previously been observed to hold across experiments with differing stimulus material and subject populations.

Categorical Properties Of Words

Converging evidence for the interpretation of the word advantage in terms of the hierarchical model, as opposed to hypotheses assuming global features of words, is forthcoming from a recent study conducted by Allmeyer and myself (Estes & Allmeyer, in preparation). We compared the recognition of letters in word, pronounceable nonword, and unpronounceable nonword letter strings with four subjects who were already highly practiced in standard tachistoscopic report and detection methods. The apparatus and display conditions were the same as those of the study reported by Estes, Allmeyer, and Reder (1976). On each trial, a patterned premask appeared, then an exposure of a horizontal array of four letters either to the left or to the right of a fixation point, and finally a patterned postmask. The words were four-letter English nouns with a single vowel in either the second or the third position. Each of the pronounceable nonwords was generated by changing the vowel in one of the word strings, and

TABLE 3
Measures of Discriminability (d') and Proportion
of Correct Recognitions as a Function of Cuing
Procedure and Context (WW versus NN)

Procedure	Discriminability		Proportion correct	
	WW	NN	WW	NN
Precue item	1.05	.98	.70	.71
Postcue item	1.30	.96	.73	.70
Postcue position	1.29	.87	.76	.71

the unpronounceable nonwords were obtained by permuting the letters so as to produce an unpronounceable sequence. Following a practice series each subject yielded data on 16 lists, each of which comprised 24 words, 12 pronounceable nonwords, and 12 unpronounceable nonwords presented in random sequence. One-fourth of the trials of each type for each subject were conducted at each of the exposure durations: 25, 60, 95, and 200 msec.

One purpose of the study was to give yet another chance for the appearance of evidence revealing the use of global features of words as a basis for recognition. To this end, the subject's first task following the display of the letter string on each trial was to indicate whether he believed it was a word or a nonword. After giving the categorization response, the subject filled in an answer card with the letters he had been able to identify from the display. We wished to see whether subjects would be able to categorize a word string correctly as a word either at durations too short to permit identification of the constituent letters or, at any duration, on trials when too few letters were identified to permit recognition of the particular word.

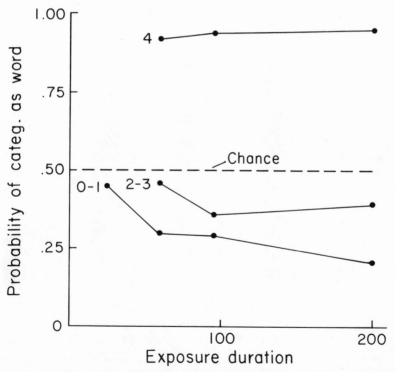

FIG. 5 Proportions of instances in which 4-letter word displays, intermixed with nonwords in random sequence over trials, were categorized as words when 0–1, 2–3, or all 4 of the constituent letters were correctly identified. The independent variable is exposure duration in milliseconds.

The answer to both questions is apparent in Fig. 5, in which I have plotted the probability of categorizing a display string of either of the three types as a word at each exposure duration, with the number of letters identified as a parameter. Considering the solid curves, representing data for the W strings, it may be seen first of all that when fewer than all four of the letters of a string were identified, the probability of correctly categorizing it as a word was less than chance. Further, under these circumstances, the probability of correct categorization did not increase as a function of exposure duration even though information concerning any type of overall features of words would surely have become clearer with increasing durations. In sharp contrast, when all four letters of a word were identified, the probability of correct categorization was near unity, independently of exposure duration. (The missing point for the shortest exposure duration on the topmost curve of Fig. 6 simply reflects the fact that the

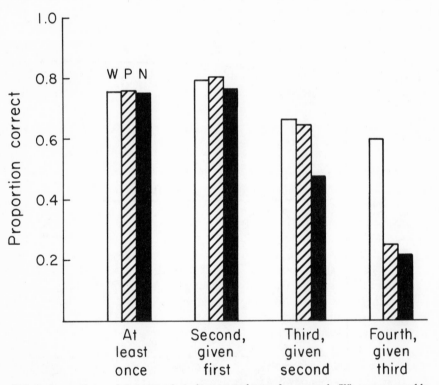

FIG. 6 Proportions of reports of at least one letter from word (W), pronounceable nonword (P), or unpronounceable nonword (N) displays, together with proportions of these instances in which a second letter was reported, proportions of a third reported given at least two, and proportions of a fourth reported given at least three.

subjects were never able to identify all four letters at the shortest exposure). The data for nonword strings, omitted from the figure since they are not especially germane to the present problem, showed better than chance accuracy in categorizing the P and N strings as nonwords at all durations.

The Dependence of Word on Letter Recognition

A more constructive picture of the way in which recognition of a letter depends on information concerning other elements of the same display is presented in Fig. 6. The leftmost set of bars represents the proportions of instances in which at least one letter was correctly reported from a W, P, or N display, the data being pooled over exposure durations. Clearly, the overall or global properties of words as distinguished from either type of nonword confer no advantage whatsoever with respect to the likelihood that at least one letter is identified from a display. Further, nearly the same is true for the probability of identifying a second letter from a display given that at least one has been correctly reported – the second set of bars in the figure. But when at least two letters have been identified from a string, the probability of recognizing a third is substantially higher for the word and pronounceable nonword strings. The fact that the results for these two types are so similar suggests that the critical variable is that the three letters identified constitute a pronounceable trigram. Pronounceability per se should not be overemphasized, for orthographic regularity is inevitably confounded with pronounceability in our displays. However, the confounding is of no great import with respect to our interest here. From the standpoint of the hierarchical model, the crux of matters is that an orthographically regular and/or pronounceable trigram would be a frequently recurring unit in English text and therefore likely to be represented in a readily accessible form in the memory system. When the input from a segment of a display closely matches such a representation, the output of that level of the filter system may be expected to yield a correct report of the given trigram.

In a final aspect of these data, the proportions of correct recognition of the fourth letter of a string given that three have been identified (the rightmost set of bars in Fig. 6) show for the first time a substantial difference between the W and P strings. This result also conforms precisely to expectations on the basis of the hierarchical filter model, for four-letter words certainly have representations in the memory system, whereas four-letter pronounceable nonwords (as we constructed them) generally must not. Thus, for example, the word WORD would have a readily accessible representation in memory. When it is converted into a pronounceable nonword by changing the O to an E, the segment WER is a frequently recurring trigram that might have an accessible representation in the memory system, in contrast to the full string WERD, which might well have never been previously encountered.

SUMMARY REMARKS ON VISUAL PROCESSING IN READING

It will be apparent, it not from this chapter, then certainly from others in this volume, that an adequate theory of reading will be a towering, multistoried edifice. My concern in this brief essay has been the situation on the ground floor, with attention to the lines of communication running further downward to visual theory and upward to semantic memory.

The Feature–Letter–Word-Processing System

An overall characterization of the view of reading developed here is one of a continual interaction between sensory inputs and memory structures. Input from text is filtered through successive levels of memory trace structures, eventuating in the recognition of letters, letter groups, or words, but with information from other sources combining with outputs of the higher levels to determine the various aspects of the individual's response to printed material— Perception, comprehension, and decision. Differing degrees of specificity of response are associated with different sources of information: Linguistic context acts, often in advance of a target letter or word, to partially activate memorial representations of subsets of words with common semantic attributes; global features of words activate smaller subsets; letter sequences are the most specific, normally leading to the activation of only a single word.

In the case of several examples considered in some detail, we have seen that the multilevel filter model, even in an incomplete and provisional form, helps provide a coherent account of a variety of findings that otherwise would appear unorganized and sometimes even contradictory. Perhaps most has been accomplished with regard to interpretation of the "word advantage," that is, the facilitated recognition of a letter embedded in a word as compared to a letter embedded in a random letter string or presented alone. Among the facts that seem both quite well established and well accounted for in terms of the model are the following:

1. No word advantage appears for forced-choice detection of targets known in advance when the WW–NN control is in effect; neither is there an effect in WN–NW comparisons if the target and context letters are displayed simultaneously for a brief interval, but a word advantage appears if the context letters remain in view beyond offset of the target, the effect growing systematically as a function of processing time.

2. When letter identification is examined by means of a single-letter probe appearing before or after a brief display, the word advantage increases as conditions require full identification of the target letter rather than simply a response on the basis of feature differences between alternative targets.

3. In the full-report task, words and random letter strings do not differ with respect to the probability that some information (typically, one or two letters)

can be extracted from a brief display; but given that some subset of the letters is recognized, the probability of the accrual of additional letters to the report is greater for pronounceable than for random strings and much greater still for words.

In general, the advantage of words and word-like letter sequences appears to lie in the attributes that provide alternative routes to the activation of representations of higher-order letter groups in the memory system and therefore alternative routes to identification of the constituent letters. Among the critical attributes that have been clearly identified are pronounceability, orthographic regularity, letter redundancy, and positional redundancy.

Reaction time data are more difficult to interpret theoretically than measures of accuracy of recognition because of the always complex determination of overt responses by stimulus, context, and often motivational variables. Up to a point, reaction time comparisons for responses to targets embedded in word versus nonword strings fit quite well with expectations from the filter model. In a forced-choice detection task with known targets, we expect response to be based on feature differences between the alternative targets and thus to be relatively immune to effects of context. This implication of the model is well born out by the results of Bjork and Estes (1973), showing virtually identical reaction times for detection of letters embedded in words versus nonword strings (1.02 and 1.00 sec, respectively), a result that was closely replicated (though the data were not included in the published report) in the study of Estes, Bjork, and Skaar (1974).

When the experimental task requires naming of a target letter, then a number of other factors must be expected to enter, including positional uncertainty and response competition. One cannot claim to predict from the filter model, at the present stage of development, such results as the common observation that a common word can often be named more rapidly than an isolated letter, or the finding of Johnson (1975) that a word can be named faster than a particular constituent letter. But neither do these phenomena appear to raise special problems for the model. I think that an understanding of comparisons of this kind will at the very least require much more extensive study of long-term practice effects. After all, accomplished readers must have had great amounts of practice at suppressing naming responses to constituent letters when reading words, and we know little about the ease with which these performance tendencies can be modified or reversed on the basis only of instructions or very limited practice.

Higher-Order Attributes and Auxiliary Information

Inevitably, the model outlined here will have to be modified in details as research continues, but what can we say at present with regard to evaluation of our basic assumptions and overall organization? The principal issue in the literature at present seems to be one dividing models like the one discussed here, which assume reading to be primarily a process of sifting sensory information through a succession of levels of memory comparisons, and more holistic models, which assume that a reader normally goes more directly from stimulus pattern to meaning and only secondarily, when a task requires it, proceeds through more analytic operations to the identification of individual letters. The latter view is represented, for example, by Osgood and Hoosain (1974) and Smith (1971).

The issue concerning the role of higher-order attributes of words or even syntactic units is not whether but how they enter into the reading process. Unfortunately, there has not been a great deal of research bearing sharply on the question of whether information from higher-order attributes of a segment of text actually becomes available earlier than that from individual letters. However, the several attempts, discussed earlier, to approach this question from different angles in our own research program have yielded a consistent pattern of results. When we follow the time course of accrual of information during individual trials in a letter recognition task, we find that information from context enters later, not earlier, than information from the target letters themselves. When we look for direct evidence that the outline shape or other overall attributes of letter strings can enable an individual to determine whether the string is or is not a word prior to the point at which he can identify the letters, the results are negative. Rather, we obtain quite direct evidence that the function of auxiliary information from orthographically regular or meaningful sequences is to enable individuals to complete imperfectly perceived letter groups.

Taking together the large literature showing facilitating effects of context on word and letter recognition with the more analytical experiments discussed here that reveal sharp limitations on the role of context, we may be led to some useful generalizations about the current state of methodology. In particular, it becomes clear, I believe, that experiments in this area need always to take full account of the character of reading as a communication process whose function is to alter the prior state of information of the reader, whether he is perusing a page of text, searching columns of stimuli for targets, or responding to tachistoscopic displays.

The important yet limited role of global features of words such as length and outline can be understood in this framework. Information concerning these features certainly may be stored with the representation of a word in memory, but just as clearly this information does not in general suffice to identify a word uniquely, or even to distinguish words as a class from nonwords that have some orthographic regularities. Thus, if an individual is entirely uncertain as to the nature of a to-be-displayed letter string, he evidently obtains no useful information from the global attributes. If he knows that the string is to be a word, these attributes narrow down the possibilities; if he knows that the word is to be chosen from a limited set of alternatives, the global features may even suffice to enable him to select the correct word uniquely. Consequently, we must expect that comparisons made without regard to the individual's state of information prior to exposure of a stimulus display can yield any possible result. Theoretically significant interpretation of experiments in this area must always depend on adequate specification of prior information and accurate monitoring of the points in time during the following exposure of stimulus material at which information from various aspects of the target stimulus and context exert their effects.

The special importance of the hierarchically organized critical feature—letter—word filter system in reading is that, without interfering with the individual's ability to take account of other sources of information, it sifts sensory information largely independently of the context and thus enables the reader to "see what is there" regardless of his prior expectations. Unlike the information obtained from various sorts of redundancy or from higher-order attributes of words and syntactic units, that obtained through the feature—letter system is nearly independent of the individual's prior state of information and consequently provides an almost fail-safe mechanism for response to printed messages that occur in unexpected circumstances.

Individual Differences

Although firm evidence is scanty, there seems little reason to doubt that both in tachistoscopic experiments and in ordinary reading, individuals have considerable flexibility in their ability to shift their degree of reliance on different types and levels of information. The filter system is always available, and, since it leads to unique identification of letter sequences, must be heavily relied on whenever accuracy is valued. In ordinary reading, where considerable accuracy can safely be sacrificed to gain speed since redundancy provides correction of gross errors, doubtless many letters of a printed line never yield inputs capable of activating their critical features and individual letter recognition is supplemented by considerable reliance on other attributes.

Studies providing comparisons between reading speed and performance in more controlled laboratory situations (e.g., Jackson & McClelland, 1975) suggest that there may be relatively little variance among reasonably accomplished readers with respect to the operation of the filter system for letter and word recognition, but much wider variation in the utilization of auxiliary information. Whether the more important differences between slow and fast readers lie in their states of prior information concerning the material, in the degree to which they have stored in memory higher-order attributes that are useful in discriminating words and syntactic groups, or in habits or strategies for accessing these auxiliary sources of information remains to be determined.

ACKNOWLEDGMENTS

Research reported in this chapter was supported in part by Grants GB 41176 and BNS 76-09959 from the National Science Foundation and MH 23878 from the National Institute of Mental Health.

REFERENCES

Anderson, J. A. A theory for the recognition of items from short memorized lists. *Psychological Review,* 1973, **80**, 417–438.
Baron, J. The word-superiority effect. In W. K. Estes (Ed.), *Handbook of learning and cognitive processes* Vol. 6. Hillsdale, N.J.: Lawrence Erlbaum Associates, 1977, (in press).
Bjork, E. L., & Estes, W. K. Letter identification in relation to linguistic context and masking conditions. *Memory & Cognition,* 1973, **1**, 217–223.
Cattell, J. M. The time taken up by cerebral operations. *Mind,* 1886, **11**, 220–242, 377–387, 524–538.
Coltheart, M. Visual information processing. In P. C. Dodwell (Ed.), *New horizons in psychology,* 2. Baltimore, Md.: Penguin Books, 1972. Pp. 62–85.
Estes, W. K. Interactions of signal and background variables in visual processing. *Perception & Psychophysics,* 1972, **12**, 278–286.
Estes, W. K. Memory, perception, and decision in letter identification. In R. L. Solso (Ed.), *Information processing and cognition: The Loyola symposium.* Hillsdale, N.J.: Lawrence Erlbaum Associates, 1975. Pp. 3–30. (a)
Estes, W. K. The locus of inferential and perceptual processes in letter identification. *Journal of Experimental Psychology: General,* 1975, **104**, 122–145. (b)
Estes, W. K., & Allmeyer, D. H. Word recognition in relation to the identification of constituent letters and lexical features. Manuscript in preparation, Rockefeller University, 1977.
Estes, W. K., Allmeyer, D. H., & Reder, S. M. Serial position functions for letter identification at brief and extended exposure durations. *Perception & Psychophysics,* 1976, **19**, 1–15.
Estes, W. K., Bjork, E. L., & Skaar, E. Detection of single letters and letters in words with changing versus unchanging mask characters. *Bulletin of the Psychonomic Society,* 1974, **3**, 201–203.
Geyer, L. H., & DeWald, C. G. Feature lists and confusion matrices. *Perception & Psychophysics,* 1973, **14**, 471–482.
Gibson, E. J. *Principles of perceptual learning and development.* New York: Appleton-Century-Crofts, 1969.
Huey, E. B. The psychology and pedagogy of reading. Cambridge, Mass.: MIT Press, 1908.
Jackson, M. D., & McClelland, J. Sensory and cognitive determinants of reading speed. *Journal of Verbal Learning and Verbal Behavior,* 1975, **14**, 565–574.
Johnson, N. G. On the function of letters in word identification: Some data and a preliminary model. *Journal of Verbal Learning and Verbal Behavior,* 1975, **14**, 17–29.
LaBerge, D., & Samuels, S. J. Toward a theory of automatic information processing in reading. *Cognitive Psychology,* 1974, **6**, 293–323.
Lindsay, P. H., & Norman, D. A. *Human information processing.* New York: Academic Press, 1972.
Massaro, D. W. Primary and secondary recognition in reading. In D. W. Massaro (Ed.),

Understanding language: An information processing analysis of speech perception, reading, and psycholinguistics. New York: Academic Press, 1975. Pp. 241–289.

Murdock, B. B. *Human memory: Theory and data.* Hillsdale, N.J.: Lawrence Erlbaum Associates, 1974.

Osgood, C. E., & Hoosain, R. Salience of the word as a unit in the perception of language. *Perception & Psychophysics,* 1974, 15, 168–192.

Reicher, G. M. Perceptual recognition as a function of meaningfulness of the stimulus material. *Journal of Experimental Psychology,* 1969, 81, 275–280.

Rumelhart, D. E. A multicomponent theory of confusion among briefly exposed alphabetic characters. Tech Report. Center for Information Processing, University of California, San Diego, 1971.

Smith, E. E., & Spoehr, K. T. The perception of printed English: A theoretical perspective. In B. H. Kantowitz (Ed.), *Human information processing: Tutorials in performance and cognition.* Hillsdale, N.J.: Lawrence Erlbaum Associates, 1974. Pp. 231–275.

Smith, F. *Understanding reading.* New York: Holt, 1971.

Smith, P. T., & Jones, K. F. Phonemic organization and search through long-term memory. In P. M. A. Rabbitt & S. Dornic (Eds.), *Attention and performance.* Vol. V. London: Academic Press, 1975. Pp. 547–562.

Thompson, M. C., & Massaro, D. W. Visual information and redundancy in reading. *Journal of Experimental Psychology,* 1973, 98, 49–54.

Woodworth, R. S. *Experimental psychology.* New York: Holt, 1938.

2
Neural Models with Cognitive Implications*

James A. Anderson

Brown University

INTRODUCTION

What a brain does when it functions should be intimately related to how a brain is constructed. An engineer builds a system with the best compromise between specifications and costs with what he has available, and the devices and techniques he has determine in large part the nature of the systems he builds. Although we can view the brain in many ways, often it is profitable to view it as an engineering solution to a set of evolutionary problems, given the material at hand at the time. Thus, the brain need not necessarily be a general purpose device; it need not be "logical"; and it may not be as fast as it might be; but whatever approach is taken is liable to be optimal in terms of its use of biological components to solve the problems with which it is faced.

Why Neural Models in Psychology?

Can the properties of the biological hardware really make any difference to the way we think about a psychological process? Let us consider one example, which we will discuss later in this chapter.

Reading, and many kinds of language behavior, often involve contacting in some fundamental way material that may be located anywhere in memory. For those who study reading and language, assumptions about the way a sensory input interacts with memory can profoundly influence the kinds of language

*Expanded text of a lecture given at the Summer Institute for Perception and Comprehension, Center for Research in Human Learning, University of Minnesota, Minneapolis, Minnesota, July 2, 1975.

models that will be considered. To take one not entirely random case (which will be discussed further in later sections), suppose we have to search our vocabulary item by item looking for a word when we see a pattern of letters. When we have a vocabulary that contains tens of thousands of items, this could be extremely time consuming, since our brain is composed of rather slow neural elements with time constants, at the very fastest, on the order of a millisecond, and actually operating much more slowly than this. On the other hand, if we assume that some kind of process exists that allows us to search a large part of memory at the same time, we can replace thousands of separate actions with a very few steps, a number that is well within the reasonable temporal characteristics of the brain. Parallel systems that can do this exist, and one version will be discussed in this chapter. However, it must be appreciated that parallel systems often have some unusual and unfamiliar properties, and have some very serious limitations as well as some spectacular capacities. If these properties are appreciated and understood, they may allow us to make models for reading and language that make full use of the strengths of distributed parallel systems and, at the same time, can compensate for their weaknesses.

Neuron Models

Our concept of the function of neurons in mammals has changed considerably in recent years. From an understandable, but misleading, fascination with the all-or-none action potential, most neurophysiologists have now generally come to accept neuron models that are basically analog with neuron output given in terms of firing frequency rather than in terms of the presence or absence of an action potential, and in which neurons act as integrators of synaptic potentials, coding the summated membrane potentials as an output firing frequency. For an exceptionally lucid introduction to this point of view, see Stevens (1966).

In the mammalian thalamo–cortical system, where most of the behavior of interest to cognitive psychologists probably occurs, we find a fairly small number of cell types (only two fundamental kinds in neocortex – pyramidal and stellate cells, with numerous anatomical variants), with many individual cells of each type arranged in two-dimensional layered structures. One layer of neurons has rich lateral interconnections and projects to other two-dimensional layers over pathways composed of many parallel fibers, with a moderate amount of convergence and divergence. This architecture suggests that sets of more or less equally important neurons operating as analog integrators and transducers project to other sets of analog transducers simultaneously over parallel pathways.

We should realize that such architecture – large groups of anatomically similar cells projecting to other large groups of cells – need not be universally characteristic of a nervous system. Many invertebrates seem to have highly specialized neurons in their 'higher' centers, single, identifiable, one-of-a-kind cells, whose properties are constant from animal to animal, each cell sometimes controlling a significant bit of behavior. *Tritonia,* a gastropod mollusc, is a good example, (See Dorsett, Willows, & Hoyle, 1973; Willows, Dorsett, & Hoyle, 1973a, b). There appears to be a great deal of inbuilt highly specific, genetically determined pre-wiring in many invertebrates. One might conjecture that many single cells in these animals, particularly near the motor output, may act as cellular "stored subroutines" rather than as small parts of a large-scale pattern of neural activities. Considering the vast number and variety of animals that may be organized this way, this approach to nervous system organization may be a major alternative form of "cognitive" architecture, in direct competition with our more diffuse, but hopefully more flexible, neocortex.

Computers and Brains

The organization — arrays of parallel analog integrators — that seems to occur in the mammalian central nervous system is quite different from the kinds of hardware found in the digital computer, an electronic device that has served as a powerful theoretical metaphor in psychology in recent years. Computers have undergone their own kind of rapid evolution in a few decades of widespread use and have become specialized to do well what humans do badly — in particular, to be fast, error free, and logical and to handle efficiently and accurately immense amounts of detail. We should be extremely careful of computer-based models of human cognition, since the capacities of the mammalian brain and the computer are very different, the divergence in abilities occurring by deliberate and conscious design over the past quarter-century. The talents of the brain and the computer complement each other, rather than mimic each other, and we should be wary of using one as a metaphor for the other.

  As we shall mention later, a much better electronic metaphor for the brain is the transistor radio, since both the brain and the radio are concerned with the retrieval of signals in noise using primarily analog circuitry.

  Ironically, the first important mathematical neural model, that of McCulloch and Pitts (1943), had an important theoretical influence on John von Neumann when he sketched the organization of EDVAC, the first modern stored program electronic digital computer (Goldstine, 1972, p. 197). However, the aspects of the McCulloch—Pitts neuron central to the digital computer — the all-or-none binary neuron and the use of binary neurons to implement formal logic — are, when taken literally, exactly the properties now felt to be unphysiological.

THEORETICAL MODELS

Let us make a couple of statements about what is of significance in the function of the nervous system when we want to model its operation. Some of these dogmatic assertions are justified at greater length elsewhere (Anderson, 1968, 1970, 1972, 1974; Cooper, 1974). First, we have a system in which large sets of more or less equivalent neurons project to other large sets. It seems then most likely that what is of interest to the nervous system is the pattern of simultaneous, individual neuron activities in this large set of neurons. Second, changes in synaptic strength at the synapses connecting these two groups of neurons are responsible for the modifications of behavior that we call memory.

Although cells in cortex are finely tuned, in that they respond to certain specific aspects of their inputs (orientation, say, in the visual cortex), they are not so exquisitely tuned as to fail to respond to more than one stimulus. An orientation detector will respond over several tens of degrees of orientation and different velocities of movement. Cells in the cerebral cortex are highly interconnected. They also often show considerable spontaneous activity. We may reasonably conjecture that a single synapse may be involved in the storage of many separate events. That is, its strength has been modified by numerous past events rather than serving to store information about a single past event. Eccles (1966, 1972) has considered this question in detail and has concluded that "any cortical neuron does not exclusively belong to one engram but, on the contrary, each neuron and even each synaptic junction would be built into many engrams" (Eccles, 1972, p. 59).

Profound consequences flow from this simple conclusion. This suggests that memory traces somehow mix together in a very fundamental way at the storage sites. Given this potential confusion, we become very restricted in the ways we can potentially use a system containing such elements as a memory.

Memory systems in which distinct stored items are spread over the storage elements and in which items can mix with each other are often referred to as "distributed" or "holographic." Technically, the models discussed here are not Fourier transform holograms, the most commonly described type, associated with lasers, but contain a different integral transform kernal.

We will define a trace as the elementary unit of memory that tends to be processed as a whole and is the large, widely spatially distributed pattern of individual neuron activities shown by the neurons in a group of neurons. An example is given later. Let us represent these traces by real-valued, N-dimensional vectors, where each element in the vector represents the activity of a single neuron. We will see that it is possible, appropriately viewed, for these activity patterns to start to act as units and to take on an independent life of their own. Partly for mathematical covenience (the analysis is far simpler) and partly because it seems to correspond to the physiology, where inhibition is as important as excitation, we let our activities, the elements in the vectors, have both positive and negative values. In some cases, this can be immediately related to positive and negative deviations of firing frequency around the spontaneous-activity level. A good example of this is the vestibular afferents recorded in the squirrel monkey eighth nerve by Goldberg and Fernandez (1971), in which there is unmistakable positive and negative transduction around a very high resting spontaneous activity level. In other cases, the presence of neuronal systems signaling stimulus changes in opposite directions (on-center and off-center cell systems in the visual system, for example) suggest a more complex interpretation of negative activity, perhaps more akin to one of the two parts of a push–pull amplifier. The conclusion that both positive and negative elements are present seems both natural and inevitable.

Patterns of *individual* activities are stressed in our assumptions because particular activities (vector elements) need not be correlated with each other. Indeed, the available physiological evidence indicates that cortical single units are surprisingly individualistic in the details of their response to stimuli, suggesting that this is a realistic approximation. For example, interneuronal spike activity correlations of nearby cells recorded with the same microelectrode in parietal cortex (classical "association" cortex) are low when the brain is doing "interesting" things, that is, when the animal is awake or in REM sleep. However, the same cell pairs in deep sleep show high neuronal firing correlations (Noda & Adey, 1970). The same result is found in the hippocampus (Noda, Manohar, & Adey, 1969). Somewhat surprisingly, even in primary visual cortex, where cells in a single column are known to respond to some common aspects of a stimulus (orientation, rough location in visual space), cells in the same column seem to show little commonality of specific synaptic input and great variability in their response properties aside from orientation (Creutzfeldt, Innocenti, & Brooks, 1974).

I have developed two primary models of memory function based on these assumptions. I attempt to model two reasonable psychological memory functions: recognition, where, given a new input, it is determined whether or not this input was stored in the memory, and association, a more general function, where, given an input, an output is generated which was associated with that input in the past.

An Example

Let us consider a set of six identical neurons, each responding only to a line segment of a particular orientation at a specific location in visual space. Assume that each neuron responds with excitation to stimuli at over $60°$ of angle. Assume that cells are slightly inhibited by stimuli at right angles to their preferred orientation. We assume that each cell has a spontaneous activity rate of 15 spikes per second. We set this value to equal zero, so with no stimulus the activity pattern, $\bar{f}_0$, is a six-element vector:

$$\bar{f}_0 = (0,0,0,0,0,0).$$

We assume that the first cell has a preferred orientation for line segments zero degrees from the vertical, the second cell has a preferred orientation at $30°$, the third at $60°$, and so on.

Now, suppose a line segment at $30°$ from the vertical appears. The first cell responds a little, since the cells respond to stimuli at over 60 degrees, say at 50 spikes per second, or 35 spikes per second above spontaneous rate. The second cell responds very strongly, say at 200 spikes per second (185 above base rate). The third cell responds at 50 spikes per second. The fourth and sixth cells do not respond. The fifth cell, since it has a preferred orientation 90° from the input, is inhibited; say it fires only at 5 spikes per second, or 10 less than the spontaneous rate. Thus, the pattern of activity corresponding to the stimulus, $\bar{f}_1$, is as follows:

$$\bar{f}_1 = (35, 185, 35, 0, -10, 0).$$

Assume that another line segment appears, oriented at 90° from the vertical. The neural firing pattern, $\bar{f}_2$, then would be as follows:

$$\bar{f}_2 = (-10, 0, 35, 185, 35, 0).$$

If we look at the overall pattern, the vectors $\bar{f}_1$ and $\bar{f}_2$, there is no question which stimulus appeared. But if we look only at cell number 3, we see that the vector element corresponding to this cell is the same in $\bar{f}_1$ and $\bar{f}_2$, that is:

$$f_1(3) = 35 = f_2(3).$$

Given only this one cell, we could not tell which stimulus occurred. The more cells we have in our activity pattern, and the more individualistic their discharges, the better able we are to discriminate different stimuli.

Recognition

Let us assume that we have K different traces, represented by K N-dimensional vectors, $\bar{f}_1, \bar{f}_2, \bar{f}_3, \ldots \bar{f}_K$, corresponding to the neural activity patterns of the items. For ease in calculation, we will assume that the vectors have zero mean; that is, the sum of the elements is zero, or

$$\sum_{i=1}^{N} f(i) = 0.$$

The value of the ith element is a single number, and is written $f(i)$. In the recognition model, we form the memory, $\bar{s}$, in the simplest way possible: We take the vector sum of the individual traces, that is,

$$\bar{s} = \sum_{k=1}^{K} \bar{f}_k.$$

A vector is written $\bar{f}_k$ and corresponds to a set of numbers. Clearly, much information is lost. However, this memory can still perform the function we have called "recognition" although not with perfect accuracy.

Suppose we present the memory with an input item giving rise to a pattern of activity, $\bar{f}$. We wish to know whether or not $\bar{f}$ is part of the sum making up $\bar{s}$. Since we know the exact form of $\bar{f}$ (it is, after all, the input), we are faced with a problem in signal detection. The optimal way to detect the presence of the trace in the noise generated by the sum of the "interfering" traces is given by the so-called "matched filter." The spatial matched filter takes an exceptionally simple form here: It is the dot product (inner product) of the input trace with the memory. This product will give a single number, which will be "large" if $\bar{f}$ was indeed present, and "small" if $\bar{f}$ was not present. If $\bar{f}$ was present, then

$$\begin{aligned} \text{output} &= \bar{s} \cdot \bar{f} \\ &= \bar{f} \cdot \bar{f} + \text{(noise).} \end{aligned}$$

The noise term can be shown to be zero on the average if the other traces are independent. The dot product, $\bar{f} \cdot \bar{f}$, is always positive, since it is the sum of squares.

As an important special case, assume that the stored traces, $\bar{f}_i$, are orthogonal; that is, $\bar{f}_i \cdot \bar{f}_j = 0$ if $i \neq j$. Suppose $\bar{f}_j$ is input and is in the memory. Then

$$\begin{aligned} \text{output} &= \bar{f}_j \cdot \bar{s} \\ &= \bar{f}_j \cdot \bar{f}_j + \sum_{i \neq j} \bar{f}_i \cdot \bar{f}_j. \end{aligned}$$

But all the dot products in the second term are zero by our orthogonality assumption. Thus, the system gives a positive output and successfully recognizes the presence of $\bar{f}_j$.

Clearly, if the $\bar{f}_j$ are not orthogonal, or if the input is not exactly what is stored, the system will make errors of recognition. In many ways the errors and limitations of this model are more interesting than the correct responses. We are, after all, trying to model a brain that is, as we know too well, error prone and unreliable in many ways.

Capacity

We can get a rough idea of the capacity of this system quite easily. Since there are N orthogonal N-element vectors, if we restrict our allowable traces to orthogonal vectors, then we can store only N of them before we run out of different allowable inputs. The system abruptly ceases to function perfectly after it has stored N orthogonal traces. Thus, we should expect the capacity of the system to be on the order of N distinct traces.

It is not clear that it would be of any use to an animal to make too many discriminations. The problem of a behaving organism in many cases is to analyze the complex and varied inputs it receives, so a good guess at an appropriate output behavior can be made from a small number of possible responses. We want an operating brain to lump inputs into equivalence classes that are recognized as similar, but not necessarily identical to what had been encountered in the past. Clearly, a system of the type proposed here will do this, since input vectors close to (correlated with) a stored trace will also give a large output. This system will tend to classify traces as similar based on correlations between their neural activity patterns (Cooper, 1974).

A more subtle property of the summed vector model along these lines is its ability to abstract from noisy examples, a matter to be discussed later.

Letter Confusability

As an almost obvious example of this process at work in the perception of letters, we predict that the confusability of two letters should be a function of the correlation between their neural codes. Since we know the visual system has a very powerful, topographic, space-preserving aspect, we might expect to find that simple correlation of visual form would provide a first approximation to the confusability of letters.

Exactly this was done by Engel, Dougherty, and Jones (1973). They drew lowercase letters on a 15-by-15 grid and gave a positive value of 10 to a grid square if it contained more than half a letter; otherwise it was given the value 1. This ordered array of many numbers is a vector. They formed the dot product of the arrays with themselves (the autocorrelation) and with every other letter (the cross correlations). They then showed that, first, the autocorrelation (equivalent to "strength" in this chapter) agreed reasonably well with the rank order of absolute number of errors for different letters in a tachistoscopic recognition task. Second, they showed that size of cross correlation and rank order of letter confusability in the same tachistoscopic task gave fairly high (.56) correlations. They also pointed out that their predicted rank orderings were in satisfactory agreement with a considerable body of work in the earlier part of this century on "confusability" as measured in reading experiments.

Since we know the visual system modifies the simple spatial representation in ways that were not considered in this work — lateral inhibition, edge detection, orientation selectivity, and so forth — which would strongly affect the neural code, the finding of this powerful effect is striking, since it is a direct prediction of the approach to perception sketched here.

It would be of interest to do a similar study with letter codings that incorporated the other kinds of neural coding that are known to exist.

A Slightly More Detailed Calculation

Let us assume that all traces are composed of independent elements. We assume that all traces, $\bar{f_i}$, are equally "strong"; that is, $\bar{f_i} \cdot \bar{f_i} = P$ for all $\bar{f_i}$. We assume (as mentioned before) that each trace has zero mean. We also assume that all the elements of a trace, $f_i(j)$, have the same average mean and variance over sets of allowable traces.

To get an idea of how our model might work in some more realistic situation, we will assume that we are storing sets of K random vectors of zero mean and equal variance. We will try to get an estimate for how the system will perform, on the average.

We form our memory as follows:

$$\bar{s} = \sum_{k=1}^{K} \bar{f}_k.$$

Suppose an input $\bar{f}$ comes in which may also be present. An appropriate number to look at in this context is the signal-to-noise ratio of the output of our matched filter. A customary definition of signal-to-noise ratio, s/n, is as follows:

$$\frac{s}{n} = \frac{(\text{signal out})^2}{E[(\text{noise out})^2]}.$$

Since nothing is known about the other stored traces except their average mean and variance, when we want to calculate the average signal-to-noise ratio of the system, the other stored traces are approximated by the values taken by independent random variables with zero mean. Since the mean is zero, the total variance of the entire trace will be P because

$$P = \sum_{i=1}^{N} f(i)^2$$

and the average variance per element will then be P/N.

To get the mean square noise (the denominator of the s/n), we sum this variance over elements and traces:

$$E[(\text{noise out})^2] = \sum_{i=1}^{N} \text{var} \left[\sum_{k=1}^{K} f(i) f_k(i) \right]$$

$$= \sum_{i=1}^{N} \sum_{k=1}^{K} [\text{var} f(i) f_k(i)].$$

Here $f(i)$ is the input. Thus, it can be taken outside the parenthesis, since it is a constant multiplying the random variables approximating the different $f_k(i)$. But since it is a constant, we can use the statistical identity,

$$\text{var} (aX) = a^2 \text{ var } X,$$

where a is a constant and X is a random variable. Then

$$E[(\text{noise out})^2] = \sum_{i=1}^{N} f^2(i) \sum_{k=1}^{K} (P/N)$$

$$= KP^2/N.$$

This follows, since

$$\sum_{i=1}^{N} f^2(i) = \bar{f} \cdot \bar{f} = P.$$

The output of the filter if $\bar{f}$ is present in $\bar{s}$ is simply $P = \bar{f} \cdot \bar{f}$. Then

$$s/n = P^2 /(KP^2 /N)$$
$$= N/K.$$

We see that the system stops working very well when N and K are roughly equal, agreeing with our earlier estimate. This result has the interesting qualitative feature that as N, the number of elements in the vector, increases, the memory works more accurately and has larger capacity. This is encouraging since a common finding in neuroanatomy is that the volume and number of cells involved in a particular structure increase as the structure increases in behavioral importance. Our own large cortex is presumably an example of this pheno-menon. This is not quite such an obvious result as it first appears since large neural structures consume a great deal of metabolic energy and are vulnerable, and many other organizational structures tend to break down and lose flexibility when they get large: Bureaucracies and large libraries are good examples.

Associative Model

We will next sketch the more general and more interesting model, which is capable of using what are formally large weighted sets of recognition memories of the type just described to associate an input and a desired output.

We assume that we have two groups of neurons, α and β (see Fig. 1). We will assume that every neuron in α projects to every neuron in β. This somewhat unrealistic assumption need not be made (Anderson, 1972), but it greatly simplifies calculations.

We assume that there is a synaptic strength, a_{ij}, that couples the ith neuron in β with the jth neuron in α. In order to proceed with our model, we must make an approximation as to the way a neuron's firing frequency is related to its synaptic inputs.

Linearity of Synaptic Addition

Very surprisingly, considering the gross nonlinearities found in the neuron membrane and synapse, a reasonably good approximation to the behavior of some (not all) neurons can be made by assuming that the activity of the ith neuron in β is given by the weighted sum of its synaptic inputs, that is,

$$g(i) = \sum_{j=1}^{N} a_{ij} f(j).$$

It should be pointed out that this relationship speaks of firing frequencies (or increments in firing frequency). Some highly nonlinear preliminary sensory transduction and spatial preprocessing have also occurred. However, in terms of

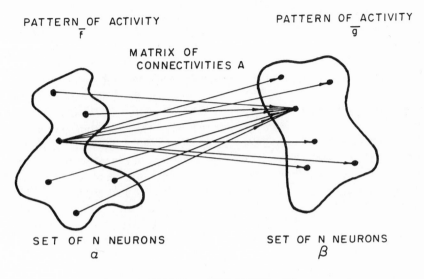

PATTERN OF ACTIVITY
$\overline{f}$

PATTERN OF ACTIVITY
$\overline{g}$

MATRIX OF
CONNECTIVITIES A

SET OF N NEURONS
α

SET OF N NEURONS
β

i) EVERY NEURON IN α PROJECTS TO
EVERY NEURON IN β

ii) EVERY NEURON IN β RECEIVES INPUT
FROM EVERY NEURON IN α

FIG. 1 Abstraction of a neural projection system. A group of neurons projects to another group of neurons – every neuron in the first group is connected to every neuron in the second group.

pre- and postsynaptic firing frequency this simple linear relationship is a useful approximation. There is diverse physiological support for this notion. Sensory neurons are often highly linear in their conversion of current from the transduction process into firing rate (Fuortes, 1971). The best characterized neural system, that of the lateral eye of *Limulus,* appears to be a nearly perfect linear system in terms of its synaptic interactions (Knight, Toyoda, & Dodge, 1970; Ratliff, 1965; Ratliff, Knight, Dodge, & Hartline, 1974). Mountcastle (1967) has hypothesized that most of the observed nonlinearities of neuron response in the mammalian central nervous system are introduced very early, in the spatial arrangement and generator potentials of the first-order sensory fibers, and a reasonably linear (though very complicated) transmission of the output of these fibers follows. Calvin (1972) reviews some of the data supporting this approximation in mammals. From a mathematical point of view, it is generally wise to defer complications until they are forced on us, since a linear system is often a useful indicator of the behavior of the more realistic, but intractable, nonlinear system.

Structure of the Model

We will assume that the following situation is a common mode of operation of our cognitive hardware: The set of neurons α shows an activity pattern $\bar{f}_1$. The set of neurons β shows an activity pattern $\bar{g}_1$. We wish to associate pattern $\bar{f}_1$ with pattern $\bar{g}_1$ so that later presentations of $\bar{f}_1$ alone will give rise, through synaptic effects, to pattern $\bar{g}_1$ in β. Since this situation involves some mechanism for actively impressing pattern $\bar{g}_1$ on β and pattern $\bar{f}_1$ on α and then somehow modifying the synapses, perhaps through a chemical "now-print" order as hypothesized by Livingston (1967) it has been called "active" learning. A model with the same modification scheme, which is self-organizing since it requires only that there be *some* output pattern on β, has been called "passive" learning and has been studied by Cooper (1974) and applied to the development of "feature-detecting" cells in primary visual cortex by Nass and Cooper (1975).

We must now specify the precise form taken by modification at the synaptic junction.

Let us ask what detailed, local information might permanently influence a synaptic junction. Clearly, it is influenced by the presynaptic activity that makes use of the junction constantly. We hypothesize that it is also influenced by postsynaptic neuron activity. This assumption requires some information about postsynaptic activity to migrate from the axon hillock, where spikes are usually initiated, to the synapse. Since there is a direct cytoplasmic connection between hillock and synapse this is not implausible. Many mechanisms for this reverse information transfer have been suggested: chemical diffusion, recurrent collaterals, impedance mismatches reflecting some spike activity toward the dendrites. However, hard physiological evidence is not available.

It should be pointed out that virtually any distributed model will be quite difficult to verify at the cellular level. This is because we should expect distributed changes to be relatively small; to be rather unpredictable, since we would have to have details about the activity of cells on both sides of the synapse for prediction; and to be unlikely to show learning all the time. The time scale for permanent synaptic learning involving protein synthesis and biological change is likely to be on the order of days. All these properties make this system experimentally very difficult to study and suggest that the most direct verification of some of these physiologically based distributed models may be through the properties of the global system or, restated, in terms of the "psychology" of the whole system.

For the recognition model, all we need is a modification of the basic element, be it cell or synapse, proportional to its past activity.

For the association model, as our basic assumption, let us assume that to associate pattern $\bar{f}_1$ in α with pattern $\bar{g}_1$ in β we change the set of synaptic weights coupling α and β proportional to the product of presynaptic activity at a junction with the activity of the postsynaptic cell. Thus, the change in the ij^{th}

synapse is proportional to $f_1(j)\, g_1(i)$ when patterns $\bar{f}_1$ and $\bar{g}_1$ are to be associated. For convenience, let $\bar{f}_1 \cdot \bar{f}_1 = \bar{g}_1 \cdot \bar{g}_1 = 1$. Then let the change, a_{ij}, in the ijth synapse be given exactly by $f_1(j)\, g_1(i)$. The set of connectivity changes form a matrix A_1 given by

$$A_1 = \begin{bmatrix} g_1(1)\,\bar{f}_1 \\ g_1(2)\,\bar{f}_1 \\ \cdots \\ g_1(N)\,\bar{f}_1 \end{bmatrix}$$

where the $\bar{f}_1$ are row vectors.

In recent years, a number of models of brain activity have postulated similar synaptic modification schemes. This seems to be partly because it is very difficult to make a formal learning system do anything "interesting" unless such an assumption is made. Kohonen (1972) has independently proposed an associative matrix memory formally quite similar to that proposed here. Willshaw, Buneman, and Longuet-Higgens (1969) proposed a closely related correlational digital model. Recently, Wilson (1975) and Little and Shaw (1975) have made and discussed the consequences of similar synaptic modification assumptions. Hebb (1949) made a synaptic learning hypothesis that, although stated in words, can be interpreted as similar to the model discussed here. The convergence of many theoretical approaches, often starting from quite different origins, toward the same kinds of requirements for synaptic modification is encouraging.

Assume that after we have "printed" the set of connectivities A_1, pattern of activity $\bar{f}_1$ arises in α. Then, by our assumption of linear synaptic summation, we see that the activity of cells in β is given by the following:

$$\begin{aligned} A_1 \bar{f}_1 &= \bar{g}_1\,(\bar{f}_1 \cdot \bar{f}_1) \\ &= \bar{g}_1, \end{aligned}$$

so we have $\bar{g}_1$ appearing as the pattern of activity in β, which corresponds to our definition of association.

Two comments should be made here. First, the exact form of synaptic modification can be viewed as only the first term in the Taylor expansion containing both $f(j)$ and $g(i)$ of a more complex synaptic modification function. The earlier terms depending on $f(j)$ and $g(i)$ alone (not considered here) might correspond to something like the recognition model. Second, we again note that synapses can be both increased and decreased in strength, so a_{ij} can be both positive and negative.

Now, it is very unlikely that these large sets of neurons only associate a single set of activity patterns. Let us assume that we have K sets of learned associations, $(\bar{f}_1, \bar{g}_1), (\bar{f}_2, \bar{g}_2), \ldots, (\bar{f}_K, \bar{g}_K)$, each generating a matrix of synaptic increments, $A_1, A_2, \ldots, A_K$. Then, since we have assumed that a single synapse participates in storing many events, we form an overall connectivity matrix, A, given by

$$A = \sum_{k=1}^{K} A_k.$$

Note that the rows of A will be recognition memories of the summed vector type discussed earlier, each vector weighted by the postsynaptic activities, $g_k(j)$. Thus, the two models are very similar in many qualitative properties.

Let us assume, for an informative calculation, that the $\bar{f}_i$ are orthogonal. Then, if pattern $\bar{f}_j$ is impressed on set of neurons α, we have

$$A\bar{f}_j = \sum_{k=1}^{K} A_k \bar{f}_j$$
$$= A_j \bar{f}_j + \sum_{k \neq j} A_k \bar{f}_j$$
$$= \bar{g}_j + \sum_{k \neq j} \bar{g}_k (\bar{f}_j \cdot \bar{f}_k)$$
$$= \bar{g}_j.$$

Thus, the system associates $\bar{f}_j$ with $\bar{g}_j$ perfectly. Of course, an operating system will produce noise as well, but the system is quite functional in many contexts.

Note that to a first order we need consider only the orthogonality properties of the inputs, the $\bar{f}_j$. The system works well when more than one $\bar{f}$ is associated with a particular response, that is,

If the $\bar{f}$s associated with the same $\bar{g}$ are not orthogonal, interesting possibilities for interaction between the $\bar{f}$s appear. These interactions, which can be constructive or destructive, give rise to the system's potential for abstraction and generalization, discussed in the next section.

The situation in which a given $\bar{f}$ is associated with more than one $\bar{g}$, that is,

causes serious problems and requires a modification of our model to fit the data. In the linear model just presented, the output pattern, when $\bar{f}$ is presented, will be a superposition of the two associated outputs. Since this result is rarely found – usually one or the other response will dominate – it is necessary to incorporate some essential nonlinearities into the model. Some initial suggestions as to what these nonlinearities might be and how they might operate are proposed later in the chapter.

Memory as a Filter

It should be clear by now that in this formulation, memory looks both formally and intuitively very much like a filter. In the recognition model, a novel input orthogonal (i.e., very dissimilar) to stored traces will give zero response. Similarly, in the association model, an orthogonal input that has not been associated with an output pattern of activity will also give rise to zero activity in set of neurons β. *Thus novel inputs are not seen by higher levels until they are learned.* Notice that this is purely a result of the structure of the system. Novel inputs simply do not give rise to much activity, while familiar inputs do. Qualitatively, we might speculate that the system should be agonizingly difficult to teach in its earliest stages, since in a real system inputs would not give rise to much activity leading to synaptic modification at the output. Once some experience has modified the synapses, the system should be capable of rapid learning (see Nass & Cooper, 1975). The initial biases of the network, especially if associative networks of this kind are cascaded as they would be in a real system, will have a profound influence on later learning since they will govern what gets through to higher levels to be learned.

Summary

The preceding discussion was intended to make several points. A great many consequences flow from the hypothesis that whatever the storage elements are in memory, they superimpose many distinct memories on top of one another; that is, distinct memory traces add together and interact. Therefore, since the value of any particular element contains contributions from a great many traces, we must look at a great many elements to detect the presence or absence of a trace. We have shifted emphasis to what are called "distributed" systems. Much information is lost and the basic problem in memory becomes that of retrieving a particular item in the presence of large amounts of noise, which is due to the other stored traces. The most appropriate mathematical techniques and metaphors to apply to memory become those of communication theory or signal detection theory: The brain is more like a transistor radio than a digital computer.

We showed that the simplest example of a memory of this kind, in which we assumed that traces added together, was capable of storing and recognizing a great many separate items with a satisfactory error rate. Similarly, a more complex system could be made that could associate one pattern of activity with another. For particular sets of input patterns, patterns mathematically describable as "orthogonal" to each other, the system could be shown to work perfectly in that a particular input presented to the system would produce an output associated with that input in the past. Both systems discussed would produce errors and noise when new inputs were correlated with previously learned inputs, but could still work adequately for many applications.

ABSTRACTION

Situations rarely repeat themselves exactly. One of the most useful functions of a nervous system would be to be able to learn from varying and noisy experience. In particular, the system might seek to reduce the immense number of possible inputs into a relatively few equivalence classes that could be maneageably associated with learned responses: This is food, this is danger, this is a friend.

It is important to observe that the nervous system is the product of a long evolution. Even in our own highly generalized cortex, there are overwhelming indications of substantial amounts of prewiring, strongly influencing *a priori* the kinds of events that will be responded to. In the visual system there is compelling evidence for substantial genetic prewiring of some aspects of stimulus analysis, especially properties like binocularity and orientation detection, and spatial location of the receptive field (Hubel & Wiesel, 1974a, b; Wiesel & Hubel, 1974). There also appears to be a substantial learned component in the responses of cells in primary visual cortex (Hirsch & Spinelli, 1971; Pettigrew, 1974). This is a matter currently under intense physiological investigation (see the review in Nass & Cooper, 1975). A combination of prewiring and learned connection presumably occurs elsewhere in cortex, to a greater or lesser degree, depending on the area.

Thus, the *kinds* of things we will abstract out of the inputs to our nervous system have a strong built-in bias, so the approximations we use in models must be chosen with care.

A good example of the kind of simple abstraction that is useful, common in humans, based on genetically specified structures, and rather remote from physical reality is color. We can tell a child that a desk is blue, that a chair is blue, that the sky is blue and by the age of three or four he is quite capable of telling whether something is blue or not. The neurophysiology of color is understood in sufficient detail to conclude that a great many cells in the visual system will have their discharges modified by the presence of particular spectral components. Yet there is no such thing as blue, per se, only blue *things*. The theoretical approach we have been taking would simply suggest that a consistent neural pattern has developed corresponding to blueness that arose from the presentation of numerous noisy examples. Many neurons responding to blue also respond to other aspects of the stimulus. The color system in vision is biologically constructed to facilitate this abstraction. Presentation of an input that is often, but not always, linked to certain wavelengths of light evokes the pattern blueness, as well as the patterns corresponding to the other features of the input, which will vary from input to input.

The powerful innate physiological component to color perception suggests that color names might not be free to be culturally defined, as has been claimed, but would be biologically determined to a large degree. Rosch (1973, in press) presents compelling evidence that this is indeed the case: The biology of our visual system seems to restrict us in the way we define the best examples of colors so that some kinds of abstraction are far more natural than others.

Mathematical Models

Let us consider the following situation: Suppose we have several, say K, possible highly discriminable (i.e., approximately orthogonal) inputs, $\bar{f}_1, \bar{f}_2, \ldots, \bar{f}_K$. A subject is attempting to associate these inputs with particular outputs, $\bar{g}_1$, $\bar{g}_2, \ldots, \bar{g}_K$ by means of one of our association matrices. Thus, the overall matrix will be given by

$$A = \sum_{k=1}^{K} A_k.$$

If a stored input comes in, say $\bar{f}_1$, then the output will be as follows:

$$A\bar{f}_1 = \bar{g}(\bar{f}_1 \cdot \bar{f}_1) + \sum_{i \neq 1} \bar{g}_1 (\bar{f}_1 \cdot \bar{f}_i).$$

The second term is zero, by the orthogonality of the $\bar{f}$'s. We pointed out in the previous section that the rows of A are simply recognition memories weighted by the elements of the associated $\bar{g}$.

We are now going to assume that the association matrices A_k are really built up of numerous presentations of noisy examples of the $\bar{f}_k$ associated with a $\bar{g}_k$. To a reasonable statistical approximation, if the added noise is random we can consider the recognition memories associated with the rows. Added noise causes the orthogonality assumption to hold only statistically.

Thus, we have simplified the problem into consideration of K recognition memories, each associated with a response. It is usually easier and more intuitive to work with recognition memories, so we shall consider them in this section and the following one, but they are an approximation to the A matrix representation.

A Model for Some Kinds of Abstraction

We will now assume that when a subject is taught to classify a group of noisy input stimuli into a small number of equivalence classes, what he is doing is forming several memories of the simple recognition type, an approximation justified earlier. Thus, if $\overline{s_i}$ is the recognition memory associated with output pattern i, and if we have a number of noisy inputs associated with output pattern i, then

$$\overline{s_i} = \overline{f_i} + (\overline{\text{noise}})_a + \overline{f_i} + (\overline{\text{noise}})_b + \overline{f_i} + (\overline{\text{noise}})_c + \ldots$$

We can now see how abstraction occurs. If we assume that the noise terms are uncorrelated from trial to trial, then after n presentations of $\overline{f_i}$ we would have, on the average,

$$\overline{s_i} = n \overline{f_i} + \sqrt{n} \, (\text{noise}),$$

where the noise term has the mean square amplitude ("average power") of the individual noise terms $a, b, c, \ldots$. This occurs because with uncorrelated noise, the noise *variances* will add linearly, while the *amplitudes* of the common part, $\overline{f_i}$, will add linearly. Thus, the representations of the common part will *constructively* interfere and the representations of the noise will *destructively* interfere, and these effects will become relatively stronger with increasing numbers of presentations. The common part, $\overline{f_i}$, is enhanced with respect to the noise.

Experiments

Can we see this process in operation? Possibly yes. Mechanisms somewhat similar to this kind of abstractive process have been suggested many times as a basic strategy of memory function. Recent models are discussed in considerable detail in Reed (1973) and in a review article by Posner (1969). Many models for perceptual and memory function consider judgment and classification as based upon the "distance" (defined variously) of new material from a stored abstraction, or a "prototype," as it is sometimes called.

   For example, Franks and Bransford (1971) used stimulus sets composed of geometric figures that had undergone simple logical transformations and succeeded in showing effects qualitatively similar to those predicted earlier. In this case, however, the similarities between the prototypes and the noisy examples presented to the subjects were defined in terms of "transformational" distance. Reed (1972) generated sets of cartoon faces varying in simple ways from each other and, in an extensive series of experiments, concluded that the "predominant (classification) strategy was to form an abstract image or prototype to represent each category and to classify test patterns on the basis of their similarity . . . to the prototypes. Similarity was determined . . . by placing a greater emphasis on these features which best discriminated between the two categories" (p. 401).

Rosch, in several recent studies (Rosch, 1973, in press; Rosch & Mervis, 1974), argues that the formation of prototypes is perhaps the central feature of human categorization. Categories, instead of being composed of clusters of properties that are either there or not, are coded in "analog" fashion; that is, the "distance" between an input and a prototype for the category is measured, and categorization proceeds on this basis. In one of her examples, a German Shepard is usually felt to be a very "doggy" dog (i.e., it is near most people's prototype), but a Pekingese is not as good an example of a dog, although it is just as much a member of the biological species dog. Similarly, a robin or a sparrow is a very good example of what most people mean by "bird," while a penguin or an ostrich, though still a bird, is not.

This kind of "analog" theory of categorization and classification is in agreement with the natural kind of structure that arises from our modeling approach: As we shall see, from a careful study of a tractable example, we have a mechanism that (a) forms prototypes (by a simple averaging process) and (b) naturally uses the distance of an input to the prototype, as a metric, by forming the correlation between input and prototype.

Since our modeling approach requires at least some qualitative insight into the neurophysiological activity underlying the representation of the stimulus, and since the neurophysiology of all but the most elementary stimuli is obscure in the extreme, to look more carefully at these effects we should try to find experiments that may allow a simple, biologically based interpretation. It is possible that the series of "prototype abstraction" experiments performed by Posner and Keele (1968, 1970) and by others (Homa, Cross, Cornell, Goldman, & Schwartz, 1973; Peterson, Meagher, Chait, & Gillie, 1973; Strange, Keeney, Kessel, & Jenkins, 1970); allows such an interpretation.

Visual Prototype Experiments

The experiments to be described are all variants of the paradigm first used by Posner and Keele (1968, 1970). In a typical experiment, they used as stimuli patterns of nine dots randomly placed in a 30-by-30 matrix. Several highly distinguishable dot patterns were produced. These original patterns were referred to as the prototypes. Then these prototypes were distorted by moving dots random distances and directions. The average distance the dots shifted was manipulated as an experimental parameter so that *examples* of prototypes could be produced that were either grossly distorted or only slightly changed from the prototype.

Experiments usually took the following form: Several prototypes were constructed and a number of distortions at various levels of distortion were constructed. Subjects were then presented several (three to nine) distortions of a small number of prototypes (three to four) to learn. In the learning procedure,

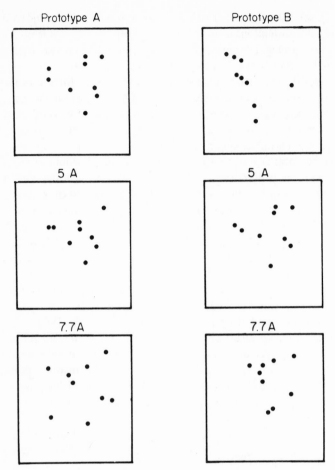

FIG. 2 Example, taken from Posner (1969), of two random dot prototype patterns (top row) and two moderate ('5A') and two extreme ('7A') distortions of prototype A. (Reprinted by permission.)

subjects were simply taught to classify examples of the same prototype together, by providing feedback as to whether or not the classification was correct. Subjects were trained to a criterion, usually two complete classifications of all the patterns in the learning set.

After learning, the subjects were tested on another set of patterns. There could be a time delay from a few minutes to as long as a week before testing started. Subjects were told to classify the new patterns "as rapidly as possible, based on their previous learning" (Posner & Keele, 1968), or to push the "most appropriate" button (Strange et al., 1970), each button having been associated with a particular class during learning. The test patterns could be either (a) patterns in the learning set; (b) the prototypes, which the subjects had never seen; or (c) new distortions of the prototype.

The results seem quite reproducible, and similar qualitatively for the various experimental permulations that have appeared in the literature.

In the original experiments four distortions of each of three prototypes were in the learned set. Subjects correctly classified most often the patterns they had seen before, as might be expected. However, subjects correctly classified the prototypes that they had never seen, nearly as well. New distortions of the prototypes were classified significantly less well.

The relative advantage of the prototype over new distortions of the prototype became even more pronounced when the delay between learning and testing was increased to a week. The prototype hardly changed in percent correct classification after a week's delay, while the percent correct classification of previously presented patterns dropped to about equal to that of the prototype (Posner & Keele, 1970). This result was replicated by Strange et al. (1970). This finding was interpreted by Posner and Keele to mean (a) that the prototype was less susceptible to decay than the representations of the specific examples and (b) that abstraction of the prototype appeared to occur at the time of learning rather than at the time of testing.

In another experiment (Experiment II in Posner & Keele, 1968), one group of subjects learned highly distorted examples. Another group learned less distorted examples. The subjects were then tested on highly distorted examples of the prototypes they had learned. Subjects who had learned highly distorted prototypes did better in classification than subjects who had learned the slightly distorted examples. Posner and Keele interpret this result to mean that some information about the variability of the examples is stored as well as the prototype. (See the discussion and additional experimental data in Posner, 1969, p. 67.) This result was not duplicated by Peterson et al. (1973, Experiments III and IV).

Another important experimental finding was reported by Homa et al. (1973). They reasoned that the *number* of distortions of a particular prototype presented during learning should be an important experimental variable. They used random dot patterns generated identically to those of Posner and Keele. They presented three, six, or nine examples of the prototype to subjects during learning. Half the subjects were tested immediately, and half after a four-day delay. For both conditions, but most strikingly for the delayed condition, the percent correct classification of the prototype was an increasing function of the number of examples presented. In the delayed condition, percent correct classification with nine examples presented was roughly equal for old examples and for prototypes, with both about 30% higher than new distortions of the prototype.

If prototype formation does play as central a role in human memory, as held by Rosch and others mentioned previously, careful study of this ability in a precisely controlled experiment might have important implications.

Posner and Keele's experiments clearly seem to show the formation of something like the prototypes that have been held to be central to higher cognitive function. What is the exact meaning of a word? An understanding of why a carrot is a very good vegetable, while a pumpkin is not, may illuminate key issues in language. The choice of the proper word may be a reflection of the strength and discriminability of prototypes formed from past experience in simple ways.

Posner and Keele's interpretation of their original experiments and the importance they attached to their results was clearly indicated by the titles they chose for their papers: "On the Genesis of Abstract Ideas" (1968) and "Retention of Abstract Ideas" (1970). Somehow, it is implied, formation of prototypical dot patterns bears a close relation to the means we use to form our abstractions, and even our concepts and ideas. Posner and Keele also pointed out that, besides clearly suggesting the presence of something that was not presented to the subject but was created internally, information about particular presented examples was retained to some extent and information about the expected variability of examples from the prototype was stored as well.

Localization in the Visual System

Perhaps the most striking aspect of the neurophysiology of the visual system at its lower levels is its very strong topographic organization. This has sometimes been referred to as the "cortical retina," meaning that adjacent points on the retina map, on the average, into adjacent points on primary visual cortex and that, to a certain extent, the spatial pattern of the stimulus is preserved, although with fascinating magnifications and distortions (Whitteridge, 1973; Brodal, 1969, p. 465). The actual situation is far more complex than a simple point-to-point map, since a single retinal receptor can excite a large number of cells in cortex, many of which are responsive to specific attributes of the spatial pattern of excited receptors feeding them (orientation, movement, contrast). The observed mapping is generally found to be accurate in the large but with a considerable amount of jitter and local discontinuity in the small. Cells in the same cortical column may have small, nonoverlapping receptive fields scattered over several degrees of visual space (Hubel & Wiesel, 1974b; Creutzfeldt et al., 1974). A tiny spot of light on the retina would influence the activity of many more cells than would be predicted by perfect point-to-point mapping. The "blur circle" (speaking optically) of a point in visual space on the cortex is large and complicated. (See McIlwain, 1975, 1976, for discussions of related problems.) Cells in monkey cortical area 17 have receptive fields on the order of a degree wide, several degrees from the fovea, and of a fraction of a degree in the fovea. (The receptive field is the area of visual space producing a response to a stimulus. In area 17, experimental stimuli are usually oriented bars.) We know average receptive field size increases linearly with angular distance from the fovea in both cat (Fischer, 1973) and monkey (Hubel & Wiesel, 1974b) cortex.

Cortical Model

Let us ignore most of these inconvenient complications and consider a cortical model as a two-dimensional spatial array of neurons, with a precise topographic representation of the outside world. A small spot of light in the visual field would give rise to a distribution of activity in the cortex, the width of the distribution corresponding to the "blur circle." Figure 3 shows the activity due to a point of light somewhere in the visual field.

Let us consider the stimuli used by Posner and Keele: nine randomly placed dots. The overall pattern of activity on the cortical surface (see Fig. 4).

To generate an example from the prototype, dots are displaced in random directions and amounts, thus displacing the bumps representing the neural activities.

We now form a recognition memory: we simply add the activity patterns from different examples.

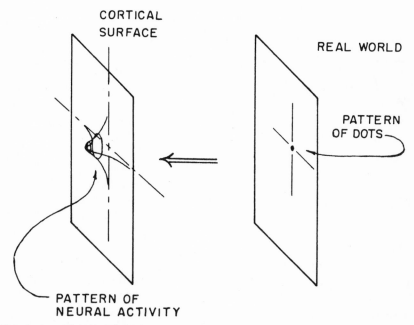

CORTICAL
SURFACE

REAL WORLD

PATTERN
OF DOTS

PATTERN OF
NEURAL ACTIVITY

FIG. 3 A small spot of light (or a small black dot) gives rise to a two-dimensional pattern of excitation on the cortical surface. The amplitude of excitation falls away from a central maximum.

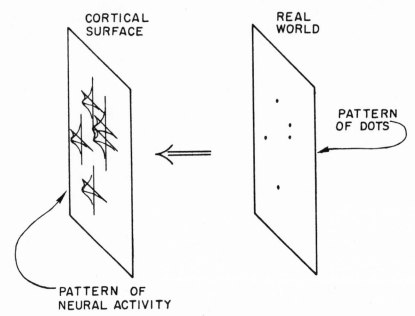

FIG. 4 A pattern of dots gives rise to a pattern of activity distributions on the cortical surface.

We have four memory arrays corresponding to the response categories. When an input comes in, we simply take the dot product between each array and the input array, and make the response with the largest output. (Remember, this is really a matrix, and this is a convenient approximation.)

Let us consider the activity corresponding to a single dot so we can see how this model will work, qualitatively.

We represent the location of the dot in the prototype by the origin of coordinates. If d is the average displacement of a dot from the prototype, then when two examples are stored we will have something like the cross section shown in Fig. 5. We see that the value of the function at the origin is less when d is larger than when d is small. However, the average value of the function, away from the prototype location when many examples are stored, is larger when the memory is formed from highly distorted examples (large d) than when it is formed from slightly distorted examples. Conversely, the amplitude of the sum at the origin will grow faster when the memory is formed from slightly distorted examples, since the activity patterns will then nearly superimpose.

Qualitatively, if the subject learns from highly distorted examples, his memory representation for a single dot will be smeared over a large area, whereas if he learns from only slightly distorted examples, his memory representation will contain a relatively narrow peak.

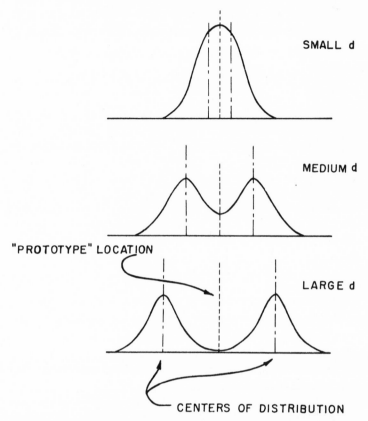

FIG. 5   The memory is formed by adding the activity patterns presented at different times. The location of the prototype is assumed to be at the origin. Large average displacements ('d') give rise to little activity at the location of the prototype. Medium 'd' gives significant prototype enhancement, and small 'd' has an activity pattern with more amplitude at the origin than anywhere else.

Thus we can predict that if the subject learns highly distorted examples, he will take longer to learn to criterion, since the memory representations of different examples will not add together very much, but he may be better at recognizing highly distorted examples, since he will have a more "broadly tuned" memory.

In Posner and Keele's original study (1968, Experiment 1), subjects learning from slightly distorted prototypes made on the average about five errors to criterion, whereas subjects learning from highly distorted prototypes made about twelve errors to criterion. Effects of this type are universally found in the experimental literature. This study also found that subjects who learned on the highly distorted examples were significantly better than the group trained on slightly distorted examples at recognizing new highly distorted examples. This result is not universally found (see Peterson et al., 1973), and does not appear to be particularly strong when found. However, all of these experiments involve learning relatively small numbers (typically 4 to 6) of examples, so the memory filter would be very "lumpy." The statistical approximations made earlier are really only valid for large numbers of stored distortions. This is clearly a matter to be investigated further experimentally since data discussed by Posner (1969, p. 67) seem to indicate that variability around the central tendency is stored in many tasks. Our model predicts that variability should be represented.

Peterson et al. (1973) suggest two models, one they call "additive" and one they call "averaging," which they seem to regard as somewhat exclusive. However, both models are incorporated in the model presented here.

As a final qualitative prediction that can be checked in the literature, we can easily see that as we store more examples we will relatively enhance the prototype, since it will be the spatial average of our noisy inputs. Homa et al. (1973) varied the number of moderate distortions of the prototype presented to subjects from three to nine. Over their experimental conditions, the percentage correct classification of old examples remained nearly constant with the number of examples, between 85 and 95% correct. We should expect this since moderate distortion means that cortical activity patterns are presumably moderately well separated, and their peaks would not interfere very significantly. (Averages over conditions went from 91% correct with three examples presented to 88% correct with nine examples presented. Data here and in later discussion are taken from Homa et al.'s Figure 1.)

The percentage of correct classifications of both prototypes and new examples of the prototypes climbed dramatically with increased number of presentations in almost all the conditions of the experiment. The average percentage correct for prototypes increased from about 62 to 85% as the number of examples presented increased from three to nine. This is what we should expect from our theoretical discussion: an increased enhancement of the prototype over the old examples with more presentations. Correct classifications of new distortions of the prototype also increased strikingly, from 49 to 66%. We should also expect new distortions to be recognized better as the memory filter gets "smoother," although not as greatly enhanced as the prototype.

Prototypes and Letter Perception

A simple prototype, of the kind illustrated here, is only a first step in understanding categorization and abstraction. When feedback and the nonlinearities proposed later are considered, the formal system becomes much more complicated, although not approaching the complexities of the real system. However, one is tempted to think that some of the phenomena observed in reading should be consistent with this model. Recognition of a letter expressed in different type faces, or in different handwritings, might be examples. I would expect the distance of a particular type face or handwriting sample from our internal prototype, formed from years of constant viewing of samples, to correspond in some way to "readability." Many distortions of letters and words produce readability effects that might be due to something as simple as the stimulus almost, but not quite, corresponding to the tuning of our internal filters.

We should be wary of one particular problem. Where memory storage elements are plentiful, it may be easier and more practical for the memory to learn separate associations than to look for commonalities, when the stimuli are different enough. Exactly where this effect occurs depends on the details of the task and the stimuli. A familiar example would be lower- and uppercase letters, which are probably learned separately. As mentioned earlier, many stimuli can be associated with the same response with little interference, if the stimuli are sufficiently different in their neural codes. It would be about as easy for the brain to learn 52 letters as 26. Trying to look for abstraction where it does not exist could be vexing. Separate association might also occur with very unfamiliar type faces – some of the letters in German Fraktur for example – and with some of the more extreme variants of handwriting. When storage elements are cheap, a balance can be struck between abstraction and learning many special cases. Exactly where this balance falls would be of great interest.

Comments on Other Abstraction Phenomena

Considerable time was spent on the Posner and Keele experiments with regard to our model, since the data for this paradigm seem reasonably clear-cut and suitable for analysis with a simple model. However, we may ask if there are other visual phenomena that could lend themselves to a similar analysis.

A well-known example might be the set of experiments by Haber and his co-workers (reviewed in Haber, 1967) on the effects of repetition on tachisto-scopic perception (see also the theoretical paper by Dodwell, 1971). Haber and his co-workers used a word stimulus, presented tachistoscopically in a very brief flash, with a duration chosen to be so short that the subject rarely perceived the word on the first presentation. The same word was then presented over and over, with the same stimulus duration, at a fairly lengthy interstimulus interval of eight seconds or more. Subjects typically report that the stimuli seem to get successively clearer and clearer, until a stimulus that initially could not be perceived at all is plainly recognized, although the *physical* stimulus has re-mained the same. The improvement in perceptibility with repetition can be extremely dramatic, with increases in correct perception of 50% or more, depending on conditions.

We might suggest that somehow the individual, extremely weak and noisy presentations are indeed summating, as suggested by our model, and that we are seeing the formation of an enhanced memory filter that interacts with the weak input to give a clear perception. The published data are not really sufficient to check this suggestion in detail, although results are certainly consistent with it.

However, the most intriguing aspect of these experiments, and the aspect that makes them difficult to handle cleanly with a physiologically based model, is the overwhelming implication from the data that the structure of long-term memory is involved in these tasks. Haber reports in this experiment that familiar words are perceived significantly better than rare words, other conditions being equal, and that English words are perceived significantly better than pronounceable Turkish words.

Thus, the structure of long-term memory has directly entered into a task that at first sight appeared to be primarily perceptual. This result is somewhat similar to the so-called "word superiority" effect that has recently been an object of intense study. Discussion of first steps toward a possible way to analyze these effects will be deferred to a later section.

As the interstimulus interval gets shorter and shorter, effects start to appear that are clearly beyond our simple model. Some stimuli summate in some cases over very brief time intervals, when they are presented sequentially. In vision, some summation effects — summation of quanta at low light levels over considerable temporal intervals and spatial areas — have been known for years (Cornsweet, 1970, Chap. 2). Both Jackson and Dick (1969) and Eriksen and Collins (1968) have reported effects that look like summation of two inputs, using, in one case, very weak visual presentation of single letters and, in the other, two meaningless dot patterns that became meaningful only when added together. Summation seemed to occur over intervals to about 60 msec. It is important, I think, to note that summation seems to occur in many tasks when stimuli are very weak, very noisy, or meaningless. However, when two strong visual stimuli are presented successively at short time intervals (say, under 100 msec), some very powerful effects can appear. These effects are often termed "metacontrast" or "masking" and are beyond the scope of a simple linear model. (See Weisstein, 1972, and Turvey, 1973, for discussion of some of these effects.)

Moral

For those with a taste for it, there is a moral of some kind to be drawn from this discussion. Here we have a system that loses the details of particular events, but has the capacity to generalize and to abstract common parts of separate events. Yet the loss and the gain are two facets of the same process, one inversely related to the other. Perhaps this balance between memory for detail and memory for generality is another example of the kind of engineering compromise that is struck everywhere in the central nervous system. One is irresistibly reminded in this context of Luria's famous mnemonist (Luria, 1968), who was rendered nearly incapable of normal functioning by his marvelously detailed memory, which proved to be more of a burden than a gift.

LIST-SCANNING EXPERIMENTS

The Sternberg Experiments

Occasionally an experiment is described that excites great interest because it is conceptually simple, gives generally reproducible results, and seems to offer the promise of significant theoretical interpretation. Such an experimental paradigm was described and analyzed by Saul Sternberg of the Bell Telephone Laboratories (1966, 1969a, b, 1975) and has been the focus of much recent work. It deals with the recognition of items from short memorized lists.

Subjects learn a short list of items, which are usually letters or digits but may also be geometric forms, pictures of faces, or words. They are then presented with a test item that may or may not have been on the list they just learned. Subjects push one of two buttons or levers, indicating whether or not the item was on the learned list. Reaction time for a response is the experimental measure. Instructions to the subjects emphasize that the subject is to respond "quickly but accurately." These slightly ambiguous instructions give subjects no difficulty, and the error rate is usually low, almost always less than 5%.

The most significant result is quite striking and has been duplicated by most experimenters who have used this task. In the "typical" experiment, there is a linear relationship between number of learned items and reaction time to items that were on the learned list ("positive items"). There is also a linear relationship, with approximately the same slope, for reaction times to items that were not on the learned list ("negative items").

There are two major variants of the experimental procedure. In the first, the "fixed-set" procedure, the same learned list is tested with many different items. In the second, the "varied-set" procedure, the learned list is changed after each test. Both seem to give essentially the same results (Sternberg, 1969a, b).

If we assume that the cognitive apparatus acts in any way like a digital computer, this is a somewhat puzzling result. Suppose that memory representations of the list items repose in separate locations somewhere in our memories. If we were writing a computer program to perform this quite simple task, we would probably, although not necessarily (see Sternberg, 1975), take the incoming test item and compare it with the list items in memory. When we made a successful match, we would exit from our scanning subroutine and make the positive response. If we made no match, after checking all the items on the list, we would exit and make the negative response. If it takes a certain amount of time to make a comparison, we would find (as we do) a linear relationship between list length and reaction time, other times being equal. However, we would also predict a different slope for positive and negative reaction times since in one case we must scan, on the average, half the items, and in the other we must scan all the items. Thus, there should be a two-to-one slope ratio of the plots of negative reaction times versus list length and of positive reaction times versus list length. This two-to-one ratio is found in some special cases, but is not found in the typical experiment.

Other experiments also argue against a simple scan of an internal list. Clifton and Birenbaum (1970) showed that there are strong recency effects when the last list item and the test item occur within two seconds of each other. Also, Theios and his co-workers (Theios, Smith, Haviland, Traupmann, & Moy, 1973; Theios & Walter, 1974) have demonstrated in several fixed-set tasks that there is a powerful effect of probability of presentation of a particular item on the reaction time to that item, more frequently presented items having generally shorter reaction times. It is possible to use list-scanning models to explain these results, but the models require some mechanism to manipulate the order of items on the internal list (Theios, 1973; Theios et al., 1973).

Exhaustive Scanning

The results imply that we seem, at least metaphorically, to scan the entire stored list in both positive and negative cases, an interpretation of this result described by Sternberg and others as "exhaustive scanning."

It seems reasonable that there is a function (a "black box") that might be loosely described as "memory scanning," where incoming sensory information meets stored information in memory and some kind of interaction occurs. What does not seem likely, however, is that this function can be described as an item-by-item comparison of stored and input information.

In many applications of long-term memory, we are usually performing what might be regarded as "exhaustive scans" of memory. For example, if we are presented with a set of letters, we can say very quickly, and in roughly the same time, whether or not the letters form an English word (Rubenstein, Garfield, & Millikan, 1970).

Most of the published work on the Sternberg paradigm has used lists that are from one to about six items long. However, several experiments, necessarily fixed set, because of the need to put a very long list into memory, have used what is essentially a Sternberg task extended to larger numbers of items.

Standing (1973) has performed the most extensive series of experiments along these lines as an adjunct to a recognition experiment involving the learning of very large numbers of items. He used both words and pictures and varied the number of learned items from five to 160. The recognition test was given ten minutes after the end of learning. The subjects did not learn the list to a fixed criterion, but error rates, even for 160-item lists, were low, 13% for pictures and 18% for words. Error rates increased sharply from 5 to 10 items for pictures

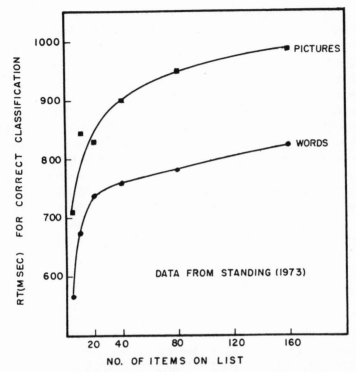

FIG. 6 Graph of reaction time for number of list items for words and pictures (data taken from Standing, 1973, Experiment IV, Table 5). Reaction times are for 'correct classification', that is, recognition as to familiarity or unfamiliarity.

(from 4 to 7%) and for words (from 4 to 13%), and seemed fairly stable after 20 items for pictures (9%) and after 10 items for words (13%).

Standing's data (his Experiment IV, data given in his Table V) are shown in Fig. 6. Only the reaction times for correct "classification" (i.e., familiar or unfamiliar) are given in the table. Positive and negative times are not given separately, but averages over conditions are nearly identical, 876 msec for positive trials and 864 msec for negative trials for pictures, and 715 and 738 msec, respectively, for words.

This curve is markedly negatively accelerated and has an interesting feature, pointed out by Standing. The slope of the curve gives the increment in reaction time caused by adding another item to the list. Standing estimates (using his own theoretical approach, approximating the curve by a power law function) that adding an additional picture to a set of one previous picture would require an additional 40 msec in reaction time, while adding an item to a list of five pictures would require 12 msec additional, and adding an item to a 160-items list would only require an additional .5 msec. An additional word adds 36 msec to reaction time for a one-element list, 11 msec to a five-word list, and .5 msec to a 160-word list. The times for short lists are somewhat comparable to the times found in Sternberg tasks, which are typically found to be in the neighborhood of 35 msec per item for letters and digits, and somewhat longer for other material, about 47 msec on the average for words and in the neighborhood of 55 msec for such visual material as random shapes, geometrical forms, or faces (Cavanagh, 1972; Sternberg, 1969a).

Burrows and Okada (1975) performed an experiment where list length was varied from 2 to 20 items. Subjects learned a list of common two-syllable words to criterion (two complete recalls) and were tested either (in Experiment 1) once on each list item or (in Experiment 2) several times on each list item. Results were qualitatively similar in each case. Plots of reaction time versus list length were fairly linear up to about six items in length, and then became markedly negatively accelerated, with slopes changing from 57 msec per added item (Experiment 1) and 37 msec per added item (Experiment 2) to 13 msec. per added item (Experiments 1 and 2) from the first portion (six items and under) of the curve to the second section of the curve (over six items). Burrows and Okada point out that the complete curve is rather well fit by a logarithmic function, which is, of course, a strongly negatively accelerated function of list length.

Perlmutter, Sorce, and Myers (1974), in a related task that might bear on the shape of the curve at longer list lengths, had subjects learn varying numbers of paired associates, ranging from 3 to 24. They conclude that the curves of reaction time for saying the paired associate versus list length are strongly negatively accelerated in most of their experimental conditions. Although there is some variation with practice, inspection of their figure 1 indicates that the per-association reaction time increase is in the neighborhood of 25 msec per association for a list 3 associates long, dropping to perhaps a 3-msec increase per association for a list 15 associates long.

Implications

These results seem to imply that the rate of memory scanning speeds up as the number of items on the list increases. This certainly seems to be a useful property for a biological memory, since otherwise we might be forced to add several milliseconds to the time required to search our vocabulary, every time we learned a new word. (A restatement – the more we know, the less we can say – seems neither true nor entirely desirable.)

Parallel models, in which the entire memory is scanned at once, seem to be the way around this problem. We have been developing a parallel model in this chapter, and we would like to see if it is capable of explaining these results.

Our discussion of prototypes in the previous section was concerned with constructing a sharp and strong memory filter from noisy inputs. Now we shall consider a more complex filter, formed the same way, that can effectively act like a memory for a list. We shall see that the stronger the representation of the item in the filter, the quicker the reaction time; conversely, the more interference from other items, the slower the reaction time. These implications seem clear if we think of memory as a filter responding to an input signal; they do not seem so clear if we think of a "memory scan" as proceeding in a series of discrete steps.

Memory "Scanning"

I would like to agree with a suggestion of Standing's. Sternberg's linear graphs are an accurate approximation for small numbers of items, but form the initial part of a negatively accelerated continuous function relating list length to reaction time.

It is argued in Anderson (1973) that very large lists (vocabularies, for example) seem to show the exhaustive "scanning" property, as do the very short lists, which have been studied by Sternberg and others. Data are not currently sufficient to determine if intermediate-length lists (10 to 100 items) also show the exhaustive scanning feature.

Let us hypothesize that the box labeled "memory scanning" represents in many cases a single, unitary operation. This operation seems to take on the order of a second for a full memory "cycle," which is roughly the time for a complete search of a very large vocabulary. It is exhaustive in the sense of Sternberg, in that every item is checked during the "scanning" process. The "scanning" rate increases rapidly with time, being slow at first and then accelerating to completion.

If the memory scan, part of a noisy system, does not make a satisfactory match or retrieval at first, presumably higher-level strategies, taking far longer to operate, could be started. These additional processes could be, and probably are, very complex indeed. However, the basic, unitary operation would take roughly a second.

A Model for Scanning

It should be no surprise to the reader that the model developed in previous sections seems to have, at least qualitatively, the properties indicated earlier. A more detailed description of the application of the model to the Sternberg experiments can be found in Anderson (1973).

Basically, we view this task as involving the operation of a memory filter, or an attentional filter. A filter is formed from the items on the list, as discussed previously. A test item appears, and interacts with the filter.

We approximate the connectivity matrix by recognition memories. The elements of the vector forming the memory of the list and the test item interact at elementary multipliers, forming the dot product. The outputs of the elementary multipliers are summed by a summing device.

If the input item as one of the list items, then the output of the filter triggers the positive response.

In the particular subset of the Sternberg experiments chosen to be modeled quantitatively (several fixed-set experiments), the negative set is as well defined as the positive set, since digits were used and hundreds of trials were given for each list. The general problem of the nature of responses to negative items is discussed later.

For this particular set of experiments, we assumed a negative filter in parallel with the positive filter. The output of the negative filter triggers the negative response. This model is shown in Fig. 7.

In order to fit the data quantitatively, several additions to the model are necessary.

The model as presented is purely parallel, and the time for filter operation is independent of the number of stored items. We must introduce a time-dependent process into the system. Something must add up all the outputs from the elementary multipliers. Since neurons, and presumably systems of neurons, often act, as has been discussed, as integrators, it seemed most natural to assume that the summer acted as a long time-constant integrator. As the simplest long time-constant integrator, and as a first-order approximately to more complex ones, let us simply assume that the summer adds up the outputs of a fixed number of elementary multipliers per unit time.

If ΔRT is the time required for the filter to operate and if the time, RT_0, required for other mental operations remains constant, which seems to be a good approximation in this task (see discussion in Sternberg, 1969a), then

$$RT = \Delta RT + RT_0.$$

By our assumption of a fixed rate of element summation, if c is the time for a single element to be summed, then

$$RT = c N_\Sigma + RT_0,$$

where N_Σ is the number of summed elements.

The subject must now look at the output of the summer and decide what to do with it. We will assume that the subject, with years of experience in doing cognitive tasks, will usually decide to try to keep his error rate constant over experimental conditions. This will involve setting the response threshold so as to accomplish this. In our approach, this would correspond to keeping the signal-to-noise ratio constant. (Rough constancy of error rate is found for lists up to about six items in length.)

Earlier in the chapter, we derived a formula for signal-to-noise ratio. With N_Σ elements and K independent list items, the signal-to-noise ratio, s_0, is

$$s_0 = N_\Sigma / K.$$

Thus,

$$N_\Sigma = K s_0.$$

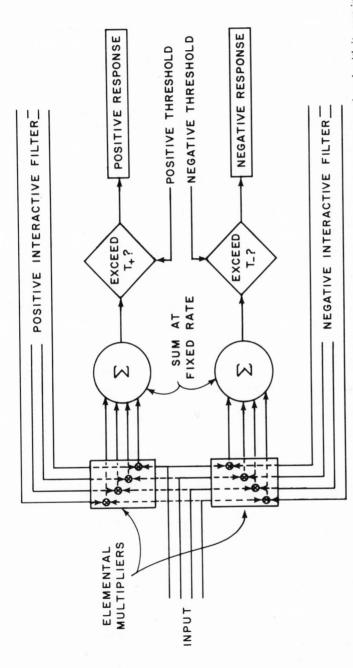

FIG. 7 A model for the Sternberg list-scanning tasks. The model assumes that two parallel systems have been constructed, each with its own interactive filter, one for the positive-stimulus set and one for the negative-stimulus set. The interactive filters bias the sets of elemental multipliers. The sensory input from the test item is multiplied together with the value of the filter at the elements and the output is summed by a summer that appears to operate at a fixed rate. A response is made when one of the summer outputs exceeds a preset threshold. The outputs of the two summers inhibit each other by means of nonrecurrent lateral inhibition. (Copyright 1973 by the American Psychological Association. Reprinted by permission.)

61

Inserting into our formula for reaction time,

$$RT = c\, s_0\, K + RT_0,$$

we have a linear increase of reaction time with number of list items, K.

This calculation is only indicative of the approach; a more detailed calculation is given in Anderson (1973). Quantitative fits of data from several published experiments are also given there.

At this point, we encounter a problem that presents difficulties for this theoretical approach: what to do, in general, about negative items.

The Negative-Item Problem

The entire theoretical approach we have been presenting is oriented toward positive items. Our memory filters, in the extreme approximation, only let through positive items, and negative items give rise to no output at all.

A few moments' thought will suggest several ways to handle this problem for particular cases: For fixed-set procedures with very well learned positive and negative sets, the parallel system described earlier seems justifiable.

Another idea arose from trying to fit the experimental data. Quantitative analysis suggested that the model is incomplete without incorporating *lateral inhibition* at the level of the summers. The output of the positive summer is subtracted from the negative summer, and vice versa. This has the effect of powerfully coupling the positive and negative filters. With appropriate values of coupling, the negative set reaction time can be made almost entirely a function of the positive set. Lateral inhibition is nearly universal in the nervous system.

Since we know that in the real nervous system all test items will get through the filters to a greater or lesser extent, the negative filter will always give some kind of output, whereas the positive filter will give a large output only when there is a match between the test item and an item stored in the filter. This is sufficient to give a reasonable explanation of negative set responses.

We should note that, when we consider only the two filter outputs, we have a model very similar to counter models and random walk models for reaction time, in which we are basing a response on the difference between two processes that are developing in time. Models of this type are impressively successful at explaining much reaction time data, and the strong similarity between these two approaches is very pleasing (see Link, 1974; McGill, 1963; Nickerson, 1969).

An Instructive Analogy

The characteristics of the integrator determine the properties of the reaction time to a very large extent. We can do a pretty good job of matching data for short lists with a fixed-rate summer. However, the negative acceleration of the curve of reaction time versus number of items indicates that the summer speeds up as it operates.

A familiar example of such a process, with a similarly shaped time course, might be the pattern of election returns seen on TV on election night. The candidates interact with the filter: the voters. Both voting and counting ballots are parallel processes, since they occur in many locations at once. Returns are at first very slow, corresponding perhaps to the regime of the Sternberg task. Then the returns start to flood in. In a few hours, returns are complete, except for a usually negligible number of stragglers and absentee ballots. Sometimes the returns are not conclusive, or seem to be noisy, whereupon complex higher-level processes are called into play — the courts or the legislature — and the unitary election process may be repeated.

The TV networks have dramatically demonstrated that only a very small number of returns need to be present to make accurate judgments as to the final outcome of the election. The number of returns required for a judgment of a winner is a function of the degree of risk of a miscall the network is willing to take, and of the size of the winning margin.

Scanning and Linguistic Behavior

The Sternberg paradigm, and related experiments, might at first glance seem to be rather specialized, and a topic of little immediate interest to those whose interests are primarily in the perception and processing of linguistic material. However, this is emphatically not so.

Consider, as mentioned earlier in the chapter, the necessity to continually search a large fraction of long-term memory during any kind of language use. A parallel, distributed memory of the kind discussed here allows rapid, simultaneous access to all parts of memory. The time to retrieve information is a function of the familiarity ("strength") of the item. We should emphasize an important point about this here. "Scanning" and "search" models of memory require an active process as they are usually presented. The filter approach to memory is more passive. The memory lies latent in the storage elements, and the interaction of the input and the memory causes the perception to occur. There is no active cognitive process here, merely excitation of a preexisting trace.

A frequent, somewhat puzzling finding for all kinds of perception is that long-term memory and perception interact very strongly. An example has been given in Haber's experiments on clarity, where repeated very short tachistoscopic presentations of a word caused an apparent increase in perceptibility, even though the physical stimulus was unchanged. More common words showed more enhancement of clarity than uncommon words. Yet how can one know whether a stimulus is familiar or unfamiliar before it is perceived? Numbers of other experiments (some of which are discussed briefly in the next section) have found that previous familiarity can cause enhanced perceptibility; for example, common words have shorter tachistoscopic threshold durations than uncommon words. As Krueger (1975) says in the abstract of a recent review:

> Familiar visual objects, such as normal letters and real words, are processed faster and more accurately than are unfamiliar objects. This fact is massively documented by a wide variety of studies, involving tachistoscopic recognition, visual comparison, and letter detection . . . (p. 949)

Although, as Krueger points out, several mechanisms may be involved, we can see clearly how this kind of effect grows out of the approach to memory sketched here. Since the perception is, very directly, the interaction of input and memory, the strengths of both items have an effect on the outcome. More familiar items interact more vigorously with their strong representations in the memory filter than unfamiliar items do with their weak representations. We need invoke no complex probablistic search processes to explain faster reaction times and enhanced perceptibility; it may be a matter as simple as the observation that it is easier to tune in a strong signal on a radio than a weak one.

DISTINCTIVE FEATURES AND NEURAL MODELS

Features

The notion that there are basic psychological entities, called "distinctive features" that form a kind of "atom" of perception is widely held in modern cognitive psychology. This approach is central to Neisser's very influential book *Cognitive Psychology* (1967) and appears prominently in many elementary textbooks.

This idea arose in linguistics, where it was suggested that phonemes were most usefully characterized by the presence or absence of a small set of "distinctive features." Each phoneme was uniquely represented by its own set of "features" which had the effect of greatly reducing the demands on later processing, since only a relatively small, normalized amount of information need be handled, as opposed to the excess of information contained in an enormously complex and variable speech stimulus.

This idea has frequently been used in practical pattern recognition systems, where often the most difficult task is to choose the correct kinds of primitive features to build into the preprocessing equipment.

The Physiology of Features: Theoretical Issues

Several questions about the relationship between neurophysiology and distinctive feature analysis immediately come to mind.

One might think that an appropriate way to design a brain to carry out distinctive feature analysis would be to have, somewhere, neurons that would respond when, and only when, a particular feature appeared. Evidence for "feature detectors" of this pure kind does exist. For example, the famous "bug detectors" of Lettvin, Maturana, McCulloch, and Pitts (1959) would probably fall into this category. Connections between the "orientation detectors" found in visual cortex and proposed lists of visual features are unavoidable, although misleading.

There is an obvious generalization of this approach, which is clearly and forcefully argued by Barlow (1972). It should be briefly mentioned here because it is held by many neurobiologists, and because it is somewhat opposed (although not as much as might seem at first glance) to the distributed approach that I have stressed in this chapter.

Barlow states a number of "dogmas" about neural processing and perception. He feels that sensory systems are organized to achieve as complete a representation of the sensory stimulus as possible with the least number of discharging neurons. Thus, only a very few cells (1,000, he calculates, in visual cortex) may fire in response to a given visual stimulus. Barlow (1972) feels that perception corresponds to the activity of small selections of numerous higher-level neurons, each of which, at the higher levels, ". . . says something of the order of complexity of a word." (p. 385). Given this statement, Barlow would feel, I am sure, that small, numbers of discharging neurons would correspond to single features in the sense used in psychology, although he does not say so explicitly.

Barlow presents evidence in his essay for, and many others have remarked on, the relative selectivity of response of many cortical neurons. Given the very large number of allowable stimuli, most cortical cells respond to only a minute fraction of them. However, the cells are not exquisitely finely tuned. An "orientation" detector usually responds to orientations over a range of angles $(10°-30°)$ and spatial positions, and a unit from auditory cortex may respond to tones over a range of an octave or more.

Since the strongest psychological evidence for feature analysis is in the auditory system — in the recognition of phonemes — we should look briefly at some of the available neurophysiological data. Corresponding in specificity, perhaps, to "bug detectors," Capranica, Frishkopf, and Nevo (1973) have shown precise matching between electrophysiology of cricket frog audition and the frequencies found in their mating calls.

However, the data from cats and monkeys are not so clear-cut. Wollberg and Newman (1972) recorded from the auditory cortex of squirrel monkeys, using as stimuli tape recordings of species—specific vocalizations. To quote from their abstract, "Some cells responded with temporally complex patterns to many vocalizations. Other cells responded with simpler patterns to only one call. Most cells lay between these two extremes . . ." (p. 212).

Funkenstein and Winter (Funkenstein & Winter, 1973; Winter & Funkenstein, 1973) recorded from auditory cortex of awake squirrel monkeys, using a wider range of species-specific vocalizations. Most of the cells (71%) responded to tone pips of varying frequencies. The response of the majority of the units (63%) that responded to species-specific vocalizations could be predicted from their response to simple stimuli. Of the cells responding to vocalization, 7% could not be excited by any other stimulus. Responses of these few cells were sometimes very precise, responding only to one particular pattern of vocalization. Of 48 responding units studied with a repetoire of 13 calls, 28% responded to only one call type, and 56% responded to no more than two. One could consider this as support for a single-neuron—single-feature model, but it should be pointed out that there are many units that do not show this specificity, and many units responding to a single call may also respond to tone pips or white noise.

Work on cat auditory cortex has found cells with frequency tuning curves of varying width, many sharply tuned, but over half with tuning curves over half an octave wide. Cells are described as "highly individualistic" in their response patterns (Goldstein, Hall, & Butterfield, 1968).

In most cases, the frequency spectra associated with proposed human linguistic features are quite broad, and sometimes ill defined, even though there are exceptions, for example, voicing (Lindgren, 1965).

Although there are some highly selective cells, we can argue from the evidence that a number of cells can respond to several features. Thus, we make the initial hypothesis, as a start for theorizing, that (1) a given neuron may respond to several distinctive features, and (2) conversely, a distinctive feature may not be coded by the firing of a particular, highly selective, single purpose group of cells.

We shall see later that this *approximation* allows us to approach the problem of the observed high specificity of cortical neurons from an intriguing angle.

This may seem to be a technical point, of concern only to neuroscientists, but it is not. A nervous system where single cells are very highly specialized in the way proposed by Barlow is of a quite different type than a more distributed system. Extreme selectivity of response has trouble giving the kinds of generalization and associativity that are found by psychologists to be characteristic of human memory. From a theoretical point of view as well, it is much easier to incorporate selectivity into a distributed system than to do the opposite. Therefore, let us make the *approximation* just given and see where it takes us.

A Mathematical Model for Features

We should initially observe that where distinctive feature analysis seems to play a large role in perception, it does so as part of a very well-learned perceptual system: for example, speech or reading. Almost all of the detailed published discussions of feature analysis in perception have used as data either spoken language or the visual perception of letters and words. It is possible, indeed likely, that a few other extremely well-learned perceptual tasks – in particular, some biologically meaningful and highly practiced tasks such as face recognition – may incorporate a feature component as well. However, as we shall see, there are theoretical reasons for believing that feature analysis may be characteristic of a particular type of very well-learned task.

Let us conjecture that two extremes of memory operation may occur in practice. The first might correspond to the particular details of specific complex occurrences. It is known that the recognition memory for very large numbers of pictures (up to 10,000), presented briefly, is astonishingly large (Standing, 1973). In the second extreme, a small number of very highly learned items must be quickly and reliably discriminated.

In the first mode, the number of independent elements involved (N in our notation) may be very large, allowing storage of many independent items with a high retrieval-signal-to-noise ratio. In the second mode, inputs are analyzed in terms of a small number of well-learned stimulus dimensions. How can we construct such a system using very large numbers of neurons that may respond to several dimensions?

Assume that we have an associative system coupling a set of neurons, α, to itself. We make the approximation that every neuron projects to every other neuron. (In general, this is not the case, but we could approximate a more restricted connectivity in some cases by considering the properties of a number of groups of completely interconnected neurons.) Let us assume that this feedback connection is positive and is through a matrix, A, of synaptic connectivities. This model is shown in Fig. 8.

Let us consider a case in which a pattern of activity on α is coupled to itself. The synaptic increment, Δa_{ij}, is proportional to the product of the activity shown by the ith neuron, $f(i)$, and the jth neuron, $f(j)$. Note that

$$\Delta a_{ij} = \Delta a_{ji},$$

implying that A is a symmetric matrix. Symmetric matrices in general have two properties of interest to us: (1) their eigenvectors are orthogonal and (2) their eigenvalues are real.

As with many other systems, the eigenvectors of this matrix display some interesting and significant properties.

Qualitatively, some interesting properties immediately appear. Assume that we present a number of orthogonal inputs. The matrix will tend to learn these inputs, as it would any other set of inputs. Thus, if $\bar{f}_i$ is an input,

$$A\bar{f}_i = \lambda \bar{f}_i,$$

where λ will increase as $\bar{f}_i$ is presented more often. How fast λ grows depends on the values of learning coefficients assumed (see Cooper, 1974; Nass & Cooper, 1975).

We have assumed a system with positive feedback. Thus, if an eigenvector, $\bar{f}_i$, appears at the input, it will be fed back. It will add to the input, and the

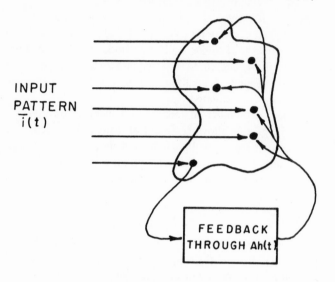

SET OF N NEURONS
PATTERN OF ACTIVITY $\bar{a}(t)$

INPUT
PATTERN
$\bar{i}(t)$

FEEDBACK
THROUGH Ah(t)

EVERY NEURON PROJECTS TO
EVERY OTHER NEURON BY
WAY OF FEEDBACK LOOP
WITH RESPONSE FUNCTION h(t)
AND·WITH CONNECTIVITY
MATRIX A

FIG. 8 A set of neurons with feedback through a connectivity matrix with a long conduction time. We have a set of N neurons. The pattern of neural activity shown by the set of neurons is denoted $a(t)$. There is an input pattern to the set of neurons, denoted $i(t)$. There is feedback from every neuron to every other neuron through a connectivity matrix, A. The impulse response function of the feedback system is denoted $h(t)$.

resulting sum will be fed back again, the amplitude of $\bar{f_i}$ growing with each trip through the feedback system. The eigenvalue (λ) will determine the gain of the feedback.

Suppose a mixture of eigenvectors with large eigenvalues and eigenvectors with small eigenvalues appears at the input of the system. The eigenvectors with small eigenvalues are fed back relatively very little and increase only slowly with time. However, the eigenvectors with large eigenvalues are fed back more and increase quickly with time. Thus, qualitatively, eigenvectors with large eigenvalues will tend to dominate the activity of the group of neurons after a brief period, and the other eigenvectors will make a relatively smaller contribution. This is exactly the behavior we wish a distinctive feature to have.

Let us identify the distinctive features of a group of neurons containing a positive feedback connectivity matrix coupling the group to itself with the eigenvectors with large positive eigenvalues of the feedback matrix.

Physiological Basis of Feedback

There is ample physiological substrate for such a feedback system. The extensive recurrent collateral system in cortex and the extensive thalamocortical and corticothalamic projection systems are prime candidates (see discussion in Anderson, 1974). Higher spine densities and more extensive high-order branching of basal dendrites of the cortical pyramids have been observed when rats are raised in an enriched environment, as opposed to littermates raised in a deprived environment (Globus, Rosenzweig, Bennett, & Diamond, 1973; Greenough and Volkmar, 1973). Recurrent collaterals in cortex seem to synapse extensively on the basal dendrites (Scheibel & Scheibel, 1970). Ingle (1975) has presented evidence and suggested that self-exciting circuits may play an important functional role in the optic tectum of the frog.

A particularly relevant series of studies has been published by Freeman and his collaborators (see Freeman, 1975 for a review). They have experimented upon and made mathematical models of the electrical activity of the olfactory cortex (prepyriform cortex) of the cat. They have had considerable success applying linear systems analysis to the activity of this primitive cortex, and have incorporated exactly the kinds of feedback loops and saturating nonlinearities that are suggested here as a model for features. An excitatory collateral system, from prepyriform pyramids onto themselves, has been described anatomically. The anatomy and physiology of this system is described in Shepherd (1974).

Stability

Whenever one has a system using positive feedback in an essential way, important questions of stability arise. Let us consider this question for a minute. In the visual system, we can approximate grossly the behavior of the system to the onset of a stimulus by assuming that the retinal neurons fire a brief, very high-frequency burst of spikes and then become relatively quiet, even if the stimulus is maintained. (See the discussion of time course of events in the visual system in Anderson, 1974.) The cortical system then responds to this brief burst with a longer time constant response. We conjecture that this long time constant response is due, at least partially, to the slow response of the feedback system, where signals slowly trickle through the feedback pathways. The decay of the slow response is very significantly lengthened by the operation of the feedback system.

Let us inspect a linear version of this feedback model.

We will assume that the cortical cell whose activity we wish to study has a rather rapid response to stimuli; that is, the membrane and postsynaptic potential time constants are fast. The feedback system, for whatever reason, is associated with a much longer time constant.

Denote the set of activities of the neurons in α by the vector $\bar{a}(t)$. The set of inputs to these cells is given by $\bar{i}(t)$. In the absence of feedback, we assume that the cortical cells follow their inputs exactly, thus:

$$\bar{a}(t) = \bar{i}(t).$$

If there is feedback through the matrix, past times will contribute significantly to $\bar{a}(t)$. Since we are assuming that the system is approximately linear and the nerve cell is acting as a linear integrator, the contribution of a past time, t_0, is given by $A\,\bar{a}(t_0)$ weighted by the value of the impulse response function of the feedback, $h(t_0)$. Thus, we can write an integral equation for the activity of the system at time t as follows:

$$\bar{a}(t) = \bar{i}(t) + \int_{-\infty}^{t} h(t-t_0)\,A\,\bar{a}(t_0)dt_0.$$

This particular equation arises frequently in linear system theory and is easily solved. Let us consider the case where there is no activity for t less than zero and where the input at $t = 0$ is an eigenvector of $A, \bar{f}$. Let us make $a(t)$ and $i(t)$ scalar functions describing the amplitude of $\bar{f}$. (We normalize $\bar{f}$, so $\bar{f} \cdot \bar{f} = 1$, as usual.) We can do this, since $\bar{f}$ is an eigenvector, allowing us to replace the matrix with the eigenvector multiplied by its eigenvalue, a great simplification. Then

$$a(t) = i(t) + \lambda \int_{0}^{t} h(t-t_0)a(t_0)dt_0.$$

The right-hand side of this equation contains a convolution integral. Thus, we can take the Laplace transform of both sides and solve for $A(s)$, the transform of $a(t)$, obtaining

$$A(s) = \frac{I(s)}{1 - \lambda H(s)}.$$

Let us consider the qualitative behavior of this system. We will assume that the input to the cortical cells is a brief burst of activity, approximated by an "impulse," $\delta(t)$. This is not a bad first-order approximation to the visual system.

Let us assume that the impulse response of the feedback system is a simple exponential decay:

$$h(t) = c\,e^{-\beta t}.$$

Inserting in our formula, we obtain, with a little algebra,

$$A(s) = 1 + \frac{\lambda c}{s + \beta - \lambda c},$$

and we find, taking the inverse transform,

$$a(t) = \delta(t) + \lambda c e^{-(\beta - \lambda c)t}.$$

We have recovered the input, $\delta(t)$, as we would have expected, but we see that the remaining activity contains an exponential time constant.

Note several things: The time constant is a function of the eigenvalue, λ. If $c\lambda > \beta$, the system is unstable, that is, grows in amplitude without limit. However, for values less than this, the time constant of the response of the system is lengthened and the multiplicative factor of λ increases the amplitude, but the activity eventually returns to zero; thus, the system is stable.

If the eigenvalue is large, the system responds to the eigenvector strongly and for a long time. If the eigenvalue is small, it responds weakly and for a short time.

We see that if an input enters that contains some "distinctive features," after a while the system activity will be composed primarily of these patterns, and the other patterns will be relatively weaker. We have thus produced an activity pattern composed primarily of independent features extracted from a complex input, which is what we wanted.

General Comment

At this point, one must take note of the very great formal similarity between this hypothesized feature extraction scheme, in a distributed neural memory system, and the Karhunen–Loève feature extraction scheme used in pattern recognition (Young & Calvert, 1974, p. 228). The Karhunen–Loève expansion reduces the dimension of a high-dimensionality stimulus space by expanding an input in terms of a subset of the eigenvectors with large eigenvalues of the covariance matrix formed from the input class of stimulus vectors. The expansion can be shown to be an optimal linear feature extractor in some senses. Although it is often used for practical pattern recognition problems, the very large amounts of computation time often needed to solve the resulting equations sometimes make applications to particular systems impractical. Use of a distributed memory, with positive feedback, as proposed here, allows us to perform this analysis automatically, again emphasizing that the kinds of calculation that can be easily performed by a distributed parallel system are often quite different from those that can be easily performed by a more serial system.

As a related mathematical point, a recent study by Pfaffelhuber (1975) discusses the general optimality of this and related memory models, and concludes that when viewed in the light of adaptive filter theory, the simple approximations made here are nearly optimal. He concludes that "correlation memory models can be looked upon as a first order approximation within a general learning scheme . . . (and) under certain well defined conditions, they are already nearly optimal in the sense that their prescriptions are close to what, in the general scheme, is achieved only after an infinite number of learning steps . . ." (p. 223).

Psychological Implications

The model as proposed is rather general, even though the phenomenon we tried to model was distinctive feature analysis. Suppose many aspects of memory reflect the operation of such a feedback system. The qualitative result is, again, that things that are familiar are better transmitted by the "memory filters." Positive feedback has the effect of more sharply tuning the filter, so it is somewhat more selective, at the cost of distorting the input. The model again suggests that unfamiliar inputs do not give the same amplitude of response, measured in cell activities, as familiar inputs. This builds in a tremendous bias in favor of the perception of patterns that are meaningful in terms of the past history of the system.

It is possible that such effects as the "word advantage" effect, where letters embedded in words seem to be detected better than letters embedded in nonwords, may reflect at least some aspects of this process.

Although it is premature to make any firm statements about the mechanisms involved in a phenomenon as complex as the "word advantage" effect, certain classes of models arise naturally from our approach to cognitive structure, whereas others require a bit of straining. We are handicapped in that we do not know much about the details of the neural representation of words and letters, other than some information about the details of the initial stages of processing of the visual image. Visually, words are composed of letters, yet, as reviewed in Estes (1975, this volume), neighboring letters have very powerful effects on the perceptibility, and presumably the neural coding, of individual letters, effects so extreme in some cases as to make letters that are legible when standing alone unidentifiable when flanked by other letters. Thus, the grouping of letters into words has caused considerable perturbation in the neural activity associated with the letters. Some of these perturbing effects, such as concentric surround lateral inhibition, operate relatively peripherally in the visual system, and we should expect even more powerful lateral interactions centrally, since receptive field sizes and complexity of structure of receptive fields increase as we progress up the visual system. Thus, we can reasonably state that the neural activity pattern representing a word is related to, but not identical with, the sum of the codes representing the individual letters, since powerful interaction terms are present.

As discussed in Anderson (1974), we may be able to view the visual system for some purposes as a series of interactive filters and feedback systems, of the type we have discussed here. Since letters are physically smaller and spatially more localized than the words composed of the letters, we might hypothesize, at least at lower levels, that the eigenstates corresponding to a letter involve activities of fewer neurons and more localized interactions than eigenstates corresponding to words. Letters, and to a lesser extent familiar letter groups, would be more common than any particular word and thus might have a larger eigenvalue and a smaller dimensionality eigenvector. We might expect the time course of the fed-back letter activity to have a somewhat faster rise time than the corresponding word activity pattern, and for the structure of the word activity to depend on the presence of strongly preprocessed elements, put into a standard form by fed-back eigenvector enhancement of the kind we have been discussing. The recognition of words would critically depend on the use of the perturbation terms, that is, the parts of the neural activity pattern not corresponding to the sum of the activity patterns due to letters. These perturbation components might loosely correspond to the "higher-level" features that have often been claimed for word perception.

Estes (this volume) suggests that the word advantage effect is primarily due to positional effects: In words the letters are held in a fixed position of known order, whereas in nonwords letter representations can "slide around" without a stabilizing framework. The word advantage effect might arise in part because, for words, the perturbing terms would be recognized, fed back, and enhanced, stabilizing the positions of the lower-level letter activities, which seem, by this interpretation, to be relatively independent of each other. Some interesting questions of visual perception arise here, since Estes' finding seems to require that the neural activity pattern corresponding to a letter contain a part that is somewhat independent of exact spatial location and, in the case of a word, is localized by cooperative neighborhood interactions.

A modified hierarchical scheme, as proposed by Estes (1975), LaBerge and Samuels (1974), and McClelland (1976), is entirely consistent with the approach to modeling sketched previously. We can metaphorically conceive of a succession of processing stages, arranged in a hierarchy, corresponding to the processing of successively more complex and "holistic" aspects of the stimulus, somewhat as sketched in Fig. 9, but now to be interpreted in a more psychological sense. It is important to note that for psychology, as well as for the physiology, the time courses of the operations performed by each level in the hierarchy are not sequential, but overlapping. That is, the later levels start to interpret incomplete, partially processed information from lower levels as soon as it becomes available, and generate outputs based on fragmentary information, as long as the information is sufficient to determine an output, perhaps by operation of a saturating positive feedback system, as proposed in the next section. As with any engineer-

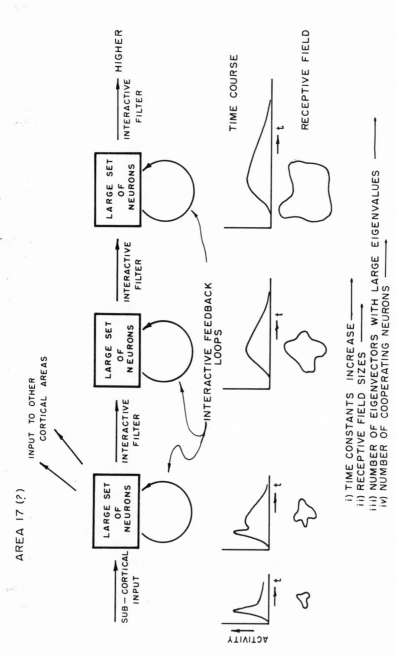

FIG. 9 A hierarchy of interactive processes in perception. We assume that large sets of neurons are coupled by interactive associative networks. At each level, positive feedback loops of the type discussed elsewhere perform a 'feature' analysis, tending to enhance the eigenstates with large positive eigenvalues. Time constants of responses to a brief input get longer and longer at higher levels of the hierarchy. Note that time courses of levels overlap; that is, one level starts processing before the earlier ones are finished. This figure is meant to be an abstraction of the kinds of projection system found in cerebral cortex, but bears a close relationship to the kinds of psychological models that would correspond to the operation of such a physiological system.

ing system, the preliminary analysis need not be very complete, just good enough to be correct a satisfactory amount of the time.

These models are similar to those found in other branches of science. For example, the "compartmental" models common in physiology and biochemistry are of this type, in which later stages of a multistage chemical reaction or physiological process will start to occur when only a few molecules of product from earlier stages appear, even though the earlier stages of the reaction are far from complete. A series of cascaded electronic filters would also be similar. A series of discrete logical steps would generally *not* be of this type.

Thus, as Estes has observed, it becomes very important to look carefully at the time courses of the component processes of these complex psychological effects, since, as he demonstrates, different aspects of the word advantage effect can have quite different time courses.

Physiological Extensions

As developed, the formal model does not make any restrictions on the form taken by the activity patterns. We could have activity patterns containing a great many small changes in activity or containing only a few large changes. All we require is that the vectors be eigenvectors and that certain normalization and statistical criteria be satisfied.

Yet we know, and some evidence has been mentioned in regard to the previous discussion of Barlow's work, that the actual coding used by the central nervous system seems to involve large changes in the activity of a fraction of the neurons; that is, the individual neurons are rather sharply tuned. Can we say anything about why this might be?

Nass and Cooper (1975) have presented a developmental model incorporating lateral inhibition that acts like a sharpening mechanism. When a cell starts to respond to a particular input pattern, it inhibits its neighbors thus preventing them from picking up that particular pattern.

Another mechanism grows out of the positive feedback notions developed earlier, and might perhaps work in cooperation with lateral inhibition. When one incorporates positive feedback into a linear system, potential for instability exists. If the eigenvalue is larger than a certain value, the amplitude of the activity grows without bound. There is no obvious mechanism to avoid this catastrophe in the model, since the "good" aspect of feedback, the relative enhancement of familiar items, is greatest when there is a large amount of feedback.

We know there is a very significant nonlinearity in neurons: they do not fire faster than a certain frequency, usually several hundred spikes per second. Thus there is an upper limit to the response of a particular neuron, as well as a lower-bound, zero firing frequency.

Suppose we incorporate this nonlinearity in our model. (A more detailed discussion of this model is in preparation.) The following discussion is accurate but qualitative. A particular activity pattern, a vector, is a point in a very high-dimensionality space. The coordinate axes correspond to activities of individual neurons. Thus, putting limits on firing frequencies corresponds to putting the allowable activity patterns in a box; that is, the activity patterns can only

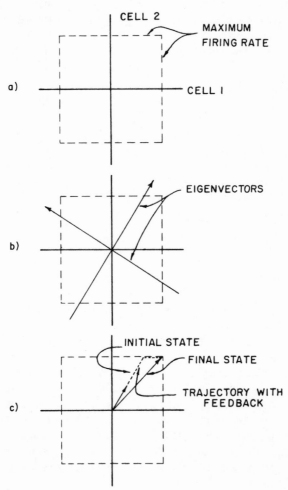

FIG. 10 Effects of saturation on the feedback model (two-dimensional example). Both Cell 1 and Cell 2 (the axes) have maximum firing rates (a). Consider the two eigenvectors shown in (b). When an eigenvector is input to the system, it lengthens owing to the positive feedback. When one component attains maximum firing rate, the continued operation of the feedback forces the vector into a corner, the final state, even though this final state is not one of the eigenvectors (c).

occupy points inside the box. Figure 10 illustrates the situation for two dimensions. There can be negative activities, it should be pointed out, and maximum negative response could correspond to either zero firing frequency, in one interpretation, or perhaps to the maximum firing rate of an "opposite-sign" cell, in another interpretation.

Suppose we start off with an eigenvector that is receiving powerful positive feedback; that is, without limits, the vector would grow indefinitely. The vector lengthens until it hits a firing limit, one of the walls of the box. Calculations are not difficult for this case, and it can be seen that the vector will continue to try to get longer, but it cannot escape from the box. Thus, it will head for one of the corners of the box, which are the points farthest away from the origin.

In the general case, when the initial state is a mixture of eigenvectors, it will try to head for the corner closest to the strongest eigenvector with a large eigenvalue in the initial state, although exactly which corner it ends up in will depend on the size of the box and the spectrum of eigenvalues associated with the eigenvectors describing the initial state.

It can be shown that only some corners are stable. How many stable corners there are appears to depend on the ratio between the largest and smallest eigenvalues and other details of the system. Interestingly, though, some corners cannot correspond to a stable state of the system.

Some intriguing properties are associated with a corner: It is a point where some cells are firing maximally and others are off (or, not responding, i.e., at zero). Thus, it conforms roughly to the observed pattern of neuron discharges as described by Barlow.

Suppose this system is a learning system; that is, the synapses are still changing. The most common pattern of activity, due to the feedback and the firing rate limitation, will be the stable corners. Thus, the synapses will tend to learn the stable corners.

Once the system has learned the corners, even the linear system that is far away from the firing limits (i.e., well within the box, that is, a short vector) will have eigenvectors that point toward the corners. A few mathematical problems can arise here if the box is not centered on the origin, but these are tractable.

It should be pointed out that the semiconductors used in computers often run in "saturation," which is formally quite similar to the system proposed here, and has the frequently desirable effects of noise immunity and speed. Perhaps more important, small nonlinearities of transduction and integration do not greatly affect the properties of a saturated system, a result true for our neural system as well.

It can be seen that as long as the positive feedback remains on, the activity pattern will stay in the corner. If a new activity pattern is impressed on the system, the pattern of activity may be made to shift corners. Or, if there is powerful adaptation, as is often found in cortex, the rapidly firing neurons will slow down with time and the system may shift to a new corner with a new set of rapidly firing neurons when the length of the initial vector decreases enough to allow it. The system can then progress from stable activity pattern to stable activity pattern with rather rapid transitions between modes.

The N-dimensional space will be partitioned into a number of regions. An initial state occupying any point in a given region will end up in the same corner. Thus, all the points in a region are "interpreted" identically by the system, since they give rise to the same final state, that is, the same corner. This is a powerful technique for putting noisy inputs into standard form, another characteristic that is associated with distinctive features but may also be typical of memory in general.

An Example

The following work was done in collaboration with Jack Silverstein, Division of Applied Mathematics, and Stephen A. Ritz, Department of Linguistics, Brown University.

The preceding section has presented a mechanism that could be used in many ways, but perhaps the most obvious function of a single stage is to take a noisy input and put into a "standard form." It becomes a kind of normalizing preprocesser. It seemed of interest to apply this model to some experimentally based data to see if it would work and to get some idea of its properties.

In its essentials, the model presented is a "categorical perceiver" in a strict sense; that is, it takes all the initial activity patterns in a region of hyperspace and lumps them together in a single corner. Thus, it has all the properties characteristic of the categorical perception phenomena that have been found in a number of linguistic contexts, particularly in the perception of consonants. Here, when a series of stimuli are constructed that vary continuously across a dimension, say, voice onset time, which is used in making the /p/ versus /b/ discrimination, the listener typically cannot make discriminations well within a category; that is, all the consonants perceived as /p/ cannot be discriminated from each other, even though their voice onset times vary considerably. Conversely, discriminations across the boundary are very good; thus, two stimuli differing only slightly in the physical stimulus can be easily discriminated when the difference falls across a category boundary.

The corner model previously described classifies all points in a region together (differences vanish) and classifies different regions apart (differences are large), and thus "categorically perceives." There is an extensive literature in this area. See, for example, Eimas (1963); Liberman, Harris, Hoffman, and Griffith (1957); Liberman, Mattingly, and Turvey (1972). The existence of this phenomenon seems well documented for consonants. It can be argued that vowel perception shows some of the properties of categorical perception, but in weaker form. This is at least partially due to the very much greater duration of vowels in speech. Vowels are perceived more categorically when their duration is artificially shortened (Fujisaki & Kawashima, 1970; Pisoni, 1971). In any case, whether or not the full picture of the strongest form of categorical perception is present, very similar physical stimuli are perceived differently, that is, named as different vowels, although discrimination is possible to some degree within vowel categories.

A good deal of detailed phonetic information is available on the acoustic structure of vowels. The frequencies present in vowels are rather constant (for pure vowels) over a hundred milliseconds or so, and the complex temporal structure characteristic of consonants and the immediately following vowel is not seen and can be ignored in our simulation. As experimentally derived data to test our model, we used the data on Dutch vowels presented by Klein, Plomp, and Pols (1970).

Klein, Plomp, and Pols analyzed the 12 Dutch vowels in their sample set by using a bank of 21 narrow band frequency filters, each one-third of an octave wide, a width chosen to approximate the critical bands of the ear and about the same width as many tuning curves of neurons in the auditory system. They then took samples of the 12 vowels, spoken by a number of male speakers, and averaged and statistically processed the filter outputs so as to get a reasonable approximation to the "average vowel." (This average vowel would correspond, quite closely, to the prototypes discussed earlier.) These were the data we used as the starting point for our computer simulation.

To a first approximation, we simply said that one filter output corresponded to the firing frequency of one of our hypothetical neural elements. Though the Dutch workers used 21 filters, our simulation involved a matrix that could lead to excessive amounts of computer time if its dimensionality was too large. By combining adjacent filter outputs, we reduced the dimensionality of the system to eight, that is, we described each vowel as an eight-element vector, each element derivable from the 21 original filter outputs. We let each one of these vector components correspond to a neural element. Finally, we adjusted each element, initially containing only positive values (decibels above a reference level), so that it had a mean of zero, averaged across vowels. Over the entire set of vowels, each neuron fired both positively and negatively. An assumption of this kind has been discussed previously, and seems reasonable in a nervous system where inhibition is as important as excitation.

In the final coding for each vowel (see Table 1), we ended up with eight neural elements and with vector representations of nine separate Dutch vowels. The number of vowels was greater than the number of neural elements, to demonstrate that the system would work when the number of elements to be categorized was greater than the dimensionality of the space. The three other vowels became, in our simplified coding, essentially identical to one or another of the nine vowels used, and were not considered further.

In the codings for each vowel (Table 1), it should be mentioned that several of these vectors are very close together. For example, the angle in hyperspace

TABLE 1[a]

Vowel	Element values							
/a/	−3	−9	17	26	18	2	5	0
/α/	−5	−5	18	22	−10	−4	2	−5
/ɔ/	−4	5	15	8	−27	−11	−4	−8
/u/	3	5	2	−8	−30	−21	−21	−5
/oe/	0	8	−1	5	9	3	−1	2
/y/	5	−2	−26	−17	9	−5	−12	2
/ε/	−1	1	13	4	16	10	7	4
/I/	1	4	−13	−14	12	14	10	5
/i/	5	−7	−28	−28	3	13	15	7

Values derived by adding filter outputs in
Klein, Plomp, & Pols

Our element	Klein, Plomp, & Pols filter
1	1–5
2	6–8
3	9–10
4	11–12
5	13–14
6	15–16
7	17–18
8	19–21

[a]Numbers are deviations from mean across all nine vowels,
separately for each component. Each unit equals .57 decibels.

between the codings for /I/ and /i/ is 32°. Also very close together are the vectors representing /ɔ/ and /u/, 45° apart, and /α/ and /ɔ/, 46° apart. Since the initial vectors were so close together, the ability to classify these vectors into different corners in the saturating learning scheme would be a rather challenging test.

The computer simulation was a straightforward application of the model as presented previously. One of the nine vowels, chosen at random, was input. The feedback matrix output added to the input and a modified input was generated. The modified input was operated on again by the feedback matrix a total of seven times. The final state was then learned, by the synaptic modification scheme we have been using, that is,

$$\Delta a_{ij} = \eta f(i) f(j).$$

The learning coefficient, η, was chosen to be 10^{-6} at first, so the matrix learned very slowly. The feedback matrix was initially set to be the identity matrix times 10^{-3}. In a real brain, there would be a very sizable genetic, prewired component to the initial state of the feedback matrix. The final diagonal values for the elements of the feedback matrix, after many learning trials, were far larger than 10^{-3}.

The limits of saturation were set at plus or minus 35, just larger than the largest initial component (30). The initial lengths of the vectors varied from 13.6 to 43.7, with a mean of 33.2. The corners were 99.0 units away from the origin, so the vectors had to expand about three times to get into a corner. (These parameters were not the result of any systematic search.)

One significant modification was made to the original learning scheme. We assumed that when a neuron reached saturation, a firing rate of plus or minus 35, in seven cycles through the feedback matrix, then the synapses associated with that neuron, both pre- and postsynaptic, did not learn. The assumption took this form in our simulation primarily for programming convenience and because it maintained the symmetry of the matrix. A similar, though not identical, assumption was made by Nass and Cooper (1975). It seems not unreasonable that a system should cease to learn when it has learned enough to cause the cell to saturate in response to a stimulus. However, the implications of this assumption are profound, and numerous reasonable variants of it are possible. This is a point that should be investigated further.

Results of the simulation were in accord with the results expected from our previous qualitative discussion. We checked the classification ability of the matrix by allowing it to operate on an initial vector for as many steps as it took to saturate all the components. When the feedback matrix was small, this might take a very large number of cycles. When the matrix had learned for a while, all the components of an input vowel would saturate in seven cycles or less. Thus, speed of classification increased greatly with learning.

Table 2 shows the corners into which different vowels were classified at various stages in the development of the matrix. To save computer time, after about 1,000 learning trials with a small learning parameter (10^{-6}), η was increased substantially, first to 10^{-4} and then to 10^{-3}. Since only a very few of the components of the vectors were remaining unsaturated, most of the matrix was not learning, and thus a greater learning rate would not distort the structure of the matrix and would save computer time. The number of learning trials quoted in the text and tables refers to estimated number of trials using the original learning parameter. Although most of the elements in the vowel vectors would saturate in seven steps by 1,000 trials, the last components did not saturate until between 10,000 and 20,000 trials.

A glance at Table 2 shows that some classifications were quite stable from the beginning of learning, while others shifted back and forth. The last change in classification was made between 10,000 and 20,000 trials. At first the system started by classifying a great many vowels together. Then, as learning continued, each grouping tended to split until, when learning ceased, each vowel was assigned to a different corner. Table 3 shows classification groups at various points in learning.

TABLE 2
Vowel Classification[a]

Approx. no. of trials	/a/	/ɑ/	/ɔ/	/u/	/oe/	/y/	/ɛ/	/I/	/i/
100	--++++++	--++-----	--++-----	--++-----	++--++++	++--++++	--++++++	++--++++	++--++++
300	+-++++++	-+++-----	-+++-----	-+++-----	+-----++++	+-----++++	+-----++++	+-----++++	+-----++++
700	+-++++++	--++-----	-+++-----	-+++-----	++--++++	+-----++-+	+--+-++++	+-----++++	+-----++++
2,000[b]	+-++++++	--++-----	-+++-----	-+++-----	+-----++++	+-----++-+	+++++++++	++--++++	+-----++++
5,000[b]	+-++++++	--++-----	-+++-----	++++++++	+-----++-+	+-----++-+	++--++++	++--++++	+-----++++
10,000[b]	+-++++++	--++-----	-+++-----	-++-----	++--++++	+-----++-+	++++++++	++--++++	+-----++++
20,000[c]	+-++++++	--++-----	-+++-----	-++-----	++--++++	+-----+--+	+++++++++	++--++++	+-----++++

[a] "+" and "_" represent positive and negative units of saturation, respectively. Each pattern of "+" and "_" represents the stable corner eventually reached by the vector corresponding to an input vowel.

[b] Increased learning parameter.

[c] Matrix has ceased to learn.

82

TABLE 3
Vowel Classifications[a]

No. of trials	ε	ɔ	Groupings
100	(a, ε)	(α, ɔ, u) (oe, y, I, i)	
300	(a)	(α, ɔ, u) (oe, y, ε, I, i)	
700	(a)	(α) (ɔ, u) (oe, y) (ε) (I, i)	
~2,000	(a)	(α) (ɔ, u) (oe, I) (ε) (i) (y)	
~5,000	(a)	(α) (ɔ) (u) (oe, ε) (y) (I) (i)	
over 10,000	(a)	(α) (ɔ) (u) (oe) (ε) (y) (I) (i)	

When misclassifications appeared or remained late in learning, they took a very long time to correct, although the final matrix correctly classified them apart. For example, /oe/ and /ε/ were misclassified in the same corner, starting at around 5,000 trials, a misclassification it took 5,000 trials to correct.

The final system contained 202 stable corners out of 256 corners. To check the size of the regions associated with corners corresponding to vowels, a Monte Carlo simulation was run with 1,000 random vectors, initially as long as the average vowel, that is, 33.2 units. It was found that about 25% of the random vectors ended up in a corner associated with a vowel, whereas we would have expected 9/202, or 4.5%, of vowel classifications, if the regions were of equal size. The learning process had greatly increased the regions associated with the vowels, at the expense of other regions.

GENERAL SUMMARY

We have covered a wide range of topics in this chapter and presented several applications of a mathematical model for memory organization that was, hopefully, a simple example of a kind of model in harmony with what we know about the brain. Thus, it was distributed in that a memory trace was spread out over many storage elements and could be realized by arrays of elements with properties somewhat like those of real neurons; that is, they acted primarily as analog integrators. The model was grievously oversimplified, as any brain model must be at this time.

The central assumptions of the model were three:

1. Nervous system activity is most usefully represented as the set of simultaneous individual neuron activities in a *group* of neurons.

2. Different memory traces make use of the same synapses. This conclusion seems unavoidable, given the first assumption and the kinds of connectivity present in the nervous system. Since the strength of connection of a single synapse is a very complex function of its past, this shifts our emphasis away from single synapses, each one of which tells us very little, to ensembles of many

synapses, which may tell us a lot. Again, we must consider the behavior of *groups* of individualistic neurons.

3. We make a specific assumption about the way a synapse responds during learning. We assume that a neuron changes strength when it learns by an amount proportional to the activity of pre- and postsynaptic cells. This is a variant of the kind of synaptic modification scheme sometimes called "Hebbian." The model that arises from this assumption is exceptionally easy to work with, and lends itself to demonstrations of the properties of distributed systems.

The kinds of mathematics appropriate for handling such systems are those arising in communication theory and signal detection theory, since the synapses, owing to their multiplicity of stored traces, conceal a desired signal amidst a large amount of noise. Observe that noise, in this system, is essential to the functioning of the memory, since what is noise on one occasion is signal on another. We view memory as essentially a complex filter, in which an input interacts with the filter to produce a large associated output, or very little output, depending on the past history of the system.

The model as presented has powerful averaging properties. Presentation of noisy stimuli, each of which was stored on top of the other, would lead to enhancement of the common portion of the patterns, exactly as an average response computer would suppress random fluctuations and reveal the desired signal. It was suggested that this straightforward, not very subtle mechanism could explain, qualitatively, some simple experiments involving random dot patterns. It was also consistent with an approach to generalization and categorization that held that inputs were categorized on the basis of their "closeness" to a stored prototype, that is, an approach that viewed categories as being "analog" in nature, with "belongingness" a continuous parameter, rather than viewing a category as a well-defined, logical cluster of attributes and relations that were either present or absent.

We next discussed how an incoming stimulus made contact with memory. A parallel distributed memory makes contact simultaneously with all of memory and is thus capable of 'scanning' an entire vocabulary in a single operation. A series of experiments (the "Sternberg paradigm") involving memory for short lists was discussed in view of our parallel model. By making assumptions about the time constants involved in the operating memory filter, it was possible to provide an alternate explanation of "memory scanning." Essentially, we assumed that the explanation for the observed time required to respond to items on a larger list was not because memory had to check, item by item, a longer list, but because more stored traces interfering with one another on the longer list required a larger filter output, involving longer integration times, to maintain the same signal-to-noise ratio. This approach generalized nicely to very long lists, where essentially all the storage elements participated fully, and predicted that, with reasonable temporal characteristics, the entire memory could be inspected in roughly a second, and that the apparent rate of memory "scanning" would increase as time progressed.

We then considered an extension of the model. We assumed a system where a set of neurons fed back on itself, allowing potential positive feedback. The presence of feedback changed the filter characteristics of the memory considerably, allowing the system to sometimes act as if it were analyzing inputs in terms of a few strong activity patterns, effectively reducing the dimensionality of the system from the order of magnitude of the number of storage elements in the system (potentially millions if elements are considered to be neurons or synapses) to very many fewer. Certain kinds of perceptual tasks — letter and phoneme perception, for example — seem to proceed by analysis in terms of "distinctive features," in which an input is represented as the presence or absence of a very small number of independent, highly discriminative traits. We formally identified the eigenvectors with large positive eigenvalues of the connectivity matrix of a set of neurons feeding back on itself with distinctive features in the psychological sense. We showed that, given a noisy input, these eigenvectors will be relatively enhanced, owing to the positive feedback, as compared with the other components of the input, so after a brief period of time only the distinctive features will remain. The input has been "preprocessed," or put into a standard form, which is a good strategy for a pattern recognition task where a potentially noisy input must be classified into a relatively small number of equivalence classes, as in letter or phoneme perception.

This first attempt at modeling perception was not entirely adequate, however, since it was a linear model that was potentially unstable and had some other undesirable traits. So we suggested a more realistic model in which neurons were allowed to saturate; that is, they could not fire faster or slower than certain limits. This assumption, coupled with the positive feedback, made the final state of the system correspond to one where the neural elements tended to be either fully on or fully off (or not responding at all). An interesting hybrid model arose, which had some of the properties of an analog system (before saturation) and some of the properties of a binary system (after saturation).

We pointed out that several recently proposed 'hierarchical' models for letter perception and reading were in harmony with this modeling approach. This view of word reception holds that perception of a complex stimulus like a word proceeds in a series of overlapped stages, each stage looking like a filter (in our terminology) that considers successively more complicated and holistic aspects of the stimulus. Stages operate in cascade, rather than discretely, so one stage starts to respond when the previous stage starts producing an output, but has not necessarily finished processing. Features, letters, groups of letters, and words correspond to successively later stages in the cascade. It is rather natural to build such a system with the kinds of distributed neural gadgetry that we have been discussing.

Finally, we checked the operation of some aspects of the system by performing a computer simulation. We used inputs that were derived from acoustic representations of spoken vowels. We hoped that our learning rule, coupled with positive feedback and saturation, would take an input, representing a single vowel, and associate it with a particular, noise-free output, corresponding to a certain pattern of saturated neurons. Thus, the system would be an effective preprocesser. After several thousand learning trials, with nine vowel codings as input, the system proved capable of associating each input, initially sometimes close together, with a separate stable activity pattern.

ACKNOWLEDGMENTS

This research was supported in part by grants from the Alfred P. Sloan Foundation and the Ittleson Family Foundation to the Center for Neural Studies, Brown University, and by a Public Health Service General Research Support Grant from the Division of Biological and Medical Sciences (No. PHS-RR-05664-08), Brown University.

REFERENCES

Anderson, J. A. A memory storage model utilizing spatial correlation functions. *Kybernetik,* 1968, 5, 113–119.
Anderson, J. A. Two models for memory organization using interacting traces. *Mathematical Biosciences,* 1970, 8, 137–160.
Anderson, J. A. A simple neural network generating an interactive memory. *Mathematical Biosciences,* 1972, 14, 197–220.
Anderson, J. A. A theory for the recognition of items from short memorized lists. *Psychological Review,* 1973, 80, 417–438.
Anderson, J. A. What is a distinctive feature? Technical Report No. 74-1, Center for Neural Studies, Brown University, Providence, Rhode Island, 1974.
Barlow, H. B. Single units and sensation: A neuron doctrine for perceptual psychology? *Perception,* 1972, 1, 371–394.
Brodal, A. *Neurological anatomy* (2nd ed.). New York: Oxford University Press, 1969.
Burrows, D., and Okada, R. Memory retrieval from long and short lists. *Science,* 1975, 188, 1031–1033.
Calvin, W. H. Synaptic potential summation and repetitive firing mechanisms: input–output theory for the recruitment of neurons into epileptic bursting firing patterns. *Brain Research,* 1972, 39, 71–94.
Capranica, R. R., Frishkopf, L. S., & Nevo, E. Encoding of geographical dialects in the auditory system of the cricket frog. *Science,* 1973, 182, 1272–1275.
Cavanagh, J. P. Relation between the immediate memory span and the memory search rate. *Psychological Review,* 1972, 79, 525–530.
Clifton, C., Jr., & Birenbaum, S. Effects of serial position and delay of probe in a memory scan task. *Journal of Experimental Psychology,* 1970, 86, 69–76.
Cooper, L. N. A possible organization of animal memory and learning. In B. Lundquist & S. Lundquist (Eds.), *Proceedings of the nobel symposium on collective properties of physical systems.* New York: Academic Press, 1974.
Cornsweet, T. *Visual perception.* New York: Academic Press, 1970.
Creutzfeldt, O., Innocenti, G. M., & Brooks, D. Vertical organization in the visual cortex (area 17) in the cat. *Experimental Brain Research,* 1974, 21, 315–336.
Dodwell, P. C. On perceptual clarity. *Psychological Review,* 1971, 78, 275–289.
Dorsett, D. A., Willows, A. O. D., & Hoyle, G. The neuronal basis of behavior in *Tritonia.*

IV: The central origin of a fixed action pattern demonstrated in the isolated brain. *Journal of Neurobiology*, 1973, **4**, 287–300.

Eccles, J. C. Conscious experience and memory. In J. C. Eccles (Ed.), *Brain and conscious experience*. Berlin: Springer, 1966.

Eccles, J. C. Possible synaptic mechanisms subserving learning. In A. G. Karczmar & J. C. Eccles (Eds.), *Brain and human behavior*. New York: Springer, 1972. Pp. 39–61.

Eimas, P. D. The relation between identification and discrimination along speech and non-speech continua. *Language and Speech*, 1963, **6**, 206.

Engel, G. R., Dougherty, W. G., & Jones, G. B. Correlation and letter recognition. *Canadian Journal of Psychology*, 1973, **27**, 317–326.

Eriksen, C. W., & Collins, J. F. Sensory traces versus the psychological moment in the temporal organization of form. *Journal of Experimental Psychology*, 1968, **77**, 376–382.

Estes, W. K. Memory, Perception, and Decision in Letter Identification. In R. L. Solso (Ed.), *Information processing and cognition: The Loyola Symposium*. Hillsdale, N.J.: Lawrence Erlbaum Associates, 1975.

Fischer, B. Overlap of receptive field centers and representation of the visual field in the cat's optic tract. *Vision Research*, 1973, **13**, 2113–2120.

Franks, J. J., & Bransford, J. D. Abstraction of visual patterns. *Journal of Experimental Psychology*, 1971, **90**, 65–74.

Freeman, W. J. Mass action in the nervous system. New York: Academic Press, 1975.

Fujisaki, H., & Kawashima, T. Some experiments on speech perception and a model for the perceptual mechanism. Annual Report of the Engineering Research Institute, Faculty of Engineering, University of Tokyo, Tokyo, 1970. Pp. 207–214.

Funkenstein, H. H., & Winter, P. Responses to acoustic stimuli of units in the auditory cortex of awake squirrel monkeys. *Experimental Brain Research*, 1973, **18**, 464–488.

Fuortes, M. G. F. Generation of responses in receptors. In W. R. Lowenstein (Ed.), *Handbook of sensory physiology. I: Principles of receptor physiology*, Berlin: Springer. 1971.

Globus, A., Rosenzweig, M. R., Bennett, E. L., & Diamond, M. C. Effects of differential experience on dendritic spine count in rat cerebral cortex. *Journal of Comparative and Physiological Psychology*, 1973, **82**, 175–181.

Goldberg, J. M., & Fernandez, C. Physiology of peripheral neurons innervating semicircular canals of the squirrel monkey. I: Resting discharge and response to constant angular accelerations. *Journal of Neurophysiology*, 1971, **34**, 635–660.

Goldstein, M. H., Jr., Hall, J. L., II, & Butterfield, B. O., Single-unit activity in the primary auditory cortex of unanesthetized cats. *The Journal of the Acoustical Society of America*, 1968, **43**, 444–455.

Goldstine, H. H. *The computer from Pascal to von Neumann*. Princeton, N.J.: Princeton University Press, 1972.

Greenough, W. T., & Volkmar, F. R. Pattern of dendritic branching in occipital cortex of rats reared in complex environments. *Experimental Neurology*, 1973, **40**, 491–504.

Haber, R. N. Repetition as a determinant of perceptual recognition processes. In W. Wathen-Dunn, J. Mott-Smith, H. Blum, & P. Leiberman (Eds.), *Models for the perception of speech and visual form*. Cambridge, Mass.: MIT Press, 1967. Pp. 202–210.

Hebb. D. O. *The organization of behavior*. New York: Wiley, 1949.

Hirsch, H. V. B., & Spinelli, D. N. Modification of the distribution of receptive field orientations in cats by selective visual exposure during development. *Experimental Brain Research*, 1971, **13**, 509–527.

Homa, D., Cross, J., Cornell, D., Goldman, D., & Schwartz, S. Prototype abstraction and classification of new instances as a function of number of instances defining the prototype. *Journal of Experimental Psychology*, 1973, **101**, 116–122.

Hubel, D. H., & Wiesel, T. N. Sequence regularity and geometry of orientation columns in the monkey striate cortex. *The Journal of Comparative Neurology,* 1974a, **158**, 267–294. (a)

Hubel, D. H., & Wiesel, T. N. Uniformity of monkey striate cortex: A parallel relationship between field size, scatter, and magnification factor. *The Journal of Comparative Neurology,* 1974, **158**, 295–306. (b)

Ingle, D. Focal attention in the frog: Behavioral and physiological correlates. *Science,* 1975, **188**, 1033–1035.

Jackson, R. H., & Dick, A. O. Visual summation and its relation to processing and memory. *Perception and Psychophysics,* 1969, **6**, 13–15.

Klein, W., Plomp, R., & Pols, L. C. W. Vowel spectra, vowel spaces, and vowel identification. *Journal of Acoustical Society of America,* 1970, **48**, 999–1009.

Kohonen, T. Correlation matrix memories. *IEEE Transactions on Computers,* 1972, **C-21**, 353–359.

Knight, B. W., Toyoda, J.–I., & Dodge, F. A., Jr. A quantitative description of the dynamics of excitation and inhibition in the eye of *Limulus. The Journal of General Physiology,* 1970, **56**, 421–437.

Krueger, L. E. Familiarity effects in visual information processing. *Psychological Bulletin,* 1975, **82**, 949–974.

LaBerge, D., & Samuels, S. J. Toward a theory of automatic information processing in reading. *Cognitive Psychology,* 1974, **6**, 293–322.

Lettvin, J. Y., Maturana, H. R., McCulloch, W. S., & Pitts, W. H. What the frog's eye tells the frog's brain. *Proceedings of the Institute of Radio Engineers,* 1959, **47**, 1940–1951.

Liberman, A. M., Harris, K. S., Hoffman, H. S., & Griffith, B. C. The discrimination of speech sounds within and across phoneme boundaries. *Journal of Experimental Psychology,* 1957, **54**, 358–368.

Liberman, A. M., Mattingly, I. G., & Turvey, M. T. Language codes and memory codes. In A. W. Melton & E. Martin (Eds.), *Coding processes in human memory.* Washington, D.C.: Winston, 1972. Pp. 307–334.

Lindgren, N. Machine recognition of human language: Part II. *IEEE Spectrum,* 1965, **2**, 45–59.

Link, S. W. A random walk theory of psychophysical discrimination. Paper presented at Advanced Workshop on Formal Theories of Information Processing, Stanford University, June 1974. To be published.

Little, W. A., & Shaw, G. L. A statistical theory of short and long term memory. *Behavioral Biology,* 1975, **14**, 115–133.

Livingston, R. B. Brain circuitry relating to complex behavior. In G. C. Quarton, T. Melnechuk, & F. O. Schmitt (Eds.), *The neurosciences.* New York: Rockefeller University Press, 1967. Pp. 499–515.

Luria, A. R. *The mind of a mnemonist.* New York: Basic Books, 1968.

McClelland, J. Preliminary letter identification in the perception of words and nonwords. *Journal of Experimental Psychology: Human Perception and Performance,* 1976, **2**, 80–91.

McCulloch, W. S., & Pitts, W. H. A logical calculus of the ideas immanent in nervous activity. *Bulletin of Mathematical Biophysics,* 1943, **5**, 115–133.

McGill, W. J. Stochastic latency mechanisms. In R. D. Luce, R. R. Bush, & E. Galanter (Eds.), *Handbook of mathematical psychology.* Vol. I. New York: Wiley, 1963.

McIlwain, J. T. Visual receptive fields and their images in superior colliculus of the cat. *Journal of Neurophysiology,* 1975, **38**, 219–230.

McIlwain, J. T. Large receptive fields and spatial transformations in the visual system. *International Review of Physiology,* 1976, **10**, 223–248.

Mountcastle, V. B. The problem of sensing and the neural coding of sensory events. G. C.

Quarton, T. Melnechuk, & F. O. Schmitt (Eds.), *The neurosciences.* New York: Rockefeller University Press, 1967. Pp. 393–408.

Nass, M. M., & Cooper, L. N. A theory for the development of feature detecting cells in visual cortex. *Biological Cybernetics,* 1975, **19**, 1–18.

Neisser, U. *Cognitive psychology.* New York: Appleton-Century-Crofts, 1967.

Nickerson, R. S. "Same" – "Different" response times: A model and a preliminary test. W. G. Koster (Ed.), *Attention and performance II.* Amsterdam: North Holland, 1969. Pp. 257–275.

Noda, H., & Adey, W. R. Firing of neuron pairs in cat association cortex during sleep and wakefulness. *Journal of Neurophysiology,* 1970, **33**, 672–684.

Noda, H., Manohar, S., & Adey, W. R. Correlated firing of hippocampal neuron pairs in sleep and wakefulness. *Experimental Neurology,* 1969, **24**, 232–247.

Perlmutter, J., Sorce, P., & Myers, J. L. Retrieval processes in recall. Report 74-1. Cognitive Processes Laboratory, Department of Psychology, University of Massachusetts, Amherst, Massachusetts, 1974.

Peterson, M. J., Meagher, R. B., Jr., Chait, H., & Gillie, S. The abstraction and generalization of dot patterns. *Cognitive Psychology,* 1973, **4**, 378–398.

Pettigrew, J. D. The effect of visual experience on the development of stimulus specificity by kitten cortical neurons. *Journal of Physiology,* 1974, **237**, 49–74.

Pfaffelhuber, E. Correlation memory models – A first approximation in a general learning scheme. *Biological Cybernetics,* 1975, **18**, 217–223.

Pisoni, D. B. On the nature of categorical perception of speech sounds. Unpublished Doctoral Thesis, University of Michigan, Ann Arbor, 1971.

Posner, M. I. Abstraction and the process of recognition. In G. H. Bower & J. T. Spence (Eds.) *The psychology of learning and motivation.* Vol. 3. New York: Academic Press, 1969.

Posner, M. I., & Keele, S. W. On the genesis of abstract ideas. *Journal of Experimental Psychology,* 1968, **77**, 353–363.

Posner, M. I., & Keele, S. W. Retention of abstract ideas. *Journal of Experimental Psychology,* 1970, **83**, 304–308.

Ratliff, F. *Mach bands: Quantitative studies on neural networks in the retina.* San Francisco: Holden-Day, 1965.

Ratliff, F., Knight, B. W., Dodge, F. A., Jr., & Hartline, H. K. Fourier analysis of dynamics of excitation and inhibition in the eye of *Limulus:* Amplitude, phase, and distance. *Vision Research,* 1974, **14**, 1155–1168.

Reed, S. K. Pattern recognition and categorization. *Cognitive Psychology,* 1972, **3**, 382–407.

Reed, S. K. *Psychological processes in pattern recognition.* New York: Academic Press, 1973.

Rosch, E. On the internal structure of perceptual and semantic categories. In T. E. Moore, (Ed.), *Cognitive Development and the Acquisition of Language,* New York: Academic Press, 1973.

Rosch, E. Human categorization. In N. Warren (Ed.), *Advances in cross-cultural psychology.* Vol. 1. London: Academic Press (in press).

Rosch, E., & Mervis, C. B. Family resemblances: Studies in the internal structure of categories. *Cognitive Psychology,* 1975, **7**, 573–605.

Rubenstein, H., Garfield, L., & Millikan, J. A. Homographic entries in the internal lexicon. *Journal of Verbal Learning and Verbal Behavior,* 1970, **9**, 487–494.

Scheibel, M. E., & Scheibel, A. B. Elementary processes in selected thalamic and cortical subsystems – The structural substrates. In F. O. Schmidt (Ed.), *The neurosciences.* Vol. II. New York: Rockefeller University Press, 1970.

Shepherd, G. M. *The synaptic organization of the brain.* New York: Oxford University Press, 1974.

Standing, L. Learning 10,000 pictures. *Quarterly Journal of Experimental Psychology,* 1973, **25**, 207–222.

Sternberg, S. High-speed scanning in human memory. *Science,* 1966, **153**, 652–654.

Sternberg, S. The discovery of processing stages: Extensions of Donders' method. In W. G. Koster (Ed.), *Attention and performance II.* Amsterdam: North Holland, 1969. Pp. 276–315. (a)

Sternberg, S. Memory scanning: Mental processes revealed by reaction-time experiments. *American Scientist,* (1969), **57**, 421–457. (b)

Sternberg, S. Memory scanning: New findings and current controversies. *Quarterly Journal of Experimental Psychology,* 1975, **27**, 1–32.

Stevens, C. *Neurophysiology: A primer.* New York: Wiley, 1966.

Strange, W., Keeney, T., Kessell, F. S., & Jenkins, J. J. Abstraction over time of prototypes from distortions of random dot patterns: A replication. *Journal of Experimental Psychology,* 1970, **83**, 508–510.

Theios, J. Reaction time measurements in the study of memory processes: Theory and data. In G. H. Bower (Ed.), *The psychology of learning and motivation.* Vol. 7. New York: Academic Press, 1973.

Theios, J., & Walter, D. G. Stimulus and response frequency and sequential effects in memory scanning reaction times. *Journal of Experimental Psychology,* 1974, **102**, 1092–1099.

Theios, J., Smith, P. G., Haviland, S. E., Traupmann, J., & Moy, M. C. Memory scanning as a serial, self-terminating process. *Journal of Experimental Psychology,* 1973, **97**, 323–336.

Turvey, M. T. On peripheral and central processes in vision: Inferences from an information-processing analysis of masking with patterned stimuli. *Psychological Review,* 1973, **80**, 1–52.

Weisstein, N. Metacontrast. In D. Jameson & L. M. Hurvich (Eds.), *Handbook of sensory physiology.* Vol. VII/4. Berlin: Springer, 1972.

Whitteridge, D. Projection of the optic pathways to the visual cortex. In R. Jung (Ed.), *Handbook of sensory physiology.* Vol. VII/3. *Central processing of visual information, Part B.* Berlin: Springer, 1973. Pp. 245–268.

Wiesel, T. N. & Hubel, D. H. Ordered arrangement of orientation columns in monkeys lacking visual experience. *The Journal of Comparative Neurology,* 1974, **158**, 307–318.

Willows, A. O. D., Dorsett, D. A., & Hoyle, G. The neuronal basis of behavior in *Tritonia.* I: Functional organization of the central nervous system. *Journal of Neurobiology,* 1973, **4**, 207–237. (a)

Willows, A. O. D., Dorsett, D. A., & Hoyle, G. The neuronal basis of behavior in *Tritonia.* III: Neuronal mechanism of a fixed action pattern. *Journal of Neurobiology,* 1973, **4**, 255–285. (b)

Willshaw, D. J., Buneman, O. P. & Longuet-Higgins, H. C. Non-holographic associative memory. *Nature,* 1969, **222**, 960–962.

Wilson, H. R. A synaptic model for spatial frequency adaptation. *Journal of Theoretical Biology,* 1975, **50**, 327–352.

Winter, P., & Funkenstein, H. H. The effect of species specific vocalization on the discharge of auditory cortical cells in the awake squirrel monkey. *Experimental Brain Research,* 1973, **18**, 489–504.

Wollberg, Z., & Newman, J. D. Auditory cortex of squirrel monkey: Response patterns of single cells to species-specific vocalizations. *Science,* 1972, **175**, 212–214.

Young, T. Y., & Calvert, T. W. *Classification, estimation, and pattern recognition.* New York: Elsevier, 1974.

3
A Pattern-Unit Model of Word Identification

Neal F. Johnson

The Ohio State University

Most individuals who are exposed to an alphabetic orthography not only learn how to read, but the ability soon becomes one of the most complex and highly developed skills they possess. While there are some clear exceptions to this generalization, reading certainly must be one of the most commonly acquired of all human skills.

Given this generality of reading, we know surprisingly little regarding the nature of the component skills and how they are acquired and performed. For example, while there seems to be some general agreement that individual letters are relevant cues in the execution of the reading skill, there are very little data, and certainly no agreement, regarding how the individual visual inputs from letters interact with one another, and with prior knowledge, to produce an appropriate word identification. The problem, then, seems to be that while we have adopted the term *reading* as a convenient label for a collection of perceptual and memorial skills, we have not developed the necessary knowledge base regarding the nature of these skills, how they are acquired, and how they interact.

READING AND THE UNIT OF INFORMATION PROCESSING

Although the issues in reading represent a rather broad set of problems, the main purpose of this chapter is to explore the organizational processes underlying the integration and identification of small orthographic units (e.g., letters and words). It is clear that such items must be treated as single units at some point in processing, but it is not clear how the unitization occurs, nor when it occurs. In addition, while there appear to be a variety of theoretical positions regarding these unitization issues, there seems to be a great deal of ambiguity in both their construction and their empirical support.

Some Conceptual Approaches to Integrative Encoding

An important reason for the ambiguity surrounding the concept of unitization comes from the fact that the term has been used in two ways. The first, and most common, refers to the process of learning a unitizing encoding for an information set (Johnson, 1970). If a subject were to learn SBJ as a response, this use of unitization would refer to those necessary processes and events that transpire between when the item is first presented and the point at which it can be retrieved and produced as a single unit.

The second meaning of the term *unitize,* and the one to be used throughout this chapter, refers to the process of utilizing an already-known encoding to integrate an information set on any given presentation. For example, once a subject had learned a unitary encoding for SBJ, that encoding could be used to integrate the letter set on any subsequent presentation. Similarly, if a word is presented to a skilled reader, some type of integrative encoding would seem to be needed before any identification could occur. The nature of this particular unitization process, then, is the specific concern of the discussion to follow.

Perceptual versus memorial integration   Given the preceding definition of the unitization issue, there are at least two general ways in which it can be construed. The first view is a memorial model, and it is predicated on the assumption that unitization is the product of some type of active memorial processing. This model assumes that the encodings that are input to memory are a spatially-ordered array of some type of perceptual atom, which are then actively integrated into higher-order units. The central points of this model are that such integrative encoding: (a) is a memorial event; (b) arises from the application of voluntary control processes; and (c) occurs only after perceptual processing has been completed. Within the context of word identification, this view has been termed the letter-integration model (Johnson, 1975a).

The perceptual model, on the other hand, has as its central assumption the idea that unitization is a prememorial phenomenon, and that information is already unitized when it is first registered in memory. In addition, this view would assume that the unitization process is relatively involuntary and may not be under the active control of the learner—perceiver. Models such as this have been described recently by Kahneman and Henik (1975) and Theois and Muise (in press), and within the context of word identification it has been referred to as the pattern-unit model (Johnson, 1975a).

A preliminary construction of the issues and some data   One primary distinction between the letter-integration and pattern-unit models concerns the form in which the information is assumed to be encoded when it is first registered in memory. The letter-integration model assumes that the processing that results in unitization occurs within memory, and consequently the initial memorial representation should be in terms of some perceptual atom. In the case of a word, this atom is likely to be a letter or some subletter feature.

The pattern-unit model, on the other hand, assumes that small patterns are already unitized when they are first registered in memory, and that no subsequent unitizing processes are needed. It would be assumed that the initial contents of memory would be a higher-order encoding that provides a single representation for the entire word, and if the subject's task were to identify a component letter, he would have to apply some active disintegration process.

This construction of the differences between these models has been operationalized in an experimental paradigm that was designed to sample the contents of a subject's memory immediately after an item had been registered. The subject was told to determine whether a presented word matched a predesignated target item, and his speed in doing so was compared to a condition in which he was to ascertain whether a presented word began with a predesignated target letter.

According to the letter-integration model, the letter information should be available before the word is integrated, with the result being that letter identification should be faster than word identification. Just the reverse would be predicted by the pattern-unit model. The first item available for response determination would be the word, and a letter would become available only after some decomposition procedure had been applied. In addition, in that a word and a letter in isolation are both small patterns, the pattern unit model would predict that they should be identified equally fast, while the letter-integration model would assume that word identification could occur only after a memorial integration process had been completed.

The results of an experiment such as this are given in Table 1, and seem quite consistent with the pattern-unit model. The subjects were faster at identifying words than at identifying letters within words, and the identification times for words and letters in isolation was about the same. In addition, the second result would suggest that the longer times for letters within words stems from the

TABLE 1
Mean Latencies

Type of response	Condition			
	Letters in words	Words	Letters	Mean
Yes	.539	.514	.493	.515
No	.590	.541	.543	.558
Mean	.564	.527	.518	.537

(After Johnson, 1975a)

retarding influence of the word context, rather than from some general difficulty subjects have in perceiving letters.

THE PATTERN-UNIT MODEL

An important point implied by both the letter-integration and pattern-unit models is the distinction between the type of information processing that occurs within a perceptual system and that which occurs within memorial systems. While there is no agreed-upon distinction between these two classes of events, it is possible to draw the distinction within the context of a model. The problem, of course, then becomes one of identifying a set of phenomena that can be clearly identified with one or the other type of processing.

The pattern-unit model is an attempt not only to represent this distinction between the two types of processing, but also to provide a characterization of the interfacing mechanism that accommodates one processing system to the other. That is, there is every reason to believe that the perceptual processing mechanisms do not encode information into a form compatible with the efficient operation of the storage and comprehension mechanisms of memory, and the interfacing processes are designed to account for the way that information transfer occurs.

An Overview of the Model

The first component of the model is perceptual processing, and its product is assumed to be a completed iconic representation, which then can be encoded into a form compatible with subsequent memorial processing and storage mechanisms. It would be further assumed that if anything interfered with the perceptual processing, or delayed the memorial encoding, the effect of such factors should be apparent in all subsequent processing stages.

The central point of the second assumption is that the only information that can be encoded into memory is the information represented by the icon at the time of memorial encoding. If the iconic representation is degraded in some way [e.g., as a result of masking (Turvey, 1973) or delying the memorial encoding (Sperling, 1960)], then any subsequent processing will not include all the original information, and any ultimate interpretation or encoding will be faulty or incomplete. In addition, whether the degradation occurs before or after the iconic representation is completed should be irrelevant. The only important issue is the state of the icon at the time of memorial encoding.

The second component of the model is the transfer mechanism which is designed to account for the way an adequate perceptual encoding is transferred into memory. It is assumed that using information stored in permanent memory, the subject attempts to assign a unitary set of memorial features to a display, followed by a testing of the extent to which that set is an adequate encoding defined in terms of the memorial task presented to him. In the event that the encoding is inadequate, the subject can either attempt to assign a different feature set to that display, or he can parse the display into components with unitary sets of memorial features being assigned to each component. The important point, however, is that the transfer occurs through the assignment of a unitary set of memorial features, and the assigned feature-set encoding is assumed to unitize the information it represents. In addition, it would be supposed that all subsequent memorial processing would be done in terms of that feature-set encoding.

At this point it is important to distinguish between features of the iconic representation and memory features assigned to that visual array by the transfer mechanism. As will be noted later, it might be reasonable to view the features of the iconic representation as little more than perceptual encodings of the physical attributes of the display, while the assigned memory features probably do not correspond in any one-to-one manner with either the physical attributes of the display or the perceptual features that make up the icon. In fact, if the memory features were found to be acoustic, rather than visual, there would be no way to even construe any such one-to-one mapping between the two feature systems (Coltheart, Lea, & Thompson, 1974; Conrad, 1967).

The final component of the model is working memory and the comparator. The major function of this component is to hold encodings relayed to it by the transfer mechanism such that either various control processes can be applied to the encodings, or comparisons can be made between these encodings and encodings retrieved from more permanent memorial representations. From a theoretical point of view, the most interesting issue regarding this component is that the encodings of information represented in working memory are not necessarily compatible with encodings of the same information while it is within the perceptual system.

The Perceptual Component of the Model

Figure 1 is a schematic characterization of the model and the perceptual component is everything up through the icon. As with all systems of encoding, this component of the model is designed to accept information encoded in one manner and recode it into a form compatible with subsequent processing mechanisms. To that extent, then, the perceptual component can be viewed as an interface between a biological system that is sensitive to energy changes in the environment and a cognitive system in which the information either can be transformed to accomplish some presented task or stored for future use.

Iconic memory   The end state of the perceptual component of the model is an iconic representation, which is assumed to be a perceptual encoding of the

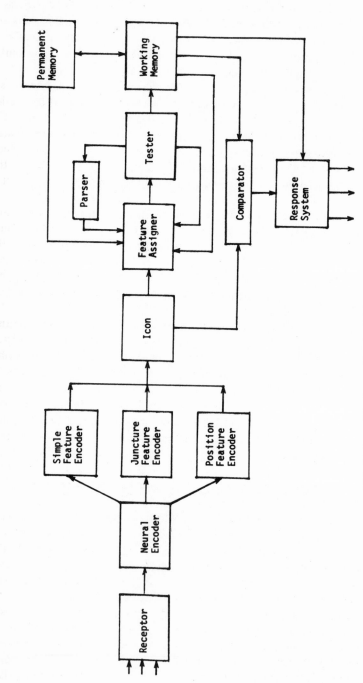

FIG. 1   A graphic characterization of the pattern-unit model.

information initially registered by the receptors, and it can be viewed as a decaying image that persists beyond the point where stimulation has terminated. The concept of an iconic image has been operationalized in terms of Sperling's (1960) task, and most of the research has been done within that experimental paradigm.

The basic task used by Sperling involves two conditions. In both conditions a small visual array (e.g., three rows of five items each) is presented for a brief interval (e.g., 50 msec), and the conditions differ in terms of whether the subjects are to report everything they saw (whole report) or just some designated portion (partial report). In the case of partial report, the cue signaling which portion to recall does not occur until after the display has terminated, and the technique has the advantage of limiting the amount of information the subject is required to reproduce.

The results from such experiments indicate that whole report yields only about four to five items, but in partial report the subjects are able to produce about that many items regardless of which portion is cued. In addition, while the level of whole report does not drop if a short retention interval is introduced, there is a rapid drop in partial-report performance if the report cue is delayed, and the partial-report advantage is completely lost if the cue is delayed beyond a few hundred msec.

The most common interpretation of these results is that a visual image persists for a brief period after a display has terminated, and the recall process involves a reading of the information from the image. If the subject is asked to report what he has seen, the image will continue to decay during recall, and it may be completely gone by the time the fifth item has been produced. The partial-report technique circumvents that problem, however, by sampling information from the image, and if the subject can report almost all of the items in any cued portion, it must be the case that he has much more information available than would be suggested by his whole-report performance. This difference in the estimate of information available based on whole and partial report has been used as a measure of information available within the image (Merluzzi & Johnson, 1974) and it disappears within a few hundred msec.

Another point suggested by the partial report data is that information can be selectively encoded into memory from the rapidly decaying image. This post-stimulus selection of information is evident from the fact that the selection criterion (i.e., the cue) is not given until after the display has terminated, and a persisting image would be the only possible source of information (see Coltheart, 1975, for a critical discussion of this issue).

In terms of the nature of the encoding, the icon is assumed to be a visual system with the features of the iconic representation being encodings of physical attributes of the display. In addition, it is not assumed that this encoding process is in any way dependent upon interactions with information stored within more permanent memory systems. For example, a number of investigators (Clark, 1969; Turvey, 1967; Kahneman & Henik, 1975; von Wright 1968, 1970) have demonstrated that while information available at the level of the icon can be processed in terms of its physical characteristics (e.g., size, color, location, etc.), any processing that requires the use of acoustic or cognitive distinctions (e.g., the difference between letters and digits) seems to be precluded (Coltheart, Lea, and Thompson, 1974; Sperling, 1960).

Stages of encoding within the icon   As the graphic representation of the model would suggest, it is not supposed that there is any direct and single-process event that encodes the initial visual representation into a completed iconic encoding of the information. Rather, it is assumed that the icon is the product of a series of encoding steps, with the initial encoding event being a transduction of the information encoded by the receptors into uninterpreted and undifferentiated neural activity. From that point on, the processing is assumed to take the form of extracting information from (i.e., interpreting) that initial neural encoding.

There are a variety of ways in which the extraction process can be construed, but one reasonable view is that the neural activity is shunted to a series of filter-like encoding mechanisms that output to the iconic representation. That is, the encoders are assumed to be similar to filters to the extent that they respond only if an incoming signal contains a certain target component (Anderson, 1973, this volume), but they are different from simple acoustic filters to the extent that their output is assumed to be an encoding of the input, rather than the input itself. Furthermore, that encoding is then assumed to be the representation of that component of the signal within the icon. To this extent, then, a critical issue in the model is the assumption that the iconic representation is an assemblage of features, with each being a code on some component of the initial neural activity.

If, as assumed, the features that make up an iconic representation are a set of encodings that are the product of separate filters or encoders, then it is necessary to assume further that at some point in the perceptual processing these features are all independent of one another, although they do seem to function as an integrated whole once the iconic representation is completely established. That is, if the perceptual component provides an independent encoding of each of the visual features that comprise a small integrated pattern (e.g., a letter), then the model also must include some mechanism to account for the way the assembly process or unitization occurs.

The empirical base for a multistage model   The major research technique that has been employed to examine levels of processing within the icon is visual masking. In the partial-report experiments described earlier, the high percentage of recall was taken to indicate a persisting visual image that contained a great deal of information. However, that was obtained when the post-display visual field was unpatterned and its illumination was quite dim or dark. If the same experiment is conducted (i.e., the same viewing conditions for the target display), but with the postdisplay field being a brightly illuminated pattern, then recall is very low, and subjects frequently report not seeing any of the letters at all. In that the viewing conditions and the visual displays to be reported were identical in the two situations, the difference in their perceptibility must be attributable to differences in what happened after the display terminated. Not only has this been taken to indicate the existence of an image that persists after the stimulation has terminated, but it also suggests that with a very brief presentation (e.g., 20 msec) most of the processing needed to perceive the stimulus may occur to the persisting image after the display has terminated, rather than to the input itself. Nothing seems to be seen when the pattern mask prevents processing of the image.

This point can be illustrated further by a number of experiments in which the mask has been somewhat delayed. In the preceding example, the target display was followed immediately by the bright pattern mask, but it is also possible to introduce a delay between the target and the mask during which a dimly illuminated unpatterned visual field is present. Under these circumstances, the longer the delay, the longer the subject can process the image before the mask interferes, and therefore, more items should be reported from the display during recall. Many experiments have supported this expectation (see Turvey, 1973, for a recent review).

Although these results appear to indicate that perceptual processing is extended in real time, they can be taken to support either a single-stage or a multistage model. For example, one could conclude either that the delay between the pattern and the mask allows more stages to be completed or that it allows more time for the single stage to occur. That point notwithstanding, however, the data do indicate that perceptual processing can continue after a visual display has terminated, and that an iconic representation can be an encoding of a persisting visual image.

Data more pertinent to the concept of stages of processing come from research on various types of mask and their differential effectiveness. Immediately after a display has terminated, almost any kind of visual input will interfere with perceptual processing. For example, a brief, but bright, flash of light will effectively mask an array of letters if it occurs within 100 msec after the display terminates (Spencer, 1969). Similarly, a black and white speckled random pattern will be an effective mask within the same temporal range (Turvey, 1973). This masking effect, then, seems to be unrelated to the similarity of the target display and the mask.

While similarity does not seem to be important in obtaining this masking effect, it does appear to be subject to some other important limitations. For example, these masks are effective only if they appear within 100 msec after the target display terminates, and within that range, the longer they are delayed the less their effectiveness. In addition, they are effective only if the target and mask are presented to the same visual field of the same eye. If the target were presented to one eye and the mask to the other, there would be no masking effect at all. Finally, Turvey (1973) has demonstrated that the magnitude of this type of masking effect is dependent upon the relative energy levels of the target display and the mask. The greater the relative energy level of the mask, the more effective it is.

A pattern mask (Turvey, 1973) is somewhat different from a randomly speckled display or a flash of light both in its appearance and in its effect. In appearance it is physically similar to alphanumeric characters (i.e., the usual target display), because it is composed of straight and diagonal lines, and such elements are generally assumed to be the critical features used in the perception of letters (see Gibson & Levin, 1976, for a review). However, in that it is also possible to control and vary the energy level of a pattern mask, the similarity between the target and the mask can be varied along both an appearance and an intensity dimension.

There are several ways in which the perceptual effect of a pattern mask is different from the other two types of mask. The most obvious difference is that while the other two masks are not effective if they are delayed more than 100 msec, there are studies that have shown an effect for a pattern mask when the delay is as long as 300 to 500 msec. In addition, while the other two types of mask are effective only if they are presented to the same eye as the target, a pattern mask is effective even if it is presented to the same visual field of the other eye. Finally, if the pattern mask is delayed beyond 100 msec, its effectiveness is unrelated to its energy level relative to that of the target, while there is such a relationship for the other two masks within their effective ranges (Turvey, 1973).

While these results have been used to answer questions regarding whether masking is a peripheral or a central process, or whether the mask replaces or integrates with the target display, they also can be used to support a model of multiple encoding stages within the perceptual system. For example, not only is the effective temporal range of a pattern mask greater than for a light flash, but it also seems to be completely effective when the target and mask displays are presented to different eyes. In that this latter effect is dependent upon an integration of the information from the two eyes, the effect must be occurring centrally. The other two types of mask, on the other hand, are effective only if they are presented to the same eye and occur in close temporal succession. That would suggest that the effects with these masks are peripheral, and may reflect much earlier stages of processing.

In terms of a multistage model, a possible interpretation of these data is that whenever the information in successive visual displays interacts, an interference effect will occur provided that the then-current encodings of the information in the two displays are sufficiently similar to allow for a confusion between them, (albeit, the exact nature of the confusion and interference will vary depending upon the stage of encoding). For example, the model assumes that visual information is first encoded peripherally as undifferentiated neural activity.

Given this assumption, it would be expected that any kind of subsequent visual input would interfere with perception, provided that the second input also resulted in neural activity, and the interaction between the two occurred before the target display was encoded into another form. That is, at that point everything is encoded as simple neural activity and everything should interfere with everything, and this seems to be the case. Furthermore, in that the only possible relevant parameter of these representations is relative energy level, it is not surprising that Turvey (1973) found it to be the primary determiner of the magnitude of the masking effect.

If perceptual processing is allowed to continue for a time before the masking display is presented, then the form of the perceptual encoding should change from simple uninterpreted and undifferentiated neural activity to a more differentiated form. If the interaction between the target and masking display occurs after that change in encoding, then it would be necessary for the two displays to share physical features so that they would retain enough similarity after the higher-order encoding for a confusion to occur. Once the process of feature encoding begins, the similarity and resulting confusion between the two displays will be maintained only so long as the features that have been encoded are the same. If there is a class of features that has been encoded from the target display that is not shared by the mask, then there would be a way to distinguish the displays and there no longer should be a masking effect.

Results reported by both Turvey (1973) and Spencer (1969) illustrate this point. Light flashes and speckled patterns lose their effectiveness to mask an alphanumeric character if they are delayed beyond 50 to 100 msec, while a pattern mask that shares more physical features with the target (e.g., a set of straight and diagonal lines) will be effective even when the mask delays exceed 100 to 150 msec.

Subsequent to encoding simple features, such as curves or horizontal, vertical, and diagonal lines, the model assumes that higher-order juncture features are encoded. These encodings are assumed to represent the intersections and physical relationships between the lower-order features, and as such, they can be used as the mechanism to account for the way simple connected patterns might be assembled within the perceptual system. In addition, these simple assemblages seem to be the highest-order units within the perceptual system, and it may be reasonable to assume that they do not depend upon more complex cognitive processing (D'Avello, 1976; Estes, 1975; Kahneman & Henik, 1975).

Unfortunately, the data supporting this view of juncture features as pattern assemblers are rather meager. Turvey (1973) did report observing that while his pattern mask (which did not have such features) did have an influence that was extended in time, letters (which would have such juncture features) had an even longer effective temporal range. In addition, Estes (1975) has recently reported studies that can be interpreted as indicating that at a certain point in processing there may be an adequate encoding of simple features, but they are "free floating" in the sense that they are not positionally tied to other features.

The final encoding process in the perceptual component of the model is the determination of positional or order information for the assemblages just discussed. While it is assumed that there is no higher-order perceptual encoding that integrates a simple display such as *cow* into a word, it is assumed that there is an encoding of the positional or order information that places the *c* first, the *o* second, and the *w* in the final position. This unintegrated but ordered character of iconic letter arrays is illustrated by Estes' (1975) finding that interletter constraints (e.g., orthographic structure) seem to have little influence on perceptual processing, although such constraints have clear effects on post-perceptual processing. That is, these constraints seem not to offer a basis for integrative encoding within the perceptual system, but the encoded positional information would allow the constraints to be used for subsequent integrative encoding within memory.

As with the concept of juncture features, the data on positional encoding are rather sparse. Estes (1975, this volume) provides some data on misplacement of letters in degraded visual displays that would suggest that item information is available at a time when there is still some positional uncertainty. In addition, den Heyer and Barrett (1971) reported a visual masking effect that seriously disrupted the subjects' ability to report the positions of letters, but had a somewhat smaller effect on item information. Finally, there is some suggestion that while dyslexic children seem to have no more difficulty than normal children when it comes to encoding letters visually, they do show a specific deficit when they attempt to order the letters (Gibson & Levin, 1976). All three of these effects would suggest that there is a point in time when the item assemblages are relatively complete, but the interrelationships among them appear to be unknown.

To summarize, then, the partial-report data suggest that there is a brief image that persists after a visual display terminates, and the masking data indicate that if the display duration is very brief (i.e., a few msec), most, if not all, of the processing that results in perceiving the display occurs after it has terminated. Furthermore, the masking data would suggest that the initial encoding seems to take the form of uninterpreted and undifferentiated neural activity, which then is successively encoded into the hierarchy of features that forms the iconic representation (albeit, the serial encoding is not an implication of the model). If the encoding is terminated by presenting a mask, the information from the already completed encoding stages seems to be available to the subject for reporting, while information that is the product of subsequent encoding stages seems to be unavailable.

Channel capacity in the perceptual system   A final issue regarding the perceptual component of the model is the extent to which there might be some limit on the amount of information that can be processed at any point in time. While there are a variety of views regarding how channel capacity could be limited (Broadbent, 1958; Rumelhart, 1970), a number of recent models have considered perceptual processing as being relatively automatic (LaBerge, 1973) and without capacity limitations (Gardner, 1973; Shiffrin, 1975; Shiffrin & Geisler, 1973). These models assume that perceptual processing is free of attentional demand and control, and any limit on a subject's ability to reproduce the information should result from postperceptual sources.

The pattern-unit model also assumes that the processing capacity of the perceptual system is unlimited, and that it cannot be influenced by cognitive intervention. This is not to say that one cannot selectively attend to information within the perceptual system, but only that such attention does not influence perceptual processing, and its primary function would be to facilitate the transfer of information from the perceptual system into memory.

The major reason for adopting such an assumption is that it appears to be the position that is most consistent with the existing data. For example, if a subject's task is to determine whether a display contains some element, presenting the elements slowly does not result in a higher probability of detection than does either a fast rate (Eriksen & Spencer, 1969) or a brief simultaneous display (Shiffrin & Gardner, 1972). In addition, if the elements are physically dissimilar, the likelihood of detecting a target item in a briefly presented array is independent of both the size of the array (Gardner, 1973) and whether the subjects have been given prior knowledge as to where they should focus their attention (Shiffrin, McKay, & Shaffer, 1976). All these data seem to be inconsistent with any position that assumes that the perceptual system has a limited processing capacity.

The Transfer Mechanism and Working Memory

The graphic representation of the model in Fig. 1 illustrates the three basic parts of the transfer mechanism: the memorial-feature assigner; the tester that determines the adequacy of the memorial encodings; and the parser that, when necessary, can fractionate the perceptual representation of a small visual pattern into its components.

As noted earlier, the overall function of the transfer mechanism is to act as an encoding interface between a perceptual system whose encodings provide a veridical representation of the physical features of a visual display, and a memorial system that seems unable to process and store those encodings in an efficient manner (albeit, regardless of efficiency, those features are encodable and can be stored within memory). The output of the transfer mechanism, then, is assumed to be an encoding of the iconic information that is adequate, efficient, and compatible with subsequent memorial processors.

The feature assigner   The function of the feature assigner is to accept perceptually encoded information and assign to it a set of memorial features that can be used for subsequent processing. The perceptual input to the feature assigner could be either from the icon or from the tester—parser, and the memorial input would be any rule system or systems that could be used to generate a set of memorial features. While the output of the feature assigner would be a memorial encoding, it is not necessarily the case that the encoding would be adequate to accomplish the presented memorial task, and it might take the assigner more than one attempt to adequately encode a display.

The feature assigner can be characterized in terms of a set of three assumptions. The first is that any input, whether from the icon or from the tester—parser, is processed as a single unit, and an integrated unitary encoding is assigned to the input. While any particular encoding may not be adequate to represent all the information in an input, the failure should not result from the assigner having fractionated the display in some way. The assigner always processes an input as a single unit, and attempts to assign a single encoding consistent with the complete input.

The second assumption is that perceivers have a fixed and limited number of memorial feature registers, and it is assumed that they are all used for encoding any input. If a display is processed as a single pattern, then the number of features assigned is constant, regardless of the nature of the pattern, and a *pattern unit* can be defined as any display that can be adequately represented by that fixed-size feature set. The rationale for this assumption is that the ease of processing a unitary encoding seems to be unrelated to the amount or complexity of the information it represents, regardless of whether the task is primarily perceptual (Doggett & Richards, 1975; Johnson, 1975a) or entails the storage and retrieval of information from memory (Murdock, 1961). If this is the case, there seems to be little reason to suppose that there would be any quantitative differences among encodings that would be related to quantitative differences in the information represented by the codes.

The third assumption is that the feature set assigned to an input is determined by the perceived properties of the entire input as a unit, and is independent of any features that might be assigned to some arbitrarily defined subcomponent of the input (e.g., a letter within a word). For example, the features assigned to a display such as *block* need not overlap with any features that would be assigned to any individual letter within *block* if the letter was presented in isolation. (However, it should also be emphasized that such overlap is not precluded by this assumption). In addition, this assumption would emphasize the fact that there need not be any one-to-one relationship between components of the encoding and physical attributes of the display.

Although these considerations do not require a detailed definition of the character of a memory feature, there are a number of ways in which these features might be construed. For example, they could be viewed as if they were a set of encodings of some simple attributes of the input, with that set being adequate for accessing a more permanent and complete representation of that display within memory. An alternative view might consider the features to be components of a generative plan that could be used to reconstruct the display at the time of test. In a sense, this view suggests that the features would be used to construct a template in the event that the memorial task were to identify the item, or they could be used to construct an ordered item set if the items were to be recalled. Regardless of these considerations, however, the exact nature of the memorial features can be left unspecified, with the exception that it is assumed that their number is limited and constant, and that they can be generated by using rule systems registered in permanent memory.

The operation of the feature assigner can be illustrated by describing the way it would operate on simple orthographic displays. If a word was presented, the icon would input a set of individually integrated letters, along with the appropriate positional information, to the feature assigner. In addition, the perceiver would have sets of orthographic rules and grapheme—phoneme correspondence rules available in memory that could be used for assigning a feature set, and the resulting encoding could take the form of either a phonetic or a lexical representation (C. Chomsky, 1970; N. Chomsky, 1970). This task can be contrasted with a situation in which a perceiver would not have a readily available rule set. This might be the case if the input from the icon was a consonant sequence such as SBJF. In that event, there would be no available rule system to generate an integrating feature set, and the subject would be unable to process the display as a single pattern unit.

The tester—parser   The function of the tester—parser is to determine if an encoding generated by the feature assigner is adequate to accomplish the task presented to the perceiver—learner, and if not, to find a way of fractionating the display such that the resulting components are readily encodable. As with the feature assigner, the tester—parser can be characterized in terms of a set of three assumptions. The first is that if an encoding is found to be adequate, it is passed on and registered in working memory, but if it is not adequate the feature assigner must be signaled and a new encoding assigned. This recursive property of the transfer mechanism allows the perceiver to test hypotheses regarding the best possible encoding for a display, and to try a new feature set if a previous encoding seems faulty.

Given that there may be some displays for which a perceiver is unable to generate an integrating feature set, it is necessary to make a second assumption that there is some limit (L) to the number of such recursive loops from the tester back to the assigner. Without such an assumption, the subjects could get into an endless and fruitless cycle with a display such as SBJF.

The final assumption is that if a display cannot be represented adequately by a unitary encoding after L attempts, it is necessary to subdivide the display into components and attempt to represent each with the fixed-size feature set. In that the feature assigner is assumed to process any input as a single unit, it is necessary for the parser to fractionate the display according to some system, and then input the resulting components individually and serially into the feature assigner for encoding. The result is that the display will not be processed as being a single pattern unit but, rather, as being as many pattern units as there are encoded components.

The operation of the parser assumes some basis for fractionating an input, and while the parsing scheme cannot be completely specified at this point, there are several possibilities. For example, it may be that the parser is not subject to the intervention of cognitive processes, and it may always fractionate displays into components that conform to the unitary assemblages from the icon. Following this very simple assumption, it would be expected that any letter array that cannot be assigned a single integrating feature set would be encoded with a feature set assigned to each letter. There would be no physical cues that could be used for identifying units between the level of the array and the level of individual letters.

A second possibility is that cognitive mechanisms, such as rule systems, can be applied by the parser. If this is the case, cognitive units that are smaller than the word, but larger than a letter, might be input to the feature assigner. Examples of these subword units could be such things as syllables (Spoehr & Smith, 1973), vocalic center groups (Smith & Spoehr, 1974; Spoehr & Smith, 1973), or spelling patterns (Gibson & Levin, 1976; Gibson, Osser, & Pick, 1963; Veneszky, 1970), and there are data indicating that under various conditions each of these subword units can have an impact on visual information processing. Regardless of the principle on which the parsing occurs, however, the important point is that if the subjects are not able to process a display as a single unit, it will be necessary to subdivide it in some way to find components that can be represented by memorial encodings.

As with the feature assigner, the operation of the tester–parser can be illustrated by showing how it might operate on simple orthographic displays. For example, as noted earlier, if the display were a word and the input were not degraded in any manner, it is likely that the tester would find the first encoding to be adequate and it would be passed on to working memory. However, if the illumination were low or the display duration brief, the iconic representation of the display might be degraded such that it would not contain all of the information in the original input. In that event, there might not be an available rule system for encoding the iconic display, and it would have to be parsed.

This point can be illustrated with a display such as *block*. If the degraded iconic representation was *b ck,* the subject's knowledge of English orthography and grapheme–phoneme correspondence rules would be of little help, and no single integrating encoding could be assigned. After L attempts to assign an adequate encoding, it would be necessary to parse the display into the three letters and encode them into memory separately. Given this fact, while *block* could be treated as a single pattern unit, it would be necessary to process *b ck* as three pattern units, and the word could be identified only by attempting to reconstruct it from the partial information in memory. Similarly, if the input were not degraded in any way, but consisted of something like SBJF, the subject also would have no readily available integrating encoding. Again, the input would have to parsed, and it would be necessary to process it as being as many pattern units as there are letters.

Working memory While the perceptual component of the model is assumed to have its own storage capability, it is clear that there are severe temporal limits on such storage. With a visual input, it is unlikely that there would be any useful information available within the perceptual system beyond a second or two after the display terminated. Given this fact, it is clear that if the task presented to the subject required that he make use of the information for more than two seconds after the input, some means of more permanent storage would have to be provided, and working memory is assumed to be that mechanism.

In addition to providing a means of mediating a temporal interval, working memory is used whenever an input must be compared with something already in working memory. For example, if a subject is told to look for instances of the word *block,* it will be necessary for him to compare each visual input with his memory of the target item. However, in that his memory of the item is in the form of an memorial encoding (i.e., memorial features), it will be necessary to encode each visual input into the same form before a comparison can be made.

This point can be illustrated by an experiment of Coltheart, Lea, and Thompson (1974). While we have every reason to believe that a primary component of an encoding in working memory is acoustic (Conrad, 1967), Coltheart *et al* demonstrated that acoustic information about an item is not available to the perceiver if the item is only in the icon and has not been transferred to working memory. The central point is that there is no way to map a set of visual features onto a set of memorial features in any one-to-one manner, and if a comparison is to be made between two items, it is necessary to encode them into a common form.

The comparator Stated quite simply, the comparator is the component that makes comparisons. Regardless of whether the subject's task is to determine if an item is a predesignated target, to determine if two simultaneously presented items are the same, or to read and comprehend a word, some kind of comparison process is involved. In some cases the comparison may be visual, and in others the input must be compared with the contents of memory, but in each case a judgment of *same* or *different* must be made, and it is the comparator that is responsible for this decision.

As suggested by the discussion of working memory, the primary criterion that determines whether a comparison can be made is the extent to which the to-be-compared items are encoded in a common form. In fact, the primary assumption describing the operation of the comparator is that separate items are always compared whenever they share the same form of encoding, even if the nature of the task does not demand such a comparison.

For example, suppose the top row of a display in a partial-report experiment was SBJFQ and the bottom row was LLZNG. Labeling the first two items of each row would require transferring them into working memory before comparisons could be made with acoustic information stored in permanent memory. On the other hand, a comparison that indicated that the first two items in the top row were different, and the first two in the second row were the same, would not require the transfer to working memory. This comparison would have been made the moment the iconic representations of these items were completed. Even if the subject's task had been to label the items, it is assumed that this comparison would have been made, and the only difference made by the nature of the task would be to determine whether the results of the comparison would be output to the response system.

Channel capacity and the transfer mechanism   While the perceptual component of the model may be best described as an unlimited-capacity system, there are at least two sources of limitation on information-processing capacity within the transfer mechanism and working memory. The first is the fact that working memory seems to be limited in the amount of information it can handle per unit of time. Whether the limit stems from its being a time-dependent system, a limited-capacity system, or both may be open to question, but the fact is that if a subject is given a set of digits to recall, there are severe limits on how many he can report immediately after presentation. Furthermore, recall declines rapidly if a retention interval is introduced. If subjects can rehearse the material, or if they have a way of recoding it into some higher-order unit (Miller, 1956), the amount retained can be increased, but even under these conditions there does seem to be a limit.

The other limitation on information processing occurs in the transfer mechanism, and stems from the fact that a complete encoding of the iconic information depends upon an adequate iconic representation at the time of encoding. In the event that a subject had difficulty in encoding a display, additional processing time would be needed for both subsequent attempts to assign an encoding and, if necessary, the parsing and serial encoding of each component. If the display were relatively brief and terminated before the transfer process was complete, then the iconic representation might decay before all the information was encoded and transferred to working memory. The assumption is that these processes are occurring in real time, and if any serial processing is required, then either there must be some means for restoring or maintaining the iconic representation, or the amount of information available for transfer will be a decreasing function of the time occupied by the processing.

This view differs somewhat from Gough's model (1972) in that he assumes that there is always a serial letter-by-letter transfer from the icon into working memory. Given this assumption, his model would expect the capacity limitation just described to hold regardless of the nature of the input, and processing differences between displays such as BLOCK and SBJFQ should be a function of posttransfer events.

A Summary of the Model

The model can be summarized in terms of a series of statements that reflect the set of assumptions upon which it rests. In fact, of course, the model is the set of assumptions, and they represent an attempt to characterize the processes and operations that intervene between the initial representation of information by receptor activity and an encoding of that information that can be subjected to control processes within memory (Atkinson & Shiffrin, 1968).

Statement I: *The initial encoding of information from the receptors is in terms of undifferentiated and uninterpreted neural activity.* Whether this is a coding process or one of simple transduction (i.e., a cipher) need not be specified so long as it is clear that there is no information loss in the encoding process.

Statement II: *Feature extraction is the result of a set of filter-like encoders whose input is the undifferentiated neural activity and whose outputs are iconic encodings of the features to which they respond.* In that the undifferentiated neural activity is the input to all the feature encoders, the encoders can function independently of one another, and there is no need to assume any particular order to the encoding.

Statement III: *The feature encoders respond to three types of features. Simple features are the elementary components of patterns and are composed of such things as horizontal, vertical, and diagonal lines and curves. Juncture features represent intersections and points of contact between simple features, and their encodings act as the mechanism that assembles simple features into unitary iconic assemblages that can be represented by a single iconic encoding. Finally, positional features represent the spatial relationships among iconic assemblages.* While it is not assumed that the information in two or more assemblages share any type of common iconic encoding, it is assumed that a set of simple features do share a common iconic encoding if they are assembled into a unit by higher-order juncture features. In fact, the common encoding is assumed to be the unitization mechanism within the icon, and the term *assemblage* refers to any such set of commonly encoded features.

Statement IV: *The end product of perceptual processing is a completed iconic representation. The icon is a rapidly decaying visual storage system that can hold perceptual encodings of visual information for short periods of time.* It is assumed that the encodings are constructed from the outputs of the feature encoders, and that they do not represent any cognitive information.

Statement V: *Subsequent visual inputs either interfere with the iconic representations of prior inputs or replace them, and the effect is dependent upon whether the two iconic representations share a common form of encoding.* This statement does nothing other than recognize the empirical facts of masking and metacontrast.

Statement VI: *With the exception of limitations on the visual acuity of a perceiver, and lateral masking effects, the perceptual system is not subject to any capacity limitations.* Again, this is an assumption dictated by the weight of empirical evidence.

Statement VII: *The feature assigner can accept inputs from either the icon or the tester–parser.*

Statement VIII: *Memory features are assigned through the use of rule and mnemonic systems registered in permanent memory.*

Statement IX: *The feature assigner cannot fractionate an input and therefore processes all inputs as single units and attempts to assign a unitary encoding consistent with the complete input.* This statement is assumed to be the basic unitization mechanism within the memorial system. The unitary encoding assigned to a display would provide a single memorial representation for all of the information within it.

Statement X: *The transfer mechanism has a fixed and limited number of memorial feature registers, and they are all used whenever a feature-set encoding is assigned.* If a display is processed as a single unit, then the number of features assigned is constant, and there should be no quantitative differences between the encodings for two patterns.

Statement XI: *A pattern unit is any visual array that can be represented in memory by a single set of memory features.* A pattern unit is assumed to be a visual analogue of a chunk (Miller, 1956) and shares a similar operational and theoretical definition (Johnson, 1970).

Statement XII: *The feature set assigned to an input is determined by the perceived properties of the entire input as a unit, and is independent of any features that might be assigned to any arbitrarily defined subcomponent of the input.* The main point of this assumption is that if an encoding represents a set of information, and it is not quantitatively related to the amount of information it represents (Statement X), then there can be no one-to-one relationship between components and features of the unitary encoding. Given that assumption, there would be no reason to believe that the features that would be used to encode a letter would be a proper subset of the features that would be used to encode a word that contained that letter.

Statement XIII: *The input to the tester is the memorial feature set assigned by the feature assigner, and it assesses the extent to which the encoding can be used to achieve the presented task.*

Statement XIV: *If the tester determines an encoding to be adequate it is passed on to working memory, but if it is inadequate the feature assigner is signaled and a new encoding is assigned.*

Statement XV: *If an adequate encoding has not been assigned to the display after some fixed number of attempts (L), the input is assigned to the parser and fractionated into components on the basis of some specified criterion. The components are then moved on to the feature assigner in a serial manner, and an attempt is made to encode them individually by assigning a fixed-size feature set to each.*

Statement XVI: *The comparator makes same–different decisions and does so automatically for pairwise comparisons among items that both share a common form of encoding and fall within a certain spatial–temporal proximity. The comparator signals the response system only if the task so demands.* The spatial–temporal limitation is intended to account for the fact that subjects may notice that an item is repeated in a sequence if the two occurrences are near one another, but with a greater separation the repetition might be missed.

This set of statements, then, expresses the assumptions that make up the model. The critical issues are the unitization processes that occur at each level of encoding, and it is assumed that the basic motivation for such integrative encoding is to both overcome the capacity limitations of working memory and increase the efficiency of retrieval. To that extent, this set of statements can be viewed as a perceptual front end to an earlier set of statements expressing a model of coding processes in memory (Johnson, 1970).

SOME ILLUSTRATIVE EXPERIMENTS

Two general approaches have been taken in an effort to document the model empirically. The first is an analysis of the part–whole relationships between patterns and their components, and the major issue is the fact that if a set of components has been encoded into a unit, then the unit itself should be somewhat more available for processing than an encoding of any of its components. The experiment described earlier (Johnson, 1975a) is an illustration of this point, in that words seemed to be identified faster than letters within words.

The second approach is an analysis of the length–difficulty relationship in the visual processing of orthographic arrays. If a display has been encoded into a single pattern unit, and the number of features in the encoding is constant regardless of the amount of information it represents, then there should be no relationship between the length of the array and difficulty of processing. This approach also can be illustrated by a previous experiment (Johnson, 1975a), in which increasing word length from four to six letters did not seem to slow down identification time.

The Length–Difficulty Relationship and the Issue of Word Frequency

While there has been a general assumption that word length has a retarding influence on word recognition (McGinnies, Comer, & Lacy, 1952), the effect does not appear to be all that clear, and on occasion it has not been obtained at all (Doggett & Richards, 1975). In addition, studies that have obtained the effect seem to do so only with low-frequency words (McGinnies et al., 1952), and even then the effect may disappear as the subjects become more practiced (Newbigging & Hay, 1962). Given this tenuousness of the length–difficulty relationship, it seems clear that any account of the effect must take careful consideration of the conditions under which it appears (see Doggett & Richards, 1975, for a review).

The currently available data can be explained within the pattern-unit model by noting that the difficulty and complexity of preresponse processing is assumed to be a function of both the number of pattern units into which the display is divided and the ease with which those pattern units can be encoded. If the iconic array cannot be generated by a rule system in permanent memory, or if it is unusual and the subject has difficulty generating an adequate encoding, then it is possible that the size and complexity of the array might have an influence on processing.

These two points can be illustrated by first considering the case where an iconic representation of a letter array does not conform to the orthographic structure of English. Not only would time be spent in the initial attempts to assign a unitary encoding, but there would then be additional time needed to parse the input and encode it element-by-element into memory. In the second case, in which the display was unusual in some way but did conform to the orthographic structure of English, the model would suppose that the display could be processed as a single pattern unit, but it might take the subject several attempts to assign an encoding, and again there would be an increase in prememorial processing time.

These increases in latency between the establishment of the icon and memorial encoding would cause little difficulty if the displays were presented for an extended period of time. However, most of the previous work on the length–difficulty relationship has used subthreshold displays, or else the threshold was determined using the ascending method of limits, and both procedures would result in all displays being very brief. With such brief displays, there would be no way of replenishing the icon if it began to decay before memorial encoding was completed, and it is quite likely that the transfer mechanism would have to deal with a degraded and incomplete iconic representation. In that such arrays would not conform to any known structure, it would be impossible to assign a unitary encoding, and it would be necessary to apply the parser and encode the available letters on an item-by-item basis. In that case, the ultimate response would have to be a best guess based on the available letters, and the probability of a correct response should be a decreasing function of the amount of missing information.

The point of these considerations is that a length–difficulty relationship should be apparent whenever the subject must use a parse-and-guess strategy, and such a strategy should be needed whenever the iconic representation of a display is degraded at the time when it is to be transferred into memory. In addition, anything that would delay the transfer of a briefly displayed item would increase the likelihood of needing the parse-and-guess strategy, because it would increase the likelihood that the iconic array would be degraded.

This explanation can be illustrated by applying it to the McGinnies et al. (1952) study. The display durations for an item began at some point below threshold, and they were increased in small increments until the subject gave the first identification of the word. It would be assumed that very early in a sequence of displays the subject's responses would all be based on a parse-and-guess strategy, and the likelihood of a correct guess should be a decreasing function of a word's length. To the extent that the first occurrence of the correct response would occur on one of these parse-and-guess trials, one would expect a length–difficulty relationship.

The fact that the relationship was obtained only for rare words can be explained by noting the much lower threshold obtained for high-frequency words. Such a frequency effect would be expected because it might take several attempts to assign an encoding to a rare or unusual word, and it would be necessary to compensate for the decaying iconic representation by having a longer display. However, the lower threshold for the high-frequency words also would mean that there would be fewer opportunities to parse-and-guess between the time when a word was first displayed and the time when its duration reached the point where it could be clearly read. With a reduced likelihood that the first correct response occurred on a parse-and-guess trial, there should be a reduction in the length–difficulty relationship. In addition, there were constant increments in the display duration from trial to trial, and the increments were the same for the various levels of word frequency. If the subjects approached threshold more rapidly for high-frequency words than for low-frequency words, there would be a greater chance that they would make a transition from a trial on which there was no usable iconic information (i.e., no basis for guessing at all) to one on which the iconic array was complete and could be encoded as a unit. This also would result in an attenuated length–difficulty relationship for high-frequency words, and this does appear to be the usual outcome (McGinnies, et al., 1952; Postman & Adis–Castro, 1957).

In a more recent study, Doggett and Richards (1975) conducted a similar experiment, but their identification criterion was two successive correct responses. In that it is likely that such a procedure would severely reduce the number of items for which the criterion would be met on a parse-and-guess trial, the length–difficulty relationship should be attenuated, and this appears to be what they obtained. Even when the displays are rare words, if the subject reports seeing the same word on two successive trials it is quite likely that the iconic array was complete and clear.

In a related study, with an even more rigid response criterion (three consecutive correct identifications), Richards (Richards & Hempstead, 1973) did demonstrate a length effect for orthographically regular nonsense material.

However, in that study the subjects were automatically assigned 80 msec as their score if they had not met the criterion by the time the display duration reached 75 msec. To the extent that such scores were assigned, it would suggest that mean performance in the experiment may have been below threshold where the parse-and-guess strategy might have been used. Furthermore, there is always a risk in using nonsense material, because even though an item may appear to be pronounceable, there might be just enough orthographic irregularity to preclude assigning a unitary encoding, and a parse-and-guess strategy would be needed for those items. In addition, the chance of such an orthographic irregularity should increase with word length.

Another class of experiments that has demonstrated length effects in word processing involves presenting a word to a subject and asking him to read it out loud, with the response measure being the time elapsing between the appearance of the word and the first sound in the subject's reading response. In such a task, there is evidence that both length in terms of number of letters (Gough, 1972) and length in syllables (Eriksen, Pollack, & Montague, 1970) influence response latency. However, in that the display was above threshold in both illumination and duration, it is difficult to explain the results in terms of the parse-and-guess strategy.

It is the case, however, that in such a task much more intervenes between the presentation of the word and the execution of the reproductive response than just an act of reading. For example, once the word has been identified it may be necessary to provide a phonetic encoding, and quite certainly it would be necessary to generate a motor program for producing the entire word (Johnson, 1972). The duration of either or both of these encoding stages could be related to word length, and the entire effect could result from events that occur after the word had been identified (i.e., read).

This interpretation is supported in part by the finding of Eriksen et al. (1970) that length in syllables did not influence reading time if the subjects were allowed to prepare their motor response before the timing began. In addition, Gough (personal communication) has suggested that some of the length effects he has reported (Gough, 1972) may have been influenced by the visual angle of the display. With large displays, it may be necessary to scan a letter array before it can be read, and the scan time should be an increasing function of the size of the array.

One situation in which length effects for words are not usually obtained involves presenting the word at some above-threshold level and asking the subject to simply indicate whether it matched some predesignated target item. In the experiment described earlier (Johnson, 1975a), the subjects were shown a series of 24 single-word displays, and each time an item appeared they were to press one of two buttons indicating whether or not the display conformed to the predesignated target for that series. The target appeared in half of the displays, and the other half of the time some other word appeared. Within a series, then, there were 24 displays, with 12 being instances of the target and the other 12

TABLE 2
Effect of Word Length and Frequency
on Recognition Time

	Word length				
	3	4	6	8	$\bar{X}$
Yes	.495	.489	.491	.514	.497
No	.486	.472	.475	.485	.480
High frequency	.488	.469	.490	.513	.490
Low frequency	.494	.492	.475	.486	.486
$\bar{X}$	.491	.481	.483	.499	–

being 12 different words. There was no attempt to control the similarity between targets and foils. The results indicated no difference in reaction time to four- and six-letter words, and this was true of both the "yes" and the "no" responses.

In a similar experiment, the word lengths employed were three, four, six, and eight letters, and within each length either the displays were all high-frequency words (Thorndike–Lorge A and AA) or they occurred less often than twice per million. The subjects were presented with a series of 25 displays, and within a series there were five instances of each of five different words, with one of them being designated the target (i.e., the target occurred on 20% of the trials, as did each of the foils). In addition, the five different words in a series were homogeneous with respect to length and frequency, and each subject was presented with eight such series conforming to the eight combinations of length and frequency. The procedures were the same as those described in Experiment II of Johnson (1975a).

The results are summarized in Table 2. Again, there was no reliable length effect, and the effect of frequency also was not significant. In addition, none of the interactions was significant. These data, then, also appear to be consistent with the pattern-unit model.

The length and frequency effects demonstrated in the preceding experiment were replicated in two other experiments using somewhat different procedures. In these experiments, a different target was used for each item in a series, rather than a single target for a whole series as in the experiments described earlier. In addition, in one experiment the displays were all six-letter words, but for four series of 24 displays they were high-frequency words (A and AA), and in four series they were low-frequency words (once or less per million). In the other experiment, the words all occurred 40 or more times per million, but word lengths were three, four, six, or eight letters.

The mean reaction times for the high- and low-frequency words was 478 and 482 msec, respectively, and the difference was not reliable ($F < 1.00$). The

TABLE 3
Effect of Word Length on Reaction Time

Type of response	Word length				
	3	4	6	8	$\bar{X}$
Yes	.486	.477	.466	.457	.472
No	.539	.519	.517	.503	.520
Both	.513	.498	.491	.480	.496

results for the experiment that varied word length are presented in Table 3. Again, there was no evidence of an effect of word length on reaction time ($F <$ 1.00), and the slight differences that were obtained were in the wrong direction.

The results of this set of experiments appear to be consistent with the expectations of the pattern unit model. The displays were all above threshold; the responses did not have to be vocalized; and even the longest words had a visual angle of less than a degree and a half, which would have eliminated any need for scanning. Given these conditions, then, there would be no basis for expecting a length effect, and none was obtained.

Unfortunately, while these data are consistent with the model, their interpretation relies on accepting the null hypothesis. In order to get more positive evidence supporting the model, a comparison was made between a condition in which the model would predict a length effect and one in which length should not influence the subject.

The basic task in this experiment (Johnson, 1975b) was the same as in the others, but both pronounceable nonsense words and consonant strings were used as displays in addition to words, and each display could contain either three or four letters. On the basis of the model, one would expect in a situation such as this that subjects would not be able to assign an integrating encoding to a string of consonants, and not only would there be time involved in attempting to do so, but there would be additional time needed for the parse and letter-by-letter encoding. Therefore, for the consonants the identification time should be long and an increasing function of the number of letters in the display. In that both the words and the pronounceable nonsense words conformed to English orthography, an integrating encoding could be assigned and no length effects should occur. While it is entirely possible that subjects might have more trouble assigning an encoding to an unfamiliar nonsense word than to a word, eventually they should be able to assign such an encoding, and the effect should be to just lengthen the identification time without word length having any influence.

As in the other studies, the displays were presented in series of 24 displays each, and each subject was presented with six such series, with one conforming to each combination of length and display type. Immediately before a display was presented the experimenter spelled the target for that display, and when the display appeared the subject responded by pressing one of two buttons.

The results are presented in Table 4. Not only did it take the subjects longer to identify the consonant strings than the displays that conformed to English orthography, but the reaction time was a function of the number of letters in the consonant strings, while this was not the case for the orthographically regular displays. When the consonant strings were compared with each of the other two types of display, both the effect of display type and the interaction between length and display type were significant.

These results offer somewhat clearer support for the model in that a length effect was obtained under conditions predicted by the model. If the subjects are able to assign an encoding to a display it can be processed as if it were a single unit, but if the display is not rule generated, it appears that a parse is needed, and it is processed on a letter-by-letter basis.

One final situation in which a word-length effect has been demonstrated in visual information processing involves a task used by Eichelman (1970). Two items were presented to subjects, one above the other, and the subject's task was to indicate whether they were same or different. Eichelman reported that reaction time increased with increasing length from displays of a single letter to displays with six letters, and Marmurek (1975) has recently obtained a similar finding.

In that the items to be compared are presented simultaneously, the model would suppose that they are encoded in the same form at all levels of processing. Given this supposition, it would be expected that a comparison could and would be made between the items as soon as the iconic representation was completed. However, in that the integrating encoding would not have been assigned at that point, the display should be processed on a letter-by-letter basis, and processing time should be an increasing function of display length. This point is further supported by the fact that Eichelman's (1970) subjects reported that they did not read the word but, rather, made a letter-by-letter comparison.

In a related study, Marmurek (1975) also found a length effect when two items were presented simultaneously and could be compared within the perceptual system. However, he demonstrated that the effect disappeared when the same items must be compared within memory. In addition, he demonstrated

TABLE 4
Mean Reaction Time for Each Condition

Condition	Consonants	Nonwords	Words	Mean
Three letter	.527	.483	.464	.491
Four letter	.561	.494	.459	.505
Both lengths	.544	.489	.461	.498

that physical similarity between targets and foils had a retarding influence on comparisons within the perceptual system, but that the similarity effect was much reduced when the comparison was made within memory after the integrating encoding had been assigned.

Part—Whole Relationships in Pattern Identification

According to the model, if an item has been processed into memory, and it conforms to an array for which the perceiver can generate an integrating encoding, then the components of the array should not be immediately available for identification. That effect should occur both because it is assumed that items lose their individual identity when they are encoded into a single unit (Statements IX, X, and XI), and because of the fact that it is assumed that there is no necessary relationship between the encoding for an item and the encoding for a pattern that contains that item as a component (Statement XII). Furthermore, even if a pattern could not be encoded as a unit, there should be a delay in identifying a component of the pattern relative to the time needed to identify the component when it is presented in isolation. This should occur because when the array is presented there would be several initial attempts to encode it as a unit, followed by a parse and a serial encoding of the letters. Only then could the component be identified.

One demonstration of effects such as these is the series of experiments described earlier (Johnson, 1975a). Given a display such as *block,* subjects can respond faster if they are asked to determine whether it conforms to a predesignated word than if they are to determine whether its initial letter conforms to a predesignated letter. Furthermore, identification of a letter in isolation was about the same as for a word, indicating both that length was irrelevant and that the slow reaction times for letters in words stemmed from the retarding influence of the word context.

While these results can be interpreted as indicating that words were available for identification before their component letters, and that the words were the basic unit of processing at the time of comparison, another possible interpretation has been suggested (e.g., Henderson, 1975). This view would suppose that the letters are processed in parallel and are available to the subject prior to the availability of the words. The reason word identification is faster than finding a letter within a word is that a decision regarding the word can be made on the basis of the very first letter processed. If it is consistent with the target word, a "yes" response occurs, and a "no" occurs if it is inconsistent. If a single letter within a word needs to be identified the response must be delayed until that particular letter is processed, and that may not be the first letter whose processing is completed. The implication, then, is that in both tasks the subjects respond on the basis of a single letter, and the word-search advantage occurs because the response can be made on the basis of the first letter processed, while in the letter-search task it is likely to be some subsequently processed letter.

This particular construction of the letter-integration model could be examined if it were possible to ensure that in all cases the response could be based on the first letter processed. For example, identifying a letter in isolation and identifying a letter within a larger array should take equal amounts of time if both identifications occur on the basis of the first letter processed. Within this view, it would be possible to predict a single-letter advantage if one were to additionally assume, like Rumelhart (1970), that subjects have a limited amount of attention that must be distributed over the array, with a decreasing amount for each item as array size increases. With decreasing attention available for each item, there should be an increase in processing time. This assumption, however, seems not to be viable, considering the data reviewed earlier on both channel capacity within the perceptual system and the effects of length on identification in tasks such as these.

Given the negative evidence regarding the limited-capacity assumption, it does seem that this parallel-processing model would predict that reaction time for identifying a single letter in isolation would be the same as for identifying a single letter within an array if the response could be based on the first letter processed. The pattern-unit model, on the other hand, would predict that whenever an array is presented some fractionation would have to occur before a component could be identified, and this would increase the reaction time over a condition in which fractionation was not necessary. Even if the critical item in the array was the first one processed, the processing would occur only after the delay from the fractionation had already been encountered.

This issue was examined in an experiment in which subjects were to identify a single letter in either a display consisting of a single letter or a display consisting of an array of five consonants. When the array consisted of five consonants, they were either all different (e.g., SBJFQ) or all the same (e.g., SSSSS). According to the letter-integration model, if the subject's task was to determine whether a display contained an S, he could do so on the basis of the first letter processed for both the case in which the display consisted of a single S and the case in which it consisted of five S's. This would not be the case, however, for a display such as SBJFQ, and the processing time should be much slower than for the other two conditions.

The results of the study were not consistent with the letter integration model. While it did take the subjects longer to identify the target letter when all the consonants were different than when they were the same, processing a single-letter display was considerably faster (i.e., 100 to 200 msec) than processing a display that consisted of five instances of the same letter. In addition, the difference occurred for both a condition in which the target letter could have occurred anywhere within the array and a condition in which the subjects were instructed to confine their search to the initial position of the five-letter arrays. If the subjects were simply responding on the basis of the first letter processed, this difference should not have occurred, but the effect does seem consistent with a view that subjects first attempted to encode the entire five-letter array as a unit, with letter identification occurring only after those attempts had failed.

The component of the model of concern in this issue is the general assumption that the transfer mechanism will either unitize an input or delay memorial processing in the event that an integrating encoding is difficult or impossible to assign. This position seems to be a necessary implication of the hypothesis that unitization occurs at the interface between perception and memory, and it provides a basis for testing that hypothesis. That is, if unitization does occur at the interface, then the kind of effects demonstrated in the earlier study (Johnson, 1975a) should occur only after memorial processing has been initiated, and should not be apparent in tasks that entail only perceptual processing.

Marmurek (1975) has reported a very critical experiment regarding this component of the model. He capitalized on the assumption included within the model (as elsewhere)–(Eichelman, 1970; Gough & Cosky, 1977, Posner, 1969) that if two items are presented simultaneously they can be compared as iconic representations before they are processed by the transfer mechanism. If this is the case, then the comparison would occur before the display was encoded into a unit, and the units of comparison should be simple iconic assemblages, rather than the larger pattern units that would emerge after the assemblages were integrated by the transfer mechanism.

In Marmurek's task, the subjects were presented two lines of material and asked to determine whether the materials on the two lines were the same or different. In one condition both lines appeared simultaneously, but in the other condition the material on the top line appeared and then went off and it was three seconds later before the material on the bottom line was presented. In the simultaneous condition, the two lines can be compared within the perceptual system, but in order to mediate the three-second delay when the displays are successive it would be necessary to encode the top line into memory. However, if the top line had been encoded into memory, it would be necessary to encode the bottom line into the same form before a comparison could be made, with the result that the comparison could occur only after the displays had been unitized by the transfer mechanism.

Within each of these conditions, Marmurek used three types of display. In one type, the top and bottom lines were both words; in a second type, the items were both single letters; and in a third type, the top line was a single letter and the bottom line was a word. In the latter situation, the single letter appeared immediately above the first letter of the word, and the subject's task was to determine if the single letter matched the first letter of the word.

Marmurek's results were quite striking. In the successive condition, comparing two words was much faster than comparing a single letter to the first letter of a word, and comparing two single letters was about as fast as comparing two words. This part of the experiment, then, replicated those reported earlier (Johnson, 1975a), indicating that under a successive presentation the pattern unit was more available for comparison than was a component of the display.

The pattern of results for the simultaneous condition was quite different. Under these conditions comparing a letter to the first letter of a word was much faster than comparing two words, and comparing two single letters was about the same as comparing a letter with the first letter of a word. That is, under the simultaneous condition an encoding of a component of a display appeared to be more available for comparison than was any integrating encoding of the complete pattern.

These results suggest that in the successive condition, in which the comparison should occur only after the material has been encoded into memory, the basic unit of comparison was the word. On the other hand, in the simultaneous condition, in which the comparison should be between two arrays of separate perceptual encodings, the letters in the words seemed not to be integrated, and processing time was an increasing function of the number of single-letter comparisons that needed to be made. To this extent, then, the data seem quite consistent with a model that assumes that unitization occurs at the interface between perception and memory.

A FINAL DISCLAIMER

It is very easy to extend conclusions beyond the domain to which they are intended to apply. For example, it seems that one basic unitization principle is that contiguous visual elements share a common encoding. However, one can also demonstrate that there are cases in which noncontiguous elements are commonly encoded. This issue has been handled within the context of the current concern by demonstrating that a second type of encoding occurs at the perception—memory interface, and it allows subjects to integrate small patterns into single units. While this type of encoding is assumed to be based on cognitive relationships, with the processing being somewhat less automatic than that which occurs within the perceptual system, it must be clear that there is a wide range of unitization effects that cannot be handled even by this more cognitive mechanism.

For example, suppose subjects are presented with a long list of words, and their task is to recall them in any order they choose. There is evidence that under these circumstances words can be encoded into common units even when their spatial—temporal separation is such that the effect could not result from processing by the transfer mechanism. Similarly, comprehension effects in reading seem to be determined by a higher-order unitization that goes beyond anything that could be explained by the model under discussion (Bransford & Franks, 1971). Finally, there appear to be cases in which the integration includes information not provided by the current task (Bransford & Johnson, 1973; Haviland & Clark, 1974), and there would be no way such common encoding could be the product of the transfer mechanism.

Given the reality of these more complex unitization effects, it is important to note that the general type of memorial processing and unitization described by the letter integration model is probably quite common, and it will be necessary for any general model of unitization to include such a component. The current concern, however, has been somewhat more limited. The intent of the pattern-unit model is not to explain all unitization effects, but to account for the way small patterns such as words become unitized, and the more complex cognitive mechanisms appear to be unnecessary for this task.

CONCLUSIONS

The major focus of the model presented in this chapter has been on the interfacing mechanism between the perceptual system and memory. The issue has arisen because of an apparent incompatibility between the type of processing and encoding that occurs within the perceptual system and that which seems to be required for the efficient and relatively permanent representation of information within memory.

One difference between memorial and perceptual encoding lies in the fact that perceptual encoding seems to be a representation of the physical attributes of the display, while the memorial encoding represents the display's acoustic and semantic content. In addition, this difference in the substance of the encoding appears to reflect an important distinction between an encoding based on the extraction of information and one based on the assignment of information from memory, and this difference offers a preliminary basis for distinguishing perceptual and memorial processing.

In addition to the extraction-versus-assignment distinction, there also appears to be a critical difference in the basic unit of processing within the perceptual and memorial systems. Physical contiguity seems to be the basic unitization principle in perception, and higher-order cognitive rules have little or no role in determining the unit of processing. Within the memorial system, on the other hand, higher-order packaging of information according to cognitive schemes seems to be the rule. One has to contrive situations in which iconic arrays are not processed into memory as units. Even with arrays that are not normally integratable, such as consonant strings, there is evidence that they are handled as units within memory if the arrays are small enough (Johnson, 1973).

An important consequence of this difference in units of processing is that within the perceptual system the components of a perceptual array should be more available than an integrated representation, but the reverse should be the case if the array has been processed into memory. In addition, if the components of an array are individually encoded within the perceptual system, there would be a basis for supposing that display size might influence processing, but once the display has been assigned a unitary memorial encoding, no such size effects should be apparent. A number of experiments offer clear support for both of these expectations.

The general conclusion is that the encoding process integrates information into larger and larger units, and within the perceptual system noncognitive relationships appear to be the basis for the encoding. The type of cognitive unitization needed to form the somewhat larger units involved in word identification seems to occur at the interface between perception and memory, where the output of the transfer device is a unitary representation within which the components have lost their individual identities.

In terms of the reading process, these considerations would suggest that the word is the most elementary unit that can be processed using cognitive mechanisms, and any subword analyses would necessarily entail processes that are not normally used in the efficient execution of the skill. For example, while the analytic skills included within the study of phonics may have some pedagogical value (albeit unknown) in the teaching of reading, there is no reason to believe that these skills have any function in the efficient execution of the reading act.

REFERENCES

Anderson, J. A. A theory for the recognition of items from short memorized lists. *Psychological Review,* 1973, **80,** 417–438.

Atkinson, R. C., & Shiffrin, R. M. Human memory: A proposed system and its control processes. In K. W. Spence & J. T. Spence (Eds.), *Advances in the psychology of learning and motivation research and theory,* Vol. 2. New York: Academic Press, 1968.

Bransford, J. D., & Franks, J. J. The abstraction of linguistic ideas. *Cognitive psychology,* 1971, **2,** 331–350.

Bransford, J. D., & Johnson, M. K. Considerations of some problems of comprehension. In W. Chase (Ed.), *Visual information processing.* New York: Academic Press, 1973, Pp. 383–438.

Broadbent, D. E. *Perception and communication.* London: Pergamon Press, 1958.

Chomsky, C. Reading, writing, and phonology. *Harvard Educational Review,* 1970, **40,** 287–309.

Chomsky, N. Phonology and reading. In H. Levin & J. Williams (Eds.), *Basic studies in reading.* New York: Basic Books, 1970.

Clark, S. E. Retrieval of color information from the preperceptual storage system. *Journal of Experimental Psychology,* 1969, **82,** 263–266.

Coltheart, M. Iconic memory: A reply to Professor Holding. *Memory and Cognition,* 1975, **3,** 42–48.

Coltheart, M., Lea, C. D., & Thompson, K. In defense of iconic memory. *Quarterly Journal of Experimental Psychology,* 1974, **26,** 633–641.

Conrad, R. Interference or decay over short intervals? *Journal of Verbal Learning and Behavior,* 1967, **6,** 49–54.

D'Avello, D. Letter feature selection from iconic memory. Unpublished master's thesis, The Ohio State University, Columbus, Ohio, 1976.

den Heyer, K., & Barrett, B. Selective loss of visual and verbal information in STM by means of visual and verbal interpolated tasks. *Psychonomic Science,* 1971, **25,** 100–102.

Doggett, D., & Richards, L. G., A reexamination of the effect of word length on recognition thresholds. *American Journal of Psychology,* 1975, **88,** 583–594.

Eichelman, W. H. Familiarity effects in the simultaneous matching task. *Journal of Experimental Psychology,* 1970, **86,** 275–282.

Eriksen, C. W., Pollack, M. D., & Montague, W. E. Implicit speech: A mechanism in perceptual encoding? *Journal of Experimental Psychology,* 1970, **84,** 502–507.

Eriksen, C. W., & Spencer, T. Rate of information processing in visual perception: Some results and methodological considerations. *Journal of Experimental Psychology Monograph,* 1969, **79** (2, P. 2).

Estes, W. K. The locus of inferential and perceptual processes in letter identification. *Journal of Experimental Psychology: General,* 1975, **104,** 122–145.

Gardner, G. T. Evidence for independent parallel channels in tachistoscopic perception. *Cognitive Psychology,* 1973, **4,** 130–155.

Gibson, E. J., & Levin, H. *The psychology of reading.* Cambridge, Mass.: MIT Press, 1976.

Gibson, E. J., Osser, H., & Pick, A. D. A study in the development of grapheme–phoneme correspondences. *Journal of Verbal Learning and Verbal Behavior,* 1963, **2,** 142–146.

Gough, P. B. One second of reading. In J. F. Kavanagh & I. G. Mattingly (Eds.), *Language by ear and by eye.* Cambridge, Mass.: MIT Press, 1972.

Gough, P. B., & Cosky, M. J. One second of reading again. In N. Castellan & D. Pisoni (Eds.), *Cognitive theory* (Vol. II). Hillsdale, N.J.: Lawrence Erlbaum Associates, 1977.

Haviland, S. E., & Clark, H. H. What's new? Acquiring new information as a process in comprehension. *Journal of Verbal Learning and Verbal Behavior,* 1974, **13,** 512–521.

Henderson, L. Do words conceal their component letters? A critique of Johnson (1975) on the visual perception of words. *Journal of Verbal Learning and Verbal Behavior,* 1975, **14,** 648–650.

Johnson, N. F. The role of chunking and organization in the process of recall. In G. Bower (Ed.), *The psychology of learning and motivation,* Vol. 4. New York: Academic Press, 1970. Pp. 171–247.

Johnson, N. F. Organization and the concept of a memory code. In A. W. Melton and E. Martin (Eds.), *Coding processes in human memory.* Washington, D.C.: Winston, 1972.

Johnson, N. F. Higher-order encoding: Process or state? *Memory and Cognition,* 1973, **1,** 491–494.

Johnson, N. F. On the function of letters in word identification: Some data and a preliminary model. *Journal of Verbal Learning and Verbal Behavior,* 1975, **14,** 17–29. (a)

Johnson, N. F. The effect of display length on the identification of letters. Paper presented at the meetings of the Psychonomic Society, Denver. 1975. (b)

Kahneman, D., & Henik, A. Effects of visual grouping on immediate recall and selective attention. Paper presented at Attention and Performance VI, Stockholm, July 1975.

LaBerge, D. Attention and the measurement of perceptual learning. *Memory and Cognition,* 1973, **1,** 268–276.

Marmurek, H. H. C. The identification of words and letters within words: A level of processing analysis. Unpublished doctoral dissertation, The Ohio State University, Columbus, Ohio, 1975.

McGinnies, E., Comer, P., & Lacy, O. L. Visual-recognition thresholds as a function of word length and word frequency. *Journal of Experimental Psychology,* 1952, **44,** 65–69.

Merluzzi, T. V., & Johnson, N. F. The effect of repetition on iconic memory. *Quarterly Journal of Experimental Psychology,* 1974, **26,** 266–273.

Miller, G. A. The magical number seven plus or minus two: Some limits on our capacity for processing information. *Psychological Review*, 1956, **63**, 81–97.

Murdock, B. B. The retention of individual items. *Journal of Experimental Psychology*, 1961, **62**, 618–625.

Newbigging, P. L., & Hay, J. The practice effect in recognition threshold determinations as a function of word frequency and length. *Canadian Journal of Psychology*, 1962, **16**, 177–184.

Posner, M. I. Abstraction and the process of recognition. In G. Bower & J. T. Spence (Eds.), *The psychology of learning and motivation*, Vol. 3. New York: Academic Press, 1969.

Postman, L., & Adis-Castro, G. Psychophysical methods in the study of word recognition. *Science*, 1957, **125**, 193–194.

Richards, L. G., & Hempstead, J. D. Auditory pretraining as a determinant of visual thresholds for pseudowords. *American Journal of Psychology*, 1973, **86**, 325–329.

Rumelhart, D. E. A multicomponent theory of the perception of briefly presented displays. *Journal of Mathematical Psychology*, 1970, **7**, 191–218.

Shiffrin, R. M. The locus and role of attention in memory systems. In P. M. A. Rabbitt & S. Dornic (Eds.), *Attention and performance*, Vol. V. London: Academic Press, 1975.

Shiffrin, R. M., & Gardner, G. T. Visual processing capacity and attentional control. *Journal of Experimental Psychology*, 1972, **93**, 72–82.

Shiffrin, R. M., & Geisler, W. S. Visual recognition in a theory of visual information processing. In R. Solso (Ed.), *Contemporary issues in cognitive psychology: The Loyola symposium*. Washington D.C.: Winston, 1973.

Shiffrin, R. M., McKay, D. P., & Shaffer, W. O. Attending to forty-nine spatial positions at once. *Journal of Experimental Psychology: Human Perception and Performance*, 1976, **1**, 14–22.

Smith, E. E., & Spoehr, K. T. The perception of printed English: A theoretical perspective. In B. Kantowitz (Ed.), *Human information processing: Tutorials in performance and cognition*. Hillsdale, N.J.: Lawrence Erlbaum Associates, 1974.

Spencer, T. Some effects of different masking stimuli on iconic storage. *Journal of Experimental Psychology*, 1969, **81**, 132–140.

Sperling, G. The information available in brief visual presentation. *Psychological Monographs*, 1960, **74** (Whole No. 498).

Spoehr, K. T., & Smith, E. E. The role of syllables in perceptual processing. *Cognitive Psychology*, 1973, **5**, 71–89.

Theios, J., & Muise, J. G. The word identification process in reading. In N. Castellan & D. Pisoni (Eds.), *Cognitive theory*, Vol. II. Hillsdale, N.J.: Lawrence Erlbaum Associates, 1977.

Turvey, M. T. The nature of information loss in the visual preperceptual system. Unpublished doctoral dissertation, The Ohio State University, Columbus, Ohio, 1967.

Turvey, M. T. On peripheral and central processes in vision: Inferences from an information processing analysis of masking with pattern stimuli. *Psychological Review*, 1973, **80**, 1–52.

Veneszky, R. L. *The structure of English orthography*. The Hague: Mouton, 1970.

von Wright, J. M. Selection in immediate memory. *Quarterly Journal of Experimental Psychology*, 1968, **20**, 62–68.

von Wright, J. M. On selection in visual immediate memory. *Acta Psychologica*, 1970, **33**, 280–292.

4
Automatic and Controlled Information Processing in Vision

Walter Schneider
Richard M. Shiffrin

Indiana University

INTRODUCTION

In many human endeavors, be it reading, playing a musical instrument, or finding a flaw in an experimental design, there is a fundamental transition between two modes of information processing. The first mode is relatively slow, sequential, subject controlled, and attention demanding. In the case of reading, for example, the beginning reader may decode words letter by letter at rates near one letter per second (or about 10 words per minute). The attention demands of this slow, sequential process are illustrated by the fact that comprehension of the conceptual content of a message read in this fashion may be negligible. The second mode is rapid, parallel, and automatic and makes few demands on attention. In the case of reading, for example, a skilled reader may process 100 characters per second (or 1,000 words per minute), and can do so with so few demands on attention that the conceptual comprehension of the message may be extremely high. These examples not only make it clear that the two processing modes differ considerably, but also point out the importance of understanding the mechanisms of learning by which the transition is made from the first mode to the second.

We shall use the term *automatic processing* to refer to the detection and recognition of visual information in an automatic fashion not dependent on the amount or kind of other information presented simultaneously. We shall use the term *controlled processing* to refer to detection, recognition, or short-term search that proceeds in a serial, feature-by-feature fashion in an order controlled by the subject.

127

In spite of the pervasive influence of these two processes in treatments of reading and visual information processing in general, there are very few clear-cut experimental demonstrations that there exist two separate mechanisms, and there are even fewer experiments elucidating their different properties or the transition between them (a notable exception being LaBerge, 1973, 1975). It is the goal of this chapter to present a variety of empirical demonstrations that automatic and controlled processing exist as two qualitatively different mechanisms, to develop their properties, to examine the conditions of training that lead to their development, and to discuss how these mechanisms might be used in reading and used to learn to read.

A SEARCH PARADIGM FOR OBSERVATIONS OF AUTOMATIC AND CONTROLLED PROCESSING

The general paradigm in which these themes will be developed is one in which both attention and short-term search may be studied in a visual detection task. The details of the procedures may be found in Schneider (1975), Shiffrin and Schneider (1976), Schneider and Shiffrin (1977), or Shiffrin and Schneider (1977), and we will give only a summary here.

Experiment 1: A Multiple-Frame Search Task

The basic paradigm is a variant and extension of that utilized by Sperling, Budiansky, Spivak, and Johnson (1971); it is illustrated in Fig. 1. Four elements are presented simultaneously on a CRT screen controlled by a PDP-8e computer. The elements are arranged in a square around a central fixation dot, and their joint presentation for a brief period of time is termed a *frame*. A trial consists of the presentation of 20 frames in immediate succession. The elements presented can be characters (i.e., digits or consonants) or random dot masks. The time from the onset of one frame to the onset of the next is termed the *frame time*. The frame is displayed for all but the first 15 msec of the frame time, and no character or mask is ever presented in the same screen position in two successive frames.

The subject's task requires the detection of one of several items (the *memory set*) presented in advance of each trial. Either no target (probability = .5) or one target (probability = .5) is presented on a given trial, in any frame from 4 through 18. The subject presses a key when he thinks he detects a target, or presses a different key at trial's end if he does not detect a target. The frame time is kept constant across the 20 frames of each trial, and the basic dependent variable is the psychometric function relating accuracy to frame time for each condition.

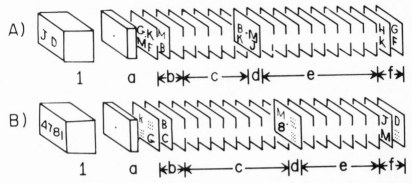

FIG. 1 Two examples of a positive trial in the 20-frame search paradigm. (A) Varied mappings: memory-set size = 2 (J, D); frame size = 4. (B) Consistent mappings: memory-set size = 4 (4, 7, 8, 1); frame size = 2. (1) Presentation of memory set. (a) Fixation dot goes on for .5 sec when subject starts trial; (b) three dummy frames that never contain target; (c) distractor frames; (d) target frame; (e) distractor frames (f) dummy frames that never contain target. Frame time is varied across conditions.

Three basic independent variables were manipulated. In order to explore the connection between selective attention and visual search, the number of characters in each frame was varied from one to four. This variable is denoted *frame size* (abbreviated F) and was held constant during all 20 frames making up a trial. When frame size was less than four, all noncharacter positions were filled by masks. Character positions were chosen randomly for each frame, subject only to certain constraints such as "no repeated elements in successive frames in the same display positions."

In order to explore the connection between selective attention and memory scanning, the number of possible targets presented in advance of the trial was varied from one to four. This variable is denoted *memory-set size* (abbreviated M). A different memory set was presented in advance of each trial.

Finally, and most important, the relationship between the memory-set items and the distractors was varied. We wished to contrast performance resulting from the two basic forms of processing. Previous work (e.g., Corballis, 1975; Briggs & Johnsen, 1973; Egeth, Atkinson, Gilmore, & Marcus, 1973; Estes, 1972; Kristofferson, 1972a) led us to suspect that automatic processing would occur when the subject had practiced a great deal at giving a consistent detection response to memory set items that were never distractors, and led us to suspect that the development of automatic processing would be speeded when the memory-set items and distractors were categorically distinct. Conversely, we expected that controlled processing would occur when responses to memory-set items were inconsistent because memory set items and distractors were mixed from trial to trial, or when subjects had been given only small amounts of training.

130

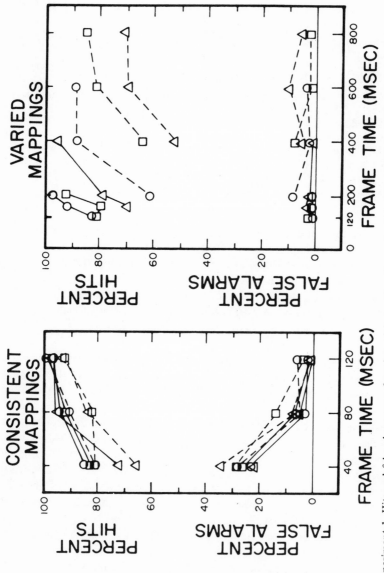

FIG. 2 Experiment 1. Hits and false alarms as a function of frame time for each of the 12 conditions. Three frame times were utilized for each condition. ○, Frame size = 1; □, frame size = 2; △, frame size = 4. Solid line: memory-set size = 1; dashed line: memory-set size = 4.

These expectations led us to utilize two conditions that differ in the manner in which they relate the memory-set items to the distractors. The conditions are denoted *consistent mapping* and *varied mapping*. The *consistent mapping* condition requires the subject to detect a digit target(s) in frames of letter distractors, or a letter target(s) in frames of digit distractors. The varied-mapping condition requires the subject to detect a digit target(s) in frames of digit distractors, or a letter target(s) in frames of letter distractors. The consistent-mapping condition keeps the targets and distractors disjoint over trials—no target is ever a distractor, and vice versa. Targets and distractors are mixed from trial to trial in the varied-mapping condition. We will refer to the consistent-mapping condition as *CM search* and the varied-mapping condition as *VM search*.

Altogether, then, there were 12 basic conditions: 2 distractor conditions (CM or VM) $\times$ 2 memory-set sizes (1 or 4) $\times$ 3 frame sizes (1, 2, or 4). In addition, each basic condition was run at three different frame times. Frame times were chosen so that the probability of correct detection or rejection varied from about .60 to 1.0. Each subject ran for a long block of trials in each condition at each frame time before switching to the next time or condition. Although a given subject ran in both CM and VM conditions, the memory-set items in his CM conditions were never used as distractors in either condition. Thus, subjects whose CM task utilized digit targets saw only letters in their VM conditions (and vice versa). The four subjects had at least 10 hours of practice distributed across the various conditions before the data to be reported were recorded.

Results of Experiment 1: Evidence for Two Processing Modes

The results of Experiment 1 are shown in Fig. 2. Frame times varied so greatly among conditions that it was necessary to graph the results in two panels, using different scalings. In the VM conditions, frame time for a given accuracy level depended strongly upon the memory-set size (M) and the frame size (F), ranging from 120 msec (for an accuracy of 80%) for the M = 1, F = 1 condition to 800 msec (for an accuracy of 70%) for the M = 4, F = 4 condition. Thus, there is an enormous "selective attention" effect, such that greater numbers of items in memory, or items per frame, yield great reduction in the speed at which frames can be presented to reach a given level of accuracy. In the VM condition, false alarms are always quite low, so that most errors are failures to detect presented targets, rather than detections when no target is present. Note that frame time to reach a given accuracy level is monotonically related to the product of memory-set size and frame size.

The CM conditions show a strikingly altered pattern of results. First, CM performance is much better than VM performance: Even the most difficult combinations of frame size and memory-set size are, at an 80-msec frame time, showing performance equivalent or better to that at a 120-msec frame time of the easiest VM conditions. Second, there is almost no effect of frame size and only a small effect of memory-set size. Thus, attention may be successfully divided in this condition. Finally, there is a large increase in false alarms (detections when no target was present) at frame times of 80 and especially 40 msec.

The results of Experiment 1 suggest the operation of two rather different detection processes. In the VM condition, the targets from some trials are distractors on other trials, and vice versa. Thus, no useful mapping of stimuli to responses, or stimuli to categories, can be learned. In such a case, a target(s) cannot elicit a response different from that elicited by the distractors, and must be found through a slow, possibly serial, item-by-item comparison of all displayed items to all items in short-term memory. We term this process "controlled search." Even if this item-by-item comparison process proceeds as fast as Sternberg (1966) found $-$ 40 msec per comparison $-$ it should be clear that large frame times would be needed to complete all comparisons in the conditions with large frame and memory-set sizes. For example, 100% detection when F = 4 and M = 4 would require an approximate frame time of 4 X 4 X 40 msec = 640 msec. In this serial model, detection would fail whenever a new frame was presented before the search of the previous frame (which contained the target) proceeded far enough to reach the target and match it to memory. If we equate a failure to detect with a failure to divide attention, then this view suggests that the failure to divide attention is due to the limited rate of search of short-term memory.

A rather different detection process appears to operate in the CM conditions. In these conditions, no target ever appears as a distractor, and vice versa. Under such conditions, a mapping of stimuli to an internal detection or attention response can be learned in long-term memory. In addition, since the memory-set items and distractors were already learned categories of numbers and letters, it could be expected that the mapping would be learned very quickly. Thus, in long-term memory an automatic attention response to each target will be learned: The subject can simply wait for the occurrence of one of the learned attention responses, check the detected item, then respond. In effect, in CM conditions the target is always matched or compared first, before any distractors, whereas in VM conditions the target is compared in a randomly chosen position. We shall term the detection process used in CM conditions "automatic detection."

When automatic detection is utilized (in the CM conditions), the only limitation on the speed at which frames may be presented should be perceptual: At fast enough presentation rates, the individual characters will not be fully processed and some characters will be confused with others. Indeed, as the frame-time approaches 40 msec the false-alarm rate climbs greatly in all conditions. Finally, if detections are again equated with the ability to divide attention, then

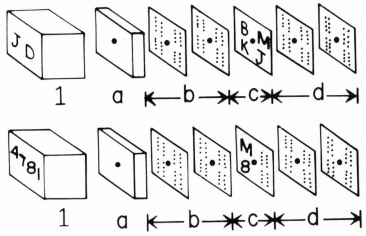

FIG. 3   Two examples of a positive trial in Experiment 2. (A) Varied mapping: memory-set
size = 2(J, D); frame size = 4. (B) consistent mapping: memory-set size = 4(4, 7, 8, 1); frame
size = 2. (1) Presentation of memory set. (a) Fixation dot goes on for .5 sec when subject
starts trial; (b) two frames of masks; (c) target frame; (d) two postmask frames. Frame time
= 160 msec for each of the last five frames.

the virtually unlimited ability to divide attention in the CM conditions may be
ascribed to the high efficiency of the automatic detection process.

Experiment 2: A Single-Frame Search Task Measuring Reaction Time

We next attempted to verify a direct relationship between the accuracy results of
Experiment 1 and the reaction time results of short-term search studies. A
sample procedure from Experiment 2 is depicted in Fig. 3. Five frames were
presented on each trial, preceded by a memory set. The first two and last two
frames contained masks only. The middle frame contained targets, distractors,
and masks. The subject was given instructions to maintain high accuracy, but to
give one of two responses as quickly as possible, indicating whether any item
from the memory set appeared in the display. Memory-set sizes were 1, 2, and 4;
frame sizes were 1, 2, and 4; and the mapping of targets to responses was
consistent or varied as in Experiment 1 (M = 2 was not examined in the CM
condition). The frame time in all conditions was 160 msec. This frame time is
much lower than that needed in Experiment 1 in many of the conditions, but
performance was expected to be accurate nonetheless because the target frame is
not followed by any additional frames requiring processing. To produce high
accuracy, the subject need only retain in short-term memory the memory set
and the (up to four) display characters during his search.

Results of Experiment 2: More Evidence for Two Processing Modes

The results are shown in Fig. 4, which gives the mean reaction time for correct responses for the various conditions. The VM condition is usually termed "varied set" and the CM condition is usually called "fixed set" in the search literature (see Sternberg, 1966). We see that there is virtually no difference in latency among the CM conditions, but a large increase in latency as the memory-set size and/or frame size increase for the VM conditions. For the VM conditions, the functions are reasonably linear and, for the larger values of memory-set size and frame size, the slope of the negative functions (target not present) is just about double that of the positive functions (target present). Such results would seem to indicate serial terminating search in the VM conditions, and direct access, parallel search in the CM conditions. These search strategies have previously been termed controlled search and automatic detection, respectively.

The variance of the reaction times is shown in Fig. 5. As was true for the means, variations in M and F have little effect in the CM conditions, but large effects in the VM conditions. It should be noted that the positive variance becomes much larger than the negative variance in the VM conditions when M = 4, F = 4, a result opposite to that obtained for the means. This finding is, however, predicted by a serial terminating search model.

Models for the controlled search process operating in the VM conditions have

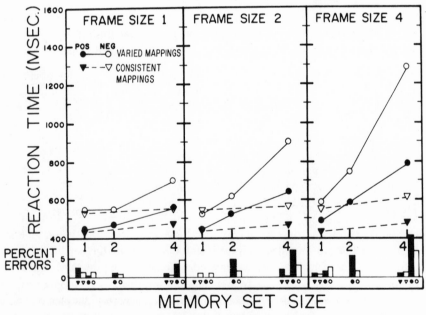

FIG. 4 Data from Experiment 2. Mean reaction time for correct responses and percent errors as a function of memory-set size, for all conditions.

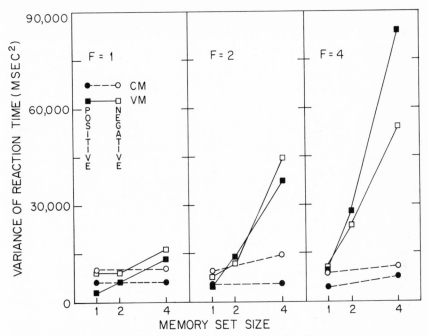

FIG. 5   Data from Experiment 2. Variance of reaction time for correct responses as a function of memory-set size, for all conditions.

been explored thoroughly in other papers, (see Schneider & Shiffrin, 1977). The quantitative model that best fits the data for the means and variances assumes that comparisons are made one at a time between members of the memory set and members of the display. Whenever a match is found, the comparisons are terminated and a positive response is initiated. If no match is found a negative response is initiated. The order of comparisons is as follows: All display items are compared to each memory item, before a switch to the next memory item occurs. Finally, each switch to a new item in the memory set is assumed to take some time. Such a model provides a close quantitative fit to the mean and variance of the reaction time data for the VM conditions, and provides additional insight into the nature of the controlled search process. Regardless of the details of the model, however, the data show clearly different patterns for the VM and CM conditions, and the serial terminating models that seem to fit the VM data would not be appropriate for the CM data.

The Relationship between the Results of Experiments 1 and 2

The case for the hypothesis that attention deficits (as seen in the accuracy data of Experiment 1) and search time (as seen in the reaction time data of Experiment 2) are intimately related is supported by the results from the two studies. In both studies, the dependence of performance upon memory-set size and frame size is very similar in pattern. To see if there might be a quantitative link, we attempted for the VM conditions to fit the model already applied to the reaction time data to the accuracy data. It was assumed that a serial search takes place through the characters in each frame, in the same fashion as was posited for the reaction time task. If a match was discovered (in the target frame) before the next frame began, then a hit occurred; otherwise a miss occurred. The means and variances of the comparison time and the time to switch to a new memory set item were assumed to have the values estimated from the fit of the model to the reaction time data. With no additional parameters, this model gave a good quantitative fit to the accuracy data of Experiment 1 (see Schneider & Shiffrin, 1977).

The fit of the model to both the accuracy and the reaction time results suggests that the same controlled search is being used in the two situations. More generally, the attentional deficits seen in the first study and the search limitations in the second study seem to be closely linked and causally related.

The CM results from Experiments 1 and 2 are also consistent, since both sets of results show memory-set size and frame size to have little effect. Thus, in both cases automatic detection is implicated to be a simultaneous, parallel, relatively independent detection process.

Additional implications concerning automatic detection may be developed by comparing the results of Experiments 1 and 2. In particular, in the second study (see Fig. 4), the CM reaction times are at least as long as the easiest VM reaction times, yet in the first study (see Fig. 2) the CM performance is much better than the performance even in the easiest VM condition. The reaction time results suggest that the time for automatic detection is at least as long as that for a very easy controlled search. Such a possibility is quite consistent with the accuracy results as long as automatic detection can occur in parallel across successive frames as well as within frames, but is not consistent with an assumption that automatic detection is serially limited across successive frames.

In conclusion, then, controlled search is used in the VM conditions and is serial in nature, while automatic detection is used in the CM conditions and is parallel and virtually independent across the characters in one display, across the characters in successive displays, and across the characters held in memory.

Multiple-Target, Multiple-Frame Studies: Qualitatively Differentiating the Two Modes of Processing

The studies in this section were designed to establish more conclusively the qualitative nature of the difference between the automatic and controlled modes of detection.

Experiment 3 utilized a 20-frame procedure just like that in Experiment 1, except that the subject (the same subjects as in the previous study) knew that multiple targets might be present and was required to note these as they occurred and respond at the end of the trial with the number detected. In fact, there were, across trials, 25% no targets, 25% one target, and 50% two targets. When two targets were presented, one-half of the time they were not identical to each other (denoted NI for *not identical*), and one-half of the time they were identical to each other (denoted II for *identical items*). The two targets were for one-quarter of the trials in the same frame (Spacing 0), for one-quarter of the trials in successive frames (Spacing 1), for one-quarter of the trials one frame removed (Spacing 2), and for one-quarter of the trials three frames removed (Spacing 4). The two targets were always in different display positions. Examples of these conditions are shown in Fig. 6. Memory-set size was set equal to 2 and frame size was set equal to 2. In VM blocks frame time was set to 200 msec, and in CM blocks frame time was set to 80 msec. These frame times were chosen to produce intermediate accuracy levels.

The results are shown in Fig. 7. The figure shows the estimated probability that the subject correctly detected one target when one was presented, or both targets when two were presented, for each condition. (The leftmost data point is the observed percent "zero" responses when "zero" targets were present.) The probabilities are estimates because a simple nonparametric correction for guesses and false alarms has been carried out upon the raw data.

Consider first the VM results. Note to begin with that the probability of detecting a single target, when squared, is about equal to the probability of detecting both targets at a spacing of 4 (the same is true for the CM condition). This indicates that at long spacings the targets are probably being detected independently. Also confirming this hypothesis is the fact that at long spacings the II and NI doubles do not differ. At shorter lags, however, large effects appear. Consider the II doubles. When both targets are in the same frame, they are detected quite well, about as well as at a long spacing. However, a target in the immediately following frame is often missed, even though it is the same target as that just detected. This inhibition probably reflects the slowing down of the search due to some time used up by the decision process that counts detections, or due to extra time spent processing the frame of the first target at the expense of the following frame. It is particularly interesting that the greatest decrement occurs when the targets are in successive frames. The attention literature on multiple-target detection indicates that a decrement occurs when targets are presented simultaneously, but the time course of the decrement has seldom been examined. Apparently, the decrement is largest in the VM conditions if there is a delay between the presentation of the two targets.

The VM–NI results show a larger decremental effect covering a longer time period than the decrement for II. There is a decrement in the same frame and also at a spacing of 2, although the largest decrement occurs for the spacing of 1. This pattern of VM results can be explained by assuming that there are two effects of target detection – first, a certain amount of decision time is lost, and

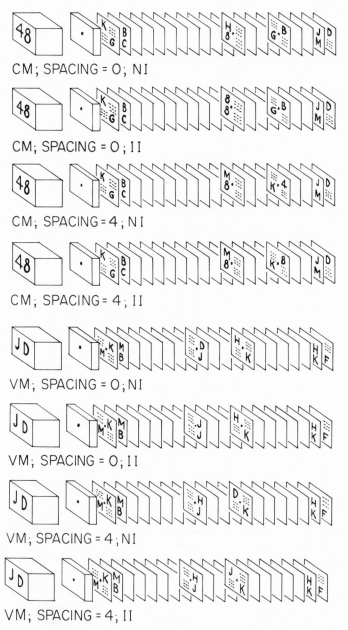

CM; SPACING = 0; NI

CM; SPACING = 0; II

CM; SPACING = 4; NI

CM; SPACING = 4; II

VM; SPACING = 0; NI

VM; SPACING = 0; II

VM; SPACING = 4; NI

VM; SPACING = 4; II

FIG. 6 Examples of trials used in Experiment 3. In each case, a trial is illustrated that has two targets, though other trials sometimes contained just one target, or no targets.

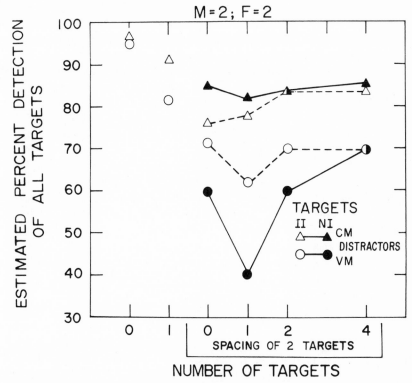

FIG. 7   Experiment 3. Probabilities of correctly detecting one target when one was presented, or two targets when two were presented, for each condition. The data shown have been adjusted to remove effects of guessing and false alarms. $F = 2$, $M = 2$; frame time = 80 msec for CM condition and 200 msec for VM condition.

second, the *order* of search is altered for a few frames so as to compare first the target already found.

Turning to the CM conditions, a radically different pattern of results is found. First of all, NI instances are better than II, the reverse of the pattern for the VM conditions. Second, there is no decrement for NI targets at any spacing, but a decrement for II targets primarily at a spacing of zero (same frame). In the CM condition, apparently, each target has an automatic learned "attention" response that can occur in parallel without inhibition. However, two identical targets in different spatial locations cannot both be detected in close temporal proximity without decrement. Perhaps attention responses occur automatically to all CM targets, but a controlled search must then be carried out to make decisions based upon characteristics internal to the automatically determined target set. In the case under discussion, some counting or discrimination mechanism might lose track of multiple identical targets.

In any event, the differing pattern of results for the CM and VM conditions is a finding of great importance. This difference in pattern indicates that what we have called automatic detection and controlled search are qualitatively different processes. One might have supposed on the basis of Experiments 1 and 2 that automatic detection is simply a faster version of controlled search, with a floor effect preventing us from seeing the effects of M and F. Such a hypothesis, however, cannot explain the results of Experiment 3.

THE DEVELOPMENT OF AUTOMATIC SEARCH, PERCEPTUAL LEARNING, AND CATEGORIZATION

The large qualitative and quantitative differences between the VM and CM conditions demonstrate with great effectiveness the existence of two fundamentally different search and detection processes. A question of considerable practical significance is, How does automatic detection develop, and how can it be altered once developed? To answer this question, we turn to the following experiments.

Experiment 4: The Learning and Unlearning of Automatic Processing

Experiment 4 was designed to watch the course of development of the automatic detection mode. The general procedure was similar to that of Experiment 1. Two character sets were chosen: the consonants from the first and second halves of the alphabet. Naive subjects were run in the multiple-frame CM procedure with one of these sets always the memory set and the other always the distractor set. The memory-set size was four and the frame size was two, so the task was quite difficult. Nevertheless, the frame time was set initially at 200 msec, a rather fast rate. The CM procedure was then run for 1,500 trials while performance improved (as automatic detection developed).

Figure 8 shows the results. The false alarms started at a level of about 10% and dropped during initial training. The hit rate rose over 1,500 trials of training to above 90%. Then the subjects were switched to a frame time of 120 msec. When the switch in frame time occurred, the hit rate dropped only to 80%; that is, performance was beginning to approach that seen in the CM conditions of Experiment 1.

These results suggest that the subjects began using controlled search at the start of CM training, and gradually learned to utilize automatic detection over several thousand trials of training. If attention responses had been learned in long-term memory to each of the memory-set items (or if nonattention responses had been learned to the distractor items), then a reversal of the roles of

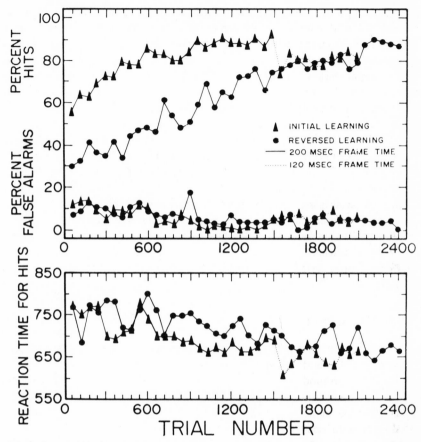

FIG. 8 Initial CM learning and reversed CM learning for target and distractor sets taken from first and second halves of the alphabet. $M = 4$, $F = 2$, and frame times are shown. Percent hits are graphed as a function of trial number. After 2100 trials, the target and distractor sets were switched with each other.

the two sets of stimuli would have been expected to result in considerable drops in performance.

Therefore, after the initial 2,100 trials were completed, the roles of the memory-set items and the distractors were reversed. The frame time was returned to 200 msec, and memory-set size was four and frame size two, as before. However, the previous distractors were now used as memory-set items, and vice versa. Under these conditions, the subjects were given 2,400 trials of CM training, which shall be termed "reversal training."

The results of reversal are also shown in Fig. 8. As shown, there was an enormous difficulty in making the reversal. In fact, at the start of reversal training performance was even below that at the start of training, when the subjects were completely naive to the task. Even assuming that reversal causes the subjects to revert from automatic detection to controlled search, this finding suggests that reversal results in negative transfer. That is, controlled search can be hampered when the distractors are items that have previously been trained to have automatic attention responses. The second result of interest is the slow rate of recovery from the effects of reversal. Apparently, subjects can learn a new set of attention responses to the new memory set items (and inhibit the old attention responses to the items that are now distractors), but this relearning process is even more difficult than the learning taking place at the start of training. In fact, it took subjects almost three times longer to reach a 90% hit rate after reversal than it did in initial learning.

The reversal learning results suggest to us that there may be two components to the perceptual learning in this task. One component is the development of a categorization such that the various targets are learned as a group. Second, there is a learned "attention" response such that both the members of a target category and the category itself acquire the ability to "interrupt" the short-term search and direct the search to themselves at once. We wish to argue that the second component is responsible for automatic detection. As this automatic response becomes learned, it becomes harder and harder to ignore, and takes increasingly long to unlearn. Thus, after reversal, the former targets, now distractors, continue to be given attention automatically and thereby harm detection of the former distractors, now targets.

Experiment 5: The Reversal of Consonants and Digits for Highly Trained Subjects

The reversal results with the two halves of the alphabet were obtained on naive subjects. We next examine the outcome when our extremely well-practiced subjects, who had taken part in Experiments 1 to 3 (and several other studies not reported in this chapter), were reversed. These subjects had spent about 20,000 trials searching for letters in number distractors (other subjects had spent equal time searching for numbers in letter distractors). In all previous tasks for these subjects, the items in the memory set for the CM condition were *never* distractor items. The memory set and distractor set were now switched: If in the CM conditions they had been searching for digits in consonants, they now searched for consonants in digits, and vice versa. If in the VM conditions they had been searching for consonants in consonants, they now searched for digits in digits, and vice versa. The conditions were the same as in Experiment 3. Multiple targets were used and $M = 2$, $F = 2$. The frame time was 200 msec for the VM conditions and 60 msec for the CM conditions.

The results of the reversal study are shown in Fig. 9. In two panels, the circles give the data prior to reversal and the triangles give the data after reversal. The

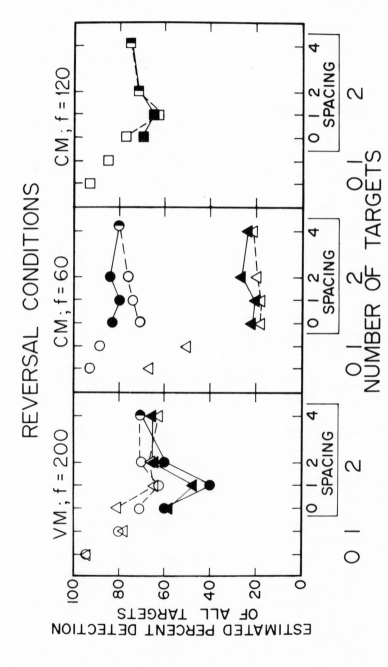

FIG. 9 Experiment 5. Circles show the estimated percentage detection prior to reversal, while triangles indicate performance after reversal. The squares in the right-hand panel show postreversal detection after frame time was raised to 120 msec. The open symbols and dashed lines indicate the II conditions (identical targets); the closed circles and solid lines indicate the NI conditions (different targets).

left-hand panel shows the VM conditions. There is essentially no performance change after reversal in the VM condition. The CM results are radically changed after reversal. As may be seen in the middle panel, performance drops very low, almost to chance levels, when the memory set and distractor sets are switched.

It seemed possible that the subjects might have been using controlled search after reversal. To check this possibility, several additional CM sessions were run with the frame time raised to 120 msec. These results are shown in the right-hand panel. The pattern is similar to that seen for the VM conditions before (or after) reversal, as may be seen through comparison with the left-hand panel. It seems likely that the subjects could not use automatic detection and switched to a controlled search strategy. Eventually, of course, because of the consistent mapping, the subjects would surely overcome the deleterious effects of the switch, as did the subjects in the pervious study, and return to automatic detection. These subjects were not given sufficient practice to demonstrate such a recovery, however.

The results of Experiment 5 also have several important implications regarding the role of category learning in automatic search. The tremendous performance decrements occurring when consonants and digits are reversed show that the presence of a well-known categorical difference between memory-set items and distractors is not sufficient for automatic detection. Rather, we suggest that it is the CM training that leads to automatic detection through the development of learned attention responses both to the stimuli making up a category, and also to the category itself, is one is known.

The pattern of results in the right-hand panel of Fig. 9 also has implications regarding the role of categorization. Compared to the results in the left-hand panel, CM performance after reversal is at least as high as VM performance, even though the CM frame time is only 120 msec while the VM frame time is 200 msec. Thus the knowledge of categories does have some benefit. Furthermore, the II and NI conditions in the right-hand panel do not differ. Both results suggest that the subjects are carrying out a controlled search after CM reversal, but a controlled search in which the category as a whole is compared to the category of each display item. This hypothesis suggests that performance levels should be comparable to those when memory-set size is one, and also suggests that the relationship between targets (II versus NI) should not matter, both results that were found in our data.

Thus while we suggest that automatic processing is caused by CM training and not by categorization, we nevertheless suggest that categorization may facilitate controlled search by reducing the effective memory-set size. Although we do not yet have firm data on this point, it also seems likely that the development of automatic detection will be accelerated when a known categorization separates the memory items and the distractor set.

The reversal results of the last two studies could hardly have provided a more dramatic demonstration of the qualitative difference between the two search modes and of the long-term learning associated with automatic processing. They suggest that the advantage of learning to use automatic detection is gained at a cost: It becomes increasingly difficult to modify or alter the process if circumstances call for a new strategy or response rule. Conversely, controlled search can be altered with little if any difficulty.

The development of an automatic response system has been demonstrated in a somewhat different paradigm by LaBerge (1973). His task required the subject to respond as quickly as possible, indicating whether two presented stimuli were physically identical. Sometimes the stimuli to be matched were well known (letters) and other times unknown (letter-like characters). In either case, the subject was led to expect at least one of the presented characters, or was led to expect neither of the presented characters. The results showed the matching time for an unexpected unknown set of characters to be slower than the matching times in the other conditions (which were about equal). These results suggest that unknown characters must be matched feature by feature, rather than as unitary entities, if they are unexpected. Next, LaBerge showed that the difference between unknown characters (when unexpected) and known characters gradually disappeared as the unknown characters were repeatedly presented over many sessions of training. Such a result suggests that the unknown characters gradually became "unitized" so that they were identified and matched in single unitary operations.

The LaBerge (1973) results demonstrated the course of learning of a "unitization," in which the features of a character become melded into a single unit in the sense that time need not be wasted processing the individual features serially. Our results demonstrate the course of learning of a "categorization," in which any of the members of a category can be detected in parallel without time being wasted searching serially for each item. These two demonstrations differ in many respects, but have in common the basic phenomenon that a process initially requiring serial controlled processing eventually is exchanged for an automatic process operating in parallel without the need for active attention.

THE ATTENTIONAL DEMANDS OF CONTROLLED AND AUTOMATIC PROCESSING

In the preceding paragraphs and in other discussions in this chapter, we have suggested that automatic detection is based upon the development of an "attention response" to the consistently mapped stimuli. The reasoning behind this terminology is better understood if we describe briefly the results of several studies directly testing the ability of stimuli to attract attention. The paradigms were similar to the multiple-frame, multiple-target procedure of Experiment 3, with the following change: One diagonal of each frame (say, the upper-left—lower-right diagonal) was defined to be irrelevant on all trials. The subject was instructed to focus all his attention upon the relevant diagonal and ignore all stimuli appearing on the irrelevant diagonal. Our first study showed that in the VM condition performance was the same when distractors appeared on the irrelevant diagonals as when masks appeared in those positions.

The conditions of interest arise when memory set items for the current trial appear on the irrelevant diagonal, or when memory set items that have previously been trained to induce automatic detection appear on the irrelevant diagonal. Let us term memory-set items on the irrelevant diagonal in VM conditions "controlled foils," and let us term previously trained targets from CM conditions on the irrelevant diagonal "automatic foils." Then the main results are as follows. Search in the CM conditions (automatic detection) is unaffected by automatic foils, except for a small decrement (about 5%) caused by an automatic foil in the same frame as the target. Search in the VM conditions (controlled search) is largely unaffected by controlled foils except for a decrement (about 11%) caused by a controlled foils in the frame preceding the target. However, search in the VM conditions (controlled search) is harmed markedly (20%) by the presence of an automatic foil in the same frame as the target, and is even harmed to a small degree (5%) when an automatic foil appears in the frame following the target. These decrements caused by automatic foils imply that attention is attracted immediately by automatic foils, even when they appear on an irrelevant, to-be-ignored diagonal. Such results make it plausible to assume that automatic detection involves the learning of an automatic attention response to consistently trained memory-set items.

SOME SUPPORTING RESULTS

In the introduction to this chapter, we set forth as a goal the demonstration that there exist two qualitatively different perceptual processes used in detection, recognition, and search. This goal has now been attained. *Automatic* and *controlled* processing have been demonstrated and differentiated in search tasks, detection tasks, and attention tasks, in some tasks using reaction time measures and others using accuracy measures, and in perceptual learning tasks. Furthermore, these various demonstrations have been closely tied together through the use of similar procedures and quantitative models.

In retrospect, it is easy to find supporting evidence for these ideas from previous studies, if one takes care to note whether such studies utilized CM or VM training procedures (or mixtures of the two). It is beyond the scope of this chapter to present such a literature review, but a very few studies are worth mentioning by way of example.

In the memory and visual search literature using reaction time as a dependent measure, a rather prominent conflict has reigned between studies showing linear set size functions with slopes near 40 msec per item (e.g., Atkinson, Holmgren, & Juola, 1969; Briggs & Johnsen, 1973; Jonides & Gleitman, 1972; Kristofferson, 1972a; Sternberg, 1966, 1969, 1975) and studies showing either curvilinear set size functions with small slopes or flat set size functions (e.g., Briggs & Johnsen, 1973; Briggs & Swanson, 1970; Egeth, Jonides, & Wall, 1972; Jonides & Gleitman, 1972; Kristofferson, 1972b; Neisser, 1974; Simpson, 1972; Sperling, Budiansky, Spivak, & Johnson, 1971). The distinctive discriminative feature between these sets of studies is of course the nature of the training procedures, flat set size functions occurring when the memory set items are consistently mapped to responses.

The divided attention literature may similarly be partitioned into two sets of studies, those showing a divided-attention deficit (e.g., Broadbent, 1958, 1971; Kahneman, 1973; Moray, 1969a, b; and the review by Treisman, 1969) and those showing no (or very little) deficit when attention is divided (e.g., Moray, 1975; Sorkin & Pohlman, 1973).[1] Once again, the nature of the training procedures provides one of the cues that allows the two sets of studies to be discriminated. In the studies consistently mapping the targets to the responses over many trials, dividing attention causes no deficits, presumably because automatic search is utilized to find the targets before memory loss occurs, or before new inputs arrive demanding attention. In the studies utilizing varied mapping of targets to responses or very low levels of practice, divided attention deficits occur, presumably because controlled search must be used, which is slowed by the presence of additional inputs needing consideration.

EXTENSIONS OF THE THEORY

The studies in the previous section have illuminated the nature of controlled and automatic processing in a wide variety of basic detection situations, but do not allow us to extrapolate directly to more complex research areas such as reading. That is, our studies have traced the development of an automatic, attention-directing detection response. In tasks such as reading, however, a much more complex and varied set of automatic processes, interwoven with a variety of controlled processes, would have to be utilized. In the remainder of this chapter, no attempt will be made to delineate the set of automatic processes used in skilled reading. Rather, the theory will be elaborated and some examples

[1] There are many studies in which subjects can divide attention without decrements in performance, but in which controlled search is probably being used. These studies usually involve threshold tasks with small numbers of inputs and are carefully designed to ensure that short-term memory is capable of retaining the features of the inputs until controlled processing can decide about them. Shiffrin (1975a) reviews one set of such studies. Such studies show that the information abstracted from inputs is sufficient to let the subject respond maximally, even if controlled processing is utilized, as long as the capacity of the controlled processing system is not stressed. In this chapter, however, our tasks always put great stress on the controlled processing system.

mentioned, in order to clarify the role of controlled and automatic processing in learning and perception situations.

To begin with, let us review the characteristics distinguishing controlled and automatic processing. The previous studies have shown these to differ in the following dimensions: (a) capacity limitations and attentional demands; (b) degree of subject control and ease of alteration; (c) the amount of training before asymptotic levels of performance are reached. In addition, we might speculate concerning one additional difference: (d) the effects upon long-term learning.

We would like to suggest a simple conception of memory (following the general suggestions of Shiffrin, 1975b) in which these characteristics of controlled and automatic processing are a natural concomitant. Suppose that long-term store is the permanent repository of the informational network, and short-term store is the temporarily activated subset of long-term store that is controlled by the subject and used for active processes like thinking, rehearsing, coding, retrieving, and deciding. Suppose long-term store to consist of a collection of nodes that are associatively interrelated in a complex fashion. Each node may itself consist of a complex set of informational elements, including associative connections, programs for responses or actions, and directions for other types of information processing. The node is a distinguishable entity because it is unitized — when any of its elements are activated, all of them are activated.

An automatic process is said to be present when a given node or sequence of nodes (nearly) always occurs in response to a particular input configuration, where the inputs may be externally or internally generated and include the general situational context. In automatic processing, the sequence of nodes is activated automatically, without the necessity of active control or attention by the subject, and the activation of one sequence of nodes may occur in parallel with another sequence without interference (at least, as long as the same nodes are not involved in the two sequences in inconsistent fashion). Since an automatic process is a permanent set of associative connections in long-term store, it will require consistent training over an appreciable period before it develops fully, and it will be difficult to suppress or alter once learned.

A controlled process is a temporary sequence of nodes activated under the control of, and given attention by, the subject. Because active attention by the subject is required, only one such sequence at a time may be controlled without interference. However, the controlled process does not require extended practice to be utilized effectively, and may be set up and altered by the subject in just a few attempts or trials.

In a variety of ways, the preceding statements about controlled and automatic processing have been supported by the studies reported in this chapter. It is important to propose one additional assumption, not directly supported by our data, in order to extrapolate to complex processing situations. Suppose provisionally that the key factor in the learning of an automatic process is the prior utilization of a controlled process linking the same nodes, a controlled process in which the subject activates, links, or attends to the elements in the sequence. In this sense, controlled processing may be described as the 'training wheels' for automatic processing. Conversely, it might be suggested that learning will not occur in the absence of controlled processing.

The advantages of a system operating in the fashion described are transparently clear. In novel situations or situations requiring moment-to-moment decisions, controlled processing may be adopted and used to perform accurately, though slowly. Then, as the situations become familiar, always requiring the same sequence of processing operations, automatic processing will develop, attention demands will be eased, other controlled operations can be carried out in parallel with the automatic processing, and performance will improve. In reading, these changes might be illustrated by the beginning reader, who struggles to identify single letters and has no spare capacity for identifying words, let alone sentences or concepts, and the experienced reader, who automatically identifies letters, words, and phrases, spending his capacity analyzing the meaning of the material.

SOME APPLICATIONS AND SUPPORTING EVIDENCE FOR THE THEORY

The proposal that controlled processing underlies learning implies a close link between attention and learning. In short, what is learned is what is attended. Evidence for such effects has been summarized by Craik and Lockhart (1972) and Craik and Tulving (1975). Conversely, unattended material is often unlearned. For example, Moray (1959) had subjects repeat aloud a prose passage presented to one ear while a seven-word list was repeated 35 times in the other ear. Later recognition for the unattended words was at the chance level. Numerous other tasks show results pointing in this general direction. To give one more example, Hyde and Jenkins (1969, 1973) had subjects perform an orthographic task (state whether the word contained a letter "e") or a semantic task (rate the pleasantness of the word). Recall of words processed orthographically was 35% less than for those processed semantically. Studies on incidental learning also support our conjecture. For example, Postman (1964) and Schneider and Kintz (1967) have shown that subjects learn the information they actually process rather than the information they are instructed to learn.

Naturally, if controlled processing is necessary for learning and memory, automatic processing will not lead to appreciable retention. Gordon (1968) showed that the distractors in a CM search task were recognized at the chance level. Gleitman and Jonides (1976) showed that the displays containing targets were recognized more poorly in a CM search task than in a VM search task. In skilled reading, one might expect surface structure features to be processed relatively automatically, while conceptual properties of the passages are given controlled processing. Indeed, Bransford and Franks (1971) demonstrated that skilled readers retain little information concerning the specific sentences they have seen. Of course, subjects may be instructed to direct their controlled processing to levels of analysis normally carried out automatically, and if they do so they will remember these attended features. One early example is found in Postman and Senders (1946), who showed that subjects instructed to attend to specific features of presented material (e.g., physical appearance, details of wording, general comprehension) improved their learning of those features at the expense of the other characteristics.

During acquisition of automatic processing, while the automatic process is still poorly developed, we might expect automatic processing to be fast but inaccurate and controlled processing of the same tasks to be slow but accurate. In such cases, the choice of processing mode would depend upon the emphasis placed upon speed relative to the emphasis placed upon accuracy. In our own search data, we sometimes find subjects in CM conditions who do not begin to show automatic processing until increased emphasis is placed upon speed rather than accuracy. LaBerge and Samuels (1974) report that for beginning readers to increase chunking, the demand for accuracy may have to be relaxed. Archwamety and Samuels (1973) report that teachers who overstress accuracy may discourage children from developing sophisticated strategies of word recognition.

Our search studies showed that targets trained to have automatic responses interfered with processing even when they appeared on a diagonal to be ignored. This finding illustrates the difficulty of ignoring responses that have become automatic. The Stroop (1935) test is the classic illustration of this phenomenon: It is difficult to read names of colors when the names are printed in ink colors that do not match the names. A different illustration comes from the reading literature. Willows and McKinnon (1973) and Willows (1974) had subjects read stories in black with alternating to-be-ignored lines of text in red. The red lines contained wrong answers to questions that followed the story. Good readers showed greater numbers of comprehension errors that were intrusions from the to-be-ignored material than did poor readers. Presumably, the good readers relied more heavily upon automatic processes and hence could not prevent processing of the irrelevant lines.

The difficulty in altering well-learned automatic processing is dramatically illustrated by our search tasks in which the memory set and distractor set were reversed (Experiment 3). Illustrations in other tasks abound. For example, interference in the Stroop paradigm continues even after weeks of training (Jensen, 1965). Such results suggest caution in improving performance early in skill acquisition through the training of an automatic process, when that automatic process is not desired in later stages of that skill. For example, subvocalization might be a desirable process early in the development of skilled reading, but might prove difficult to "unlearn" if necessary for further development of the skill.

Our search studies demonstrate beyond question the critical role of consistent mapping in the development of automatic processing. Supporting evidence may also be found in studies of the development of reading. For example, Gibson (1965, 1969) and Gibson and Levin (1975) showed that the development of higher-order units was much superior in CM training situations compared to VM training situations.

It is useful to consider briefly how a child might mature cognitively. A newborn child would be expected to process only sensory (both internal and external) and motor information. As the child learns invariant relationships (CM conditions), automatic processing will develop at various intermediate levels. A child at a stage of development where acoustic processing is developing would tend to mistake "fountain" for "mountain." Later, acoustic processing will be both automatized and accurate, and automatic processing will be developing at the semantic or conceptual level; then the child will more likely confuse "hill" and "mountain." Developmental data do tend to show such patterns (see Gibson & Levin, 1975, Chapter 3). Indeed, our framework predicts a developmental sequence similar to Gibson's (1969) on the basis of the properties of controlled processing. That is, new learning will be limited by the capacity of controlled processing, which is presumably subject to the limitations of short-term store. As new automatic processing is learned, and as unitization and categorization develop, the load on the short-term system will be effectively lessened and more complex learning can take place (see Shiffrin, 1976, for a more thorough treatment of this hypothesis).

At this point, we will terminate our meager and rather superficial review. Despite the brevity of the preceding illustrations, we hope to have demonstrated some of the applications of the processing theory developed from our studies. It should not be difficult for readers expert in areas of research such as reading to apply these conceptions more thoroughly or to develop experiments to test these ideas.

CONCLUSIONS

We have used a series of search and detection tasks to give firm experimental backing to the proposed two-process theory. The basic characteristics of controlled and automatic processing have been inferred from our studies, and the fundamental difference between these processes has been delineated. We have proposed and shown evidence that automatic processing (a) is a learned associative sequence in long-term memory that develops with consistent training; (b) operates in parallel and relatively independent of others, simultaneous processes; (c) is not under subject control; and (d) does not require the subject's attention. We have proposed and shown that controlled processing (a) is a limited-capacity, serial, short-term-memory operation; (b) can be utilized without extensive practice; and (c) requires active attention. We have also suggested that the development of automatic processing may be dependent upon the prior utilization of controlled processing. Some indications were finally given pointing to the manner in which these ideas might be applied in more complicated tasks such as reading.

ACKNOWLEDGMENTS

This work was supported by PHS Grant 12717 and a Guggenheim Fellowship to the second author, but the chapter represents an equal and joint effort by both authors.

REFERENCES

Archwamety, T., & Samuels, S. J. A mastery based experimental program for teaching comprehension skills through use of hypothesis/test procedures. Research Report No. 50. Research Development and Demonstration Center in Education of Handicapped Children, Minneapolis, Minnesota, 1973. Cited in LaBerge & Samuels, 1974.

Atkinson, R. C., Holmgren, J. E., & Juola, J. F. Processing time as influenced by the number of elements in a visual display. *Perception & Psychophysics,* 1969, **6**, 321–326.

Bransford, J. D., & Franks, J. J. The abstraction of linguistic ideas. *Cognitive Psychology,* 1971, **2**, 331–350.

Briggs, G. E., & Johnsen, A. M. On the nature of central processing in choice reactions. *Memory and Cognition,* 1973, **1**, 91–100.

Briggs, G. E., & Swanson, J. M. Encoding, decoding, and central functions in human information processing. *Journal of Experimental Psychology,* 1970, **86**, 296–308.

Broadbent, D. E. *Perception and communication.* London: Pergamon, 1958.

Broadbent, D. E. *Decision and stress.* London: Academic Press, 1971.

Corballis, M. C. Access to memory: An analysis of recognition times. In P. M. A. Rabbitt & S. Dornic, (Eds.), *Attention & performance V.* New York: Academic Press, 1975.

Craik, F. I. M., & Lockhart, R. S. Levels of processing: A framework for memory research. *Journal of Verbal Learning and Verbal Behavior,* 1972, **11**, 671–684.

Craik, F. I. M., & Tulving, E. Depth of processing and the retention of words in episodic memory. *Journal of Experimental Psychology: General,* 1975, **104**, 268–294.

Egeth, H., Atkinson, J., Gilmore, G., & Marcus, N. Factors affecting mode of processing in visual search. *Perception and Psychophysics,* 1973, **13**, 394–402.

Egeth, H., Jonides, J., & Wall, S. Parallel processing of multielement displays. *Cognitive Psychology,* 1972, **3**, 674–698.

Estes, W. K. Interactions of signal and background variables in visual processing. *Perception & Psychophysics,* 1972, **12**, 278–286.

Gibson, E. J. Learning to read. *Science,* 1965, **148**, 1066–1072.

Gibson, E. J. *Principles of perceptual learning and development.* New York: Prentice Hall, 1969.

Gibson, E. J., & Levin, H. *The psychology of reading.* Boston: Massachusetts Institute of Technology, 1975.

Gleitman, H., & Jonides, J. The cost of categorization in visual search: Incomplete processing of targets and field items. *Perception and Psychophysics,* 1976, **20**, 281–288.

Gordon, G. T. Interaction between items in visual search. *Journal of Experimental Psychology,* 1968, **76**, 348–355.

Hyde, T. S., & Jenkins, J. J. Differential effects of incidental tasks on the organization of recall of a list of highly associated words. *Journal of Experimental Psychology,* 1969, **82**, 472–481.

Hyde, T. S., & Jenkins, J. J. Recall for words as a function of semantic, graphic, and syntactic orienting tasks. *Journal of Verbal Learning and Verbal Behavior,* 1973, **12**, 471–480.

Jensen, A. R. Scoring the Stroop test. *Acta Psychologica,* 1965, **24**, 398–408.

Jonides, J., & Gleitman, H. A conceptual category effect in visual search: O as letter or as digit. *Perception & Psychophysics,* 1972, **12**, 457–460.

Kahneman, D. *Attention and Effort.* Englewood Cliffs, N.J.: Prentice-Hall, 1973.

Kristofferson, M. W. Effects of practice on character classification performance. *Canadian Journal of Psychology,* 1972, **26**, 54–60. (a)

Kristofferson, M. W. When item recognition and visual search functions are similar. *Perception & Psychophysics,* 1972, **12**, 379–384. (b)

LaBerge, D. Attention and the measurement of perceptual learning. *Memory and Cognition,* 1973, **1**, 268–276.

LaBerge, D. Acquisition of automatic processing in perceptual and associative learning. In P. M. A. Rabbitt & S. Dornic (Eds.), *Attention and performance V.* New York: Academic Press, 1975.

LaBerge, D., & Samuels, S. J. Toward a theory of automatic information processing in reading. *Cognitive Psychology,* 1974, **6**, 293–323.

Moray, N. Attention in dichotic listening: Affective cues and the influence of instructions. *Quarterly Journal of Experimental Psychology,* 1959, **11**, 56–60.

Moray, N. *Listening and attention.* Harmondsworth: Penguin Books, 1969. (a)

Moray, N. *Attention: Selective processes in vision and hearing.* New York: Academic Press, 1969. (b)

Moray, N. A data base for theories of selective listening. In P. M. A. Rabbitt & S. Dornic (Eds.), *Attention and performance V.* New York: Academic Press, 1975.

Neisser, U. Practiced card sorting for multiple targets. *Memory & Cognition,* 1974, **2**, 781–785.

Postman, L. Short-term memory and incidental learning. In A. W. Melton (Ed.), *Categories of human learning.* New York: Academic Press, 1964.

Postman, L., & Senders, V. Incidental learning and generality of set. *Journal of Experimental Psychology,* 1946, **36**, 153–165.

Schneider, W. Selective attention, memory scanning, and visual search: Three components of one process. Doctoral dissertation, Indiana University, Bloomington, 1975.

Schneider, F. W., & Kintz, B. L. An analysis of the incidental–intentional learning dichotomy. *Journal of Experimental Psychology,* 1967, **73**, 85–90.

Schneider, W., & Shiffrin, R. M. Controlled and automatic human information processing: I. Detection, search, and attention. *Psychological Review,* 1977, **84**, 1–66.

Shiffrin, R. M. The locus and role of attention in memory systems. In P. M. A. Rabbitt & S. Dornic (Eds.), *Attention and performance V.* New York: Academic Press, 1975. (a)

Shiffrin, R. M. Short-term store: The basis for a memory search. In F. Restle, R. M. Shiffrin, N. J. Castellan, H. Lindman, & D. B. Pisoni (Eds.), *Cognitive theory,* Vol. I. Hillsdale, N.J.: Lawrence Erlbaum Associates, 1975. (b)

Shiffrin, R. M. Capacity limitations in information processing, attention and memory. In W. K. Estes (Ed.), *Handbook of learning and cognitive processes.* Volume 4: *Memory: Processes.* Hillsdale, N.J.: Lawrence Erlbaum Associates, 1976.

Shiffrin, R. M., & Schneider, W. Towards a unitary model for selective attention, memory scanning and visual search. In S. Dornic & P. M. A. Rabbitt (Eds.), *Attention and performance VI.* New York Academic Press, 1976.

Shiffrin, R. M., & Schneider, W. Controlled and automatic human information processing: II. Perceptual learning, automatic attending, and a general theory. *Psychological Review,* 1977, **84,** 127–190.

Simpson, P. J. High-speed memory scanning: Stability and generality. *Journal of Experimental Psychology,* 1972, **96,** 239–246.

Sorkin, R. D., & Pohlman, L. D. Some models of observer behavior in two channel auditory signal detection. *Perception & Psychophysics,* 1973, **14,** 101–109.

Sperling, G., Budiansky, J., Spivak, J. G., & Johnson, M. C. Extremely rapid visual search: The maximum rate of scanning letters for the presence of a numeral. *Science,* 1971, **174,** 307–311.

Sternberg, S. High speed scanning in human memory. *Science,* 1966, **153,** 652–654.

Sternberg, S. Memory scanning: Mental processes revealed by reaction time experiments. *American Scientist,* 1969, **57,** 421–457.

Sternberg, S. Memory scanning: New findings and current controversies. *Quarterly Journal of Experimental Psychology,* 1975, **27,** 1–32.

Stroop, J. R. Studies of interference in serial verbal reactions. *Journal of Experimental Psychology,* 1935, **18,** 643–662.

Treisman, A. Strategies and models of selective attention. *Psychological Review,* 1969, **76,** 282–299.

Willows, D. M. Reading between the lines: A study of selective attention in good and poor readers. *Child Development,* June, 1974.

Willows, D. M., & McKinnon, G. E. Selective reading: Attention to the 'unattended' lines. *Canadien Journal of Psychology,* 1973, **27,** 292–304.

5
How Perception Really Develops: A View from outside the Network

Eleanor J. Gibson

Cornell University

Truth was their model as they strove to build
A world of lasting objects to believe in,
Without believing earthenware and legend,
Archway and song, were truthful or untruthful:
The Truth was there already to be true.

from 'The Truth' by W. H. AUDEN
*Homage to Clio**

Can a process so fundamental as perception be subject to the fads and fancies induced by a Zeitgeist in the minds of those who seek to understand it? Perception, the most solidly based of all cognitive processes, surely cannot be whipped about with the wind of the times, however processes like memory ("short" or "long"?), images ("reproductions" or "constructions"?), or intelligence ("normative" or "operational"?) may be conceived variously by fickle thinkers in one decade or another. And yet, signs and portents assure us (uneasy psychologists) that it is. Recall unconscious inference, dredged up from time to time ever since Hemlholtz. What about the fact that it wasn't fashionable to mention perception at all during the heyday of S—R theorizing? What about the "new look" in the early Fifties? And now, what about the craze for information-processing models of perception?

*Copyright © 1959 by W. H. Auden. Reprinted from *Collected Shorter Poems 1927–1957*, by W. H. Auden, by permission of Random House, Inc.

The craze is with us; one has only to consider other chapters in this book. How did it come about? The answer lies, I think, in the transition from S–R theories to cognitive theories via computer simultation. How respectable it is! If a computer can "model" a cognitive process, there is something substantial to take hold of. I believe people who would not have dreamed of working on what they think of as perception in 1950 are happy to now because they can invent stages of "processing" that can be duplicated in computer software, if not hardware. But there is something else that makes it acceptable to these people. It is still elementaristic, just as much as S–R theory. One starts by assuming that "input" comes in pieces or bits. The assumption is seldom defended; it is just made. And then, of course, if the input is only bits and pieces, a construction process must be devised to assemble things in the head, to reconstruct reality, because it is obvious that we don't perceive bits and pieces, but a world. The goal is how to build "a world of lasting objects," when, in fact, they are already there in the world.

I am inclined to think that many present-day cognitive psychologists consider themselves redeemed because they have foresworn behaviorism but that they are really pursuing the same course because they conceive of the stuff of the world that is available to an organism as meaningless and atomistic. Such a conception requires them to invent "processing mechanisms" to put the world together. Sensations have traditionally been the bits and pieces – unstructured, although having a few dimensions like intensity by means of which they can be arranged in a scale. Now, however, we have a mysterious construct known as a "feature detector" that implies that (for vision at least) the pieces at some early stage have a wee semblance of form, such as tiny lines in varying orientations. These may, however, have to be "coded" from the sensations; and in any case, the orientation seems to be with respect to the retina, so it still doesn't help with construction of a world.

There must in fact, to judge from the models of perception and cognition, be a series of "coding" and "decoding" processes (world to stimulus; stimulus to ikon; ikon to features; features to parsed units of some kind; those units to short-term memory; short-term memory to another code where meaning is somehow incorporated, etc.). There is a "processor" at each of these stages of recoding, and in the end cognitive psychology becomes a branch of cryptology. The tendency to homunculize appears irresistible; there are cryptologists in the brain. But how to put Humpty Dumpty back together again? No answer to this has ever been proposed, except "integration with past experience," or "inference from past experience." But what was the past experience like? How was it obtained? How did it become complete and meaningful?

Information processors quite often conclude that there is no such thing as perception, that what we experience as perception is really memory. The conclusion is almost inevitable from this kind of analysis, for indeed there is no frozen instant of time in which a perception may be said to occur. Perceiving goes on continuously; temporal information is not only available but *must* be extracted. If it were not, we would not perceive a hurled object looming at us on a collision course, or even feel our own arms reaching out toward a target. So eliminating perception may be consistent, but it leaves us where we started. If what we are talking about is really memory, where did we get the meaningful information to remember? Of course, once something gets constructed, the information processor can make progress because he can start matching the bits and pieces to the construction, but the original structure of the information and the meaning have still escaped the processors.

Suppose one does not accept this view of the way the world comes to us in experience as atomic bits or even "pictures" frozen in time and without spatial organization?[1] I do not believe it is essential to invent mechanisms for assembling what we know we actually *do* perceive: things, a spatial layout, events that take place in it. There is structure in the array, relational information that does not have to be pieced together because, like truth, it is already there. This is the assumption I want to proceed with. I do not want a construction theory, with processors at every stage like an assembly line. What kind of theory do I want, then?

I might call it a "seek and ye shall find" theory (find sometimes, at least). What do we seek? Living organisms search for information for invariant properties of the world: of the *spatial layout,* which must have a stable structure (in fact, an objective one in which not only I but other animals too can locate things); of *objects,* with constant dimensions (not shrinking, expanding, or losing and gaining substance as we move around) and reliable affordances that meet our requirements for survival; and of *events,* in which things happen with predictable relations (not randomly or chaotically).

This search is so much a part of man's nature, evolved over millions of years, that it is as ingrained, strong, and unconscious as the functions of digestion and breathing and much more elaborately provided for. We have many windows on the world: systems for listening, looking, touching, tasting, and accompanying patterns of exploration like scanning, palpating, and licking. I think we have been fooled by our own laboratory paradigms into believing that we have to bribe an animal or an infant into learning something with material rewards like food. For human infants, this procedure does not even work very well. It turns out that they learn best if they are allowed to discover an interesting source of information or a predictable contingency or a problem to be solved.

From this perspective, if I look for any mechanism at all, it will not be an associative process or a construction process, but an abstraction process. What is needed is abstraction (extraction?) of the relevant information from the flood of available information. Abstraction is supposed to be a very high level process.

---

[1] Piaget, J. *The construction of reality in the child* (Translation by Margaret Cook). New York: Basic Books, 1954. P. 4.

Can babies do it, on a perceptual level at least? It seems that they must, if only to abstract phonemes, for instance, from a continuous speech flow. That they do, indeed, abstract consonantal phonemes from vowel contexts has been demonstrated by Fodor, Garrett, and Brill (1975).

With this view that perception is not constructed from sensory particles go a few caveats. Does it carry the implication that all the information in stimulation, provided it is available to an organism, is picked up automatically, regardless of species, age, or earlier experience? Certainly not. The information has to be extracted (but it is information that is extracted, a relation, not an element). What does extraction depend on? For the sake of brevity, I note just three important points:

1. What is extracted depends on the species. Every living organism is equipped appropriately to extract the information needed for survival in its ecological niche. All get some kind of information for the spatial layout, the events, and the objects that are relevant for them, but the information differs. Recordings from single cells in the auditory system of monkeys, for instance, have shown that they are tuned so as to make it possible to hear the range of vocalizations characteristic of the species. Similar studies have shown appropriate tuning in bats and other species. Primates and birds are equipped to get excellent information for the spatial layout by visual means. Bats, on the other hand, have highly specialized systems for getting acoustic information for where they are going.

2. What is extracted depends on developmental maturity. Human infants appear to differentiate and identify stationary objects rather poorly before they are four or five months old. But they seem to locate things quite well very early. Their attention is greatly drawn to events; how soon these are differentiated in any fine-grained way we do not yet know, but highly contrasting ones like looming and zooming are probably distinguished by a month or so. Small events embedded in larger events seem to be differentiated considerably later.

3. What is extracted depends on learning. There is learning common to members of a species, who share an ecology and pickup systems, and there is also idiosyncratic learning by individuals. It is very instructive to look at what is learned, because that will give us clues to how learning itself can or cannot be understood. One of the most impressive examples of idiosyncratic perceptual learning has been provided to us in the literature on chess masters (Chase & Simon, 1973). A chess master can look for as little as two seconds at a board as it stood in midgame (although he did not play that game) and reconstruct it almost perfectly. An amateur cannot. But when the same number of chessmen have been arranged randomly on the board, the master is no better than the amateur. What has he learned? He does not "remember" that particular arrangement. It is not an image of an arrangement on a board that he once saw that gives him the advantage. He picks up quickly an order in the arrangement that results from an abstract set of rules that someone else has followed. But they are

rules that he knows. Rules are abstract, but cases are generated from them. We perceive the cases as ordered because they are derived from the rules that generated them. They are meaningful as well, because they "afford" something – in this case, what move to make next so as to win the game. The chess master is not matching to some specific stored image or schema in his brain. There is no "feature detector" for every arrangement of a chessboard. We perceive specific things, yes, but always with internal and contextual relations.

If I look for mechanisms, therefore, they are going to have to be ones that deal with relations and ones that abstract information, rather than add on or integrate pieces. I am not primarily interested in processing mechanisms. I am interested in what is learned in perceptual learning, and I am interested in trends in perceptual development, not over a fraction of a second, but in the growing individual. I have chosen to talk about the latter, but I will consider along with these trends whether I need to invoke a process of integration – of construction from elements.

TRENDS IN PERCEPTUAL DEVELOPMENT

Twice before, I have talked about "trends in perceptual development," once in my book on perceptual learning and development, and once at the University of Minnesota about two years ago. What I had to say on each occasion was quite different, five or six years having intervened, but the trends were the same. They still are, although I begin to think that two of them can be combined into one. They are descriptions that characterize perceptual development, its end points and how it moves toward them, to be authenticated and explained if one can. I have spent more time in describing them and in demonstrating their authenticity than in explaining them. I shall still do that, but I shall ask whether the concepts I have been using – differentiation; search for distinctive features, invariants, and order; a process of abstraction; and reduction of uncertainty by finding order – are sufficient for an adequate account of where perception is going developmentally.

Increasing Specificity of Correspondence between What Is Perceived and Information in Stimulation

A striking trend in perceptual development is the increasing specificity of correspondence between information in stimulation in the world and in what is perceived. I think objects and events and layout are perceived from the start, insofar as anything is, but with little differentiation. I am not persuaded by experiments that display line drawings of geometrical forms to neonates that perceiving begins with the pickup of a line, and then gradually more lines, welded together into cell assemblies by eye movements. What do babies normally look at? Not line drawings. They certainly look frequently at faces, and research has tended to focus, quite properly, on the development of perception of faces.

Unfortunately, even this research does not have all the ecological validity one might wish, because the displays used are often flat, motionless, silent, oversimplified cartoons. Real faces move and talk. But if we think of the displays used as varied degrees and types of simulation, attempting to isolate critical information, they can perhaps still tell us something. It seems pretty clear that during the first few months of life infants progressively differentiate the human face *as a face;* gross outer contour appears to compel attention very early, then internal details like the eyes; but gradually superordinate relations are noticed and right ones are differentiated from wrong ones. Only later are individual faces differentiated as unique, and properly identified. Work in our laboratory by Spelke with motion pictures of people doing things (chewing gum, nodding, yawning, and so on) shows that a person is recognized despite different activities by about 5½ months. Invariant, enduring properties peculiar to the person are picked up despite varying actions. The truly unique features seem to be discovered over change. It is impossible for me to conceive of recognition that develops over varying activities as a process of associating elements or constructing from elements a schema to be matched. There certainly is no frozen image to be viewed or "processed" by a comparator.

Since the chapters that preceded mine all deal with the perception of words (single words or alphanumeric symbols of some sort), I shall try now to choose my examples from this realm. An early case of developing specificity of correspondence is the differentiation of graphic symbols. Research by Lavine (1977) showed that children in our society differentiate "writing" from pictures (simplified line drawings) at age 3. When tested with many samples of printing, cursive writing, and scribbles simulating writing, they unhesitatingly identified them as writing, although few could identify a single letter by name. Lavine's experiments showed that the youngest children tend to make use of some class features, such as linearity, repetition, and recombination of items, for distinguishing writing from pictures. But older children, at ages 5 to 6, were making greater use of distinctive features of individual letters. They differentiated one from another (still usually without naming) and discarded scribbles and artificial characters. Many, however, classified unfamiliar characters (e.g., Hebrew and Chinese) as writing, pointing out that it was not *their* kind of writing. Differentiation of global features for writing as a class evidently preceded differentiation of *kinds* of writing and of individual letters.

I have given a good deal of attention, in the past, to an analysis of distinctive features of letters. Does that not set me up as one who calls upon "feature detectors," one who assumes that features are the elements out of which letters are constructed? Our sins do seem to come home to roost, and I have certainly been thought to hold his notion. It was my own doing, I now see, since I suggested a table of features that others interpreted in this way. But it is not too late to protest. I have always thought of distinctive features as relational, as Roman Jakobson defined them for phonemes. They are contrasting properties useful to distinguish one thing from another, not bricks. They are discovered in a "differencing process" and are abstract.

Most children seem to have little trouble learning to distinguish letters – even rather confusable ones (cf. Gibson & Levin, 1975, pp. 239ff.). When trouble comes, it generally occurs in distinguishing sequences of letters in given orders (e.g., *boat* from *baot; trial* from *trail*). Is this not a failure in, or rather a need to develop, the ability to integrate? Again, I doubt it. Perception of order requires perception of succession. Perceiving succession over time is a particularly good example of differentiation that improves with development. There is considerable evidence that temporal acuity develops in children; they become better at resolving information given over time, rather than at integrating it. The temporal relations for perception of phi movement provide one example. Younger children perceive movement rather than succession with a longer interval and a wider gap than do older children and adults. Another example is the effect of masking a visually presented target. The masking threshold – the temporal interval that must intervene between a target (a letter, say) and a mask (another letter or some figure like a grid or a dollar sign) in order to identify the target – has generally been found to be longer, the younger the child. I do not think that this is because he cannot remember the target. Rather, I think that events have to be differentiated, not integrated. Furthermore, perception of order requires ability to discriminate succession. In other words, differentiation of succession – including segmentation – is a prerequisite for pickup of order.

There is supporting but indirect evidence for this notion in studies of children's problems with segmentation when they begin to read. Words resist being broken down into sounds. Perhaps the same is true of printed letters in a string for younger children. We have recently initiated what I hope will be more focused experiments to study masking effects in second- and fifth-grade children to see whether such effects with letters and words are related to perception of order in words. Is confusion of order within visually presented words related to developing ability to detect temporal order or succession? In some sense, information for succession must be perceived, whether one reads letter by letter or not. Information processors would no doubt refer to short-term memory for letter order, but I would talk about perceptual pickup of order information – something that has to be differentiated, especially in the internal portions of words. Of course, there is not only order information in words, there is information about other structural relations too, and I want to turn to this, since it leads to the second important trend: increasing economy of information pickup.

Increasing Economy of Information Pickup

I think increasing economy comes about because the developing organism becomes more efficient in detecting and using relations that are present in the stimulus array. In general, there are two major ways of increasing the economy of extracting relevant information.

One is the detection and use of the smallest possible distinguishing feature that will permit a decision. It may sound as though relational information is not involved in detecting what some people think of as an element. But it must be remembered that it is not an element that is singled out. The differentiating process requires generalization and classification. The minimal information is relational — an abstraction of a common contrasting property that divides two sets. The two sets could be letters or artificial characters in a Sternberg type of task (Barron, 1975; Yonas, 1969) that are separable if some contrastive property is discovered; or they could be concepts that share many properties but differ critically in just one or two. It is *only* that one or two that will be retained for future classification (Vurpillot et al., 1966). Children tend to behave this way, as well as adults, but adults can accomplish a finer sifting — with word meanings, for instance.

The second way of increasing economy is the detection and use of superordinate structure that permits what has often been called "grouping information in larger units." This is a typical way of increasing economy in reading; a reader will deal with the information in the text in the largest units that are relevant for his task, if he is capable of it (Gibson & Levin, 1975). These units are not conglomerations of associated parts (whatever the parts might be — lines? letters?), but are generated by the various rule systems that characterize discourse, in this case written discourse, at all levels. There is order in the way the information is presented — within words, within sentences, and within passages of discourse.

There has been much talk of economical use of structure at the level of the word during the past decade and indeed at this symposium. I need hardly remind you that it takes as long to read a letter as a one-syllable word; that a word may be recognized at as short an exposure duration as a letter; that a letter *in* a word can (under some circumstances at least) be identified, with a short exposure, more accurately than the same letter alone; that it takes longer to identify a target letter in a word than to identify the word itself as a target; and so on.

Although we have far less research bearing on this question, there is reason to think that ability to treat words as units develops over a fairly long period while a child is learning to read. The earliest data I know of were collected by Hoffman in 1927 (reported in Woodworth, 1938, and Gibson & Levin, 1975). He compared the increase with grade level in the number of letters read correctly with tachistoscopic exposure of unconnected consonants, nonsense syllables, unfamiliar words, and familiar words. From the first to the eighth grades, there was only a slight rise in the number of randomly connected consonants and nonsense syllables read, but there was a large increase for words, especially familiar ones. The sharpest rise occurred between the first and third grades, a finding consistent with more recent data collected by me, my students, and my colleagues (Gibson, Osser, & Pick, 1963; Golinkoff, 1974; Rosinski & Wheeler, 1972).

None of our studies has covered a really wide age range, however, or compared more than two or three kinds of items (usually words, pseudo-words, and unpronounceable letter strings). I was pleased, therefore, to receive a copy of a very extensive study by Doehring (1976) comparing latencies of response to a number of kinds of verbal material, with different judgments, over a very broad age range.

I have chosen a few of Doehring's results (all typical) that make the point about growth of economical processing. When an auditory—visual match was to be made and latency recorded, children did not improve significantly after the first grade in matching single letters. But when four-letter words (presented visually) were to be matched to a sample presented auditorily, latency improved significantly to the middle of the second grade. When four-letter pronounceable syllables were presented, latency improved up to the ninth grade. The trends for purely visual matching were similar for the three kinds of material. The same trends were particularly strong for oral reading measured in mean latency in seconds per syllable. The varying rates of progress for letters, words, and syllables had nothing to do with simple motor strategies of vocalizing, since picture naming over the same period showed no change at all in latency.

One further result deserves mention. Vellutino, Smith, Steger, and Kaman (1975) found that poor readers are frequently able to copy and name letters in words correctly, with tachistoscopic presentation. But the same words were often read incorrectly. The poor readers' performance on letter reproduction and naming approximated that of normal readers, although they were typically inferior to them in reading.

The fact is indubitable that most children *do* learn to extract information from text in larger units than the letter — both actual words and letter strings with structural constraints having to do with legal positions of consonant clusters and vocalic separation of consonants and clusters of them. Table 1 illustrates these constraints. The initial clusters are constrained to that position in a monosyllabic word or in a syllable, just as the final clusters are to their position. The vowel must be present in the syllable, and if there are both initial and final consonants, or consonant clusters, it must separate them. Any such arrangement, as indicated in the table, may be a word. Even if it is not a word, it can be pronounced and read like one. Now, do I not need the concept of integration to explain such learning? Do not children forge larger units by *associating* letters into blocks or chunks from originally smaller elements like single letters (sometimes called the "bottom-up" view)?

TABLE 1
Examples of Orthographic Constraints within
the English Monosyllable

Initial consonant cluster		Final consonant cluster
qu	/a/, /i/, /u/, /ae/	ck
br	/a/, /i/, /u/, /ae/	ng
scr	/a/, /i/, /u/, /ae/	pt
gl	/a/, /i/, /u/, /ae/	rd
fl	/a/, /i/, /u/, /ae/	nch
str	/a/, /i/, /u/, /ae/	ngth

If a word has been integrated from letters, we must have "lost" the saliency of the incorporated letters, because a letter is perceived better when it is part of a word, if the word is exposed quickly. Several people have objected that this finding is due to redundancy; of course it is. The constraints that characterize a word as a word constitute first class, usable redundancy. At the same time, if one is asked to decide whether a given word or a given letter is present in a display, it is faster to detect a whole word than a letter (Johnson, 1975). The word does not decompose easily, for adults as well as young children, but for different reasons. Children must segment before they can observe order and constraints. They do not have the "pieces" to begin with. But after segmentation is possible, the constraints provide new structure. The word, or even a legal pseudo-word, has holistic properties.

How do I know that a word has holistic properties such that it resists segmentation? Numerous experiments on anagram solution provide very handy evidence. It is harder to break up a word to solve an anagram that to solve an anagram from the same letters presented in a random arrangement (Beilin & Horn, 1962; Ekstrand & Dominowski, 1965, 1968). High word frequency of the solution word may facilitate solution, as in the following examples:[2]

	Anagram	Solution Word
	sauce	cause
vs.	ceusa	cause
	bleat	table
vs.	bleta	table

On the other hand, high frequency of the anagram word may inhibit it. But the word–nonword effect holds despite varying frequency of either the anagram or the solution word (Ekstrand & Dominowski, 1968). "Pronounceable" anagrams, even though they are nonwords, are harder to solve than unpronounceable

---

[2] Taken from Ekstrand and Dominowski (1968).

arrangements, so orthographic regularity as well as familiarity and meaning again contributes to a word's integrity as a unit (Dominowski, 1969). It has often been suggested that transitional probability, or bigram frequency, is a source of the word's unity (e.g., Mayzner & Tresselt, 1959, 1962), but transitional probability of letters and summed bigram frequency have been found to have only a little and sometimes no effect on anagram solution (Beilin & Horn, 1962; Dominowski, 1967; Stachnik, 1963). Since bigram counts where letter position is given consideration[3] are confounded with pronounceability and legality of orthography, a correlation with such a count would not be surprising – a bigram like *ck* in the fourth and fifth positions of such a word would have a pretty high frequency and at the same time accord with orthographic and phonological rules of English word structure. The sample of words used (and other variables such as frequency of the anagram in relation to the solution) would interact to make conflicting results possible, of course.

How early in the development of reading skill does a word exhibit strong unity, resisting fragmentation and rearrangement? Beilin (1967) gave three-, four-, and five-letter anagrams to subjects of four age groups (8, 10, 12, and 14 years). The difference in solution times for word as compared with nonsense anagrams was apparent for five-letter but not for three- or four-letter anagrams, but it did not reach significance until age 12. Along with the fact that the children were progressively able to solve any kind of anagram faster with increasing age, structural features of the word continued to become more prominent.

What are these features? In the first place, does a word have features? What is it that resists segmenting? Consider transitional probability first, although this is a letter-to-letter property rather than a property of the word as a whole. When other factors are controlled, summed bigram frequency as such does not prohibit the word inferiority effect for anagram solution. Neither does it account satisfactorily for the word superiority effect for tachistoscopic recognition of letter strings. Biederman (1966) found a slight effect of bigram (digram) frequency, taking letter position into effect (Mayzner–Tresselt count, 1965), with five-letter words, all of low word frequency. Some were words having typical English orthographic structure (e.g., *clang,* bigram count 203) and some were not (e.g., *gnome,* bigram count 15), so it may have been a higher level of structure that was actually effective. Gibson, Shurcliff, and Yonas (1970) compared the effects of pronounceability and sequential probability (as measured by four counts) on tachistoscopic recognition of pronounceable and unpronounceable pseudowords. Pronounceability had a strong predictive relationship to correct recognitions, but of the frequency counts, only the Mayzner and Tresselt (1965) bigram count did, and it was a far less effective predictor than pronounceability ratings.

---

[3] Letter position and word length are considered in a frequency count by Mayzner and Tresselt (1965).

It stands to reason that there are structural variables in words that frequency counts (so far) have not captured.

What else characterizes a word? La Berge (1976) describes a model involving coalescing of features. If I understand him, he is thinking of the word's contour, or some kind of superordinate graphic information. I doubt that graphic information is very important in word "coalescence" (I prefer the term "unity" or "coherence"). Recent experiments by McClelland (1975) found evidence for the tachistoscopic word superiority effect despite scrambled type faces, making it unlikely that the visual outline of the word is necessary for the effect to occur. I am in agreement with McClelland that "knowledge of abstract properties of familiar stimuli, not just knowledge of specific featural configurations, can facilitate perception" (p. 42).

The effectiveness of structural properties in an expeiment in some ways analogous to the word/letter experiments was demonstrated recently by Weisstein and Harris (1974). They showed an "object-superiority effect" for the detection of line segments. A single target line (one of four oblique lines) had to be detected when it appeared as part of a display containing the same eight context lines, variously arranged so as to produce a unified pattern of connected squares in a three-dimensional relationship, or a less unified, unclosed arrangement that appeared only partially or not at all three-dimensional. The target line was detected more accurately (with tachistoscopic exposure) when it was part of a configuration that looked unitary and three-dimensional. The effect does not contradict the notion that a highly coherent whole is hard to break up; it still may be. But detecting a given line in a "muddle" of context lines is much harder when the subject has a very short time to search. Weisstein and Harris (1974) suggest that "Perhaps recognition of both words and objects depends on more general processes that make use of structural rules and meaning to determine perception" (p. 754).[4]

It is these two relational properties of words—rule-like structure and meaning — that seem to me to be the ones that confer unity and coherence; that make them easily recognizable; that make them resist fragmentation; and that yet, when time is limited, make them easier ground for detecting a subordinate part than would a random arrangement of all those parts. They are abstract properties, not concrete, physical ones. The case for the structural rules is easy to make. English words have constraints that any monosyllabic word or any syllable in a multisyllabic one must obey. I have illustrated this point in Table 1.

---

[4] The rules for unity of an object, or a pictured one, are by no means the same as the rules for words, of course. An object is perceived as having unity, I think, because it takes up space (is three-dimensional); because its parts move together when it moves, and stay together when the observer moves; because it has texture and substance different from the background; and because it has continuity of contours and surfaces. A drawing of a cube lacks many properties of a real object, but it still hangs together better than the array of discontinuous fragments.

There must be a "vocalic center" (Hansen & Rodgers, 1968; Spoehr & Smith, 1973); there may be consonants or consonant clusters in either initial or final position. The latter may be constrained as to position. Indeed, nearly all consonant clusters in English are constrained (Fries, 1963). These constraints are a source of redundancy that contributes to ease of identifying even a pseudo-word, if the rules are obeyed. The rules apply both phonologically and orthographically. Invariance of the rules over phonology and orthography may also be important, but that question is still unsettled.

Orthography alone provides further useful rules in spelling patterns – contrastive groups of words that cover a large number of cases (see Fries, 1963, pp. 171ff.). An example is the shift in the value of any vowel when a succeeding consonant has an *e* added, as in the following examples:

pan—pane	con—cone	tin—tine
dun—dune	gem—gene	

This principle, as well as others illustrated by Fries, makes individual association of letters as unnecessary as it would be uneconomical. The structure is generated by the rule. I do not need to appeal to a constructive process that integrates letter by letter. The reduction of information provided by these rules is as economical and as compulsively useful as the three-dimensional structure in the Weisstein and Harris experiment.

The orthographic structure of a word, it seems to me, is not "integrated"; I do not see how it can be and generalize the way it does to previously unseen but well-formed nonwords. The process of learning it must be akin to the way a child learns grammar, a kind of gradual abstraction. The knowledge itself is abstract, not a specific physical configuration. I am the more convinced of this by a series of experiments in which I tried to teach children about orthographic structure. None of them worked very well, including one in which we explained the rules. An abstraction has to be discovered for oneself. We can put the relevant information in the way – as we do when a child hears us talk while we provide the appropriate situational context – and hope that his endogenous motive to attend to new information, and the economy principle that leads him to reduce the information by abstraction and classification, will have their effect. Drill at least will get you nowhere, nor will M & Ms. Appropriately contrastive displays that prompt the generalizations implicit in orthography appear to be the most promising instructional aid.

THE MEANING OF WORDS

Now, what about meaning? This property of words distinguishes them from pseudo-words that are orthographically and phonologically legal, and many experiments have found that it contributes to the unity and coherence of the word, giving it an added advantage for recognition (Barron & Pittenger, 1974; Gibson, Bishop, Schiff, & Smith, 1964; Murrell & Morton, 1974), and an added disadvantage for fragmentation and recombination in anagrams. How meaning lodges itself in a word is still anybody's guess, but it is a cogent property of a spoken word very early, and makes difficult the beginning reader's task of considering the word as a phonetic object. My guess is that the meaning of a word is learned as part of a situational context in which it is invariant with an event of interest. "Here's a cookie" goes along with being offered a cookie, with all the affordances thereof. The meaning of a word is probably differentiated from both its linguistic and its situational context.

I have lately become unhappy with talk about meanings of individual words, because their derivation seems to me so obviously context dependent. But I shall describe briefly one more experiment in which three students of mine[5] studied the developmental course of abstraction of features of printed words, including meaning. This experiment was originally designed to illustrate what I have thought of as a third trend in development: the optimization of attention. It seems to me now that the phenomena that persuaded me at one time to consider such a trend as unique are well subsumed under the trend toward economy in extraction of information. I shall not argue for a third trend, therefore, but rather point out the cognitive economy and adaptiveness of increasing ability to attend readily and flexibly to those aspects of presented information that have most utility for the perceiver in his role as performer.

In several experiments with young children (Pick, Christy, & Frankel, 1972; Pick & Frankel, 1973) the subjects have been given tasks that required them to select one aspect of the information presented by some object, to the exclusion of the rest. The ability to abstract information in this way, and to change what is abstracted flexibly from one aspect to another as required, seems to increase with age. The experiment to be described made use of such a task, but words rather than objects constituted the displays from which several kinds of information — graphic, phonetic, or semantic — were to be abstracted. The subjects were children from the third and fifth grades and adults.

Supposing that children have the necessary knowledge of the graphic features, sound, and meaning of a word, do they nevertheless show progress in abstracting one of these characteristics from a given word when asked to compare it with another one? How efficiently can they select the aspect that is relevant and adapt themselves anew when asked to select a different aspect? Reading is always for a purpose, and we have generally assumed that active selection of wanted information is an important part of the development of reading skill. In this experiment, the selection process with words was investigated.

[5] Condry, S., McMahon, M., & Levy, A. A developmental investigation of extraction of graphic, phonetic and semantic information from words. (submitted for publication)

Slides were presented to the subjects portraying three words (projected on a small screen). One, a standard, was typed alone at the top center. Below it, one on the right and one on the left, were two other words. One of the other words resembled the standard by either *looking* like it, *sounding* like it (rhyming), or having a similar *meaning*. The second word was chosen as a possible distractor or else was neutral with respect to the standard. The subject was told before the slide appeared that he was to choose the word that looked (or sounded or meant) most nearly the same as the standard, and to press one of two buttons (on his right or his left, corresponding with the choice words) as soon as he had made his selection.

For example, a slide might appear in one of the following arrangements:

	cry			near			near	
high		weep	bear		close	bear		deer
	(A)			(B)			(C)	

The subject might be told before the slide (e.g., arrangement A) was projected, "Choose the word that means (or sounds) most like the top one"; or he might be told (e.g., arrangement B), "Choose the word that means (or looks) most nearly the same as the top one"; or (arrangement C) "Choose the word that looks (or sounds) most like the top one." A distractor was provided that looked or sounded like the standard if the subject was to select for meaning (cf. A or B); that looked or meant much the same if the subject was to select for sound (cf. A and C); and that sounded or meant much the same if the subject was to select for looks (cf. B and C). For each of the three tasks (looks, sounds, means), slides with neutral rather than distractor alternatives were also provided. A subject made judgments with respect to all these types of slides (nine in all: three tasks – looks, sounds, or means – and three types of distractor for each task).

Half the subjects in each age group were shown the slides for the three tasks in a mixed random order. Half were shown all the slides for each task in a block. We thought that the latter procedure, which did not require switching to a different aspect of the word from trial to trial, would be easier, particularly for the younger readers. Flexibility in this sense has increased with age in at least one other experiment (Pick & Frankel, 1973), although the materials used were different and the age range younger.

The results of this experiment, as regards main effects, were as expected. The second-grade children made most errors and were slower on every comparison than the two older groups, although errors were few overall. The fifth-grade subjects were slower than the adults. All the subjects were faster when the tasks were blocked, but, somewhat to our surprise there was a negligible interaction of blocking with age. Everyone found "switching" troublesome – but on the other hand everyone, including the second-graders, could do it. The "looks" task was easiest and the "means" task hardest. Judging synonymy is especially difficult for second-graders. The interaction of age X task was significant when "means" was compared with "looks" ($p < .01$) and when it was compared with "sounds" ($p < .01$).

The distractor items, compared with neutral items, increased decision times (e.g., it is harder to decide which word means the same as the standard when a third word is present that looks or sounds like it, than when the third word does not resemble it in any obvious way). The distractor effect held at all age levels. The younger children, however, were more distracted by a "looks like" distractor on the "sounds" task than were the older subjects. Oddly enough, the effect of distractors was not especially strong for them on the "means" task, probably because the task was so hard for them in general.

All in all, this experiment supports the hypotheses that one kind of information in a printed word can be abstracted and compared when a task requires it, and that the decision becomes more efficient with age. Random switching of the task was harder for the youngest subjects, but it was hard for everyone (even the adults commented on it). The most striking age differences showed up in length of decision time and in making the "means alike" decision. The second-grade children knew what the words meant, in the usual sense, and would have no trouble understanding them in an appropriate sentence context. The judgment of synonymy of two single words is difficult for them, however, both with and without a distractor present.

Skillful deployment of attention in extracting relevant verbal information evidently improves with age (as well as reading experience) and contributes to the economy of information pickup. I see no way of understanding this fact better, however, in the context of an information-processing stage analysis. I see instead the need for reexamining the concept of attention, and weighting heavily the role of the task assigned (either by an experimenter or by oneself). Perhaps attention is simply perceiving that information which is coincident with task demands. Skill then will vary greatly with the task, as it did in this experiment. Perceiving that something has utility for the task certainly does improve with age, but I doubt that we can understand this improvement better by inserting another stage in a processing chain and calling it "attention." The danger of homunculizing looms up, and with it comes the danger of pushing the problem further into obscurity rather than solving it.

CONCLUSION

And now, to come to a conclusion, or to put it more accurately, simply an end, am I not, in repulsing information processing, preventing myself from theorizing? Will my intention of describing what is learned in perceptual learning, and what the trends are in perceptual development, render me a mere collector of facts, a file cabinet for assorted odds and ends? I doubt it. It is the themes of atomism and construction that I have an aversion to. But I have a theme too, in Holton's (1975) sense. We all do — as scientists, we are as born and bred to seek them as Brer Rabbit the briar patch. What we have to fear is that those ideas that are easily tagged will deteriorate into "vogue words" and "vogue concepts" (Merton, 1975). Hardening them by mathematicizing them will only make things worse if they are wrong, since it will frighten the innocent into an uncritical respect for them.

My themes are that there is information in stimulation and that what we experience does not come in bits and particles (a theme I have obviously borrowed from James J. Gibson); that we should speak of learning and development in perception as differentiation rather than construction; that the relevant processes are more akin to discovery and abstraction than to association and integration; and that man evolved as a seeker of information, not an intellectual pauper who must build something to believe in, because there would be no truth otherwise.

REFERENCES

Barron, R. W. Locus of the effect of a distinguishing feature in a memory search task. *Memory and Cognition,* 1975, **3**, 302–310.

Barron, R. W., & Pittenger, J. B. The effect of orthographic structure and lexical meaning on "same–different" judgments. *Quarterly Journal of Experimental Psychology,* 1974, **26**, 566–581.

Beilin, H. Developmental determinants of word and nonsense anagram solution. *Journal of Verbal Learning and Verbal Behavior,* 1967, **6**, 523–527.

Beilin, H., & Horn, R. Transition probability in anagram problem solving. *Journal of Experimental Psychology,* 1962, **63**, 514–518.

Biederman, G. B. Supplementary report: Recognition of tachistoscopically presented five-letter words as a function of diagram frequency. *Journal of Verbal Learning and Verbal Behavior,* 1966, **5**, 208–209.

Chase, W. G., & Simon, H. A. The mind's eye in chess. In Chase, W. G. (Ed.), *Visual information processing.* New York: Academic Press, 1973. Pp. 215–281.

Doehring, D. G. The acquisition of rapid reading responses. *Monographs of the Society for Research in Child Development.* 1976, **41**, Serial No. 165.

Dominowski, R. L. Anagram solving as a function of bigram rank and word frequency. *Journal of Experimental Psychology,* 1967, **75**, 299–306.

Dominowski, R. L. The effect of pronunciation practice on anagram difficulty. *Psychonomic Science,* 1969, **16**, 99–100.

Ekstrand, B. R., & Dominowski, R. L. Solving words as anagrams. *Psychonomic Science,* 1965, **2**, 239–240.

Ekstrand, B. R., & Dominowski, R. L. Solving words as anagrams: II. A clarification. *Journal of Experimental Psychology,* 1968, **77**, 552–558.

Fodor, J. A., Garrett, M. F., & Brill, S. L. *Pi ka pu:* The perception of speech sounds by prelinguistic infants. *Perception and Psychophysics,* 1975, **18**, 74–78.

Fries, C. C. *Linguistics and reading.* New York: Holt, Rinehart & Winston, 1963.

Gibson, E. J., Bishop, C. H., Schiff, W., & Smith, J. Comparison of meaningfulness and pronounceability as grouping principles in the perception and retention of verbal material. *Journal of Experimental Psychology,* 1964, **67**, 173–182.

Gibson, E. J., & Levin, H. *The psychology of reading.* Cambridge, Mass.: MIT Press, 1975.

Gibson, E. J., Osser, H., & Pick, A. D. A study in the development of grapheme–phoneme correspondences. *Journal of Verbal Learning and Verbal Behavior,* 1963, **2**, 142–146.

Gibson, E. J., Shurcliff, A., & Yonas, A. Utilization of spelling patterns by deaf and hearing subjects. In H. Levin & J. P. Williams (Eds.), *Basic studies on reading.* New York: Basic Books, 1970. Pp. 57–73.

Golinkoff, R. M. Children's discrimination of English spelling patterns with redundant auditory information. Paper presented at American Educational Research Association, Feb., 1974, New Orleans, La.

Hansen, D., & Rodgers, T. S. An exploration of psycholinguistic units in initial reading. In K. S. Goodman (Ed.), *The psycholinguistic nature of the reading process.* Detroit: Wayne State University Press, 1968. Pp. 59–102.

Holton, G. On the role of themata in scientific thought. *Science,* 1975, **188**, 328–334.

Johnson, N. F. On the function of letters in word identification: Some data and a preliminary model. *Journal of Verbal Learning and Verbal Behavior,* 1975, **14**, 17–29.

LaBerge, D. Perceptual Learning and Attention: In W. K. Estes (Ed.), *Handbook of Learning and Cognitive Processes,* Vol. 4. Hillsdale, N.J.: Lawrence Erlbaum Associates, 1976.

Lavine, L. O. Differentiation of letterlike forms in prereading children. *Developmental Psychology,* 1977, **13**, 89–94.

Mayzner, M. S., & Tresselt, M. E. Anagram solution times: A function of transition probabilities. *Journal of Psychology,* 1959, **47**, 117–125.

Mayzner, M. S., & Tresselt, M. E. Anagram solution times: A function of word transition probabilities. *Journal of Experimental Psychology,* 1962, **63**, 510–513.

Mayzner, M. S., & Tresselt, M. E. Tables of single-letter and digram frequency counts for various word-length and letter-position combinations. *Psychonomic Monographs* (Suppl.), 1965, **1**, 13–32.

McClelland, J. Preliminary letter identification in the perception of words and nonwords. Tech. Report No. 49, Center for Human Information Processing, University of California at San Diego, 1975.

Merton, R. K. Thematic analysis in science: Notes on Holton's concept. *Science,* 1975, **188**, 335–338.

Murrell, G. A., & Morton, J. Word recognition and morphemic structure. *Journal of Experimental Psychology,* 1974, **102**, 963–968.

Pick, A. D., Christy, M. D., & Frankel, G. W. A developmental study of visual selective attention. *Journal of Experimental Child Psychology,* 1972, **14**, 165–176.

Pick, A. D., & Frankel, G. W. A study of strategies of visual attention in children. *Developmental Psychology,* 1973, **9**, 348–357.

Rosinski, R. R., & Wheeler, K. E. Children's use of orthographic structure in word discrimination. *Psychonomic Science,* 1972, **26**, 97–98.

Spelke, E. Infants' recognition of moving faces. Paper presented at meeting of the American Psychological Association, Chicago, Ill., September, 1975.

Spoehr, K. T., & Smith, E. E. The role of syllables in perceptual processing. *Cognitive Psychology,* 1973, **5**, 71–89.

Stachnik, T. Transitional probability in anagram solution in a group setting. *Journal of Psychology,* 1963, **55**, 259–261.

Vellutino, F. R., Smith, H., Steger, J. A., & Kaman, M. Reading disability: Age differences and the perceptual-deficit hypothesis. *Child Development,* 1975, **46**, 487–493.

Vurpillot, E., Lacoursière, A., de Schonen, S., & Werck, C. Apprentissage de concepts et différenciation. *Bulletin de Psychologie,* 1966, **252**(XX), 1–7.

Weisstein, N., & Harris, C. S. Visual detection of line segments: An object-superiority effect. *Science,* 1974, **186,** 752–755.

Woodworth, R. S. *Experimental psychology.* New York: Holt, 1938.

Yonas, A. The acquisition of information-processing strategies in a time-dependent task. Unpublished doctoral dissertation, Cornell University, Ithaca, N.Y., 1969.

6
Mechanisms for Pronouncing Printed Words: Use and Acquisition

Jonathan Baron

University of Pennsylvania

INTRODUCTION

The mechanisms of reading are of interest both because of practical problems in teaching people to read and because of what we might learn about complex skills in general by studying reading. By studying tasks that are of practical importance, experimental cognitive psychologists can guard against the possibility that the mechanisms we discover are used only in the tasks we invent. Moreover, some day we might even surprise ourselves and discover something useful.

The commonalities between reading and other skills also make reading an excellent model of complex skills in general. As pointed out by Bryan and Harter (1899), many other tasks besides reading involve the integration of subskills into higher-order skills. Many of these skills, like reading, can be broken down into hierarchies or levels, such as the levels dealing with phonemes, words, and meanings. As pointed out by LaBerge and Samuels (1974), many complex skills seem to require automatization of their component subskills before fluent integration can occur. Even such subskills of reading as those involved in reading nonsense words seem to be automatic, enough to interfere with naming pictures when nonsense words are embedded in the pictures (Rosinsky, Golinkoff, & Kukish, 1975). Yet, while the subskills of reading become automatic with practice, they seem to be extremely difficult for the beginner (see Rozin & Gleitman, 1976). Overcoming the initial difficulties may thus be a prerequisite for ultimate fluency.

In what follows, I want to focus on the role of a particular subskill, the ability to pronounce printed words aloud, in both the mature skill of fluent reading and the acquisition of reading by children. This subskill is of particular interest because it is one of the most difficult to learn and yet, apparently, one of the most essential. I shall address questions about the mechanisms for this subskill itself, and about the use of this subskill in fluent silent reading. I shall try to argue that knowledge of spelling–sound correspondences is used in pronouncing printed words, in addition to knowledge of associations between whole words and their respective pronunciations. I shall also argue that the subskill of pronouncing words aloud is used in reading fluently for meaning. These arguments together lead to the conclusion that knowledge of spelling–sound correspondences is important in fluent reading. This conclusion leads to a further question, Can knowledge of correspondences be acquired *implicitly* (Reber, 1976) as a by-product of practice at other mechanisms, or are conscious, intentional strategies for learning required? I shall try to argue for the importance of intentional learning strategies. I shall then conclude with some speculations about the role of intentional learning strategies in acquiring complex skills with automatic subskills, thus completing the circle.

ANALYSIS OF THE POSSIBILITIES

Before turning to experimental attempts to answer the questions I have posed, I want to introduce a framework that may be helpful in discussing possible mechanisms of pronunciation. This is shown in Fig. 1. We shall be concerned with the connections between three kinds of representations, which we shall loosely call print, sound, and meaning. In Fig. 1, there are two main ways to read aloud: through meaning or directly. Anyone who has been forced to learn to read Hebrew to prepare for a Reformed Jewish Bar-Mitzvah can testify that one can learn to read without any awareness of meaning whatsoever. Thus, the direct link between print and sound is clearly possible. The indirect path through meaning to sound must be involved when we read such sentences as, *"TO WIND UP THE PLAY, BEFORE TAKING A BOW, THE LIVE LEAD READ HOW TO USE THE HEAVY LEAD BOW IN THE POLISH WIND."* (Here, of course, we include syntactic functions as part of what we loosely call meaning.) Other evidence for the existence of a pathway to sound through meaning comes from studies of patients with brain damage, who will sometimes give a semantically related word when asked to read a word out loud (e.g., Shallice & Warrington, 1975).

Similarly, we may extract meaning from print either *directly* – as when we use pictures or maps, and possibly when we read a sentence like *I saw the son* – or *indirectly*, through sound, as when we first read a word we have only heard before. Interesting evidence for the existence of both of these pathways from print to meaning can also be found in neurological patients (Marshall & New-

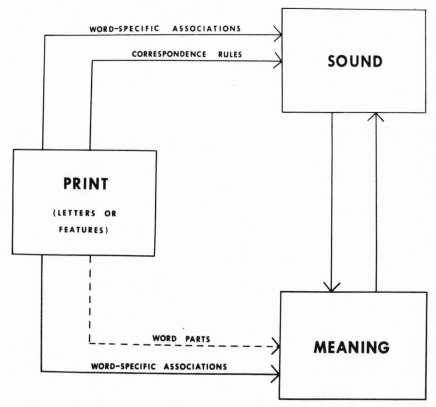

FIG. 1   A framework for discussing the extraction of sound and meaning from print.

combe, 1973), some of whom make clear semantic errors (mentioned earlier) and others of whom make phonological errors, indicating absence of the direct pathway to meaning. Allport (1976) has also found that normal readers make both types of errors under certain conditions of masking of the printed word.

Each of the main pathways in Fig. 1 can be broken down into a number of alternative pathways. Beginning with the link between print and meaning, the two major alternatives are direct associations between printed words and meanings, and, alternatively, associations between parts of printed words and parts of meanings. The first type of pathway needs no explanation, although in fact we have lumped together several distinct possibilities under this heading. The second is a possible link between prefixes and suffixes and the meanings they represent. Evidence of a direct link between a suffix and a meaning comes from an anecdotal account (Gleitman & Rozin, 1973) of a child given the word "child + s" to read and pronouncing it "children." Other evidence (Rozin & Gleitman,

1976) is our own ability to say something about the meanings of the nonsense words *bratian* and *bration*, which are pronounced the same. It is clear which one means the act of brating and which a person from Brate. Other examples of this are *bracked* and *bract*, and *drays* and *draze.*

Turning to the mechanisms for going from print to sound directly, we may again divide up the possibilities in terms of whether the relevant units of print—sound association are as large as words or not. We shall call pathways using smaller units, such as letters or letter groups, *rules*, and we shall call the pathways with word-sized units *word-specific associations.* The existence of rule pathways is shown by our ability to pronounce names or words we have never seen before with at least some accuracy. The existence of word-specific associations is suggested by our ability to pronounce words that are exceptions to the rules, such as *one, sure, lb,* or *Ag.* This ability might rely on associations between print and *meaning*, but it seems of interest that there are similar examples in the kind of Hebrew that people learn to read without understanding: In particular, the name of God is usually abbreviated in phonetically unrelated letters. It thus seems likely that direct associations between print and sound are used.

There is a second distinction to be made besides that between rules and word-specific associations. The first distinction concerned the size of the relevant units for accessing sound, while the second concerns the level at which these units are themselves accessed. The two main possibilities are the level of visual features and the level of letter identities. We clearly use the level of identities to some extent, as we can read words printed in novel typefaces, or in uppercase when we have seen them only in lowercase. The question is whether we also use visual features, particularly at fluency. Note that this distinction is relevant whether the units for accessing sound are words or letter groups, although it becomes degenerate if the units are individual letters. Note also that the visual features at issue may either be features of letters or features of a whole form (such as symmetry, regularity) that arise when letters are combined. As Smith (1971) has pointed out, different features of a letter may be used as a function of the context in which the letter occurs. For example, the existence of a vertical line in the letter "t" might be more salient in the context "th," but the horizontal line might be more salient in the context "to"; perception of certain features of the second letter might direct attention toward certain features of the first. This is another reason why we might learn to use word-specific information. I shall refer to any mechanism that uses visual features to access pronunciations of whole words as a *whole-word* mechanism, unless the features are just those used to access letter identities.

While it is clear that most or all of the mechanisms I have discussed are used in various situations, it is not clear which of them are used in fluent reading, or which must be acquired in learning to read. It is these questions that we shall try to answer.

PRONOUNCING WORDS ALOUD

The first question I shall discuss concerns the use of orthographic rules in reading words aloud as a mature skill. While it is practically obvious that orthographic rules are useful in the early stages of learning to read, it is not quite so obvious that the rules are useful after extensive experience with individual words. There are a number of ways in which rules are more complicated than word-specific associations, and it thus seems possible that after sufficient practice, the associations take over.

Artificial Alphabet Experiment

One way to find out whether rules are used is to make up two sets of words using an artificial alphabet, each word paired with a spoken response consistent with rules, and then to re-pair the stimuli and responses in one of the sets so that the alphabet is no longer useful as a guide to pronunciation. Subjects can then learn both sets of associations between printed words and sounds, one with the rules and one without, and then practice them for some extended period. If, with practice, the rules become as useless for the rule words as for the others, the speed of reading the two sets of stimuli should approach the same asymptote.

Brooks and I (see Brooks, 1976) did just this. We taught eight subjects associations between printed stimuli and spoken responses, as shown in Fig. 2. Each subject learned the *orthographic* responses to one set of stimuli and the *paired-associate* responses to the other set. In the orthographic condition, each artificial letter corresponds to an English letter. In the paired-associate condition, the stimuli are re-paired with the responses so that the orthographic regularity is lost. Half of the subjects learned the first set of stimuli in the

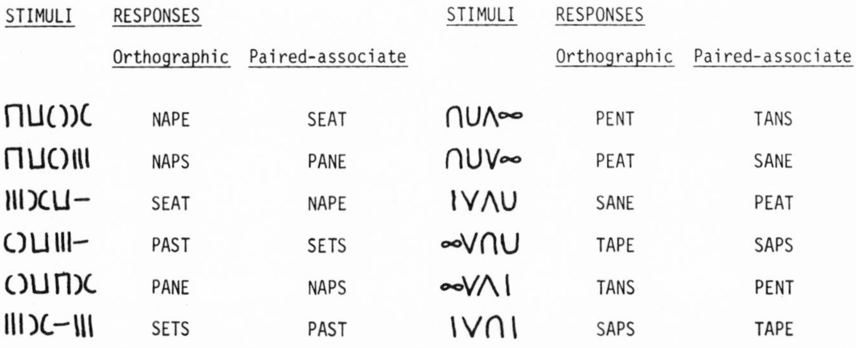
STIMULI
RESPONSES
Orthographic
Paired-associate
NAPE
SEAT
NAPS
PANE
SEAT
NAPE
PAST
SETS
PANE
NAPS
SETS
PAST
STIMULI
RESPONSES
Orthographic
Paired-associate
PENT
TANS
PEAT
SANE
SANE
PEAT
TAPE
SAPS
TANS
PENT
SAPS
TAPE

FIG. 2 Stimuli and responses for artificial-alphabet experiment.

orthographic condition and the second set in the paired-associate condition; for the other half, the conditions were reversed. The subjects were then given the stimuli in different random lists of six at a time and were asked to produce the six spoken responses in order as fast as possible. The subjects did this for 400 trials for each condition.

The mean times per list are shown in Fig. 3 as a function of practice. The orthographic condition starts out slower than the paired-associate condition, presumably because the subjects find it easier to use six associations between whole words and their responses than six associations between letters and their responses. In the orthographic condition, several associations need to be recalled for each response instead of just one. However, after extensive practice the orthographic condition speeds up, and actually approaches a lower asymptote than the paired-associate condition. This result suggests that orthographic rules, that is, spelling—sound correspondences, can facilitate reading words aloud in spite of extensive practice that would encourage the use of word-specific associations. The word-specific associations are available to an equal extent for both conditions, but the orthographic rules are available only in the ortho-graphic condition. These rules apparently make this condition faster.

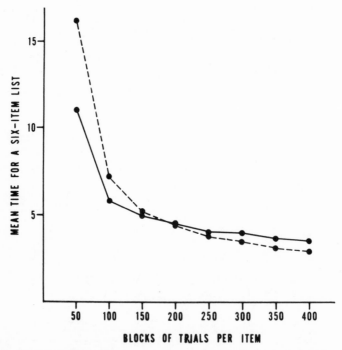

FIG. 3 Results of artificial-alphabet experiment: Dashed line is orthographic condition; solid line, paired-associate condition.

How Rules Could Be Used

Before turning to another study that supports the idea that rules are used in reading aloud, I would like to point out that there are three ways in which rules could be used to extract pronunciations in these experiments as well as in real reading. First, the reader might use direct *component correspondences* between individual letters and sounds, possibly taking into account the context in which the letter occurs, or between letter groups and sounds. A second way to use the rules is to form *analogies* between words. To use analogies, it is not necessary to store in memory any knowledge about particular correspondences. It is necessary to have available some general strategies for inferring the pronunciation of a word from the ways in which it resembles other words, and it is also necessary to have a number of associations between printed words and their respective pronunciations. One might, for example, infer the pronunciation of *red* from that of *rat, at,* and *ed* without having any idea that individual letters stand for phonemes (in prinicple, of course). The existence of rules allows the analogy strategy to be useful, but the rules themselves need not be directly represented in the reader's memory. More generally, we may distinguish between the analogy strategy and the correspondence strategy along two dimensions. The analogy strategy makes use of larger units of known correspondences, whole words instead of letters or letter groups, and the analogy strategy places greater reliance on strategies brought to bear at the time a word is pronounced, as opposed to the time the rules are learned (for component correspondences).

The third mechanism, the *similarity* mechanism, is even simpler. This mechanism relies only on the fact that similar printed words have similar pronunciations. In principle, this mechanism could work even in the absence of rules, as long as the similarity relations still held. For example, we might expect some facilitation of responding if we used random abstract geometric forms to represent words, with all words starting with a certain sound represented in different shades of the same color. The use of a similarity mechanism in real reading might create a tendency to assign to a new word the pronunciation of the most similar old word one can recall. Such a mechanism is practically a necessity if we are to avoid being confused by occasional mispellings. Later I shall discuss the role of all three of these mechanisms in pronouncing words encountered for the first time.

Exceptions and Regular Words

Let me turn now to some further work concerning the question of how skilled readers read words aloud. Given the superiority of the orthographic condition in the preceding experiment, it ought to be possible to show that orthographic rules are used in reading real words as well as artificial ones. The simple way to do this seems to be to try to find words that differ along the same dimension as our orthographic and paired-associate conditions in the experiments I just discussed. English does have words that seem to break orthographic rules, no matter how the rules are written, so as a first attempt it seems reasonable to compare the time required to pronounce regular words, which follow the rules, and irregular words, which break them.

In a first experiment, Strawson and I (Baron & Strawson, 1976) asked subjects to read lists of words. We used regular words such as *glue, chant, joker, fresh, yarn, boxer, loan, twig, ankle,* and *thigh,* and exceptions to the rules such as *epoch, tongue, answer, vise, beige, schism, cough, chute, should, whore.* The regular words and the exceptions were approximately matched in frequency. In addition, we used pronounceable nonwords such as *laf, caik, skail,* and *secks.* The mean time to read words was 428 msec for the regular words, 594 msec for the exceptions, and 778 msec for the nonwords. The error rates were 0.5% for regular words, 4.5% for exceptions, and 5.6% for nonwords. Further, the percentage of words on which errors were made by at least one subject was 10% for regular words, 48% for exceptions, and 56% for nonwords. Clearly, the exception words were much more difficult than the regular words, and almost as difficult as the nonwords. Since the exception and regular words were matched for frequency, it would seem likely that word-specific mechanisms were equally available for both. The orthographic mechanism, however, could be used efficiently for the regular words only. It thus seems likely that the orthographic mechanism is used in reading real words aloud.

But from these data alone we cannot state conclusively that the exceptions are pronounced less quickly because they break the rules. Even though the words are roughly matched for frequency, they may be harder to read for other reasons. For example, they might contain sequences of phonemes that are harder to pronounce, or their meanings might be stranger in some way because of historical factors that led these words to have irregular spellings in the first place.

Further, we cannot conclude from these results that word-specific associations are used for exception words. The exception word might not really be an exception at all. It might just obey more complex rules. Every attempt to write the rules of pronunciation usually includes a number of complex conditions that indicate how the pronunciation of a given letter depends on what follows it, or, alternatively, conditions that specify the assignment of pronunciations to spelling patterns rather than letters. By extending this procedure for writing rules it is possible to account for every single exception, so long as we do not require that a rule account for more than a certain number of instances. For example, to account for the pronunciation of *s* in *sure,* we might propose a rule of the form "Pronounce *s* as *sh* when it is followed by *ug* or *ur* and then a vowel." Such a rule accounts for *sugar* as well. Note that this rule is no more complex than other rules that are usually counted as productive, such as the rule for *i* followed by *gn,* which might be stated, "Pronounce *i* as long when followed by *gn* except when this is followed by a vowel not part of a new morpheme." This rule accounts for *signer, signing, signet*, and *signal.* It is hard to find some number of instances a rule has to account for in order to count as a real rule. Most exceptions are part of groups of two, three, or four words that break the rule in the same way, such as *tough* and *rough* or *cough* and *trough.* Even when there is only one of a kind, it almost seems reasonable at times to count a rule as psychologically real. For example, given the spelling of *said,* is it *totally* unreasonable to spell the past tense of *feed* as *faid*? Thus, it is not as obvious as it might first appear to be that the exceptions really differ from regular words. The exceptions might just use more complicated rules.

To examine this issue, as well as to remove the possible confoundings mentioned earlier, we used a different approach in a second experiment. We tried to select subjects who were either relatively good at the word-specific mechanism or relatively good at the orthographic mechanism. Let us call the subjects who are good at the word-specific mechanism and bad at the orthographic mechanism the Chinese, and those who are good at the orthographic mechanism and bad at the word-specific mechanism the Phonecians. What we will try to show is that the Chinese are relatively good at the words that are exceptions and the Phonecians are relatively good at regular words, discounting whatever differences exist between the words to begin with. The tests we used to select the two groups of subjects had nothing to do with speed of pronouncing exception and regular words, so if we succeeded in finding reliable individual differences, these differences could not be ascribed to differences in sensitivity to one of the confounding variables mentioned earlier. Note that it was not assumed that people who are good at one mechanism are bad at the other. In fact, our measures suggest that the two abilities are uncorrelated within our sample.

To measure ability at the orthographic mechanism, we gave college students a test that involved applying orthographic rules to nonwords of the sort I have already described. Twenty-two nonwords were used, and only thirteen actually sounded like words when pronounced according to the rules. The subjects were asked to check off those words that sounded like words when pronounced according to the rules. They were given the examples of *caik* and *burb* which do and do not sound like words, respectively. The score on this test was defined as the number of errors made, which ranged from zero to 11 out of a possible 22. Subjects with a low error score were assumed to be more likely to be Phonecians.

The test for use of the word-specific mechanism involved the use of that mechanism in spelling. Often when we write or type a word, we spell it using the rules for converting *sounds* to *spellings*, then look at the word we have written, decide it does not look right, and go back and try again. The idea of this test is that if we do this repeatedly, we ought to be classified as Chinese, assuming that application of the orthographic rules alone is not sufficient to rule out the spelling we have written down. Thus, the test for the word-specific mechanism involved asking subjects to spell, in written form, difficult words. They were asked not to make any changes in their spellings after they had written anything down. Then the subjects were given a forced-choice spelling test using the same words. Among the alternative spellings given were *argueable–arguable, assistant–assistent,* and *procede–proceed.* The number of errors on the initial test ranged from zero to 13 out of 25. A subject's score on this part of the selection procedure was defined as the improvement between the free spelling test and the forced-choice test. This improvement score ranged from 7 to −3. Most subjects did improve. Again, a subject with a high score should be put in the Chinese group. Since the scores on the two parts of the test had about the same range, we simply added them together to get an overall grand score for each subject. Those selected as Phonecians had a grand score of 1 or 0, usually as a result of no errors on the nonword test and no improvement in the spelling test, and those selected as Chinese had a grand score of 9 or more. There were originally 11 Chinese and 8 Phonecians, but three of the Chinese could not be induced to appear for the subsequent testing, which conveniently left us with eight subjects in each group.

In this experiment, the Phonecian and Chinese subjects were asked to read lists of exceptions and regular words aloud. Each exception was matched with a regular word that in most cases was lower in frequency and had the same spelling pattern that was "mispronounced" in the exception. For example, *honor* was matched with *holder,* and *doll* with *toll.* Each word was used in three different lists, which differed in type case. Lower case, uppercase, and mixed-case lists were used. The mixed-case lists consisted of words that began with a lowercase letter, followed by an uppercase letter, and so on, with the letters alternating in this manner throughout the word. It is assumed that the mixed-case words are not only less familiar but also consist of spelling patterns that are less familiar as visual units. The significance of the manipulation of type case will, I hope, become clear shortly.

Table 1 shows the mean times per list as a function of regularity and type case, across all subjects. First, it is clear that the manipulation of word frequency, so that the regular words were less frequent than the exceptions, succeeded in eliminating the overall difference between exceptions and regular words found in

TABLE 1
Mean Times-per-List (in Sec)
(10 Words per List)

| | Words | | |
Case	Exception	Regular	Exception–regular
Mixed	4.97	4.71	.27
Upper	4.52	4.67	−.16
Lower	4.49	4.51	−.02

the last experiment. This made it easier to interpret any interactions we found in looking for differences between groups. Second, there appears to be a small difference between upper- and lowercase letters for both exceptions and regular words, presumably due to the greater experience that the subjects had with lowercase letters. Third, there is no interaction at all between exceptions versus regular words and upper- versus lowercase type.

Of greater interest is the fact that there *is* an interaction between exceptions versus regular words and mixed versus same case. This interaction is significant across subjects. In particular, the exceptions are more affected by printing them in mixed cases than the regular words. This indicates that some mechanism is used more for the exceptions than for the regular words, and this mechanism relies more heavily on the letter groups that are broken up by the mixed-case condition. (These letter groups may be as large as whole words.) If we assume that the difference between exceptions and regular words is the possibility of relying on the orthographic mechanism in the latter case but not in the former, this result indicates that the alternative mechanism, the word-specific mechanism, is more disrupted than the orthographic mechanism by the breaking up of familiar letter groups or whole words.

The results concerning individual differences are shown in Table 2. In general, for the lower- and uppercase words, the exceptions were read more slowly than the regular words for the Phonecians, but more quickly for the Chinese (for whom the higher frequency of the exceptions could speed performance without opposition from an opposing effect of regularity). The interaction was significant for lowercase alone as well as for the means of upper- and lowercase. Moreover, in spite of the difference in frequency, the Phonecians actually did better on the regular words than the exceptions in lowercase type, although this result was only marginally significant.

From these results, we may conclude three things. First, different mechanisms, at least roughly those I have called word specific and orthographic, do exist for

TABLE 2
Mean Times-per-List (in Sec) by Group

Group/case	Words		
	Exception	Regular	Exception–regular
Phonecians:			
Mixed	5.06	4.69	.37
Upper	4.66	4.73	−.07
Lower	4.67	4.53	.15
Chinese:			
Mixed	4.89	4.72	.17
Upper	4.38	4.61	−.23
Lower	4.30	4.48	−.18

fluent reading of printed words. Second, fluent readers differ in the extent to which they rely on one mechanism or the other. Third, the exceptions really are treated differently from the regular words. That is, the word-specific mechanism is used more and/or the orthographic mechanism is used less for exceptions. This experiment thus confirms and extends the conclusions of the experiment using artificial materials and the experiment that simply compared regular words and exceptions. By showing individual differences in the mechanisms used to read aloud, we can conclude that both postulated mechanisms exist — the orthographic mechanism and the word-specific mechanism. If only one was used, individual differences in the relative strengths of two mechanisms, as measured by speed of reading regular words and exceptions, would not be found. Moreover, if exceptions were simply treated as words with more complicated rules, it would be hard (at best) to explain the individual differences in the time required to read them, relative to regular words. These results thus raise questions about how these two different sorts of mechanisms, orthographic and word specific, could both be used. I shall return to these questions after discussing a couple of other experiments.

The Whole-word Mechanism

I want now to examine more carefully the finding that there was no interaction between upper- versus lowercase type and exceptions versus regular words. We might have expected otherwise. In particular, let us make three assumptions: (1) a whole-word mechanism exists; (2) the whole-word mechanism is used more for exception words than for regular words; and (3) the whole-word mechanism is used more for lowercase than for uppercase words. The second assumption is reasonable if we assume that the whole-word mechanism is part of the word-specific mechanism, and that the word-specific mechanism is used more for exceptions than for regular words. The third assumption is reasonable both on the basis of the likelihood of greater familiarity with whole words in their lowercase forms and on the basis of the likelihood of greater distinctiveness of word shapes for lowercase than for uppercase words. Given these assumptions, we would expect the impairment due to uppercase type to be greater for exceptions than for regular words, since the exceptions would be relying on a whole-word mechanism that was impaired by printing them in uppercase letters. The uppercase regular words, however, could continue to rely on the orthographic mechanism.

Since there was no such interaction (and in fact any interaction was slightly in the opposite direction), one of these assumptions must be wrong. To find out which, another experiment was done. The idea was to look for an interaction between words versus nonwords and upper- versus lowercase letters. If assumptions (1) (existence of whole-word mechanism) and (3) (use of this mechanism more for lower- than for uppercase words) are correct, we ought to find that words are impaired more than nonwords by putting them in uppercase letters. This is because the whole-word mechanism is, by definition, useless for non-words, which are novel and thus cannot have word-specific associations. The lowercase words would thus be helped by the whole-word mechanism, but not the lowercase nonwords. In the experiment, the nonwords were unambiguously pronounceable pseudowords that were matched to the words in the distribution of initial consonants and final vowel—consonant groups. For example, the first few words in one list were *jet, found, land, more,* and *not,* and the matched nonwords were *fet, lound, mand, nore,* and *mot.* In fact, no difference was found; the advantage of lower- over uppercase type was 2/msec per item for words and 18 msec for nonwords, well within the range expected by chance, even with 30 subjects and 35 words per list. (The fact that both of these differences were small may be accounted for by yet another factor, the small size of lowercase type, which makes it harder to read in all conditions; a smaller typeface was used in this experiment than in others described.) We can conclude that at least one of the two assumptions, (1) and (3), must be wrong. There is either no whole-word mechanism, or it is used equally for uppercase and lowercase words.

The next step seemed to be to find a way to test for the existence of a whole-word mechanism more directly. Perhaps the reason for our failure to find a difference between upper- and lowercase words is that we have in fact seen most words in both type cases often enough for the whole-word mechanism to be equally useful in both cases. A more extreme situation exists in the case of proper names, which appear only very rarely with their first letter in lowercase type, and many other words that practically never begin with an uppercase letter. If there is a whole-word mechanism, we would expect these kinds of items to be read more quickly if they appear in their familiar form (starting with uppercase letters for names, lowercase letters for words) than in their unfamiliar form (vice versa). Similarly, there are some abbreviations (such as those for states of the United States) that normally appear with the first letter in uppercase type, and others (most measures) that normally appear with the first letter in lowercase type. In all of these kinds of material, the difference in frequency between the familiar and unfamiliar forms would on the face of it seem to be much greater than the difference between the frequencies of words in upper- and lowercase type, which was manipulated in the last experiment.

Accordingly, an experiment was done using a list of 13 measure abbreviations in a familiar form (in., qt, yd, gal, etc.) and an unfamiliar form (In., Qt, etc.); a list of 13 state abbreviations in a familiar form (Conn., Fla., Ind., Mass., etc.) and an unfamiliar form (conn., etc.); a list of thirty words not usually found at the beginning of sentences, and of three letters or less, in a familiar form (at, ate, ant, dip, end, dim, etc.) and an unfamiliar form (At, Ate, etc.), and a list of thirty names of three letters or less, matched closely to the words, in a familiar form (Al, Abe, Ann, Dan, Ed, Don, etc.) and an unfamiliar form (al, abe, etc.).

These eight lists, one familiar and one unfamiliar for each type of material, were all presented to each of 31 subjects, in a balanced order, with the constraint that the two forms of the same list were separated from one another by three other intervening lists. The task was to read each list out loud (pronouncing the entire word in the case of abbreviations). The results are shown in Table 3.

The effect of familiarity was significant across subjects for all lists combined ($t(30)$ = 4.30, $p < .001$) for the names ($t(30)$ = 2.12, $p < .025$), for the words ($t(30)$ = 1.70, $p < .05$), and for the abbreviations combined ($t(30)$ = 2.38, $p < .025$), but not for the two kinds of abbreviations considered separately (recall that these lists were only 13 items long, and that the entire words had to be pronounced). The effect of familiarity was also significant across the four types of material ($t(3)$ = 16.1, $p < 0.001$), and was in fact of almost equal magnitude for the four types.

It seems safe to conclude that there is in fact a whole-word mechanism. (See Brooks, 1976, for further support for this idea.) Information other than that from identities of letters is used to identify words, even for pronouncing them. (Conceivably, this mechanism may be used only to extract meanings, which in turn may be used to access pronunciations.) Putting this conclusion together with the last experiment, it would seem that our original assumption (3) (whole-word mechanism used more for lowercase than for uppercase words) is wrong; we seem to have had enough exposure to uppercase words so that the whole-word mechanism works for them as well as for lowercase words. This leaves assumption (2) in doubt; we are not in a position to say whether the whole-word mechanism is used more for exceptions than for regular words.

Summary: Parallel Pathways

To summarize our main conclusions about reading words aloud, it appears that some sort of orthographic mechanism is used even after considerable experience with a given word. It also appears that the word-specific mechanism is used as well. This mechanism uses, at least in part, a whole-word mechanism, one relying

TABLE 3
Time (in Msec per Word) to Read Familiar and
Unfamiliar Forms, where Familiarity Is
Determined by Case of First Letter[a]

Material	Familiar	Unfamiliar	Difference
Measures	503 (2)	537 (3)	34
States	486	516	30
Names	405	430 (2)	25
Words	401	431 (1)	30

[a]Errors (total) in parentheses, for 31 subjects.

on visual information rather than just letter identities. Evidence for the ortho-graphic mechanism comes from the artificial alphabet studies in which the availability of that mechanism was manipulated, from the finding that excep-tions take longer to read than regular words, and from the individual differences in the magnitude of the exception—regular difference. Evidence for the word-specific mechanism comes from the same individual differences and from the effect of changing the case of one letter of a word (Tom versus tom).

How can two different mechanisms, the orthographic and the word-specific pathways, be used at once? One possibility is that they are *not* both used at once, but if this were true the subject would be faced with the additional task of deciding which path to use. A more likely possibility, it seems to me, is that they are both automatic paths. Since automatic paths do not require capacity (La-Berge & Samuels, 1974; Norman & Bobrow, 1975), both may be used without taking capacity from each other. Moreover, since the two paths ordinarily lead to the same response, they do not interfere with each other. Thus, it is to the subject's advantage to use both of them. In any case, since the paths are presumably automatic as a result of extensive practice, there is little the subject can do to avoid using both of them. Conflict may thus occur for words that are exceptions even when the subject knows in advance that the words are excep-tions, as in the experiments we did (or in even more difficult cases such as the word *menus*).

EXTRACTING MEANING

I want to turn now to the question of how we extract meaning from printed words, and in particular, whether the indirect pathway through some sort of phonemic representation is of any use to a fluent reader. If the indirect pathway through a phonemic code is useful, then the mechanisms I have been discussing up to now are of some use even to a person reading silently to himself.

Before becoming involved in this issue, I should point out that there is some confusion about what is meant by "extracting meaning from words." I share that confusion. However, when we examine this question in the laboratory, it seems to me that there are certain tasks that clearly do not qualify as measures of extracting meaning, although performance on them may often involve the extraction of meaning. Among these tasks are the pronunciation tasks I have been discussing up to now, tasks involving tachistoscopic perception, same—different comparison of words, and lexical decision tasks (in which a decision must be made about whether something is a word or not). While these tasks might involve the use of meaning, they do not require it. A person who can read Hebrew out loud without understanding the meaning of a single word, for example, could very likely do all of these tasks with Hebrew stimuli, even the lexical decision task (on the basis of rote memory of which letter strings had been seen before in real text). Tasks that do require the use of meaning, I shall assume, are those that require the subject to decide whether something makes sense, whether a sentence or phrase is ambiguous, whether one word is a member of a category described by another, which of several items a word refers to, whether a word matches a picture, or how an ambiguous word such as *read* is to be pronounced. Another task that has been used to examine meaning is short-term memory for sentences. While this task certainly is facilitated if the sentences are meaningful, we must be cautious in inferring that some particular manipulation affects the use of meaning in this task rather than some other sort of representation.

Homophone Experiments

Let me begin by reviewing an earlier experiment that at first seemed to indicate very little use of the indirect path to meaning in fluent reading (Baron, 1973). In this experiment, I presented subjects with printed phrases such as those shown in Table 4. Their tasks were to decide as quickly as possible whether each phrase made sense or not, in one task according to spelling, in the other according to sound. The stimuli of interest were the *homophone* phrases such as *tie the not*, which made sense according to sound but not according to spelling. There were also *sense* phrases such as *he is ill* and *its not so* and *nonsense* phrases such as *ill him*. Each homophone word occurred in both forms, such as *knot* and *not*, and each form occurred in both a sense and a homophone phrase. For each homophone pair, another pair of words differing in the same way, such as *kill—ill*, was used to make up another four phrases, two sense phrases and two nonsense phrases.

If the indirect path is used at all in the task in which the subject judges in terms of spelling, this path ought to lead to incorrect answers for the homophone phrases (*tie the not*); the subject should at least be tempted to say that

TABLE 4
Reaction Times (in Sec)

		Task	
		Spelling	Sound
Sense	its not so	1.02^a	$.81^a$
Sense	he is ill	1.01^a	1.01^a
Homophone	tie the not	1.06	$.86^a$
Nonsense	ill him	1.05	1.10

[a]Yes responses (given by pressing a button) to the question of whether the phrase made sense (according to its spelling or its sound).

these phrases make sense. However, no such confusion should occur for non-sense phrases, where both spelling and sound lead to the same conclusion. However, the results for the spelling task, shown in Table 4, showed no difference in the time required to say that the homophone phrases did not make sense. Thus, there was no evidence for any use of the indirect path (except for a difference in error rates that was small compared to the 100% error rate that would be expected for homophone phrases if we assume that the indirect path is always used).

By analogous reasoning, we can ask whether the direct path was used in the sound task, in which the subject had to judge according to the sound of the phrases. If the direct path was used at all, it ought to make it easier to say that the sense phrases make sense, as compared to the homophone phrases, since the direct path would lead to the same answer as the indirect path for the sense phrases. (The relevant comparison here is between the matched sense and homophone phrases, such as *its not so* and *tie the not*, since both of these phrases received equal benefit from the subject learning that he could respond "yes" on the basis of part of a phrase, such as *tie the,* for these items – both phrases were associated with "yes" answers.) As Table 4 shows, the sense phrases were responded to more quickly (and in fact also more accurately) than their matched homophone phrases. Thus, the direct path seems to be used even when it is not required. This finding in itself may not be surprising, but it does show that the task is sensitive to differences in the use of different paths, and thus suggests that the failure to find a difference in the spelling task was not due to procedural insensitivity.

Baron and McKillop (1975) extended this study, using a much larger population of subjects, in the hope of finding some subjects who used the indirect path. We asked subjects to perform three different kinds of tasks instead of two. Each task required the subject to distinguish two different kinds of phrases, mixed together randomly in a list, by placing a check next to one type and an X next to the other as fast as possible. One task, the sense-versus-homophone, or SH, task, required the subject to place a check next to the sense phrases and an X next to the homophone phrases. This forces the subject to rely on the direct pathway, so that differences in the speed of performing this task reflect differences between subjects in the speed of this pathway. The homophone-versus-nonsense, or HN, task required the subject to use the indirect path, since both phrases would not make sense if judged according to the direct path. The speed of performing this task thus provides a measure of the speed of the indirect path. In the third task, the sense-versus-nonsense, or SN task, the subject was free to use either path. This allows us to measure the speed when both paths are available. The questions of interest concerned the determinants of individual differences in this task.

First of all, we picked two groups of five subjects, out of the sample of 40 who were under study, according to the ratio of each subject's SH time to his HN time. Since the SH lists force the use of the direct strategy and the HN lists force the use of the indirect strategy, a subject with a low SH:HN ratio can be said to be faster using the direct path, and a subject with a high SH:HN ratio can be said to be faster using the indirect path, relative to other subjects. The result of interest is that the group that was faster using the direct path was also faster on the SN lists, where either path could be used. In particular, the group with the low SH:HN ratios took an average of 15.7 sec to read the SN lists, and the group with the high SH:HN ratios took an average of 20.5 sec, which was significantly higher. This result can be seen as confirming the conclusion of the last experiment, that the direct path is faster when the subject is free to use either one, for it tells us that a subject's speed on the direct path is a better predictor of his reading speed than is his speed on the indirect path measured independently.

From the results I have described so far, it is entirely possible that the direct path was faster for every single subject, and the indirect path slower by a varying amount. In this case, the SN and SH lists would serve as independent measures of a single speed, the speed of the direct path. To check this possibility, we estimated this speed by combining the estimates derived from both the SN and SH tasks. We then found, for each subject, the ratio of this estimate to the HN time, which should estimate the speed for the indirect path. This ratio would thus tell us the relative speed of the two paths for each subject, if our hypothesis that the SN and SH times measure the same thing is true. Further, if we pick subjects who have high or low values of this new ratio, there should be no differences between the SH:SN ratios for these two new groups. However, this result was not found. It turned out that the group with the relatively slow indirect path had a lower SH:SN ratio than the group with the relatively fast indirect path. In other words, some of the subjects, at least, *were* using the indirect path on the SN lists.

Of course, this study does not conflict with my earlier conclusion that the direct path is the fastest one for a mature reader. It is quite possible, given their slower times on the SN lists, that those subjects who used the indirect path were less mature readers. This could be the result of their failure to learn fully the mature strategy of word recognition, or, as I shall discuss later, they might have had to use a different strategy for the actual semantic decisions because of poorer linguistic skills having nothing to do with reading per se.

Memory and Phonemic Mediation

In spite of the rather straightforward appearance that I hope these results present, there are two serious problems with these experiments. The first problem is that these tasks might differ from real reading in some crucial respect. In particular, a number of people have suggested that real reading involves the use of short-term or primary memory as an intermediate stage in comprehending sentences. A number of results suggest that phonemic codes have an advantage over visual codes in short-term memory, at least when the stimuli are printed words. Thus, the reader might have to rely on the indirect path to meaning simply because he has to remember the words before he understands them, the easiest way to remember them is phonemically, and the phonemic representation used is easily extracted from the print. Another difference between reading and the tasks we have examined so far is that in reading, the reader occasionally intends to store something in long-term memory, in addition to merely under-standing it. The second problem concerns the use of homophones. We have assumed up to now that homophones have exactly the same representation in the phonemic code that is used in the indirect path to meaning. This assumption might well turn out to be wrong. As I shall discuss at greater length later, there might well be a kind of representation that is phonemic in terms of what interferes with it and what capacities it draws on, yet that is closer to spellings than to sounds in terms of the relations of similarity and identity that exist within the code. This code might be in essence what Chomsky (1970) has called a deep phonemic level, as opposed to the surface phonemic level within which homophones are in fact identical.

There are at least two experiments in the literature that bear on the role of short-term memory in reading, and the question of whether the need for memory encourages the use of an intermediate phonemic representation. Both of these studies have been based on the idea that formation of a phonemic representation can be selectively interfered with by asking the subject to do certain tasks while he is doing the reading task of interest. Levy (1975), in one of these experiments, asked subjects to count out loud while they were reading sentences that they would be required to remember. Counting almost totally obliterated the memory for the sentences. However, when the subjects had the sentences read to them through earphones, counting while listening had no effect at all on the ability to remember sentences (except for the last of three sentences read). Levy concluded that counting specifically disrupted the conver-sion of print into a phonemic representation and that once the information was in this form, it was no longer subject to disruption. The counting presumably influenced the conversion from print to sound because it tied up the articulatory mechanisms, and it was thus concluded that these are involved in reading for memory.

A second relevant study was done by Kleiman (1975). He asked subjects to search through a printed sentence for a particular word, a member of a certain semantic category, or a rhyme of a word, in different conditions. In another condition, subjects had to judge whether entire sentences were acceptable. Subjects performed each task with or without a concurrent shadowing task. The shadowing task disrupted the sound and acceptability judgment tasks consider-ably, but had only a very small effect on both the semantic-relatedness and same—different tasks. Kleiman concluded that the indirect path to meaning is not involved in just any semantic task, but only in one that places demands on memory. Hence, the acceptability task was disrupted but not the semantic-relatedness task.

It seems to me that both of these studies suffer from a similar problem of interpretation. It is not clear from either of them whether the interference manipulation had a greater effect on one task than on another because of the modality of the code used in the task in question or because of other influences on the difficulty of the task. In both experiments, it is assumed that the differential interference results from the similarity of the interference to a postulated process in the tasks that are interfered with the most. However, it is also possible that the interference effects were due to a drain on general capacity rather than to competition with specific processes.

To spell out this argument more clearly, it might be helpful to use the distinction recently made by Norman and Bobrow (1975) between data-limited and resource-limited tasks. Norman and Bobrow postulate a function relating performance level on a given task to the amount of processing resources devoted to that task. Level of performance is measured by time or errors, and resources are manipulated by the simultaneous requirement to do other tasks, among other things. For the curve representing each such function, there is a region in which performance increases with increasing resources, and a further region in which the curve becomes horizontal. In the latter region, changes in resources devoted to the task do not affect performance as long as those changes stay within a critical range. Each task thus has its own characteristic point above which further increases or decreases in resources do not matter. Above this point, the tasks are said to be data limited; below it, resource limited.

In essence, then, the argument against the conclusions of Levy and Kleiman is that the tasks not affected by concurrent verbal activity might be in their data-limited ranges. In Levy's case, this might be because the information from the auditory input persists in a passive, echoic memory. The resources required for using this memory for the task might be small enough so that no interference occurs. Reading the sentences, as opposed to listening to them, might be interfered with simply because reading is in the resource-limited range, even if the direct pathway is used, possibly because the direct path to meaning might not have an echoic memory available. In Kleiman's experiment, the acceptability task might have been interfered with because it is poorly practiced, or because it requires suspension of normal strategies for understanding prose. (It is irrelevant to this argument how the phonemic task is interfered with.) The point here is that the greater susceptibility of this task to interference need imply nothing about the form of the memory that was used.

In order to gather more conclusive evidence, it may be helpful to restate the claims that Levy and Kleiman are making:

1. Reading sometimes involves short-term memory of particular words or phrases before their significance is fully understood. This is especially true for difficult material.

2. A phonemic code is a useful form in which to remember words or phrases for a short time while reading. Eventually, the meaning will be understood, at least in part, through sound—meaning associations of the sort used in understanding speech.

There is little doubt about the first claim. It seems to me to be confirmed by the fact that we sometimes have to reread the beginning of a sentence we do not at first understand. The second claim is the weaker of the two, for it is possible that we remember meanings, for example, rather than sounds, even when there are several possible meanings that have yet to be sorted out. Such a possibility, however implausible it may seem on its face, is consistent with the evidence for the relative absence of phonemic memory when words are presented visually rather than auditorily (Crowder & Morton, 1969), and with the evidence for reliance on semantic codes in short-term memory for words (Crowder, 1974).

I have done an experiment that I think provides some support for the second claim. The purpose of the experiment is to show that when a subject has to make a judgment about the meaning of a word, he relies more heavily on a phonemic representation of the word when he has to remember it than when he does not. In other words, requiring him to remember specific words encourages him to code the words phonemically. On each trial, the subject was given a card with five words on it, all uppercase homophones, such as PAIN, SUN, GUEST, SUM, POUR, or SOME, WEIGHS, WEEK, SELLER, MIST. The task was always to decide whether the list contained a member of a certain semantic category, such as *building materials, pronouns, body parts, drink or food, animals,* etc. On half of the trials, the no-memory trials, the category was given first. On the memory trials, the category was given after the card, thus requiring the subject to remember the words on the card. On half of the memory trials and half of the no-memory trials, the subject was told to make his judgment according to spelling, and on the other half of the trials he was to use sound. Blocks of five spelling trials alternated with blocks of five sound trials, until all 180 cards had been used for each of 12 undergraduate subjects. Half of the subjects did the first 90 trials in the memory condition, half in the no-memory condition. Thus, each card appeared in both conditions for different subjects. For about one-third of the cards, there was in fact a member of the specified category, and the data from these cards were not analyzed. Except for these "yes" trials, error rates were very low.

Table 5 shows the mean times taken to read the five words on each card for the four conditions. In general, the sound trials took longer than the spelling trials, and the memory trials took longer than the no-memory trials. But the result of interest is the interaction. The difference between sound and spelling conditions decreased significantly ($t(11) = 2.43$, $p < 0.025$, one-tailed) in the memory condition. We may take the difference between the sound and spelling conditions as a measure of the relative usefulness of phonemic codes and other codes (visual or semantic) in this task; if the sound code were relied upon

TABLE 5
Mean Time to Read 5 Words (in Sec)
(12 Subjects)

	Spelling	Sound	Difference
No memory	3.15	4.12	.97
Memory	5.47	6.06	.59

completely, there would be no difference between the sound and spelling conditions. In other words, a smaller difference between the sound condition and the spelling condition indicates greater reliance on the phonemic code in the spelling task. Since this difference between sound and spelling conditions is smaller in the memory conditions than in the no-memory conditions, we may conclude that the phonemic code is more useful in the memory conditions. Thus, a requirement that words be remembered makes a phonemic representation more useful than when this requirement is absent. This is one of the claims that Levy and Kleiman were trying to make. (Note that the particular kind of phonemic code used is one in which homophones are represented as identical, as this is required by the task.)

What remains to be shown is that the sort of phonemic short-term memory required in this experiment is actually required for reading, at least some of the time. Introspection suggests that this sort of memory is used frequently, especially when reading difficult scientific papers. Often one must read a sentence and then make several passes through a phonemic representation of it before understanding it. What is needed is a type of experimental procedure that allows us to analyze the reading of difficult material.

I believe I have found an experimental procedure that captures this sort of difficulty. The subject was given a card with two sentences expressing relations, for example, *John is taller than Jack. Jim is shorter than Jack.* Each sentence was on a separate line, and (for our convenience) all used names and comparative terms pertaining to persons; the names on each card began with the same first letter; and different names and comparatives were used for each of 32 cards. The main task was to read the card as fast as possible and then turn it over and recall what was on it, either by combining the information in some way or by repeating it verbatim. The experience of doing this task seems to me to be similar to what I experience when I read difficult material on academic subjects. To show that phonemic memory was involved in the task, one of two "interfering" tasks was performed while reading each card. The interfering task of interest consisted of saying "oh" after reading each sentence for the first time. The control task consisted of tapping the table instead of saying "oh." The idea is that the effect of the "oh," over and above the difficulty of performing any simple response while reading, would be to disrupt a phonemic memory. The idea, of course, came from Crowder and Morton (1969), who used such a procedure for a different purpose. In the experiment, the 32 cards were presented in the same order twice. On each presentation of the stack, the subject either tapped or said "oh" to each set of 8 cards, alternately. Those for which the used for tapping in one presentation were used for "oh" in the second, so that every card appeared in each condition, in a balanced design.

The "oh" had a pronounced effect, so to speak, on the time to read the card. For the four subjects who recalled the information verbatim (on all but one or two trials each), the "oh" condition took 7.6 sec per card, and the tap condition, 6.7 sec. For the three subjects who combined the information on the cards before reporting, the times were 12.5 sec for "oh" and 11.3 sec for taps. And for the remaining three subjects, who mixed their strategies, the times were 10.0 sec for "oh" and 9.1 sec for taps. The overall difference of 1.0 sec was significant across subjects ($t(9) = 5.75, p < .001$). The error rate, including cases of forgetting to say "oh" or tap, was 12.2% for "oh" and 9.7% for taps. Subjects' introspections agreed with our conclusion that the extra time required was due to having to go back and reread the card after the "oh" had disrupted phonemic memory.

When these results are placed alongside those I have already discussed, the case for the claims about the involvement of phonemic memory in reading difficult material is strengthened. We may conclude that experiments, such as the *tie the not* experiment described earlier, that do not involve memory, do not allow a fair test of the use of the indirect path to meaning. When memory is required, it seems that phonemic memory is used, at least to some extent. This phonemic memory thus serves the function of acting as a link between print and meaning over a delay. The translation of printed words into this phonemic representation would most likely involve the same mechanisms that are used to read printed words aloud, the mechanisms discussed earlier in this chapter. (However, it is still possible that phonemic memory is accessed from word *meanings*, which might still be extracted directly from print.)

Mediation by Deep Phonemic Representations

It is possible that a phonemic representation may be used even when memory is not required. While experiments with homophones, such as the *tie the not* experiment, suggest that the phonemic representation is not used, such experiments are inconclusive because they rely on the assumption that if there were an intermediate phonemic code, homophones would be identical when represented in it. To see more clearly what might be wrong with this assumption, consider the possibility, raised by Chomsky (1970), that there is actually a deep phonemic representation, different from the surface representation of speech which we use when we read. The words *sign* and *sine* are homophones in their surface representation but not in their deep representation. The value of assuming a different deep representation is in our ability to account for the relationship between such pairs of words as *sign—signal* or *sign—signature*, and for the predictability of this relationship from phonological rules unrelated to reading. The particular rule at issue in this example deletes the *g* from a *gn* occurring at the end of a word in the deep representation, and changes the vowel. Perhaps such a rule is needed because of the difficulty of pronouncing *gn* at the end of a word. In any case, there is reason to suppose that this deep level, in which the *gn* is represented in both members of each pair, exists even in nonreaders. Another example of a rule relating deep and surface phonology is the rule relating such pairs of words as TELEGRAPH-TELEGRAPHY, MIGRATORY-MIGRATE, AMBIGUITY-AMBIGUOUS,   FRIVOLOUS-FRIVOLITY,   HORIZONTAL-HORIZON, etc.; in the second vowel in the first member of each of these pairs, the rule has reduced the vowel to a neutral "schwa", which makes it impossible to identify the original vowel from the surface phonology alone. For some reason, our orthographic system has evolved so as to be closer to deep than to surface phonology. Some of these correspondences may be due to historical processes; spelling may have reflected sound more closely in the past. Yet it seems unlikely that the n in *sink* or the g in *sign* were ever pronounced "literally." A theory that denied the reality of deep phonology would be hard put to explain how these spellings arose. (Note, however, that many of the spellings can be accounted for in terms of the preservation of correspondences between spelling and *meaning*.)

Of course, Chomsky's theory is only one version of the more general hypothesis that printed words map into a code that differs substantially from speech and yet is still phonemic in modality. But Chomsky's hypothesis is one specific spelling out of this general hypothesis, one that does have some inherent plausibility. In what follows, I shall be talking about the general hypothesis rather than Chomsky's specific version. This general hypothesis holds that a phonemic representation is used in accessing meaning; that this representation is closer in its form to the spellings of words than to their sounds; and that in spite of this difference in form, the capacity that is drawn on by processing this code is the same one that is drawn on by processing articulation or speech comprehension.

The general deep-phonology hypothesis I propose thus makes a distinction between two different ways of inferring that a representation takes a certain form (in this case, a phonemic form). One way of making this inference is to look at the effects of similarity or identity of stimuli; homophones, for example, are identical in a surface phonemic code. Another way of making the inference is to look at what disrupts the formation or use of the code. If, for example, a certain representation is disrupted specifically by concurrent use of the speech system, this would be evidence for the articulatory nature of that representation. The hypothesis I propose is that the representation used to access meaning is phonemic only in terms of the second kind of inference. The first kind of inference would be possible if we knew what the representation was (for example, if we knew it was identical to a surface phonemic code), but we do not know this.

The *tie the not* experiment is not the only one that is complicated by the general deep-phonology hypothesis. Another experiment with the same problem was done by Szumski and Brooks (Brooks, 1977). Szumski and Brooks asked subjects to learn "meanings" such as "coffee" as responses to spoken nonsense words such as *pite* and to practice reading "pite" out loud from print. Half of the subjects were also given training at producing the meaning response to the written form of the word as well, thus giving them word-specific practice at "reading" the meaning of that nonsense word. Then both groups were asked to make semantic judgments about the printed nonsense words, such as deciding whether *pite* is something to drink. On at least the first couple of trials the subjects who had gotten specific experience at associating a word with its meaning were faster than those who had not gotten it. Moreover, these subjects were not impaired by the presence of acoustic confusability within the list of nonsense words they had learned, and the others were. However, in order to manipulate acoustic confusability without at the same time manipulating visual confusability, the acoustically confusable items used different spellings of the same sounds. For example, the item confused with *pite* was *jight*. Clearly, then, all of Szumski's results can be accounted for by assuming that the subjects with specific experience associating each word with its meaning were using well-learned associations between spelling and a deep phonological code, while those who only had experience associating the sounds with the meanings, and pronouncing the words, were using a surface code. The deep code was easier to use, possibly because it is closer to the orthography in form, and this accounts for the overall superiority of the direct-association training. Also, within this deep phonological code, acoustically confusable words were no longer acoustically confusable. Hence the lack of an effect of confusability in those subjects with the training in direct print-to-meaning association.

Effect of Orthography on Phonemic Mediation

Clearly, another approach to the question of the use of the indirect path (when memory is not required) is needed, an approach not subject to objections based on differences between surface phonemic codes and the ones used. An approach was suggested by the experiment with artificial alphabets performed by Brooks and this author. Perhaps we could show that the orthographic relationship between print and sound was useful not only in reading the print out loud, but also in extracting the meaning from print. In fact, as part of the original experiment comparing orthographic and paired-associate pairings, we asked four subjects who had been through the entire experiment to learn associations between the six stimuli in each condition and written responses consisting of the digits 2 through 7. The subjects practiced these responses for 400 trials, and the superiority of the orthographic condition was apparent even over the last 100 trials.

Glenn and Baron (1975) extended this finding. We asked five subjects to learn associations of the sort shown in Fig. 5, with partial counterbalancing of conditions and stimuli. The stimuli consisted of lists of three-letter items printed in our artificial alphabet, which I shall refer to as Greek, since many of the letters were actual Greek letters. Subjects learned pronunciations for each stimulus in three conditions, two of which are relevant here. In the orthographic condition, there was a simple letter–phoneme correspondence. In the other relevant condition, the binary condition, only two different spoken responses were used for the six stimuli in the condition, each response paired with three stimuli. Subjects also practiced making motor responses – drawing simple figures – to the six stimuli in each condition. Making these responses was about as difficult as writing an Arabic digit (after practice), but the drawn responses had no obvious names. The motor responses were assumed to represent the simplest sort of meaning that could be extracted from a printed word – analogous to the meaning of the word "two" when the response required is to write the corresponding digit. Subjects simultaneously practiced drawing and pronouncing from Greek for several weeks, until an apparently stable asymptote was reached (defined in terms of a low degree of improvement from day to day). In the orthographic condition, the simultaneous practice at pronouncing and drawing would be optimal for development of an indirect pathway, in which the phonemic representation was used as (at least) a partial cue for the "meaning"

STIMULUS	DRAWING RESPONSE	VOCAL RESPONSES	
		Orthographic condition	Homophonic condition
Σ√Σ		kok	kok
Σ√T		kob	beb
T√Σ		bok	beb
T√T		bob	kok
TΩΣ		bek	kok
TΩT		beb	beb

FIG. 4   Stimuli and responses for second artificial-alphabet experiment.

response, since the phonemic representation could be extracted in the best way, with correspondences, and since each spoken response could be associated with a unique meaning reasonse. In the binary condition, however, the correspondences between spelling and sound were absent, and the spoken response was almost useless in extracting the meaning response; spoken responses were nonetheless used in order to prevent subjects from developing their own, idiosyncratic, phonemic mediating responses. In sum, an indirect path should be used in getting the meaning responses without speaking aloud, only for the orthographic condition.

To test this hypothesis, we asked the subjects to draw silently, and to draw with concurrent vocal interference, which consisted of their saying "another, another, another . . ." while drawing from Greek. If the indirect path was used more for the orthographic condition, this condition ought to be more subject to interference. (We could not simply compare the times to draw from Greek for the two conditions because of the large variability due to the specific stimuli used, and the impossibility of removing the effects of this variability with so few subjects.) The effect of the interference, expressed as the ratio of the mean time to read lists with interference to the time without interference, was 1.085 for the orthographic condition and 1.058 for the binary condition. This difference was significant across subjects at the 0.02 level by a t test. The magnitude of the difference might have been larger if the effect of the interference had not disappeared completely for all conditions after a few trials. This finding thus supports the hypothesis that the indirect path was used in the orthographic condition. If this had not been the case, both conditions would have been affected equally by the interference.

Two other experiments that I shall describe support the conclusion that the indirect path may be used even in the simplest sorts of tasks, when the smallest possible demands are placed on short-term memory. In these experiments, the stimuli are either the Roman numerals I through IV or the English words "one" through "four." Both kinds of stimuli may be associated with the same meaning responses and with pronunciations (the spoken words that are their names). The difference of interest between Roman and English stimuli is that the English stimuli are associated with their corresponding spoken responses by spelling–sound rules, in large part, while the Roman stimuli must rely on specific associations. Since we have shown that the possibility of using correspondence rules can speed up the extraction of pronunciation, we ought to expect the indirect path to meaning, which uses this pronunciation, to be more useful for English than for Roman stimuli. If this is the case, we ought to find that making "meaning responses" is impaired by vocal interference more for English stimuli than for Roman stimuli.

Two different kinds of meaning responses were used. In both tasks, the subjects were given lists of Roman or English stimuli with 16 stimuli per list. The *comparison* task required the subject to check off each item that was larger than

TABLE 6
Mean Times-per-List (in Sec), Roman–English
Interference Experiment

	First task (comparison)		Second task (adding)	
	Roman numerals	English words	Roman numerals	English words
With vocal interference	36.0 (2.5)	38.4 (2.3)	15.0 (.3)	15.7 (.8)
Without interference	35.8 (1.6)	34.6 (1.3)	11.9 (.8)	11.9 (.4)
Effect of interference	.2	3.8	3.1	3.8

[a]Percent errors in parentheses.

the item preceding it in the list. The *adding* task required the subject to add one to the number represented by each item and write the answer as an Arabic numeral. Thirty-one subjects performed each task. There were four Roman lists (R1 to R4) and four English lists (E1 to E4). The tasks were performed for half of the lists of each type with vocal interference and half without, by each subject. The interference (int.) consisted of counting backward from 10 to 1 as quickly as possible while doing the meaning task. The design was balanced: 15 subjects went through the conditions in the order E1, R1, E2-int., R2-int., E3, R3, E4-int., R4-int., E1-int., R1-int., E2, R2, E3-int., R3-int., E4, R4; and 16 subjects performed in the reverse order. (Means were computed by first finding the mean for each order, and only then taking the mean of these two means.)

Table 6 shows the results. The effect of the interference on English, measured as the difference in times with and without interference, was greater than for Roman, for both tasks ($t(30) = 2.54$, $p < .01$, for the comparison task; $t(30) = 1.85$, $p < .05$, for the adding task).

The most plausible explanation of these results is that the existence of spelling–sound correspondences for the English stimuli made it easier to extract a phonemic code in time to use this code to make the meaning response (at least in part), and the formation of this code was disrupted by the vocal interference. These results thus allow us to speculate about the relationship between spelling–sound correspondences and the use of the indirect path in accessing meaning in reading. It appears likely that the advantage of the indirect path results, in part, from the use of spelling–sound correspondences in extracting the phonemic code that is used. As we saw earlier, the availability of spelling–sound correspondences speeds up the extraction of the phonemic code itself.

Summary: Parallel Pathways Again

To summarize this section, we may conclude that there is considerable evidence for the use of the indirect path to meaning, in spite of earlier studies that suggested otherwise (Baron, 1973). When demands are placed on short-term memory, a surface phonemic representation (in which homophones are identically represented) seems to be used, as shown by the preceding experiment on category decisions by sound and spelling, with and without memory demands. Moreover, situations resembling real reading seem to place the necessary demands on memory, as shown in the Levy (1975) experiment, the Kleiman (1975) experiment, and the experiment reported earlier with the subject saying "oh" to disrupt memory.

Further, there is evidence for some use of the indirect path (with a phonemic code that may differ from that used in speech) for even the simplest tasks, with the fewest possible demands on memory, such as the Glenn and Baron (1975) experiment with artificial alphabets and the Roman–English experiments just described. This evidence is puzzling, since it is hard at first to see how an indirect path, with two steps, can be used when a direct, one-step path is available. One possibility is that the indirect path is used because it relies on associations between sounds and meanings, which are used in spoken language as well as reading and thus receive more practice than direct associations between print and meaning. But this hardly seems likely to be the whole story, since it would also seem likely that years of practice at reading (if not much less practice) would establish associations between print and meaning that worked just as quickly as those between sound and meaning.

A second possible explanation of the use of the indirect path is that the advantages of accessing meaning with sounds instead of letters are sufficiently great to compensate for the extra time required to get to sound in the first place (rather than going directly from print to meaning). By using the indirect path, *three* letters, for example, might be first translated into *one* syllable. It might be easier to extract meaning from one unit than from three. Further, extracting the syllable from the letters is facilitated by the spelling–sound correspondences, as already discussed. According to this proposal, the advantages of the indirect path would largely disappear for a syllabic alphabet (of the sort used in Japanese), since such an alphabet has as many printed symbols as syllables. While there is no evidence against this explanation, it is clearly ad hoc, and therefore unsatisfying.

A third – and to me most satisfying – explanation of the use of the indirect path when memory is not required, is that it is used in parallel with the direct path. If this is the case, we can expect it to be useful even if it is usually slower than the direct path in providing information about meaning. If we imagine the two paths as hoses that can be used to fill up a bucket with information about meaning, we can see that the addition of a second hose can speed up the filling of the bucket even if it provides less water than the first. Of course, this idea assumes that using the second hose does not decrease the flow through the first one. This assumption, however, is a natural one if we assume that the hoses are used automatically, in the sense of LaBerge and Samuels (1974). Since automatic paths do not require attention, they do not take attention away from other paths. Ordinarily, simultaneous use of two automatic paths results in conflict (as in the Stroop effect), but in this case the two paths lead to the same outcome, so that facilitation occurs instead of interference.

Note that this explanation, in its general form, also explains why both orthographic and word-specific paths can be used to extract sound from print. Again (except for words that violate spelling–sound rules), both paths lead to the same outcome, and both paths have become automatic by virtue of extensive practice. It may thus be a general principle of skills that when several paths that produce the same outcome become automatic from practice, all of these paths are used. For skilled performance, the general answer to the question "Which path is used?" may be "All of them."

Note, however, that while all paths may be used when they are automatic, according to this account, some of the paths, such as the orthographic path to sound, may not be strictly necessary. While this path seems helpful in fluent reading, it is also difficult to learn. I now turn to the question of how this particular subskill is acquired, and ultimately to the question of the relationship between acquisition and skilled performance.

LEARNING THE ORTHOGRAPHY

I have argued so far that orthographic rules are important in fluent reading. Their availability is helpful in reading words out loud. Given this, it is likely that they are just as helpful in converting print into the kind of surface phonological representation that seems to be useful when short-term memory is required. Finally, they seem to be useful even when no short-term memory is required, although here we may be talking about a deep phonological representation rather than a surface one.

This, of course, is only part of an argument that spelling-to-sound rules are important for the beginning reader to learn. We have shown so far only that he must learn them eventually if he is to have a full battery of reading skills. However, there is a great deal of evidence that orthographic rules are if anything *more* important for the beginning reader than they are for the fluent reader. Rozin and Gleitman (1976) and Gibson and Levin (1975) have recently summarized this evidence, but it would be useful to review some of the high points.

One study by Firth (1972) examined correlations between ability to read out loud (as measured by errors) in first- and second-graders and a number of variables that might be basic to learning to read. With I.Q. scores partialed out, the speed of learning to associate names with strings of nonsense forms, essentially the paired-associate condition that Brooks and I used, did not correlate at all with reading ability. Tests of ability to discriminate and classify phonemes, however, did correlate significantly with reading ability. Other tests measured what the child had learned so far from his reading instruction. Among these variables, ability to use context to guess what a word would be had a very low correlation with reading ability, while the ability to pronounce nonsense words had a correlation of over 0.90. In fact, when intelligence and the ability to pronounce nonsense words were partialed out, all other correlations with reading ability essentially disappeared. The nonsense-word test is about the most direct measure there could be of knowledge of orthographic rules, so it would seem that learning these rules is quite important in the early stages of reading. (This is not to say that nothing else is important. See, for example, Samuels & Anderson, 1973.)

Other evidence suggests that poor readers not only do not know the rules, but do not even know the principles behind the rules. Rozin, Bressman, and Taft (1974), for example, found that students selected from classes of poor readers in the second grade could not tell which of the printed words *mow—motorcycle* matched up with which spoken word. These readers knew so little about the principles of orthography that they could not even tell that the longer word would most likely have the longer spelling.

Aside from such experimental evidence, there are practical arguments for the importance of the rules in early learning. The most convincing of these is the fact that a beginning reader who knows the rules can in essence teach himself to read, without continual feedback from a teacher who tells him the identity of each new word he encounters. Even though the rules in English are far from perfect in their ability to specify a pronunciation uniquely, they are usually good enough, with the help of context.

Two questions arise at this point. Once we have established the importance of rules for the learner, it is of interest to know what sort of knowledge about rules is most useful. Recall the three mechanisms I described earlier that might be used in pronouncing words written orthographically: component correspondence, analogy, and similarity. All three of these strategies are plausible contenders for the strategy used by the beginner. They may be distinguished here according to the size of the units that are used at the time new words are decoded and according to the way that knowledge is used. The analogy and similarity strategies use large units, possibly even the associations between whole words and their respective pronunciations. The correspondence strategy, on the other hand, uses smaller units such as single letters or letter pairs. The difference between the analogy and similarity strategies is that in the analogy strategy the pronunciation of a known word is modified, while in the similarity strategy the old pronunciation is taken over entirely. Ordinarily, the similarity strategy seems of little help, except when we encounter new spellings of words we already know, such as *Phonecian*. Clearly, the differences between these strategies are not absolute, as intermediate cases are possible. However, in discussing the experiments to be described, I shall treat these strategies as if they were distinct categories, for the purpose of analyzing data.

The second question is that of how the rules are acquired. In particular, we will ask whether the most useful principles of decoding may be acquired without the prior acquisition of certain strategies, strategies for learning or for transfering what has already been learned to new words. The alternative to this idea about strategies is the idea that the rules are learned best from instruction that completely ignores their existence and simply teaches children to pronounce words as if the words were pictures to be named. Such is the claim of those who favor the idea of implicit learning (e.g., Reber, 1976) as opposed to explicit learning. The essential issue here is whether the mechanisms for learning the rules are already present in the beginning reader, ready to do thier work on pairs of printed and spoken words, or, alternatively, whether the ability to learn the rules requires effortful acquisition of a new ability, or learning set, for this purpose.

In this section, I shall report two sets of experiments. The first set deals with the question of the size of the units used in decoding new words; I argue that large units are important for both adults and children. The second set deals with the question of whether acquired strategies are useful in decoding. Here, I argue that what I have been calling an analogy strategy is improved by training in both children and adults. Decoding new words improves when people are taught to find analogies with words they already know.

Using Large Units

The first experiment provides evidence that adults use large units in reading nonsense words aloud. It is based on an earlier experiment (Baron, 1976) in which it was shown that subjects tend to pronounce words such as *yeart, yopy,* and *yave* so as to rhyme with *heart, copy,* and *have,* in spite of the fact that the latter three words are unique exceptions to any rules for pronunciation that have been proposed. This experiment indicates that the effective units of transfer, from old words to new, are at least as large as *eart, opy,* and *ave.* A possible problem with this experiment, however, is that the subjects were given all the time they wanted. The chance to reflect might have encouraged the use of otherwise unnatural strategies.

In the current experiment, subjects were asked to read the following list of nonsense words, as fast as possible, in groups of five words at a time (so that times and pronunciations could be recorded by the experimenter): *yave, tive, zew, tey, fut, yord, flont, yoes, wrom, yash, minth, yatch, whon, proad, nonth, dongue, yeart, poth, thoe, topy, douch, bint, fliend, yon, thoot, kome, faid, deen, yaugh, plove.* Responses to *tive* and *plove* were not analyzed because I found more than a single analogy in these cases (*give, live, prove, move*). Fourteen percent of the responses to the 28 remaining words were based on a one-of-a-kind analogy, and only 5% were errors, that is, responses that could not be accounted for by any analogy or correspondence rules; this difference was significant across the 37 subjects ($t(36) = 6.02, p < .001$) and across the 28 words ($t(27) = 2.96, p < .005$). This result indicates that large units of correspondence are readily accessible when we try to decode novel words. If these adult subjects had decoded these words in terms of the smallest possible units, they would not have produced one-of-a-kind analogy responses any more frequently than responses that conformed to no rules or analogies at all.

It remains to be shown that large units are as natural for children to use as for adults. To show this, I will report an experiment performed in collaboration with June Hodge, and with the able assistance of Joy Delman, on kindergarten children (in Fitzpatrick Elementary School, a primarily middle-class school, in May 1975). In essence, the children were taught four "training" words by rote, such as *at, bat, ed, red,* and were then asked to try to decode four "test" words, such as *bed, rat, bad, bet.* Two of the test words (here, *bed* and *rat*) could be decoded by "analogy," that is, by using relatively large units from the training words – in some cases, the entire words. The other two test words could be decoded only by a correspondence method, that is, by using knowledge of the correspondence between single letters and sounds, the smallest possible units. Of course, for all of these words a similarity strategy would lead to incorrect responses; *bed* might be pronounced as "red," for example.

Table 7 shows the training and test words used (although one, *ug,* is more an exclamation than a true word). Note that along with each set of four words, we included a single letter from one of the words. The sound taught for this letter was the standard sound used in synthetic phonics instruction, that is, the shortest and most neutral syllable starting with the corresponding phoneme (*buh, duh, ss,* and *rr*). This was to see whether such phonics training would help over and above the analogy training. Note also that there were four different kinds of test words. The first two kinds (e.g., *bed, rat*) could be figured out by the analogy principle already described. The first type had the possible additional advantage of the phonics instruction and the second did not. The third type (*bad*) could be figured out by putting the first two letters of one training word together with the third letter from another. The fourth type of test word

TABLE 7
Words Used in Analogy Experiment

	Set 1	Set 2	Set 3	Set 4
Training:	*b*	*d*	*s*	*r*
	at	*ug*	*in*	*ug*
	bat	*bug*	*pin*	*mug*
	ed	*am*	*at*	*an*
	red	*dam*	*sat*	*ran*
Test:				
Type 1	*bed*	*dug*	*sin*	*rug*
Type 2	*rat*	*bam*	*pat*	*man*
Type 3	*bad*	*bum*	*pit*	*rag*
Type 4	*bet*	*bag*	*sit*	*run*

(*bet*) involved taking the first and third letters from one training word and the middle letter from another. Both this and the third type of test word could be figured out by the use of component correspondence, if we assume that the subjects learned anything about component correspondence from the training words.

The training stimuli were printed by hand in lowercase letters on the bottom of 3 in. × 5 in. index cards and the test words on the top, in order to encourage the subjects to note the similarities and differences by placing the test cards next to the training cards. For each set of cards, the five training cards were laid out in front of the subject, and the experimenter told the subject how each card was pronounced, going through the set twice. Then the subject was questioned on the set over and over, being told the answer when he did not know it, until he was correct on all five cards for two successive trials. This took between 0 and 8 trials. (In one case, pictures were placed next to the cards as an aid to memory.) The order of questioning the five cards was changed from trial to trial, as were the positions of the cards in front of the child.

In the test part of the experiment, after each set of five training cards had been learned to criterion, the subject was given one test card at a time, and asked if he could figure out what it was. The four types were given in a balanced order across sets. All guesses were noted. If the child said he did not know, he was encouraged to compare the test card to the training cards, to recall the sounds of the training cards, and to note similarities and differences in both the spellings and sounds. Phonic sounds were never used as part of this training procedure, nor did the experimenter pronounce any of the sounds for the subject. If the subject finally got the right answer, he was asked how he knew, although in many cases it was already obvious that the subject had used the analogy strategy, slowly and painstakingly. If he did not get the answer, it was given to him and explained.

Six out of a total of 30 subjects who began the experiment got tired and decided to quit before they had mastered the original five cards. These subjects were dropped from the experiment at that point. Of the remaining subjects, all but 13 failed to complete the entire experiment, in one case because the subject already knew how to read, in one case because of an erratic attention span, and in the other nine cases because the children were unavailable at a convenient time for the experimenter after the first set had been learned. The remaining subjects took from two to four testing sessions to complete the entire series, each session lasting about half an hour. Eight of the subjects did the four sets in the order in Table 7, and 5 in the reverse order, with the order of presenting the test words reversed as well.

Table 8 shows the main results. Clearly, the test words that could be figured out with the analogy strategy were easier than those that could not. All 13 subjects seemed to learn the analogy strategy by the third set, and most of the subjects figured it out immediately. One might suspect that the subjects already knew how to read, except that they did so poorly on the nonanalogy test words,

TABLE 8
Number Correct out of 13
(Examples from Training Set: *b, ed, red, at, bat*)

Test type	Set of words				Total (in %)
	1st	2nd	3rd	4th	
1. Phonics + analogy (*bed*)	9	11	13	13	88%
2. Analogy (*rat*)	11	11	13	12	90%
3. Correspondence (*bad*)	1	1	1	1	8%
4. Correspondence (*bet*)	1	0	2	5	15%

and when they were asked how they figured out the words, there were only two cases in which a subject said he already knew the analogy test word (e.g. *bed, rat*).

(One might think that the superiority of the analogy words, Types 1 and 2, might be due to the fact that the subject could figure them out by using two "parts" experienced elsewhere, the first letter and the last pair of letters, while at least the Type 4 words required three parts experienced elsewhere as parts – the three letters. We can test this possibility by counting the number of "parts" correct; this is a stringent test, because the last two sounds both had to be correct for the analogy words to count as a single correct part, and because the maximum number of correct parts would be two for the analogy words and three for the nonanalogy words. In spite of this lower ceiling for the analogy words, there were more parts correct for these words (1.88) than for words of Types 3 and 4, the nonanalogy words ($1.26; t(12) = 3.8, p < .005$).)

Some evidence for the use of a similarity strategy comes from the errors. Of those 56 cases in which a word was given as an incorrect response, there were 8 for which one of the training words was given as the response, and 18 for which one of the other test words was given. The errors in which another test word was given as a response were likely to be due to overextension of the analogy strategy rather than use of similarity, however, as 10 of these 18 responses were given before the test word in question was presented and 16 of them were in fact appropriate responses for one of the analogy test words. Also, strangely enough, 16 were on Type 3 words, 2 on Type 4, suggesting that this overextended analogy strategy was triggered by similarity with training words. (Note that the 18 errors are far too few for this overextension to account in full for the overall success of the analogy strategy.)

Two results suggest that the "phonics" training on the single letter presented alone was nearly useless to these children. First, performance on the Type 1 words, where the phonics training was designed to help, was no better than performance on the Type 2 words, as shown in Table 8. Second, we can look at all the words of Types 3 and 4 to see if the subject was more likely to get the first letter correct when it matched the single letter he received in training (bed, bad, bet, dug, etc.) than when it did not. Excluding the 37% of the trials for these words on which the subject made no guess, subjects were correct on the first phoneme 77% of the time when they had been given the letter alone in training and 65% of the time when they had not. This difference was not significant. (While the single letter did not seem to help, it should be noted that children referred to it frequently in justifying their responses to the test words. However, they also, on occasion, referred to a letter or letter pair embedded in one of the training words.)

In sum, these results suggest that it is natural for young children to decode words by putting together large pieces of words they have learned, rather than proceeding letter by letter. Moreover, observation of the children suggests that doing this was a difficult task, more like solving a problem than like uttering a sentence for the first time. These observations are thus consistent with my claim that learning to read involves the application of acquired strategies, beyond the "implicit" learning mechanisms that – according to some – allow us to learn spoken language.

Acquiring Strategies for Transfer

Recall that I began this section with two questions, the first pertaining to the size of the units of decoding, and the second to the value of acquired general strategies in learning to decode. The results discussed so far indicate that large units are important for both adults and children. I now turn to evidence about the value of acquired strategies. Rather than attempting to enumerate all of the strategies that might be helpful in learning to transfer correspondences from old words to new words, I shall use one strategy as an illustrative example. This is the strategy of decoding new words on the basis of similarities to old words. I shall present evidence that both adults and children perform better at decoding new words if they are taught to use this strategy. (By "this strategy" I mean, of course, this set of strategies.) Conceivably, there are many different activities involved in the process of decoding new words by comparing them to old ones, processes such as deciding what the relevant units of the new words are, searching memory for words with these units, and modifying the pronunciations of the remembered words in appropriate ways. However, all of these strategies are part of a superordinate strategy that can be described simply as using one's knowledge of old words to help one learn new words. Once a person has learned to try to use this superordinate strategy, its components may be learned more easily.

I have described the first relevant experimental result in more detail elsewhere (Baron, 1976), so I shall simply review the findings here. Adult subjects were asked to pronounce a list of 35 nonsense words, including items such as *cen, fign, knif, hamb,* and *psoal.* The experimental group was then asked to perform the task again, this time trying to use words they already knew to help figure out the new ones. The control group was simply asked to perform the task again, with no analogy instructions. In all cases, subjects were asked to produce all of the responses they thought might be correct. The number of correct responses increased (from 91% to 96% of the stimuli) for the experimental group only, even though the total number of responses decreased. Errors involving general rules, such as the rule for pronouncing vowels as a function of whether a vowel follows the next consonant, also decreased significantly; for example, subjects were less likely to pronounce *cip* as if it were *sipe*. In general, this experiment indicates that whatever other strategies adults have for pronouncing new words are less reliable than the analogy strategy, and that use of the analogy strategy may be increased by instructions.

The second result I want to report concerns the opposite end of the age continuum of interest: 5-year-olds in a middle-class nursery school. The experiment was run in collaboration with Elizabeth Valori. Its purpose was to try to teach a simple analogy strategy to these nonreaders, all but one of whom failed a simple segmentation test (with items such as "What happens to *man* when you take away the *m* sound?"). The idea was to measure the use of this strategy by looking for transfer of learning between related pairs of words. For example, a child would be asked to learn the pair of words *mat* and *mug* (printed on index cards in lowercase letters). The number of trials to criterion (two successive correct trials on both words) and the number of errors were recorded. The child would then be asked to learn the "words" *at* and *ug* under exactly the same conditions. Transfer was measured by subtracting the number of errors made while learning the second pair from the number of errors made with the first pair. Each subject learned six sets of pairs with four words in each set, as in the example just given, in this way. Our hypothesis was that the transfer scores should increase across the six sets, that is, that there should be more transfer from the first pair to the second in each set across trials as a result of learning the analogy strategy. To encourage the children to learn the analogy strategy, hints were provided during the learning of the second pair; children who said they did not know a word were asked to think of a similar word they had just learned.

The subjects were five boys and three girls with a mean age of 5 years and one month. Half of the subjects always learned the three-letter words first, the other half, the two-letter words. The three-letter words from each set were *mat, mug; box, bus; hum, his; leg, law; pin, pal; wit, wax.* The two-letter words were all constructed by removing the first letter from the three-letter words. Half of the subjects learned the list in the order just given, and half in the reverse order. Finally, half of the subjects learned the second pair in each set with the first pair in view (for the first three sets only); all other subjects did not have the first pair in view and thus had to rely on their memories. To our surprise, this variable, face-up versus face-down, made no difference in amount of transfer or in increase in amount of transfer, so I shall not discuss it further. Each set was learned on a different day.

The main results, the number of errors on each pair, for each of the six sets in order of presentation, are shown in Table 9. It can be seen that the transfer did increase, as predicted. (We shall return to the other obvious property of the data, that the transfer was mostly negative rather than positive.) To test the significance of this result, we determined the slope of the line that best fit each subject's transfer scores as a function of sets (in order of presentation); a positive slope would mean increased positive transfer or decreased negative transfer over the six sets. Across the eight subjects, the mean slope (.80) was significantly greater than zero ($t(7) = 1.94, p < .05$, one-tailed). In general, then, we can conclude that the children learned something that enabled them to do better on the transfer words, the second pair in each set. Whatever they learned did not seem to affect their learning of the first pair in each set, so it is appropriate to say that they learned something about transfer.

The fact that most of the transfer was negative, however, is disturbing. We had hoped to find no transfer at all in the early sets, and positive transfer in the later ones. It is indeed true that there is positive transfer on the last set ($t(7) = 3.24, p < .02$, two-tailed), but we cannot yet claim that positive transfer increased. The entire effect we found might be due to the disappearance of negative transfer. To test this possibility, we examined the most likely source of negative transfer: use of the similarity strategy. In fact, 24% of the errors were repetitions of the training word most similar to the test word (e.g. *man* instead of *an,* when *man* had occurred in the first pair). To find out whether decreases in repetition errors could account for the apparent increase in transfer, we simply reanalyzed the data, counting repetitions of a training word as correct responses to the corresponding test word and maintaining the criterion of two "correct" trials. When the data were analyzed in this way, the increase in transfer over the six sets was still present (mean slope of .33, $t(7) = 2.45, p < .025$). Moreover, there was no evidence of any negative or positive transfer in the early trials, once these

TABLE 9
Mean Number of Errors before Criterion, for the 6 Sets of Pairs[a]

Set	First pair	Second pair	Difference (transfer)	Corrected difference
1	4.75	8.00	−3.25	.50
2	2.88	4.75	−1.87	−1.75
3	2.38	2.75	−.37	.25
4	2.50	3.75	−1.25	.25
5	2.75	3.38	−.63	−.25
6	3.50	2.00	1.50	1.88

[a]Corrected differences count similarity responses as correct.

repetitions were counted as correct. We may conclude that there was a real increase in the tendency to make use of the first pair of words in a set when learning the second pair, over and above any decrease in the tendency to use a similarity strategy.

In sum, the last two experiments reported provide evidence that both adults and young children can be given instruction or practice that will improve their ability to decode new words on the basis of similarities and differences with old ones. In the experiment with adults, the words on which the analogies were based were already known. In the experiment with children, the words had just been learned. In spite of these differences, it seems likely that roughly the same strategy was used in each case, a strategy of trying to think of similar words as a way of dealing with new ones. However, we must also keep in mind the possibility that, for the children, this strategy was already available, and that what changed over the course of training was the method of learning the first pair of words. Possibly, the children might have paid more attention to the parts of the word and the parts of its spoken response as a result of their having learned that this would pay off when the second pair was presented. Even in this case, however, we could still conclude that the children had learned new strategies (or had learned to use certain strategies) that resulted in an increased ability to transfer effective knowledge of correspondences from old words to new ones. We have thus provided strong evidence against the view that mechanisms of learning and transfer naturally used by the child are sufficient to ensure such transfer. It seems worthwhile, then, to try to teach children the relevant strategies for learning and transfer before trying to teach them how to read, or at least to test for the presence of these strategies.

CONCLUSIONS

Let me conclude by summarizing the points I have been trying to make in the context of a general argument about the acquisition and performance of complex skills such as reading. Part of this argument is addressed to the question of the use of different pathways, associations, or connections in skilled performance, and part is addressed to the question of the role of acquired strategies in acquiring (in turn) some of these connections.

In activating one code or representation on the basis of other codes, there may be different paths connecting the relevant sets of codes. For example, representations of letters or visual features may be connected with representations of sounds or articulations either through direct, word-specific pathways or through pathways based on smaller units, that is, spelling—sound correspondences. Or, for another example, meanings may be connected with print directly or through phonemic representations. In cases in which two pathways between one set of codes and another set receive extensive practice, both pathways will tend to become automatic. As a consequence, the use of one pathway will not take capacity away from the use of another, and both paths will be used. If, further, the two paths are nearly equal in effectiveness, both will contribute to the speed of activating the codes they lead to. This is especially true if we imagine both paths adding information to the critical codes continuously over some time span, rather than in an all-or-none manner.

Evidence for the use of multiple paths has been presented in this chapter. We first found, on the basis of artificial-alphabet experiments and experiments with words that are exceptions in English, that both spelling—sound paths and word-specific paths are used in deriving sound from print. Then I presented other evidence that both a direct path and a path through sound are used to derive meaning from print. The indirect path seems to be more useful when memory is required, presumably because of the durability of a phonemic representation in short-term memory. But we cannot rule out some involvement of a phonemic representation even in tasks placing minimal demands on memory, such as the experiments comparing Roman numerals to English words in susceptability to vocal interference, which in fact suggested some phonemic involvement. These experiments cast some doubt on earlier demonstrations purporting to show no involvement of phonemic representations, especially in view of the fact that the earlier demonstrations assumed that homophones were represented identically in the phonemic representation used, which need not be true.

Turning now to the question of the acquisition of skills, we may divide processes of acquisition (very roughly) into those that require prior acquisition of strategies for learning or transfering the skills and those that do not. Some of the paths used in fluent reading may require very little in the way of special strategies in order for a child to acquire them; this would most likely be true for the direct, word-specific paths from print to sound or to meaning. (However, even here general strategies for learning may be required.) Other paths seem to require strategies that are only weakly developed in many beginning readers, and not even fully developed in college students. One of these strategies may be the use of "analogy," the strategy of decoding new words by comparing them to old ones in terms of fairly large units of spelling and sound. In the last section of this chapter, I presented evidence both for the naturalness of using large units for both children and adults and for the improvement of the ability to transfer as a result of appropriate training, again in both adults and children.

Putting together the arguments about the usefulness of multiple paths and those about the value of acquired strategies in learning to use some of these paths, we may conclude that mature and fluent use of what may appear to the user to be a simple and straightforward skill may require considerable intellectual effort in the early stages of learning that skill. The learning and transfer strategies used at these stages must themselves be acquired, often with difficulty.

It is thus not surprising that only intelligent creatures seem to be able to learn to read the way we do.

ACKNOWLEDGMENTS

Alan Allport, Rod Barron, Max Coltheart, Floyd Glenn, John Jonides, James McClelland, Linda Midgley, Dom Massaro, and the editors made helpful comments on earlier drafts. The research was supported by grants from the National Science Foundation (U.S.) and the National Research Council (Canada). Donna Ducanis provided able assistance in running the experiments.

REFERENCES

Allport, D. A. On knowing the meanings of words we are unable to report: The effects of visual masking. In S. Dornic & P. M. A. Rabbitt (Eds.), *Attention and Performance VI.* Hillsdale, N.J.: Lawrence Erlbaum Associates, 1976.

Baron, J. Phonemic stage not necessary for reading. *Quarterly Journal of Experimental Psychology,* 1973, **25**, 241–246.

Baron, J. What we might know about orthographic rules. In S. Dornic & P. M. A. Rabbitt (Eds.), *Attention and performance VI.* Hillsdale, N.J.: Lawrence Erlbaum Associates, 1977.

Baron, J., & McKillop, B. J. Individual differences in speed of phonemic analysis, visual analysis, and reading. *Acta Psychologica,* 1975, **39**, 91–96.

Baron, J. & Strawson, C. Orthographic and word-specific mechanisms in reading words aloud. *Journal of Experimental Psychology: Human Perception and Performance,* 1976, **2**, 386–393.

Brooks, L. R. Visual pattern in fluent word identification. In A. Reber & D. Scarborough (Eds.), *Toward a psychology of reading.* Hillsdale, N.J.: Lawrence Erlbaum Associates, 1977.

Bryan, W. L., & Harter, N. Studies on the telegraphic language. *Psychological Review,* 1899, **6**, 345–375.

Chomsky, N. Phonology and reading. In H. Levin & J. P. Williams (Eds.), *Basic studies on reading.* New York: Basic Books, 1970.

Crowder, R. G. The absolute limit on phonological confusability in memory. Paper presented at the meetings of the Psychonomic Society, Boston, November 1974.

Crowder, R. G., & Morton, J. Precategorical acoustic storage (PAS). *Perception and Psychophysics,* 1969, **5**, 365–373.

Firth, I. *Components of reading disability.* Ph.D. Thesis, University of New South Wales, 1972.

Gibson, E. J., & Levin, H. *The psychology of reading.* Cambridge, Mass.: MIT Press, 1975.

Gleitman, L. R., & Rozin, P. Teaching reading by the use of a syllabary. *Reading Research Quarterly,* 1973, **8**, 447–483.

Glenn, F., & Baron, J. Orthographic factors in reading for pronunciation and meaning. Paper presented at the meetings of the Psychonomic Society, Denver, November 1975.

Kleiman, G. M. Speech recoding in reading. *Journal of Verbal Learning and Verbal Behavior,* 1975, **14**, 323–339.

Levy, B. A. Vocalization and suppression effects in sentence memory. *Journal of Verbal Learning and Verbal Behavior,* 1975, **14**, 304–316.

LaBerge, D., & Samuels, S. J. Toward a theory of automatic information processing in reading. *Cognitive Psychology,* 1974, **6**, 293–323.

Marshall, J. C., & Newcombe, F. Patterns of paralexia: A psycholinguistic approach. *Journal of Psycholinguistic Research,* 1973, **2**, 175–199.

Norman, D. A., & Bobrow, D. G. On data-limited and resource-limited processes. *Cognitive Psychology,* 1975, **7**, 44–64.

Reber, A. S. Implicit learning of synthetic languages: The role of instructional set. *Journal of Experimental Psychology: Human Learning and Memory,* 1976, **2**, 88–94.

Rosinski, R. R., Golinkoff, R. M., & Kukish, K. S. Automatic semantic processing in the picture–word interference task. *Child Development,* 1975, **46**, 247–253.

Rozin, P., Bressman, B., & Taft, M. Do children understand the basic relationship between speech and writing? The *mow–motorcycle* test. *Journal of Reading Behavior,* 1974, **6**, 327–334.

Rozin, P. & Gleitman, L. R. The structure and acquisition of reading. II. The reading process and the acquisition of the alphabetic principle. In A. Reber & D. Scarborough (Eds.), *Toward a psychology of reading.* Hillsdale, N.J.: Lawrence Erlbaum Associates, 1977.

Samuels, S. J., & Anderson, R. H. Visual recognition memory, paired-associate learning, and reading achievement. *Journal of Educational Psychology,* 1973, **65**, 160–167.

Shallice, T., & Warrington, E. K. Word recognition in a phonemic dyslexic patient. *Quarterly Journal of Experimental Psychology,* 1975, **27**, 187–199.

Smith, F. *Understanding reading.* New York: Holt, Rinehart and Winston, 1971.

7

Integrative Processes in Comprehension

Patricia A. Carpenter
Marcel Adam Just

Carnegie—Mellon University

Even though we acquire much of our knowledge by reading or listening to other people, we sometimes have difficulties in understanding them. The problem often lies *not* in understanding the words that the other person is using, but in understanding "what the speaker is talking about." These difficulties arise in understanding how the words and clauses in a sentence are related to other sources of information, such as the previous sentences in the discourse. One simple example of this interrelation among sentences is the way a pronoun is used to refer back to a previously mentioned item. For example, if the sentence *He just bought a car* occurs within a paragraph, then the referent for *he* must have been previously established. Comprehension requires more than retrieving a representation of the word *he* that specifies (+ male) and (+ human). It requires that the comprehender determine the referent of *he.* This is an example of relating the information in the sentence to other knowledge in order to understand "what it is about."

In this chapter we will examine the process by which information in the sentence is related to other sources of information, such as a preceding paragraph, a question, or the perceptual context. We will also examine a number of linguistic devices that indicate how the sentence is related to its context; and we will examine how the cues are used during comprehension.

To talk about the psychological process of integrating information, we will introduce the concept of a *discourse pointer.* A discourse pointer is a symbol in the comprehender's mind that indicates the current topic of the discourse or the perceptual context. The discourse pointer activates either a single concept or an entire relational structure. The activated constituent then plays a central role in how the currently comprehended sentence is integrated with other information.

As an initial example of the psychological function of the discourse pointer, consider the process of comprehending a very simple paragraph:

> Cecil, the aardvark, was a strange pet. Because of his exotic eating habits, he was able to rid the house of insects. What he devoured most often were the little, dark ants. He was often seen routing these out with his long, ugly snout. Granted, his snout made him an excellent exterminator. However, it also made him an unusual household pet.

Various linguistic devices in this paragraph set the discourse pointer and indicate how the sentences relate to one another. The opening sentence initially sets the discourse pointer to the proposition that the aardvark is a strange pet. Opening sentences play a major role in paragraph comprehension because they determine the initial state of the pointer. The initial state may also serve as a default state, to which the pointer returns unless it is explicitly set to another concept or proposition. That is why it is important to place the topic sentence at the beginning of a paragraph.

The second sentence exploits the preceding context by referring to the aardvark with the pronoun *he*. The discourse pointer is moved to the topic of eating habits by the sentence describing the nature and consequences of those habits. The third sentence expands on this topic. The sentence presupposes that Cecil devours things. This presupposition matches the contents of the discourse pointer. The sentence also adds the new information that the insects most often eaten are ants.

The fourth sentence changes the discourse pointer to the topic of Cecil's snout. Both the fifth and sixth sentences expand on this subject, referring to the snout with pronouns. The connectives *granted* and *however* establish the relationship between these propositions and the primary topic, that Cecil is strange. *Granted* signals a concession to an opposing argument. *However* signals a return to the main argument.

This short paragraph provides a number of examples of linguistic devices that signal how the current sentence relates to the representation constructed from the previous discourse. Determining these relationships is part of the integrative process. We will argue that the content of the discourse pointer plays a special role in integration: It is the first candidate to be examined when one is trying to relate a sentence to previous information.

In the first section of this chapter we will present a series of studies examining how the information designated by the discourse pointer influences the comprehension of a sentence. We will show that the function of a number of linguistic devices used in discourse is to set the pointer appropriately, and to organize and program integrative processes. Several experiments will explore the parameters of the processes initiated by these devices and how they interact with the contents of the discourse pointer.

While in the first section we discuss integrative processes from the viewpoint of mental operations and linguistic structures, in the second part of the chapter we look at integrative processes from another viewpoint, namely, the rules for writing comprehensible prose. Teachers of prose composition have provided some rules of "good writing." These rules are often concerned with the linguistic devices that make sentences fit together. We will show how their analyses are based on implicit models of human comprehension processes. Many of the guidelines can be thought of as rules for appropriately setting the discourse pointer. We will analyze these rules and relate them to psychological models of the reader's comprehension processes.

The mental operations of chief interest here are those that find and represent higher-order relationships between constituents such as clauses and sentences. The duration of these integrative processes is very short; under optimal circumstances, it may take only a fraction of a second to determine how one sentence is related to another. In order to tap into these rapid mental operations, it may be necessary to monitor the processes as a sentence is being read and integrated with the previous ones. One such methodology (to be reported in this chapter) asks the reader to read each succeeding sentence of a passage and decide if it is consistent or inconsistent with the previous sentences. The decision times can be analyzed as a function of the semantic and anaphoric relationships between the current sentence and previous ones. This methodology gives some measure of the duration of an integrative step. Another possible approach is to monitor eye fixations during reading (Carpenter & Just, 1977). The duration of fixation on a particular constituent may reflect how long it takes to relate that constituent to previous information from the passage. Furthermore, regressive eye movements to previous mentions of a concept may externalize the search for the constituents to be integrated. By directly monitoring the integrative process, these methodologies may reveal the nature, sequence, and duration of the mental operations that are used in integration.

Relating New Information to Old Information

Each sentence of a connected discourse contains some new information as well as some old information that is redundant with the preceding sentences (Chafe, 1970; Halliday, 1967). The new information fulfills the function of communicating new knowledge. By contrast, the primary role of the old information may be integrative (cf. Haviland & Clark, 1974). But how does the reader know what information is old and what information is new? The distinction must be communicated because the two kinds of information are treated quite differently during comprehension, as we will document later in the chapter.

There are various linguistic devices that signal to the reader which constituents are old and which are new. In fact, the linguistic structure that a writer uses depends upon what he thinks his reader already knows and what he is trying to communicate as new information. Consider the writer who wants to say something about the event of John painting a barn. If the reader has already been told that John painted something, but does not know precisely what was painted, the writer might say *It was a barn that John painted* but not *It was John who painted the barn*. By contrast, if the reader knew that the barn had been painted, but did not yet know who painted it, the writer might say *The one who painted the barn was John*. Thus, the same event would be described differently, depending on the reader's previous knowledge.

This linguistic marking of the old and new information has an important consequence for the discourse pointer. The information marked as old in the sentence should usually correspond to the contents of the pointer. We will demonstrate that such correspondence facilitates comprehension by examining some linguistic structures that explicitly mark the old and new information in a sentence.

Cleft and pseudocleft sentences, which occur primarily in written rather than in spoken English, clearly demarcate the old—new distinction. A pseudocleft sentence presents the new information at the end of the sentence. For example, *The one who painted the barn was John* marks the identity of the painter, *John*, as new information. In a cleft sentence, the new information comes in the introductory clause, for example, *It was John who painted the barn*. It is possible to vary the semantic role of the new constituent. As an example, we have listed the pseudocleft and cleft constructions in which the agent or object is the new information (indicated by italics).

Pseudocleft agent: The one who painted the barn was *John*.
Pseudocleft object: What John painted was *the barn*.
Cleft agent: It was *John* who painted the barn.
Cleft object: It was *the barn* that John painted.

A writer can use these structures to mark the old and new components such that they correspond to the reader's state of knowledge.

Relating a Sentence to a Preceding Picture

To examine how the information structure of a sentence relates it to its context, we studied the comprehension of a sentence that was preceded by a picture. The picture depicted only one person. This contextual information should set the discourse pointer to a representation of that person. Then the sentence was presented; it described the relative positions of the depicted person and another person. The sentence should be easy to integrate if its linguistic structure marks as old the constituent designated by the discourse pointer. By contrast, the sentence should be difficult to comprehend if it marks as old a constituent that does not correspond to the setting of the pointer.

The subjects were told that the sentences always concerned two people, John and Barb, who were walking one behind the other either from left to right or from right to left. They were first shown a line drawing of a male or a female

FIG. 1   A typical picture used in Experiment I; it provides the reader with information about Barb's position. An appropriate sentence to follow this picture would be *The one who is leading Barb is John,* since it correctly presupposes that Barb is part of the old information.

(John or Barb) walking either to the left or to the right. Then they were shown a sentence like *The one who is leading Barb is John.* Figure 1 shows a typical picture and sentence. The subject had to indicate whether the person not depicted would be to the left or to the right of the depicted person. In the example shown in Fig. 1, the subject would answer that John was on the left, by pushing the left-hand response button. The critical variable was whether the picture depicted old or new information as defined by the sentence structure. Responses should be faster when the person shown in the picture was also the person marked as old in the subsequent sentence.

All four sentence types (pseudocleft agent, pseudocleft object, cleft agent, and cleft object) were combined with the verbs *leading* and *following* and the two orders of names (Barb–John and John–Barb), for a total of 16 possible sentences. The 16 sentences and the 4 possible pictures (John or Barb facing right or left) produced 64 different picture–sentence combinations. Twelve subjects, college students, underwent three blocks of 64 randomly ordered test trials. The picture appeared in the upper channel of a tachistoscope for half a second, then disappeared as the sentence appeared in a channel immediately below until the subject responded.

Results.   Responses were faster (by 189 msec) when the person shown in the picture was also marked as old in the subsequent sentence, $F(1,11) = 43.08, p < .01$. The mean latencies are shown in Table 1. The main effect was highly consistent across subjects; all 12 of them responded faster when the picture depicted the old information. As Table 1 shows, the effect occurred for six of the eight sentences. The exceptions were the cleft agent sentences like *It is John who is leading/following Barb,* where the responses were faster when the picture depicted the information marked as new in the sentence. It is possible that with practice, our subjects treated the cleft agent sentences like simple actives, which they resemble. Such an interpretation would be consistent with the obtained result.

TABLE 1
Mean Response Latency in Msec and (% Error) in Picture–Sentence Experiment

Stimulus sentence	Picture depicts			
	Old		New	
Pseudocleft agent:				
The one who is leading/following Barb is John.	2,447	(2%)	2,764	(6%)
Pseudocleft object:				
The one who Barb is leading/following is John.	2,355	(2%)	2,780	(4%)
Cleft agent:				
It is John who is leading/following Barb.	2,276	(4%)	2,164	(4%)
Cleft object:				
It is John who Barb is leading/following.	2,622	(6%)	2,750	(7%)
	2,425		2,614	

In general, performance is facilitated when the old–new information structure of the sentence corresponds to what is pragmatically old and new to the reader. The previous context establishes what information is pragmatically old. In the current task, the reader knew that two people were walking one behind the other. The picture established the direction of walking and the identity of one of the people. Thus, a picture such as the one in Fig. 1 would set the discourse pointer to the propositions (WALK, BARB) and (LEFT, WALK). The information marked as old in a subsequent sentence should be compatible with the contents of the discourse pointer. For example, the information marked as old in *The one who is leading Barb is John* is that Barb is being led. The fact that Barb is being led can be related to the contents of the discourse pointer because they both concern Barb's position. The next step is to add to memory the new information from the sentence, namely, that John is ahead.

The integrative process is more difficult when the sentence is inappropriate to the pictorial context. For example, the picture of Barb in Fig. 1 could be followed by an inappropriate sentence like *The one who is following John is Barb*. The information marked as old in this sentence is that John is being followed. It is difficult to relate this fact about John to the discourse pointer, which concerns Barb's position. The reader must discover this mismatch and reinterpret the sentence before adding the new information from the sentence to memory. It is this mismatch and reinterpretation that results in the longer latencies for sentences that are inappropriate to the context.

The Discourse Pointer in Paragraph Comprehension

The discourse pointer should play an especially important role in integrating the sentences of a paragraph. In particular, the setting of the discourse pointer by an early sentence should influence the comprehension of a subsequent sentence that refers back to it. To study this comprehension process, we varied the semantic relationship between a sentence at the beginning of the paragraph and a subsequent sentence that we will call the target sentence. This relationship should affect the time subjects take to read and process the target.

We constructed 32 simple paragraphs that shared certain structural properties. The following is a typical paragraph:

(1) The ballerina captivated a musician in the orchestra during her performance.

(2) The one who the ballerina captivated was the trombonist.

(3) It was the conductor who arranged the choreography.

(4) The one who arranged the choreography was the stagehand.

(5) It was the costume designer who worked the hardest.

The opening sentence always described how a person interacted with some unspecified member of a group. In the preceding example, the ballerina interacted with an unspecified member of the orchestra. This sentence initially set the discourse pointer to information that was relevant to a later target sentence. The target sentence provided new information as to the identity of the member of the group. In the example, the target sentence appears in Position (2) and identifies that the previously unspecified orchestra member as the trombonist. This target sentence was to be integrated with the opening sentence. The target sentence had an old–new structure that was either appropriate or inappropriate to the opening sentence.

To ensure that successive sentences were integrated, the subject was asked to judge whether each sentence was consistent or contradictory with the preceding sentences. The subject's decision time was measured from the onset of the sentence. The sentences were presented on a video monitor one at a time and removed as soon as the subject made his judgment of "consistent" or "contradictory." A contradictory sentence clearly contradicted a previous filler sentence. [For instance, in the preceding example the sentence in Position (4) contradicts the sentence in Position (3).] The contradictory filler never preceded the target. The fillers and the target were cleft or pseudocleft sentences, so that the superficial form of the sentences did not distinguish the fillers from the target.

This task was designed to study how appropriate or inappropriate marking of old and new information affected integrative processes in the comprehension of the paragraph. A target sentence with an appropriate information structure marks as old the information that was communicated in the opening sentence. For example, the appropriate target in the paragraph given earlier marks as old the fact that the ballerina captivated someone, a fact communicated in the opening sentence. An example of an inappropriate target would be *The one who captivated the trombonist was the ballerina;* this sentence inappropriately marks as old the fact that the trombonist was captivated by someone. In the latter case, the reader must detect the incongruity and reinterpret the sentence before integrating the new information.

A second way in which we varied the relationship between the discourse pointer and the target sentence was by inserting intervening sentences between the opening sentence and the target. That is, the target sentence could appear in Position (2), (3), (4), or (5). The filler sentences were only tangentially related to the opening sentence. The intent of the slightly incoherent filler sentences was to dislodge the discourse pointer from the representation of the opening sentence. Thus, when the target sentence was separated from the opening sentence by fillers, its old information would not be compatible with the contents of the discourse pointer. The reader would be forced to search his memory to retrieve the relevant information. The duration of the search process should be reflected in the subject's response latency. For example, Sentences (3) and (4) discuss choreography and may set the discourse pointer to this topic. If the target sentence appeared after Sentence (3), the information marked as old would not match the contents of the discourse pointer. The reader would have to continue his search beyond the contents of the pointer in order to integrate the information.

The paragraphs were randomly assigned to the 32 different conditions formed by three orthogonal factors: (1) the target sentence had an information structure that was appropriate or inappropriate to the opening sentence; (2) the target sentence was a pseudocleft agent, pseudocleft object, cleft agent, or cleft object; and (3) there were 0, 1, 2, or 3 filler sentences between the opening sentence and the target. The 12 subjects were college students.

Results. Subjects took less time to integrate the target sentence when its information structure was appropriate with respect to the content of the opening sentence, as shown in Fig. 2. Overall, sentences with an appropriate structure were verified about 991 msec faster than sentences with an appropriate propriate structure, F' (1,39) = 10.11, $p < .01$. (The F' statistic is used to test the reliability of this effect over populations of subjects and paragraphs.) The information structure of the sentence being processed provides an important cue for relating the sentence to the preceding discourse. The reader uses the information that is marked as old to determine how the current sentence relates to some aspect of the discourse. When this old information matches what is designated by the discourse pointer, or when it matches what the subject already knows, then the integrative process is relatively fast. When the information structure of the target sentence was inappropriate, the information marked as old did not match any of the propositions in the reader's memory. The sentence had to be reinterpreted before it could be correctly integrated with the previous information. These additional processes contributed to the longer response latencies for sentences with inappropriate information structures.

The time taken to integrate a target sentence with the opening sentence increased as the number of intervening filler sentences increased, as shown in

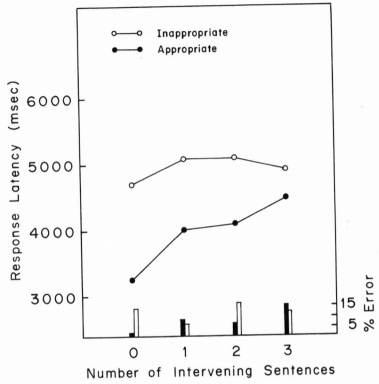

FIG. 2   The mean response latencies for appropriate and inappropriate target sentences as a function of the number of filler sentences that intervened between the opening sentence and the target.

Fig. 2. Responses were fastest when the information structure was appropriate and there were no fillers. In that case, the discourse pointer was set appropriately for the immediately following target. In all of the other cases, the intervening fillers displaced the discourse pointer to concepts unrelated to the target. The memory search for information relevant to the target presumably took longer when there was more information from filler sentences to search through.

Although certain conditions of the current experiment resemble the previous experiment, there is a much larger effect of an inappropriate information structure in the current task. For example, in the previous experiment, when the target sentence immediately followed a picture, an inappropriate structure increased the response time by 189 msec. In the condition of the current experiment, in which the target immediately followed the initial sentence, an inappropriate structure increased the response time by 1,444 msec. One possible explanation for the difference in magnitude involves the variety of sentences in the two tasks. In the previous experiment, the sentences varied only in the names of two people and the subject may have known exactly how to interpret an inappropriate sentence. By contrast, each paragraph in the current experiment involved different people and objects, and it may have been harder to formulate a reinterpretation of an inappropriate structure.

The performance in our paragraph comprehension experiment provides firm evidence that the effect of the discourse pointer is more than just a general context effect. In all the experimental conditions, the relevant preceding information had been read and internalized by the reader. What determined the speed of response was the information-structure relationship between the sentence being processed and the preceding context. The discourse pointer designated the current theme or topic of the discourse. If the content of the pointer corresponded to what an ensuing sentence marked as old, then the sentence was integrated quickly. In other words, what was important was how the reader found the relevant information in his representation of the preceding information, and how the sentence he was processing guided his search.

We have not thoroughly explored the factors that control the movement of the discourse pointer in the course of comprehending a paragraph. We have assumed that the opening sentence sets the pointer to its own content, and this is probably a good assumption. After the first sentence, there are a number of factors that could control the movement of the pointer. One operative device is an intersentential connective that explicitly denotes the relationship between the sentence being processed and the previous context. A connective like *For example* should move the pointer from its previous location to a new one, with the labeled relation "is an instance of." A phrase like *To return to the main point* should move the pointer to the structure that it had previously designated at the next highest level. We will return to the role of such connectives later in the chapter. As a first step, we have been content to assume that in our simple narrative paragraphs the pointer does move from sentence to sentence.

Relating Answers to Questions

A question—answer sequence provides another opportunity to examine the role of the discourse pointer during intersentence integration. When a question is asked, the discourse pointer is set to some old information. This old information will be either implicitly or explicitly presupposed by the answer. The answer's main role is to provide the requested information, and this information should be marked as new. As an example of how this works in ordinary questions and answers, consider the following set:

(1) Who painted the barn?   John.
(2) Who painted the barn?   It was John.
(3) Who painted the barn?   It was John who painted it.

All of these answers either implicitly or explicitly assume that someone painted the barn and that his identity has been requested. The answer provides his identity and marks it as new information.

The consequences of a mismatch between the discourse pointer and the answer are jarring:

(4) Who painted the barn?   *It was the barn that John painted.

This response is inappropriate; it incorrectly marks *the barn* as though it were the requested, new information. The answer in (4) is not a bad sentence in itself; it would be an appropriate reply to a question like *What did John paint?* These examples demonstrate how the new information in the answer must conform to the structure established by the preceding question.

We designed an experiment to study the comprehension of question—answer pairs in which the answer's information structure was either appropriate or inappropriate to the question. The experimental procedure required a subject to read a question like *Where is John?*, and then a sentence like *It is John who is leading Jim,* and use the information in that sentence to answer the question. The subject responded either "ahead" or "behind" to indicate John's relative position by pressing one of two buttons. The main variable of interest was whether the question probed information that was marked as new in the subsequent sentence or information that was marked as old. The response latency for answering a question should be shorter when the question probed the information marked as new.

Thirty-two different question—sentence pairs were constructed by using four kinds of sentences (pseudocleft agent, pseudocleft object, cleft agent, and cleft object), the predicates *leading* and *following,* the names *John* and *Jim,* and a question that probed either the name marked as new or the name that was part of the old information in the sentence. Each of 12 subjects was presented with two blocks of 32 randomly ordered trials.

Results. Responses were considerably faster, by 284 msec, when the question probed the new information in the sentence, $F(1,11) = 9.19, p < .01$. Thus, the main hypothesis was confirmed: Performance was facilitated substantially when the information structure of the sentence corresponded to the question's request for information. The mean latencies and error rates for the various question—sentence pairs are shown in Table 2.

The advantage of questions that probed the new information was present for seven of the eight sentences. The only exception was the pseudocleft object sentence with the verb *leading* (i.e., *The one who John is leading is Jim*), which had faster responses when the question probed the old information. This reversal occurred only for this sentence and only in Block 2, suggesting that it may be due to random fluctuation.

A question sets the discourse pointer to a proposition with a constituent missing. For example, asking "Where is John?" sets the pointer to (LOCATE,

TABLE 2
Mean Response Latency in Msec and (% Error) in Question–Answer Experiment

Stimulus sentence	Question interrogates			
	New		Old	
Pseudocleft agent:				
The one who is leading/following Jim is John.	3,860	(6%)	4,276	(9%)
Pseudocleft object:				
The one who Jim is leading/following is John.	4,071	(14%)	3,952	(2%)
Cleft agent:				
It is John who is leading/following Jim.	3,282	(1%)	3,745	(4%)
Cleft object:				
It is John who Jim is leading/following.	3,960	(2%)	4,336	(18%)
	3,793		4,077	

JOHN, ?). An easily comprehensible answer not only provides the requested information, but also marks it as new. In ordinary discourse, the information structure of sentences corresponds not only to explicit questions, but also to implicit questions (Halliday, 1967). For example, a listener's quizzical facial expression during a conversation is an implicit request for information. The speaker may mark as new whatever information he believes his listener desires.

Comparing a Sentence to a Picture

The previous experiments have demonstrated how the information structure of a sentence can influence the way the sentence is related to preceding information stored in memory. Can this information structure also influence the way the sentence is related to perceptual events that follow? To examine this question, we designed an experiment in which subjects read a sentence describing the relative positions of two people, followed by a schematic array that depicted two people walking in a particular direction. The task was to verify whether the sentence was a true description of the picture. The following is an example of a true sentence and the accompanying picture:

The one who is leading Dave is Jill.

Jill   Dave
←   ←

The array consisted of a woman's name, a man's name, and two arrows to indicate the direction in which each of them was walking. The woman in the array was always located on the left, and the man on the right, as shown. Thus, the subject always knew where to look for information corresponding to the new or old constituent. We were interested in whether the subjects would first check the information marked as new or the information marked as old in the sentence.

The main contrast we wanted to make concerned the cases when the picture falsified the information marked as new and those in which it falsified the information marked as old. An example of a display that falsified the new constituent would be

The one who is leading Dave is Jill.

Sue   Dave
←   ←

An example of a display that falsified the old constituent would be

The one who is leading Dave is Jill.

Jill   Mike
←   ←

Let us assume that the sentence–picture comparison proceeds as follows. First, the name of one of the people mentioned in the sentence is compared to the name in the corresponding slot in the picture. If the names mismatch, the comparison can terminate, with a response of *false*. If the names match, then the other pair of names is compared. If the second pair of names match, then the verb can be compared to the relationship depicted in the picture. If the comparison process does terminate on a mismatch, then the response latencies can indicate the order in which constituents are compared. Mismatches on constituents compared earlier will yield shorter response latencies than mismatches on constituents compared later. Thus, the relative response latencies for the two kinds of false trials should indicate whether the information marked as old or new is compared first.

There were 48 distinct sentence–picture combinations composed of the four types of sentences (pseudocleft agent, pseudocleft object, cleft agent, and cleft object), whether the new information referred to a male or a female, and six different pictures. Three of the pictures correctly depicted what was described in the sentence. The other three pictures falsified the sentence by mismatching the agent, the object, or the verb. Different pairs or triplets of names were used in the 48 trials. Twelve college students ran through three blocks of 48 trials.

Results. Latencies were shorter when there was a mismatch on the new information than when there was a mismatch on the old information. This result held for all four sentence types, as shown in Table 3. The mean difference was 167 msec, $t(11) = 2.90, p < .01$. This result suggests that subjects first compared the new information from the sentence to the appropriate part of the picture. If there was a mismatch, then the comparison process terminated and there was a quick response. If the new information matched, then they went on to compare the old information. If it mismatched, then the comparison process terminated.

In a follow-up study, we looked for an overt difference in the perceptual encoding of elements in the display, as a function of the sentential information structure. We designed an experiment very similar to the one just described,

TABLE 3

Mean Response Latency and (% Error) in Sentence–Picture Verification Experiment

	Picture falsifies			
Stimulus sentence	New		Old	
Pseudocleft agent:				
The one who is leading/following Barb is John.	2,917	(1%)	3,180	(0%)
Pseudocleft object:				
The one who Barb is leading/following is John.	3,020	(0%)	3,228	(0%)
Cleft agent:				
It is John who is leading/following Barb.	2,680	(0%)	2,821	(0%)
Cleft object:				
It is John who Barb is leading/following.	2,880	(8%)	2,933	(0%)
	2,874		3,041	

except that the subject heard the sentence and we monitored his eye movements while he scanned the perceptual display. There was a significant tendency to look first at the part of the display that contained the element corresponding to the word marked as new. For example, when a female name was marked as new, the subject tended to fixate first on the part of the display that contained the female name. This result confirms the conclusion from the latency study, that new information is verified first.

These results are consistent with another study that used a very different methodology. Cleft and pseudocleft sentences like *The one who is petting the cat is the girl* were presented auditorily, and followed by a picture presented for only 50 msec (Hornby, 1974). The subject's task was to decide whether the sentence was an accurate description of the picture. The false pictures incorrectly depicted either the constituent marked as old or the constituent marked as new, as shown in Fig. 3. Of key interest were the false cases that were erroneously labeled 'true' by the subjects. Subjects made significantly fewer of these errors when the picture falsified the new information than when it falsified the old information. If the information marked as new were verified first, then the representation of the picture would still be fresh during verification, and verification accuracy would be high. This representation would decay with time, so that when the subject subsequently verified the old information, his accuracy would decline.

The order in which the constituents are verified in all these studies may be explained by considering the normal communicative function of the old–new distinction. When information is marked as old, it is a signal to the reader that he already has identical or very closely related information stored in memory. Normally, he should not have to check whether it is true of the perceptual environment. By contrast, when information is marked as new it is a signal to the reader that he has not yet heard this particular bit of news. Thus, it might

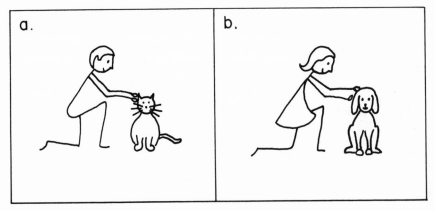

FIG. 3 One of these two pictures might follow a sentence like *The one who is petting the cat is the girl.* Picture (a) falsifies the new information in the sentence. Picture (b) falsifies the old information.

well be subjected to a validity check before being integrated into memory. Evidence concerning the information marked as new is verified before evidence concerning the information marked as old.

The discourse pointer indexes the current topic of discourse, regardless of whether the discourse is written or spoken. However, the devices that control the pointer differ across communication media. In spoken discourse, the speaker can employ intonation patterns to reflect the old or new status of various constituents. For example, the old information receives less vocal contrastive stress than the new information; this is particularly true for nouns (Chafe, 1974; Halliday, 1967). The speaker can appeal to the perceptual context to supply information for the listener's discourse pointer, and thereby make assumptions about the shared contextual information. In written discourse, the writer and reader are removed in time and space, so the pointer must be controlled almost entirely through the devices of language itself.

USING THE DISCOURSE POINTER IN WRITING

In the preceding section, we explored the cognitive processes used in integrating information across sentences. The primary focus was on the processing mechanisms and the time they take to integrate a sentence as a function of its linguistic status. This section explores the problem from the viewpoint of writing. We will explore the correspondence between the rules of writing and the mechanisms of comprehension.

Stylists and writing teachers have evolved certain guidelines for writing good prose by analyzing examples of good and bad writing and by relying on their own trained introspection. These rules are often compiled in books with titles such as "The Art of Readable Writing" or "How to Speak, Write, and Think More Effectively." The rules concern the kinds of words or sentences that a writer should use, as well as more global guidelines for organizing various kinds of prose. In this section, we will be concerned primarily with rules for making sentences fit together. We will show that these rules tend to generate prose that facilitates the reader's comprehension.

The Serial Order of Old and New Information

The processing distinction between old and new information that we have examined has also been discussed by writing teachers. In particular, they have been concerned with the serial order in which the old and new components occur. One standard guideline is to place the new information at the end of a sentence. For example, Strunk and White (1959) advise writers to "place the emphatic words of a sentence at the end":

> The proper place in the sentence for the word or group of words that the writer desires to make most prominent is usually at the end. The word or group of words entitled to this position of prominence is usually the logical predicate, that is, the *new* element in the sentence . . . (p. 26)

Similarly, Flesch (1946) advises writers to "Go from the rule to the exception, from the familiar to the new." The implicit psychological assumption is that the old information will establish a framework. Establishing this framework is equivalent to setting the discourse pointer to a particular concept before presenting the new information. After the pointer has been set, it is easier to integrate the new information with the previous context.

In sentences that do not have an explicit marking of the old and new information, the information at the end of the sentence is usually assumed to be new (Halliday, 1967). For example, in a simple active, transitive sentence such as *John loves Mary,* the fact that John loves someone is interpreted as old information and the identity of that someone, Mary, is interpreted as new. Of course, the context can change this. For example, in response to *Who loves Mary?* it is appropriate to say *John loves Mary.* But in the absence of any other context, the last part of the sentence tends to be interpreted as new information.

The judgments of naive subjects tend to corroborate Halliday's linguistic analysis of active and passive sentences (Hornby, 1972). When asked to judge what active sentences were about (i.e., what the old information was), 62% of the raters said that the sentence was about the agent. For passives, 65% said that the sentence was about the recipient. In both these cases, the constituent at the beginning of the sentence was judged to be the old information, and by default the constituent at the end was judged as new. In sentences like clefts and pseudoclefts, which explicitly mark the old—new distinction, the agreement between the subjects' judgments and the linguistic analysis was even higher. But in sentences that don't explicitly mark the distinction, about two-thirds of the subjects interpreted the element at the end of a sentence as the new one.

One literary device that makes use of the old–new structure to integrate two successive sentences is dovetailing. Two sentences are dovetailed if the beginning of the second sentence has the same referent as the end of the first sentence (Eastman, 1970). Consider the following two dovetailed sentences:

> What we must never neglect is the will to win. The determination to survive can extend a man's resources.

The new information in the first sentence emphasizes "the will to win" and the discourse pointer is set to the proposition that the will to win is important. Then the second sentence refers to this proposition at the very beginning with the words "the determination to survive" and adds the new information ". . . can extend a man's resources." The same two sentences are less comprehensible when they are not dovetailed:

> What we must never neglect is the will to win. A man's resources can be extended by the determination to survive.

In this case, the passive sentence signals that "a man's resources" should be old information, but there has been no mention of this concept and so the discourse pointer does not index it. Consequently, the reader must temporarily store that element until the pragmatically old information is introduced at the end of the sentence. Dovetailing is an effective writing device because it uses the information structure of the sentences being combined to optimize the integrative processes in comprehension.

Guidelines for writing may suggest placing the new information at the end of a sentence, but do good writers take this advice? An essay by Bertrand Russell, "The Elements of Ethics," has been analyzed in terms of the information structure of the sentences (Smith, 1971). The sentences in this essay are quite long and generally complex. However, Russell consistently constructed the sentences so that the most important information unit, the new information, occurred in the final position. Of the sentences Smith was able to classify, 86% had the new information at the end. The analysis of Russell's essay indicates that effective communication of complex ideas is mediated by a prose style that facilitates comprehension. Moreover, it shows that literary analysis need not remain the exclusive domain of the artist, but can be opened to a science of literary aesthetics based on psycholinguistic processes.

Repetition of Key Words

Another device that facilitates the integration of ideas from different sentences is the repetition of a key word or concept. In fact, recent experiments indicate that it is easier to comprehend a paragraph that has several references to a restricted number of concepts than one that introduces many new, different concepts (Kintsch, Kozminsky, Streby, McKoon, & Keenan, 1975). An example of a passage that contained many repetitions and a small number of different concepts is the following:

> The Greeks loved beautiful art. When the Romans conquered the Greeks, they copied them, and thus learned to create beautiful art.

Notice that the passage above has two repetitions of *the Greeks,* two repetitions of *beautiful art,* and two instances of pronominalization. The reading time for this kind of passage was compared to a passage with approximately the same number of words, but few pronominal referents or repetitions:

> The Babylonians built a beautiful garden on a hill. They planted lovely flowers, constructed fountains, and designed a pavilion for the queen's pleasure.

This passage has no repetition of key words and only one instance of a pronominal referent, and refers to many different concepts.

The passages with repetitions and pronominal reference took less time to read than the passages without repetitions. Moreover, subjects also remembered the passages with repetitions better, perhaps because the repetitions resulted in a more integrated memory structure. A passage with many repetitions has a relatively small amount of new information in each sentence and instead has more familiar, old elements. It is easier to process propositions that build upon old information rather than ones that continually introduce new concepts. Kintsch and his colleagues suggest that "propositions that contain new concepts require an additional processing step on the part of the reader. Not only must a proposition itself be inferred from the text, but the new concept apparently requires some special processing in that it must be encoded. Old concepts, on the other hand, need not be reencoded. A reference to the already encoded representation is sufficient, in this case." This research demonstrates how repeated reference to a central concept affects the way sentences are integrated during comprehension. Not surprisingly, writing stylists have suggested that "the repetition of the key word or synonyms of those words will build the coherence of a passage" (Eastman, 1970, p. 217).

Intersentential Connectives

Another device that establishes the relationship between sentences is the intersentential connective, such as *therefore, because, however,* and *on the other hand.* Consider the following paragraph:

> Edgar wanted to go into forestry. Granted, the hours were long and the pay was low. Nevertheless, he wanted to become a forest ranger.

This paragraph flows relatively smoothly from sentence to sentence primarily because of the information provided by the intersentential connectives. The first sentence sets the discourse pointer to the propositions stating that Edgar wanted to go into forestry. Then the connective *granted* indicates that the second sentence will provide an opposing argument. Without this connective, the second sentence would appear to present a supporting argument, which is contrary to the notion that long hours and low pay are negative attributes of a job. So the connective indicates how the second sentence is related to the proposition designated by the discourse pointer. Similarly, the connective *nevertheless* indicates that the third sentence will return to the original line of argument. In general, the connectives indicate the relationship between the proposition designated by the pointer and the current sentence.

Connectives can be classified in terms of the intersentence relations they denote. The following list (adapted from Brooks & Warren, 1970; Eastman, 1970) provides a representative analysis of connectives.

To show that the same topic continues: this, that, these, such, the same.

To introduce another item in the same series: another, again, a second (third, etc.), further, furthermore, moreover, similarly, likewise, too, finally, also.

To introduce another item in a time series: next, then, later on, afterwards, finally.

To introduce an example or illustration of what has been said: for instance, for example, specifically.

To introduce a consequence of what has just been said: accordingly, thus, therefore, then, as a result, hence, consequently, so.

To introduce a restatement of what has just been said: in other words, to put it differently, that is to say.

To introduce a concluding item or summary: finally, altogether, all in all, the point is, in conclusion, to summarize.

To introduce material that opposes what has just been said: but, however, on the other hand, on the contrary.

To introduce a concession to an opposing view: to be sure, undoubtedly, granted, of course.

To show that the original line of argument is resuming after a concession: still, nevertheless, nonetheless, all the same, even though.

Intersentential connectives relate the sentences of a paragraph to each other much as verbs relate the constituents of a sentence. In cases where the connective does not appear in the text, the reader must infer the relationship between the sentences by drawing on his knowledge of the referential situation. The integrative process should be shorter in duration when connectives do appear and thus make the inference process unnecessary.

Anaphoric Reference

Anaphoric reference is a device that allows a writer to refer back to a previously mentioned concept by appealing to the previous mention. For example, in the sentences, *Edgar certainly loves cars. He dotes on his '56 Chevy, he* in the second sentence refers back to Edgar. The two sentences are integratable because the referent of the pronoun in the second sentence is designated by the discourse pointer at the time the second sentence is being processed. By contrast, consider a different version of these sentences: *Edgar certainly loves cars. Joyce hates them. He dotes on his '56 Chevy.* The reader might have some difficulty in comprehending the referent of *he* in the third sentence, even though it is logically unambiguous. The reason for the difficulty is that after the second sentence the discourse pointer is set to the proposition that Joyce hates cars. The *he* in the third sentence does not refer to Joyce, so the reader is forced to search for the appropriate referent elsewhere. This example indicates how anaphoric reference interacts with the discourse pointer. We will consider this interaction in more detail for two kinds of anaphoric reference, pronominalization and definite description.

The use of a pronoun to denote a concept presupposes that the concept is known to the listener. The referent may have been communicated in the preceding discourse, as in the example of Edgar and the car, or the referent may be obvious from the perceptual context, for example, *Look out! It's falling!* Pronominalization requires that the listener search his representation of the discourse for the referent of the pronoun. The search will start at the contents of the discourse pointer.

A recent study externalized some of the search processes in comprehension triggered by pronouns in a text (Cooper, 1974). The subjects in this experiment listened to a passage; for example, one passage concerned a trip to Africa, mentioning a dog, a zebra, a group of peacocks, and so forth. At the same time, subjects were looking at a set of pictures that included these objects. As one might expect, subjects tended to look at the picture of the object that was being mentioned. Subjects also tended to fixate the referential picture when a pronoun occurred. Looking at the appropriate picture presumably correlates with the memory search for the referent of the pronoun.

When two sentences are linguistically related by pronominal reference, they tend to be comprehended and remembered together. In one interesting demonstration of this phenomenon, subjects listened to compound sentences whose clauses were linked by the conjunction *and* or by pronominal reference (Lesgold, 1972). For example, among the sentences conjoined with *and* was the following:

The blacksmith was skilled and the anvil was dented and the blacksmith pounded the anvil.

The following is the same sentence with a pronominal reference:

The blacksmith was skilled and he pounded the anvil which was dented.

After listening to a series of such sentences, the subjects were given prompt words and were asked to recall the gist of the sentences. Recall was better in two ways when the sentence had pronominal reference than when it was conjoined with *and*. First, subjects recalled more words from the pronominal sentences. Second, they recalled more words of the clause that *did not* contain the prompt word. The latter result is important because it suggests that the information from the two clauses was more likely to be integrated in memory when a pronominal referent linked them.

The definite article *the* is another type of anaphoric reference, one that can indicate that the modified noun has been referred to in the preceding context. By contrast, the indefinite article *a* often modifies a noun whose referent is new (cf. Karttunen, 1971). The role of the article is especially important within discourse, since the choice of a definite or indefinite article may signal whether two nouns are coreferential. For example, the sentences *Yesterday, Beth sold her Chevy. Today, Glen bought the car* imply that the same car entered into both transactions. The sentences would have a very different meaning if the indefinite article *a* replaced *the: Yesterday, Beth sold her Chevy. Today, Glen bought a car.* Hence, the definite or indefinite articles tell the listener how to integrate the two clauses.

The definite article, like a pronoun, assumes that the referent exists. As an example, consider the following sentences from Karttunen (1971):

(1) a. Bill has a car.   b. It is black.
         c. The car is black.

Either sentence (1b) or (1c) could plausibly follow sentence (1a). However, consider the following sequence:

(2) a. Bill doesn't have a car.   b. *It is black.
         c. *The car is black.

Neither sentence (2b) nor (2c) can follow sentence (2a) because they presuppose the existence of a car that does not exist. When such existential presuppositions are violated comprehension takes longer, as has been demonstrated by Haviland and Clark (1974). Their subjects read pairs of sentences like the following and pressed a button to indicate when they had understood the second sentence:

(3)   a. We got some beer out of the trunk.
       b. The beer was warm.
(4)   a. Andrew was especially fond of beer.
       b. The beer was warm.

The definite article in sentences (3b) and (4b) presupposes the existence of some particular beer. Sentence (3a) establishes the existence of some particular beer (namely, the beer that was taken from the trunk), but sentence (4a) does not. As predicted, subjects had longer comprehension times for sentence (4b) than for sentence (3b). The difference in comprehension times demonstrates that the reader tries to relate the meaning of the second sentence to the representation established by the prior sentence.

Inappropriate anaphoric reference can also disrupt the comprehension of larger units of text, such as passages. Presenting the sentences of a passage in a scrambled order disrupts shadowing performance to a greater degree if the passage contains more anaphoric reference (Rosenberg & Lambert, 1974). In other words, the more closely the original sentences were related, the more disruptive was the violation of the passage structure. The results show that even in a shadowing task, people use anaphoric reference as a cue to comprehension; scrambling the passage structure makes the cue misleading.

Much like pronouns, definite articles encourage people to integrate sentences in comprehension and in memory. This was demonstrated in an experiment in which subjects read a list of sentences that could form a coherent passage (de Villiers, 1974). The subjects were not told that the sentences could be related to each other. In fact, when the sentences contain indefinite articles they seem to be unrelated, as the following excerpt demonstrates:

A man bought a dog.
A child wanted an animal.
A father drove to his house.
A cottage stood near a park.
A boy was delighted with a gift.
A twosome went exploring along
   a path into a woods.

When the indefinite articles are replaced with definite articles, the same sequence forms a story:

A man bought a dog.
The child wanted the animal.
The father drove to his house.
The cottage stood near the park.
The boy was delighted with the gift.
The twosome went exploring along
   the path into the woods.

Each subject was presented one of these versions, a single sentence at a time. About half of the subjects in the definite article condition reported that the sentences seemed to form a story. These subjects recalled more sentences and had more intersentence lexical substitutions (e.g., substituting *dog* for *animal* in recalling the second sentence). By contrast, the subjects in the indefinite-article condition did not think that the sentences formed a story. Their recall was poorer, and they did not make coreferential substitution errors. The definite articles increase the probability that readers will integrate the sentences, and when they do integrate them, recall is improved.

Summary

In this part of the chapter, we examined a number of linguistic devices and literary rules from the viewpoint of comprehension processes. Devices such as dovetailing, repetition of key words, and intersentential connectives set the discourse pointer so that the reader is prepared to integrate the next clause or sentence. This approach suggests that "good" writing may optimize the reader's comprehension processes. However, not all good literature is written to be optimally comprehensible. For example, stream-of-consciousness writing is not meant to facilitate comprehension, but rather, to induce a sense of confusion. While our approach is not appropriate for all writing and comprehension tasks, it is applicable in the many cases where the primary goal is efficient communication of information.

OVERVIEW

At the beginning of this chapter, we argued that understanding spoken or written discourse involves more than just deriving an abstract semantic representation for each individual sentence. Comprehension involves relating the words and clauses in the sentence to other information, often information in the previous part of the discourse or information encoded from the perceptual context. At this point, it might be helpful to review some of the properties of this integrative process.

The integrative process includes a search through the working memory to find information related to the current phrase or sentence. The search seems to begin at the contents of the discourse pointer, the current topic. The search is fastest when the currently processed sentence is directly related to the contents of the discourse pointer. However, the search can go beyond the discourse pointer to other information in the working memory. One of the reported experiments demonstrated that the duration of the search increases as the reader searches through more information in memory.

The search process is directed, in part, by various linguistic devices. We have examined some of these devices, such as the clause structure of cleft and pseudocleft sentences, question-and-answer sequences, definite and indefinite articles, pronominal reference, key-word repetition, and the intonation patterns in spoken discourse. What a device marks as old information is to be matched with other information in memory. What is marked as new may have to be added to previous knowledge in the working memory. Thus, these devices function as instructions to the listener to either find certain pieces of information in memory or construct a representation of new information. If the device is used inappropriately – for example, if the reader does not possess some information that the sentence directs him to find – then integration takes longer. The additional time (between .2 and 1.4 sec in the reported experiments) may reflect the time needed to reinterpret the sentence or build a new structure in memory.

The effect of these various linguistic devices demonstrates that the search for relevant information is more than a generalized search for related concepts, more than a spreading activation among concepts in semantic memory with a search for intersections among the concepts (cf. Collins & Loftus, 1975; Quillian, 1968). In all of the experiments reported here, the same concepts were mentioned when the linguistic device was appropriate and when it was inappropriate. Presumably, spreading activation would operate similarly in both cases. The pronounced effects of the linguistic structure indicate that these devices direct and program the search processes.

Finally, we argued that theoretical models of integrative processes can be closely related to models of prose writing. Prose is easily comprehensible if it makes optimal use of linguistic devices to guide psychological processes. The structure of a paragraph guides the reader's comprehension processes, from the old to the new. Various rules of writing that have been induced intuitively can be understood in terms of their processing implications for the reader.

In summary, it is clear that integrative processes play a primary role in language comprehension. We now have techniques to study how these processes are executed in various circumstances. The studies reported here have demonstrated that the integrative processes influence the speed with which we understand sentences in context and the accuracy with which we later remember them.

ACKNOWLEDGMENTS

The order of authors is arbitrary. This chapter represents a collaborative effort. The project was supported in part by the National Institute of Education, Grant NIE-G-74-0016, and by the National Institude of Mental Health, Grant MH-07722, U.S. Department of Health, Education and Welfare.

REFERENCES

Brooks, C., & Warren, R. P. *Modern rhetoric.* (3rd ed.). New York: Harcourt, Brace & World, 1970.
Carpenter, P. A., & Just, M. A. Reading comprehension as eyes see it. In M. A. Just & P. A.

Carpenter (Eds.), *Cognitive processes in comprehension.* Hillsdale, N.J.: Lawrence Erlbaum Associates, 1977, in press.

Chafe, W. L. *Meaning and the structure of language.* Chicago & London: University of Chicago Press, 1970.

Chafe, W. L. Language and consciousness. *Language,* 1974, **50,** 111–133.

Collins, A. M., & Loftus, E. F. A spreading activation theory of semantic processing. *Psychological Review,* 1975, **82,** 407–428.

Cooper, R. M. The control of eye fixation by the meaning of spoken language. *Cognitive Psychology,* 1974, **6,** 84–107.

de Villiers, P. A. Imagery and theme in recall of connected discourse. *Journal of Experimental Psychology,* 1974, **103,** 263–168.

Eastman, R. M. *Style.* New York: Oxford University Press, 1970.

Flesch, R. *How to write, speak, and think more effectively.* New York: Harper, 1946.

Halliday, M. A. K. Notes on transitivity and theme in English: II. *Journal of Linguistics,* 1967, **3,** 199–244.

Haviland, S. E., & Clark, H. H. What's new? Acquiring new information as a process in comprehension. *Journal of Verbal Learning and Verbal Behavior,* 1974, **13,** 512–521.

Hornby, P. A. The psychological subject and predicate. *Cognitive Psychology,* 1972, **3,** 632–642.

Hornby, P. A. Surface structure and presupposition. *Journal of Verbal Learning and Verbal Behavior,* 1974, **13,** 530–538.

Karttunen, L. Discourse referents. Bloomington, Indiana: Indiana University Linguistics Club manuscript, 1971.

Kintsch, W., Kozminsky, E., Streby, W. J., McKoon, G., & Keenan, J. M. Comprehension and recall of text as a function of content variables. *Journal of Verbal Learning and Verbal Behavior,* 1975, **14,** 196–214.

Lesgold, A. M. Pronominalization: A device for unifying sentences in memory. *Journal of Verbal Learning and Verbal Behavior,* 1972, **11,** 316–323.

Quillian, M. R. Semantic memory. In M. Minsky (Ed.), *Semantic information processing.* Cambridge, Mass.: MIT Press, 1968.

Rosenberg, S., & Lambert, W. E. Contextual constraints and the perception of speech. *Journal of Experimental Psychology,* 1974, **102,** 178–180.

Smith, C. S. Sentences in discourse: An analysis of a discourse by Bertrand Russell. *Journal of Linguistics,* 1971, **7,** 213–235.

Strunk, W., & White, E. B. *The elements of style.* New York: MacMillan, 1959.

8

Inferences in Comprehension

Herbert H. Clark

Stanford University

One evening as Margaret and Jeffrey were relaxing at home, the telephone rang and Margaret answered.

"It's George," she told Jeffrey after a short time. "He's having a party Saturday night and wants us to come. Are you interested in going?"

How should I answer? Jeffrey asked himself. From the way she asked the question, she can't be very anxious to go. Yes, I'd very much like to go, but it wouldn't be fair to drag her to something she doesn't like. I'd better give her a way out.

"It doesn't make much difference to me one way or the other," Jeffrey answered.

His answer is so neutral, he can't really want to go, thought Margaret. And if he doesn't want to go, I certainly wouldn't want to force him. He'd be hard to live with all day Sunday.

"Okay, then, I will make excuses for us," she said, and after a short interchange with George, she said goodbye, hung up the telephone, and sat down.

"George's party sounded as if it would be a lot of fun," she said after a moment. "I'm sorry you didn't want to go."

"*Me* not want to go? But it was *you* who said you didn't want to go. I was just giving you a way out."

The twists and turns of this conversation illustrate nicely how much of what we understand comes from what we infer. Jeffrey had quite legitimately understood Margaret as having said she didn't really want to go, even though the words she used – *Are you interested in going?* – by themselves hardly convey this message. Jeffrey understood what he thought she meant by drawing an inference. If Margaret had genuinely wanted to go, he thought, she would have said *I'd love to go – how about you?* or *We can make it, can't we?* or *It sounds great and Saturday night is free, isn't it?* – a question revealing enthusiasm while asking Jeffrey for his answer. What she did say, however, was *Are you interested*

243

in going? This was a noncommittal question that put the burden of the decision on Jeffrey. And when Margaret put the burden of the decision on him, Jeffrey knew, she wanted him to decide because she wouldn't go otherwise. As a result, Jeffrey decided that she meant she didn't want to go. Margaret's understanding of Jeffrey's answer took just as complicated a route. She saw that his answer, *It doesn't make much difference to me one way or the other,* was noncommittal, and for Jeffrey a noncommittal answer really meant "no." Hence, what he meant here was that he didn't want to go. Although Margaret made the mistake of asking so noncommittal a question in the first place, they were both right from then on to infer what they did. Margaret conventionally *did* mean she didn't want to go when she used a noncommittal question, and Jeffrey conventionally *did* mean he didn't want to go when he used a noncommittal answer.

Authorized Inferences

What is illustrated in this conversation is something I will call the *authorized* inference, an inference the speaker intended the listener to draw as an integral part of the message being conveyed. Jeffrey meant Margaret to understand that he didn't want to go to the party when he said *It doesn't make much difference to me one way or the other.* He would judge her as having misunderstood if she hadn't taken it that way. On the other hand, many inferences we draw in conversations are unauthorized, inferences the speaker did not necessarily mean to convey with a particular sentence. I will return to the distinction between authorized and unauthorized inferences later on, for it turns out to be crucial for theories of comprehension.

In the study of comprehension, it is important to discover how we draw authorized inferences as we listen to people talk. Comprehension is best thought of as problem solving. The problem to be solved is, What did the speaker mean? or more accurately, What did the speaker intend us to understand by what he said? We solve this problem, as Margaret and Jeffrey's conversation suggests, using three main ingredients:

1. The explicit content of the sentence.
2. The circumstances surrounding the utterance.
3. A tacit contract the speaker and listener have agreed upon as to how sentences are to be used.

Roughly speaking, we take what is actually said (1), register the relevant features of the present circumstances (2), implicitly consult the contract we have with the speaker about what such a sentence would mean under such circumstances (3), and from this deduce the intended meaning of the utterance. To illustrate, Margaret took what Jeffrey actually said (*It doesn't make much difference to me one way or the other*), registered the relevant circumstances (he is answering a question about going to a party; he and I are on intimate terms), and consulted their tacit contract about the use of such sentences (a noncommittal answer between intimates means a qualified "no"). From the ingredients as she perceived them, she deduced that Jeffrey meant "No, I don't really want to go to the party."

This, of course, is only a rough characterization of how we understand what other people say. Before it can have any real substance, we must be able to specify (a) the tacit contracts people have with each other; (b) the inferences these contracts lead to; and (c) the way listeners actually use the contracts in drawing authorized inferences. In this chapter, I will take up a fundamental type of authorized inference and follow it through these three specifications with some care. In the first section, I will take up a tacit contract called the given—new contract, one that Haviland and I have recently discussed in a series of papers (Clark & Haviland, 1974, 1977; Haviland & Clark, 1974). In the second section, I will present a taxonomy — as yet incomplete — of the inferences people draw on the basis of this contract. In the final section, I will discuss some ways in which listeners draw the inferences they do. Now, although I will be concerned with one particular type of inference, its lessons are very broad indeed. Above all else it reaffirms how much of comprehension is problem solving of the most sophisticated kind, for it demands extensive use of general knowledge, subtle judgments about the circumstances present, and in the end just plain skill.

THE GIVEN—NEW CONTRACT

What I will be concerned with is reference — to objects, events, and states of affairs. When someone says *The man over there is gullible,* he is using part of the sentence, namely, *the man over there,* to refer to a particular object, and he is leaving it to us to infer what object that is. We draw this inference by consulting the content of the sentence (*the man over there*), the circumstances surrounding the utterance (e.g., the direction of the speaker's gaze), and a tacit contract about the use of noun phrases for reference. On the basis of all this, we decide that he is referring to Gerald, a man standing nearby. Reference of this kind, then, is an example par excellence of authorized inference. The definite noun phrase, however, is not the only linguistic device available for referring, and the referents themselves do not have to be objects. When someone says *What Maxine did was leave,* he is using *what Maxine did* to refer to an act Maxine carried out, and when he says *What Maxine was was brave,* he is using *what Maxine was* to refer to some state of affairs that holds for Maxine.

The Function of Given and New Information

All these instances of reference fall under what linguists have called given information as distinguished from new information (see Halliday, 1967, 1970; Chafe, 1970, 1974; Kuno, 1972, 1975; and with the terms *presupposition* and *focus* in place of *given* and *new,* Akmajian, 1973; Chomsky, 1971; Jackendoff, 1972). In English, each assertion is said to convey given information and new information, a distinction that is obligatorily indicated in its syntax and intonation. The part of the sentence said to convey given information is conventionally required to carry information that the listener already knows or could know. The part of the sentence said to convey new information is conventionally required to convey information the listener doesn't already know but that the speaker would like to get across. In *What Maxine did was leave, Maxine did something* conveys given information — the listener is expected to know that Maxine did something — and *Maxine left* conveys new information — the listener is not expected to know that Maxine left. As this example makes clear, the distinction is not reflected in one set of words versus another, but in one set of underlying propositions versus another.

Why are we obliged to distinguish between given and new information? The obvious answer is that they serve an important function in communication. But for them to be useful, the speaker and listener must agree to use them in the conventional way. The speaker must try to construct his utterances so that the given information actually *does* convey information he believes the listener already knows or could know, and so that the new information actually *does* contain information he believes the listener doesn't already know. The listener, for his part, agrees to interpret each utterance on the assumption that the speaker is trying to do this. In short, the speaker and listener agree to hold to what Haviland and I have called the given–new contract, a tacit agreement between the speaker and listener about how given and new information are to be used in sentences. It is only by holding to this agreement that the speaker and listener can gain any advantage from the distinction.

For the listener, the main consequence of this tacit agreement is that he can make use of the given–new strategy. (For more detail, see Clark & Haviland, 1974, 1977; Haviland & Clark, 1974). He is assumed to absorb each assertion into memory in three steps:

Step 1: Identify the given and new information.
Step 2: Search memory for a proposition matching the given information and call it the "antecedent."
Step 3: Add the new information to memory by replacing the given information by its antecedent.

To see how this strategy works, imagine that the listener is confronted with the sentence *It was Maxine who hit Max.* At Step 1, he divides the sentence into given and new thus:

1.   Given: X hit Max.
     New: X = Maxine

At Step 2, he realizes that he should already know about an event in which someone hit Max, so he searches memory for such an event. When he finds one, say, E_{31} *hit Max* ("some entity labeled E_{31} hit Max"), he assumes that it must be the event the speaker was referring to with the given information, so he labels it thus:

2. Antecedent: E_{31} hit Max.

At Step 3, he notes that since X corresponds to E_{31}, he should replace the X in $X = Maxine$ by E_{31} and add the resulting proposition to memory thus:

3. Add: E_{31} = Maxine

By this time his memory has been updated by the new information in this sentence yet has not been cluttered by all the information in the sentence he already knew – the given information. More important, he has added the new information at just that place in memory where the speaker intended it to be added.

Implicatures

This strategy works smoothly and precisely in many very simple cases. Consider Sequence (A):

(A)   I saw someone hit Max. It was Maxine who hit him.

In order to give self-contained examples, I will assume that the only information the listener hearing the second sentence has in episodic memory is the information conveyed by the first sentence. Hence, when the listener applies the given–new strategy to the second sentence, the only place he can search for antecedents is in the information provided by the first sentence. In this instance, the listener will search for an antecedent to X *hit Max* (the given information of the second sentence); he will find a matching proposition directly expressed in the first sentence; he will call it the antecedent (say, E_{58} *hit Max*); and after changing the new information to E_{58} = *Maxine,* he will add it to memory.

It is far more typical, however, for there to be no direct antecedent in memory. Consider Sequence (B):

(B)   Max had a black eye. It was Maxine who hit him.

Once again, the listener will search memory for a proposition matching X *hit Max,* but in this instance he will not find one. *Max had a black eye* simply does not say, or even necessarily imply, that someone hit Max, and Step 2 in the strategy will fail. In instances like this, Haviland and I have assumed, the listener attempts to introduce an antecedent that he connects to information already in memory in a way he thinks the speaker must have intended it to be connected. This process is called *bridging,* and it results in the addition of a set of one or more propositions to memory, a set that is called an *implicature.* In Sequence (B), the listener would most likely add this implicature to memory:

(B')   Max had a black eye because someone hit him.

Once he has done this, of course, he has a proposition that can serve as the antecedent, namely, *someone hit Max,* and he can add the new information to memory appropriately.

The implicature in (B′), I argue, is an integral part of the message the speaker of (B) is trying to get across; indeed, it is just as much a part of the message as the information (B) conveys explicitly. My reasoning here is this: If I were to say (B) to Susan Haviland, I would mean for the proposition *X hit Max* in the second sentence to refer to some particular event. More than that, I would not have used the sentence unless I was sure she could figure out precisely what event I was referring to. Of course, I know well that she does not yet realize directly that someone hit Max, and I know she knows I know it. Yet I am confident that if I pretended she knew that someone hit Max, she would be able to figure out just what event I was talking about. I am sure she would reason this way: "Ah, if Clark can pretend that I already know that someone hit Max, he must think that that should be obvious from what I already know. I already know that Max had a black eye, which could have had any number of causes. But given Clark's pretense, he must intend me to think that it was caused by someone hitting Max. Without this inference he could not expect me to identify the referent for *X hit Max.*" In listening to ongoing speech, of course, we are not aware of reasoning like this, but that makes it no less plausible. Many implicatures are difficult to account for without such reasoning.

In its most general form, then, the tacit agreement the speaker and listener have with each other on the use of given and new information goes like this:

> Given–New Contract: The speaker agrees to try to construct the given and new information of each utterance in context (a) so that the listener is able to compute from memory the unique antecedent that was intended for the given information, and (b) so that he will not already have the new information attached to the antecedent. (Clark & Haviland, 1977, p. 9)

This contract is critical to the listener. It allows him to be confident that the speaker had referents in mind in the first place, and it gives him a way to figure out what those referents are. If the speaker is cooperative and is adhering to the given–new contract, the listener should be able to identify the referents uniquely on the basis of what he can be confident the speaker thinks the listener knows. Elsewhere, Haviland and I have examined some consequences of this contract. Here I will take up the problem of implicatures.

VARIETIES OF GIVEN–NEW IMPLICATURES

The implicatures the given–new contract leads us to draw as we listen to others talk take many forms. To give some idea of their variety, I will present a brief taxonomy of these implicatures as found in naturally occurring speech. As with any taxonomy, this one is hardly complete. No taxonomy can be truly complete without a theory to explain it, and there does not appear to be any theory for this taxonomy at this time. All one can hope for is that this taxonomy will suggest the kind of theory to be worked out in the future. As before, I will illustrate each implicature with a two-sentence sequence in which the first sentence is meant to constitute all of the episodic information the listener has available to him as he listens to the second sentence. That is, the only place he can search for antecedents, or bridges to antecedents, is in the information conveyed in the first sentence. Many of the implicatures I will illustrate, however, could just as well have been inferred on the basis of nonlinguistic sources. The two-sentence sequences are simply the most convenient way of displaying the implicatures briefly and clearly.

Direct Reference

One of the commonest types of implicature is direct reference — when, for example, a noun phrase refers directly to an object, event, or state just mentioned. This type of implicature is so simple and so well known that we may overlook the fact that there is an inference required here at all. Consider the following examples:

A. Identity:
1. I met a man yesterday. The man I met yesterday told me a story.
2. I ran two miles the other day. My two-mile run the other day did me good.
3. Her house was large. The largeness of her house surprised me.

B. Pronominalization:
4. I met a man yesterday. He told me a story.
5. I ran two miles the other day. It did me good.
6. Her house was large. That surprised me.

C. Epithets:
7. I met a man yesterday. The bastard stole all my money.
8. I ran two miles the other day. The whole stupid business bored me.
9. Her house was large. The immensity made me jealous.

D. Set membership:
10. I met two people yesterday. The woman told me a story.
11. I met two doctors yesterday. The taller one told me a story.
12. I swung three times. The first swing missed the ball by a mile.

The implicatures for these four categories are straightforward. For the identity in Example (1), the implicature is roughly this:

(1') The antecedent for *the man I met yesterday* is the entity referred to by *a man*.

Obvious as this inference may be, the listener still has to draw it if he is to properly understand the second sentence in Example (1). It is conceivable that the speaker did not mean this antecedent to be the same entity as that referred to by *a man* in the first sentence, so the listener must make a leap — perhaps only a millimeter leap — in drawing the inference. I call this case identity because the referring expression *the man I met yesterday* contains all and only the information the listener knows about the entity being referred to. Examples (2) and (3) are analogous except that what is referred to in Example (2) is an event and in Example (3) a state.

For pronominalization, the principle is the same except that pronouns use only a subset of the properties that characterize the previously mentioned object, event, or state. In Example (4), the entity *he* refers to would be completely characterized as *the man I met yesterday; he* uses an abbreviated characterization that retains only the features "male" and "singular." The same goes for Examples (5) and (6). In reality, there are many expressions with which one could refer to this man, and they range in progression from the full *the man I met yesterday* down to the sparse *he: the man I met yesterday, the man I met, the man who was met yesterday, the man who was met, the man,* and *he.* Some of the conceivable expressions in this series — *the person, the adult,* and *the met one* — do not work very well in examples like (1) and (4) for reasons I do not fully understand.

Epithets, on the other hand, add information about the referent, as in this implicature for Example (7):

(7′)   The antecedent for *the bastard* is the entity referred to by *a man;* that entity is also a bastard.

Epithets turn out to be surprisingly restricted in productivity. Not just any added information will do. Replace *the bastard* in Example (7) by *the rancher, the robber,* or *the President,* and there is no longer an obvious implicature. We would normally take *the rancher, the robber,* and *the President* as referring to someone other than the man mentioned in the first sentence.

With set membership, reference is made to one or more members of a set. What the given information does is (a) identify the set and (b) provide a way of distinguishing the referent from the rest of the set. The implicature in Example (10) looks roughly like this:

(10′)   One of the entities referred to by *two people* is a woman and the other is not; this woman is the antecedent to *the woman.*

In Example (10), the noun phrase *the woman* enables us to infer (a) that its referent belongs to the set referred to by *two people* and (b) that one of the two people is a woman and the other is not. We infer (b) because if both people were women, the speaker of Example (10) could not have expected us to be able to figure out the referent uniquely. Examples (11) and (12) work along similar lines.

Indirect Reference by Association

Very often what is referred to is not an object, state, or event mentioned previously, but only something indirectly associated with such an object, state, or event (see Chafe, 1972). The associated pieces of information are sometimes completely predictable from what has been mentioned, but often they are not. Here I will give only three levels of predictability, although in reality these levels very likely lie along a continuum:

E. Necessary parts:
    13. I looked into the room. The ceiling was very high.
    14. I hit a home run. The swing had been a good one.
    15. I looked into the room. The size was overwhelming.

F. Probable parts:
    16. I walked into the room. The windows looked out into a garden.
    17. I went shopping yesterday. The walk did me good.
    18. I left at 8 p.m. The darkness made me jumpy.

G. Inducible parts:
    19. I walked into the room. The chandeliers sparkled brightly.
    20. I went shopping yesterday. The climb did me good.
    21. I left at 8 p.m. The haste was necessary given the circumstances.

The implicatures we are induced to draw here are once again obvious. In Example (13), the implicature would look something like this:

(13') The room referred to by *the room* has one and only one ceiling; that ceiling is the antecedent of *the ceiling.*

Since every room has one and only one ceiling, the ceiling is a "necessary part" of the room mentioned in the first sentence in Example (13) and is therefore easy to refer to. Similarly, the swing is a necessary event for the home run in Example (14), and the size is a necessary property of the room in Example (15). In Example (16), the implicature would be as follows:

(16') The room referred to by *the room* has more than one window; those windows are the antecedent of *the windows.*

What makes the windows only a "probable part" is the fact that not all rooms have windows, although they often do. In this example, then, the implicature adds an important bit of information, namely, that the room mentioned does have windows, and this is information that is not found anywhere else.

It is the classification "inducible parts" that shows how critical the given–new contract is for drawing these inferences. As we hear *the room* in Example (19), we could infer that the room has a floor, some walls, and a ceiling and that it might well have windows, furniture, and lights. But we would not infer, for example, that it has chandeliers. Yet this is precisely the inference that is forced by the second sentence in Example (19):

(19′) The room referred to by *the room* has chandeliers; they are the antecedent for *the chandeliers*.

Here, then, is a clear example in which the search for an antecedent has forced us to draw an inference we would not otherwise draw. By the mere act of referring, the speaker of Example (19) has induced us to build and store away in memory a piece of information that is not predictable from anything else.

Indirect Reference by Characterization

In many instances, what is referred to is an object that plays a role in an event or circumstance mentioned previously. For example, a murder is an event that requires one or more murdering agents, a murder weapon or instrument of some sort, and a victim. Once a speaker has mentioned a murder, he can refer to objects that play these roles as long as he characterizes the roles clearly. As with associated parts, roles can vary from complete predictability – all murders require a victim – to almost complete unpredictability. I will nevertheless give just two levels here:

H. Necessary roles:
    20. There was a murder yesterday. The victim was a terrorist.
    21. I went shopping yesterday. The time I started was 3 p.m.
    22. I trucked my trunk to New York. The truck was quick.
I. Inducible roles:
    23. John died yesterday. The murderer got away.
    24. John was murdered yesterday. The knife lay nearby.
    25. John went walking at noon. The park was beautiful.

The implicatures for "necessary roles" are just as we should expect. The implicature for Example (20), for example, is roughly as follows:

(20′) The event referred to by *a murder* had a murder victim; that person is the antecedent for *the victim*.

Examples (21) and (22) have similar implicatures. For the "inducible roles" we are forced to make broader leaps of inference. The implicature for Example (23) might look like this:

(23′) Some one person caused John to die yesterday; that person is the antecedent for *the murderer*.

In Example (24), we infer that the murder weapon was a knife, not a gun, a bomb, or poison. And in Example (25), we infer that John went walking in a park.

These two categories — necessary and inducible roles — cover a lot of ground, for in English, noun phrases can characterize the roles they refer to in many ways. Some have been illustrated already. The noun *victim* characterizes the role it refers to by itself, since *victim* means "person to whom something bad has happened." But the same effect could have been achieved with a noun plus restrictive adjectives or relative clauses, as in *the one who was murdered, the one who died,* or *the dead man.* Similarly, *the murderer* in Example (23) is explicitly agentive, meaning "the one who did the murder," although it could be replaced by *the one who did the murder* or something similar. Of course, the more fully the referent is characterized, the easier it is to infer its identity.

It is not always easy to separate "parts" from "roles." In Example (24), the knife was classified as a "role" in the action of murdering, not as a "part." An event, like a murder, may have another event, like stabbing, as a "part," but it cannot have a concrete object as a "part." Concrete objects play "roles" in events. Ultimately, this distinction may break down, for one could argue that stabbing, though an event, plays a role in a murder just as a knife does: The stabbing is the cause of the death. For now, it is convenient to retain the distinction. Concrete objects are "parts" of other concrete objects but play "roles" in events or states.

Temporal Relations

In many sentences — perhaps most — the given information refers back to an event — call it A (for antecedent event) — and A occurred at a particular point or period in time. Now, if A has not been mentioned before, the listener must build some temporal relationship between A and an event that *has* been mentioned before; if he does not, he will not have A anchored in time. Just as we try to anchor each object referred to to some place we already know, so we try to anchor each event referred to to some time we already know. Yet the relationship between A and previously mentioned events need not be merely temporal. It may carry an additional notion of cause, reason, or consequence. There appear to be five major classes of temporal relations:

J. Reasons:
26. John fell. What he wanted to do was scare Mary.
27. John went to the party. The one he expected to meet was Mary.
28. John had a new suit on. It was Jane he hoped to impress.

K. Causes:
29. John fell. What he did was trip on a rock.
30. John went to the party. The one who invited him was Mary.
31. John had a new suit on. It was Jane who told him to wear it.

L. Consequences:
    32. John fell. What he did was break his arm.
    33. John went to the party. The one he saw first was Mary.
    34. John met Sally. What he did was tell her about Bill.
M. Concurrences:
    35. Max lives in New York. Moritz is crazy too.
    36. Max lives in New York. Moritz isn't very sane either.
    37. Alex went to a party last night. He's going to get drunk again tonight.
N. Subsequences:
    38. John looked left. John looked right.
    39. John arrived at the party. He got himself a drink.
    40. John met Sally. They talked for ten minutes.

The implicatures in Classes J through N are easy to illustrate. A reason is something that answers the question "What for?" and a cause is something that answers the question "How come?" The implicature induced by Example (26) gives a reason:

(26′) John fell for the reason that he wanted to do something; that something is the event being referred to by *what he wanted to do.*

On the other hand, the implicature induced by Example (29) gives a cause:

(29′) John fell because he did something; that something is the event being referred to by *what he did.*

For both reasons and causes, A (the event referred to) occurs *before* the event mentioned previously. In Example (26), John's wanting to scare Mary occurred before his fall, and in Example (29) John's tripping on a rock occurred before the fall. In contrast, consequences occur *after* the previously mentioned event. So the implicature induced by Example (32) is roughly as follows:

(32′) John did something because he fell; that something is the event being referred to by *what he did.*

Thus, Examples (29) and (32) lead to exactly the opposite implicatures: In Example (29), A (the antecedent event) caused John's falling, whereas in Example (32) John's falling caused A.

The class of implicatures called concurrences are usually induced with the help of an adverb like *too, either, again,* or *still.* The implicature for Example (35) is roughly as follows (see Lakoff, 1971):

(35′) Everyone who lives in New York is crazy; therefore, Max is crazy; this state is the state being referred to by the given information *someone other than Moritz is crazy.*

In Examples (35), (36), and (37), the listener is expected to draw the implicature that being in one state, or the occurrence of one event, necessarily entails the existence of another state, or the occurrence of another event. In Example (37), the listener is expected to infer that Alex's going to the party last night necessarily entails his getting drunk at that party.

The last class of implicatures, the subsequences, are the easiest to describe but the hardest to explain. In Example (38), we would normally infer that John looked left *and then* John looked right. The second-mentioned event, we would infer, occurred immediately subsequent to the first-mentioned event. But how does this come about? The sentence *John looked right,* with the main stress on *right,* can be divided into given and new information in three distinct ways (see Chomsky, 1971; Clark & Haviland, 1977; Jackendoff, 1972):

a. Given: X happened.
    New: X = John look right
b. Given: John did X.
    New: X = look right
c. Given: John looked in X direction.
    New: X = right

These three divisions correspond to the three questions that *John looked right* can legitimately answer: (a) *What happened?* (b) *What did John do?* and (c) *Which way did John look?* Imagine that the listener takes interpretation (a). In Example (38), since it is given that something happened, the listener must find the event A that is being referred to. No event mentioned in the first sentence is compatible with John's turning right, so the listener draws the implicature that A occurred after the event mentioned previously. He would have done the same if he had interpreted *John looked right* as in (b) or (c), too. So the implicature of (38) is roughly as follows:

(38′) Something happened after John looked left; that is the event being referred to by *something happened,* the given information of *John looked right.*

Subsequences are extraordinarily common. When someone describes a number of events, allotting one event to a sentence, we normally infer that these events occurred in the order in which they were mentioned. Indeed, children are able to draw this inference before they understand words like *before* and *after* (Clark, 1971), and adults make use of this inference in reconstructing sentences from memory (Clark & Clark, 1968; Smith & McMahon, 1970). Thus, subsequence is the major way by which we sequence events as we hear them. Subsequence can be thought of as having consequence as a special case. Consequence is subsequence plus causality: The first-mentioned event not only precedes the second-mentioned event but also causes it.

From these illustrations, it is clear that the placement of two sentences adjacent to each other can be taken to imply one of at least four relationships — reason, cause, consequence, or subsequence. These are illustrated in the following four sequences:

(C) John fell.   He wanted to scare Mary.
(D) John fell.   He tripped on a rock.
(E) John fell.   He broke his arm.
(F) John fell.   He stood up.

To figure out just which of the four relationships the second sentence has to the first, the listener must look at information outside the sentences themselves. Probably the most useful information is the plausibility of the four relationships. In Sequence (E), it is implausible for John's breaking his arm to be a *reason* for his falling or for it to be a *cause* of his falling. It is quite plausible, however, that it was not only subsequent to his falling but also caused by his falling. If this is roughly correct, the route by which the listener draws the right implicature — the inference the speaker intended him to draw — is complicated. It goes something like this: The listener assumes that the speaker meant the second event to have some temporal relationship to the first. The relationship he meant could not have been an implausible one, for then the speaker could not be sure that the listener would identify it uniquely. Hence, the speaker must have meant the most obvious, the most plausible, relationship.

DRAWING INFERENCES

Here, then, is a prime example of authorized inference. The speaker wants to get his message across. As part of that message he needs to refer to objects, events, and states the listener already knows. But he cannot refer to them directly — there is no way of pointing to objects, events, and states in the listener's mind directly. He has to rely on his tacit agreement with the listener, the given–new contract. By this agreement, he is confident that if he builds sentences in a particular way, the listener will infer the identity of the referents he means. The listener views the process in much the same way. He assumes that the speaker wants to refer to objects, events, and states and that the speaker is coopera- tively relying on the given–new contract. Thus, he, the listener, can infer the identity of referents and draw other implicatures on the basis of this contract.

So far, I have briefly described the contract and classified the implicatures to which it leads. Here I turn to the process by which these implicatures might be drawn. Before I can do that, however, I must reexamine the notion of au- thorized versus unauthorized inferences.

Authorized and Unauthorized Inferences

Imagine that someone has just heard a passage describing how a washing machine works. For many investigators in psychology and artificial intelligence, this listener would be said to have understood the passage if he had come to know how a washing machine works as characterized by the passage. For them, understanding a message is synonymous, or virtually synonymous, with understanding the situation the message describes. I want to argue that this view of comprehension is incomplete because it fails to distinguish between authorized and unauthorized inferences — between inferences the speaker meant the listener to draw as an integral part of the message and inferences the listener drew without the speaker's authorization. It fails to distinguish between the intended meaning of a message and the implications of a message, a distinction that we listeners keep straight as best we can. Some examples will make this distinction clearer.

Tina is sitting in an easy chair reading a book when Michael walks into the room, leaving the door open. Tina says to Michael, "It's getting cold in here." She means for Michael to understand this as a polite request to close the door, and he understands her to mean that. Michael has thereby drawn an authorized inference, one he believes Tina meant him to draw.

Basil is a defendent in a murder trial. In his testimony, he says, "I was home at 6 p.m." By this, he means for the jury to think he believes he was home at 6 p.m. But the jury, from other evidence, realizes that Basil has just lied — he could not have been home at 6 p.m. because he was seen 60 miles away at 6:15. The jury further infers that he must have lied about the blood on his tie, too, which he said had come from a steak he had for dinner. The jury finally concludes that Basil must be the murderer. Basil, of course, did not mean this to be part of his message at all. The jury has drawn unauthorized inferences from what Basil said.

Jurgen asks Gisela the question, "Is Gordon a psychologist?" and Gisela replies, "Is the Pope Catholic?" Although Gisela's answer is not a *direct* answer to Jurgen's question, she intends him to understand it to mean, "Definitely yes," and Jurgen understands it as such. The inference that the answer is "Definitely yes," then, is one that she authorized.

Ian has just arrived home after a late night at work, and his wife Maggie calls out, "Is that you, honey?" Now Maggie meant for Ian to take this as a mere question of concern, one to be answered by "Yes" or some such response. But Ian infers something more. He recalls that whenever she has called out like this before, she has worried all evening, watched television for consolation, and been cranky all the next day. He therefore infers that she worried and watched television that night and that she will be cranky the next day. Maggie clearly did not mean to convey this by what she said, and so Ian has drawn unauthorized inferences.

Ned and Jane have just seen a very bad movie, and Jane says to Ned, "Wasn't that terrific?" She means for Ned to take this as a sarcastic exclamation about the movie, and he understands it this way. He has drawn the authorized inference that she thought the movie was terrible.

Susan is in the financial district doing business when she decides to stop at Sam's Bar for a midafternoon cocktail. As she reaches the door, a bartender steps in her way and says, "Sorry, the bar has just closed." He means her to understand this as a statement of fact – the bar has just closed – plus an apology that he cannot help it. She realizes that this is what he meant and walks away. But she draws further inferences. Since bars do not close until later, he was barring her deliberately. Financial districts are notorious for their male-only bars, so he must have been excluding her because she was a woman. Although he did not mean to insult her, she drew the unauthorized inference that he had. Susan could therefore distinguish between what the bartender meant her to understand and the other things she inferred.

From these examples, it is not hard to see what distinguishes authorized from unauthorized inferences. For each authorized inference, the speaker intended the listener to draw an inference, and the listener realized that the speaker intended him to do so. For each unauthorized inference, there was no such intention on the speaker's part nor any attribution of such an intention on the listener's part. For each authorized inference, the speaker relied on one or another speaker–listener agreement about how sentences are to be used. Tina relied on conventions about indirect requests, Gisela on conventions about indirect answers, and Jane on conventions about sarcasm. For the unauthorized inferences, there were no such agreements. The listeners in these instances drew inferences from the intended meaning together with other information, relying on logical requirements *outside* any conventions about the use of language.

The line between authorized and unauthorized inferences, of course, is not always as clean as these examples suggest. At times we may think an agreement is in force when it is not and therefore believe the inference we draw is authorized when it is not. Speakers can make mistakes too, as when they utter sentences that by normal agreements should be taken as meaning something they did not intend them to mean. Yet the distinction between authorized and unauthorized inferences is one that speakers try to keep track of. For example, Susan knew what the bartender meant her to believe when he said, "Sorry, the bar has just closed," even though she took it in quite a different light.

Inferring the Identity of Referents

Earlier in the chapter, I briefly described the given–new strategy by which listeners are assumed to integrate the novel information of an assertion into memory. It has three steps:

Step 1: Identify the given and new information.

Step 2: Search memory for a proposition matching the given information and call it the antecedent.

Step 3: Add the new information to memory by replacing the given information by its antecedent.

It is at Step 2 in this strategy that listeners infer the identity of referents, drawing all of the implicatures described in the earlier section on varieties of implicature. Yet as it now stands, Step 2 is not very illuminating. It appears to involve an intricate process of problem solving in which authorized inferences and the given—new contract play central roles. Though there is little to go on other than the logical considerations discussed so far, one can describe a rough but plausible model for the process by which listeners draw these implicatures.

Like other kinds of problem solving, the process of inferring referents has a goal, a "data base" or store of information, a set of constraints or boundary conditions, and some fundamental mental operations. Briefly, the process requires the following four components:

Goal: Identify the referent of the given information.

Data Base: Information in previous sentences; real-world knowledge of objects, events, and states.

Constraints: Given—new contract

1. The referent matches the given information.
2. The referent is one the speaker believes the listener can figure out from what he knows.
3. The referent is unique.

Mental operations:

1. Build a candidate referent from the data base.
2. Check whether a candidate referent conforms to the constraints.

To proceed, the listener sets up the goal of identifying the referent, and attempts to find a way to achieve it. To do this he builds a candidate referent from the data base and checks whether it conforms to the constraints. If it does, he assumes that his goal has been reached and that he has identified the referent. If it does not, he tries another candidate referent, and so on. For some candidate referents he will be forced to add certain assumptions, and if this candidate is accepted, so are the assumptions. This way the listener arrives at the intended referent plus the other inferences he was supposed to draw.

To illustrate, consider a simple case of pronominalization, as in Example (4):

(4) I met a man yesterday. He told me a story.

In the second sentence it is given that there is a singular male entity, so the problem to be solved is "Identify the referent of *he.*" The listener first builds a candidate referent from the data base, say, "the person referred to by *I,*" and checks it against the constraints. As it happens, it fails the first test — "The referent matches the given information" — because *I* and *he* cannot be coreferential. The listener then builds another candidate referent, say, "the person referred to by *a man,*" and then checks the constraints, finds that they are all satisfied, and accepts the problem as solved: *He* refers to the person referred to by *a man.*

A sequence like Example (19) offers a much more challenging illustration:

(19) I walked into the room. The chandeliers sparkled brightly.

Here the listener's goal is, "Identify the referent for *the chandeliers.*" As a first candidate referent, he might set up "the person referred to by *I*" and as a second, "the object referred to by *the room.*" Both candidates fail and are rejected. With no other explicit candidates to try out, the listener is forced to begin making assumptions. He might note that although there is no obvious relationship between chandeliers and people (*I*) or between chandeliers and walking, there is one between chandeliers and rooms — rooms may have chandeliers in them. He would therefore make the assumption that the room actually did have chandeliers in it and set up these chandeliers as a candidate referent for *the chandeliers.* These assumed chandeliers pass the first test (they are chandeliers), the second test (they are ones the speaker could plausibly expect the listener to think of), and the third test (they are unique). Thus, the listener accepts the chandeliers he assumed to be in the room mentioned as the referent to *the chandeliers.*

It is easy to see how this process leads to implicatures in the other sequences provided earlier. Take Example (10):

(10)   I met two people yesterday. The woman told me a story.

If the first and second tests are to be met, the referent for *the woman* has to be one of the two people mentioned in the first sentence and has to be a woman. More interesting, if the third test is to be met, the other person can*not* be a woman — it must be a man, a boy, or a girl. If the other person were a woman, the referent would not be unique. This of course is precisely the inference we draw in hearing this pair of sentences.

Or take Example (26):

(26)   John fell. What he did was trip on a rock.

If *what he did* in the second sentence referred to John's falling, the second sentence would be contradictory. If *what he did* referred to an event subsequent or consequent to John's falling, the second sentence would be implausible. But if *what he did* referred to a cause of John's falling, the second sentence would make good sense. Hence the listener assumes that something happened to cause John to fall and that that something was meant to be the referent of *what John did.* This, too, is just the implicature that was earlier attributed to Example (26).

An important consequence of this process is that implicatures are determinate. To see this, consider Example (35):

(35)   Max lives in New York. Moritz is crazy too.

If the listener had the time and inclination, he could conceivably build an indefinitely long series of assumptions linking the second sentence to the first. For example, he might assume the following: Everyone who lives in New York breathes foul air; everyone who breathes foul air develops bronchial diseases; and bronchial diseases always drive one crazy. By this circuitous route, it would follow that everyone who lives in New York is crazy and therefore Max is crazy. The last clause could serve as a referent to *someone besides Moritz is crazy,* the given information of the second sentence in Example (35). But the listener would never go to all this trouble. He would reject this chain of assumptions because the speaker could hardly have expected him to figure it out and to do so uniquely. Because of the second and third constraints, the listener will always pick the simplest assumption the speaker could plausibly expect him to make. In Example (35), the simplest assumption is the shortest chain: Everyone who lives in New York is crazy. Thus, in drawing implicatures the listener should always take the shortest route since this will make them determinate, unique.

Implicatures, or authorized inferences, differ from ordinary implications, or unauthorized inferences, in just this way. Implicatures are determinate, whereas implications may not be. On hearing *the room* in Example (19),

(19)   I walked into the room. The chandeliers sparkled brightly.

we might begin drawing unauthorized inferences that there may be windows, doors, furniture, and people in the room. There is no principled stopping rule for such inferences — we could go as far as our imagination would allow. But when we hear *the chandeliers* and draw the authorized inference that it refers to chandeliers that are in the room, the process is determinate. In this instance there is a principled stopping rule, and it is this: Make the simplest assumption possible. The rule makes good sense. If implicatures were not determinate, the speaker could not consider them an integral part of what he wants to convey, for what he conveys must be determinate.

CONCLUSIONS

Authorized inferences, or implicatures, I have argued, play a central role in communication. Speakers build utterances expecting their listeners to draw certain inferences, and listeners, in turn, comprehend utterances on the understanding that speakers mean them to draw such inferences. These inferences are therefore an integral part of what speakers try to convey. Indeed, people rarely consider them to be inferences at all — they are simply part of what the speaker said. Nevertheless, drawing inferences clearly takes skill and knowledge — children and eavesdroppers are often unsuccessful. It also consumes mental effort and time (Haviland & Clark, 1974).

In this chapter, I have taken up just one type of authorized inference — the identification of referents. I have argued three major points. First, listeners identify referents by use of an agreement they have with speakers called the given—new contract. Without that agreement they would have no basis for identifying referents — at least the ones the speaker intended. Second, in order to identify these referents listeners have to add certain bridging assumptions —

authorized inferences or implicatures – and these are limited in their variety. Third, listeners arrive at these implicatures through a process of problem solving in which they try out candidate referents, check them against constraints dictated by the given–new contract, and accept the candidate that satisfies them all.

Yet in investigating these inferences I have barely scratched the surface. Many questions remain to be answered and much work is left to be done. Is the taxonomy I have presented complete? How is it to be explained; that is, why these categories of implicature and not others? Do people identify referents by the process I have outlined? If so, how does it work in detail? These are important questions. If the approach I have suggested is roughly correct, their answers will affect the way we think about other aspects of comprehension as well. Whatever the process of identifying referents turns out to be, authorized inferences are here to stay.

ACKNOWLEDGMENTS

The preparation of this chapter was supported by Grant MH–20021 from the U.S. Public Health Service. It is based in part on a paper called "Bridging" that I presented at a workshop on "Theoretical Issues in Natural Language Processing," convened by R. Schank and B. L. Nash-Webber in Cambridge, Massachusetts, in June 1975. I thank Eve V. Clark for her suggestions in the preparation of this chapter and Susan E. Haviland for discussion over several years on the issues I have taken up here.

REFERENCES

Akmajian, A. The role of focus in the interpretation of anaphoric expressions. In S. R. Anderson & P. Kiparsky (Eds.), *A Festshrift for Morris Halle.* New York: Holt, Rinehart, & Winston, 1973.

Chafe, W. L. *Meaning and the structure of language.* Chicago: University of Chicago Press, 1970.

Chafe, W. L. Discourse structure and human knowledge. In J. B. Carroll and R. O. Freedle (Eds.), *Language comprehension and the acquisition of knowledge.* Washington, D.C.: Winston, 1972.

Chafe, W. L. Language and consciousness. *Language,* 1974, **50,** 111–133.

Chomsky, N. Deep structure, surface structure, and semantic interpretation. In L. A. Jakobovits & D. D. Steinberg (Eds.), *Semantics: An interdisciplinary reader in philosophy, psychology, linguistics, and anthropology.* Cambridge: Cambridge University Press, 1971.

Clark, E. V. On the acquisition of the meaning of "before" and "after." *Journal of Verbal Learning and Verbal Behavior,* 1971, **10,** 266–275.

Clark, H. H., & Clark, E. V. Semantic distinctions and memory for complex sentences. *Quarterly Journal of Experimental Psychology,* 1968, **20,** 129–138.

Clark, H. H., & Haviland, S. E. Psychological processes as linguistic explanation. In D. Cohen (Ed.), *Explaining linguistic phenomena.* Washington: Hemisphere, 1974.

Clark, H. H., & Haviland, S. E. Comprehension and the given–new contract. In R. Freedle (Ed.), *Discourse production and comprehension.* Norwood, N.J.: Ablex, 1977.

Halliday, M. A. K. Notes on transitivity and theme in English: II. *Journal of Linguistics,* 1967, **3**, 199–244.

Halliday, M. A. K. Language structure and language function. In J. Lyons (Ed.), *New horizons in linguistics.* Baltimore: Penguin, 1970.

Haviland, S. E., & Clark, H. H. What's new? Acquiring new information as a process in comprehension. *Journal of Verbal Learning and Verbal Behavior,* 1974, **13**, 512–521.

Jackendoff, R. S. *Semantic interpretation in generative grammar.* Cambridge, Mass.: MIT Press, 1972.

Kuno, S. Functional sentence perspective: A case study from Japanese and English. *Linguistic Inquiry,* 1972, **3**, 269–320.

Kuno, S. Three perspectives in the functional approach to syntax. In R. E. Grossman, L. J. San, & T. J. Vance (Eds.), *Papers from the parasession on functionalism.* Chicago: Chicago Linguistic Society, 1975.

Lakoff, G. The role of deduction in grammar. In C. J. Fillmore & D. T. Langendoen (Eds.), *Studies in linguistic semantics.* New York: Holt, Rinehart, & Winston, 1971.

Smith, K. H., & McMahon, L. E. Understanding order information in sentences: Some recent work at Bell Laboratories. In G. Flores d'Arcais & W. J. M. Levelt (Ed.), *Advances in psycholinguistics.* Amsterdam: North Holland, 1970.

9
Understanding and Summarizing Brief Stories

David E. Rumelhart

University of California, San Diego

INTRODUCTION

Consider the following brief fragment of a story:

> (1) Mary heard the ice cream man coming down the street. She remembered her birthday money and rushed into the house. . . .

Upon hearing just these few words most readers already have a rather complete interpretation of the events in the story. Presumably, Mary is a little girl who wants to buy some ice cream from the ice cream man and runs into the house to get her money. Of course, it does not *say* this in the story; there are other possibilities. Mary could be afraid that the ice cream man might *steal* her birthday money, and so forth. Still, most readers find the first interpretation most plausible and retain it unless later information contradicts it. What happens when we read a story such as this? The purpose of this chapter is to suggest an account for this comprehension and show how this account allows us to account for aspects of story recall and summarization. Of course, we are not yet in a position to give a complete account of this process; nevertheless, I believe we can now begin to formulate an initial account and that we can begin to get empirical leverage on the process whereby we understand.

I will begin with a general discussion of the comprehension process. I will develop, in this context, a general theoretical framework consistent with the evidence and general theoretical accounts given to data. Then, in the second section I will develop a special case of this general model and show how this special case model can account, in some detail, for the structures we find in many stories. In the third section of the chapter, I will show how the notion of *gist of a story* relates to the model of comprehension developed previously. In that section I will show how this model of gist can account for people's responses to "summarization instructions" on brief stories. In the final section of the chapter I will relate the model to the recall of simple stories.

A COMPREHENSION MODEL

The general conceptualization outlined here is, I suspect, fast becoming the *modal model* of comprehension. Although I have formulated this model in the context of the work carried out in our laboratory over the past several years (cf. Norman, Rumelhart, & LNR, 1975; Rumelhart & Ortony, 1977), I believe that the general ideas presented are consistent with those presented by Bartlett (1932), Bobrow and Norman (1975), Bransford and McCarrell (1974), Minsky (1975), Schank and Abelson (1975), and probably others. A more complete development of this general model is given in Rumelhart and Ortony (1977).

The notion central to the comprehension model sketched here is the *schema* (schemata is the plural). A schema is an abstract representation of a generic concept for an object, event, or situation. Internally, a schema consists of a network of interrelationships among the major constituents of the situation represented by the schema. Moreover, a schema is said to account for any situation that can be considered an instance of the general concept it represents.

A simple analogy will be useful. A schema can be likened to a play. The relationship between a schema and a situation for which it accounts is similar to the relationship between a play and any particular enactment of the play. Just as any enactment of a play has far more detail than the script for the play, so too a situation has more detail than the schema that accounts for it. The schema specifies certain important relationships while leaving unspecified aspects irrelevant to the schema in question. On the other hand, a schema may very well contain a good deal of information *not* apparent in the situation or passage for which it accounts. It is as if we use the first and third acts of a familiar play to determine the play in question and then infer the crucial events in the unseen second act from our knowledge of the script. To give a very simple example, we see a magician carry out a familiar motion (say, the motion typical of passing a coin from one hand to another) and presume that he has carried out the familiar action associated with that motion (even though, of course, we do not actually see the coin move from one hand to the other). Here the magician has shown us the first and third acts of the "hand switch" play and has counted on our inferring the nature of the "missing" second act. If we, in fact, determine that we have seen the familiar play, we will be fooled when it turns out that the second act was not as we had thought. Thus, although we "thought we understood" what the magician was doing, we discover only later that we had "misunderstood" (i.e., found the wrong schema for) the event in question.

Another example comes from Collins and Quillian (1972). Consider the following sentence:

(2) The policeman held up his hand and stopped the car.

Let us consider the process of comprehending this sentence. We search our memories for a schema that will account for the described event. There are probably many schemata that would account for the information at hand, but perhaps the most likely is one involving a traffic cop who is signaling to a driver to stop his car. Notice that this brings a number of concepts to the fore that are not mentioned in the sentence itself. In particular, one imagines that the car has a driver and that the policeman managed to stop the car through signaling to the driver, who then probably put his foot on the brake of the car, causing it to come to a halt. The proximal cause of the car stopping is taken to be the operation of the car's brakes. Moreover, the significance of the officer holding up his hand would be a signal to stop, a fact that is neither in the sentence nor even in the actual perception of such a situation, but rather a fact about the way traffic officers are known to communicate with automobile drivers.

On the other hand, if the policeman were known to be Superman and the cars were known to be driverless, we would require quite a different schema to allow us to understand the situation. We might well determine that the holding up of the hand was not a signal at all, but rather a mechanism for physically stopping the cars. In such a case, given our schema for one object physically stopping another, we would assume that the hand had actually come into contact with the cars, that the policeman (Superman) probably braced himself for impact, and so forth. The brakes on the car would, in this schema, not come into play.

Before leaving our general discussion of schemata and the meaning of the phrase "accounts for," I would like to make two more points: (1) schemata can differ with respect to the degree of detail with which they account for a situation; (2) ordinarily, a situation is not accounted for by a single schema, but by a set of interrelated schemata.

Consider the following dialog (from Hellman's *The Little Foxes*):

(4) REGINA: Tomorrow morning I go to Judge Simmes . . .
    OSCAR: And what proof? What proof of all this . . .
      R: None. I won't need any. The bonds are missing and they are with Marshall. That will be enough. If it isn't, I'll add what's necessary.
      O: We'll deny . . .
      R: Deny your heads off. You couldn't find a jury that wouldn't weep for a woman whose brother steals from her. *And* you couldn't find twelve men in this state you haven't cheated and hate you for it.
      O: What kind of talk is this? You couldn't do anything like that! We're your own brothers . . .

R: Now I don't want to hear any more from any of you. You'll do no more bargaining in this house. I'll take my seventy-five percent and we'll forget the story forever. That's one way of doing it, and the way I prefer. You know me well enough to know that I don't mind taking the other way.

This passage can be understood at many different levels of abstraction. At one level it can be understood as a *conversation*. At another, more detailed level it can be understood as a case of *conflict* between two parties. At an even more detailed level it can be understood as a case of *extortion* in which one party is holding a threat over another party to get some particular gain. As we discover increasingly more specific schemata to account for the passage, we have an increasing amount of structure in the schema and we find that the more specific schemata yield better fits to more of the detail of the passage. Depending on our knowledge and our purpose in reading we may settle for a more or less specific schema corresponding to a more or less deep understanding of the passage.

Finally, it must be emphasized that more than one schema must be used to account for the various parts of a situation at any one time. In fact a configuration of mutually consistent and interrelating schemata are normally found to account for a situation in its entirety. Thus, the interpretations of the dialog just mentioned are not mutually exclusive. We could very well interpret this dialog as conversation, conflict, and extortion.

The model of comprehension that I am suggesting can now be stated very simply:

(3) The process of comprehension is taken to be identical to the process of selecting and verifying conceptual schemata to account for the situation (or text) to be understood.

On having selected and verified a schema and determined that it has given a satisfactory account of the situation in question, one can be said to have understood the situation or passage. In the succeeding sections I will bring this very general theory to a level of specifics and will show how it can account for the summarization and recall of brief stories.

A PROBLEM-SOLVING SCHEMA FOR STORIES

Given the general view of comprehension outlined earlier, it would seem a productive strategy to develop, in detail, concrete modes of those schemata that play important roles in comprehending a wide range of situations. Naturally, since we want these schemata to be very generally applicable, they must be rather abstract. In a recent study (Rumelhart, 1975) I have outlined a general set of schemata that appear to be widely used in story comprehension. In this chapter I will develop those ideas further and show how they fit into the general schema theory sketched in the preceding section.

Casual observation suggests a surprisingly simple motif underlying a remarkable number of brief stories. This motif involves what I call *problem-solving episodes*. Such stories have roughly the following structure: First, something happens to the protagonist of the story that sets up a goal for him to accomplish. Then the remainder of the story is a description of the protagonist's problem-solving behavior as he seeks to accomplish his goal. The problem-solving behavior itself is usually well structured and appears to be of the form expected from such theories of problem solving as the General Problem Solver (GPS) of Newell and Simon (cf. Newell & Simon, 1972). Thus, the problem-solving portion of the story looks something like the sequence of actions attempted and goals entertained during the run of a GPS program.

There are really two schemata involved in this motif: One, which I call an EPISODE schema, specifies the relationships among the initiating event, the goal, and the attempt to accomplish the goal. The other, which I call the TRY schema, specifies the internal structure of the attempt. It is this second schema that has a structure similar to GPS.

We can express these schemata as simple computer programs.[1] First, the EPISODE schema:

EPISODE ABOUT PROTAGONIST *P.*
 (1) EVENT *E* CAUSES *P* TO DESIRE GOAL *G.*
 (2) *P* TRIES TO GET *G* UNTIL OUTCOME *O* OCCURS.

The EPISODE schema has four variables: the protagonist, *P*, the initiating event, *E*, the goal, *G*, and the outcome of the problem-solving attempt, *O*. Note here that the *variables* of schemata, unlike the *roles* or *props* of plays, can stand for abstract entities like events and goals as well as concrete entities like people and objects. It also should be pointed out that the relational terms (such as CAUSE, DESIRE, and TRY) mentioned in the EPISODE schema are really references to other schemata, each of which has its own internal structure. Thus, in order to determine that our EPISODE schema accounts for some situation, we must have evidence that the CAUSE schema, the TRY schema, etc., account for appropriate aspects of the situation. When we find a case in which all of these events can be found, then we conclude that the EPISODE schema is an appropriate account of the entire situation.

---

[1] I have chosen to represent schemata in terms of the language SOL developed to represent semantic procedures. For a discussion of SOL, see Rumelhart & Norman (1975). For an illustration of its use, see Rumelhart & Levin (1975). In what follows, I make no use of the fact that SOL is a computer language. I merely use it as a convenient formalism. In my attempts to simulate the schema ideas on the computer, however, I have made use of the fact that a schema can be represented as a procedure.

I will not attempt, here, to specify the CAUSE and DESIRE schemata, but a specification of the internal structure of the TRY schema is central to my account of problem-solving episides. The TRY schema is specified thus:

AGENT *A* TRIES TO GET GOAL *G*.
(1) *A* SELECTS A METHOD *M* WHICH COULD LEAD TO *G*.
(2) FOR EACH PRECONDITION *P* OF *M*,
      A TRIES TO GET *P* UNTIL OUTCOME *O*.
(3) *A* DOES *M* WHICH HAS CONSEQUENCE *C*.

The TRY schema has four major variables and a number of lesser ones. The main variables are the trier, *A*, the method to be employed, *M*, the goal, *G*, and the consequence, *C*, of the attempt. In addition, there may be any number of preconditions, *P*, that must be satisfied before the method can be attempted directly. Finally, for each attempt to fulfill a precondition there is an outcome, *O*, of the attempt. If an essential precondition cannot be met, the outcome may be to GIVE UP ON *M* and the attempt will be abandoned. Note that the structure of TRY is very much like that of GPS TRYing to accomplish the subgoal. Thus, stories like problem solving in general, frequently involve a whole set of embedded goals (a *goal stack*) that appear to be determining the protagonists' actions.

Before turning to some examples of how these elements can be applied to stories, it is useful to consider a graphic representation of these schemata. Figure 1 shows a structure diagram illustrating the major constituents of the schemata in question and the relationship between the structure of the EPISODE schema and the TRY schema. The diagram is in the form of a tree, with the major

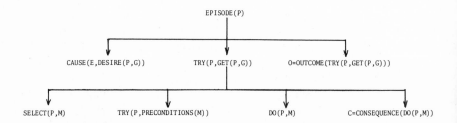

P   =   PROTAGONIST OF EPISODE
M   =   METHOD CHOSEN
G   =   GOAL OF EPISODE
E   =   INITIATING EVENT
O   =   OUTCOME OF THE EPISODE
C   =   CONSEQUENCE OF ENACTING THE METHOD

FIG. 1 Structure diagram illustrating the relationship between the EPIDOSE and TRY schemata.

constituents of a schema specified at the immediately lower level of the tree and the order of the constituents corresponding to their order of occurrence in the schema. Thus, the EPISODE schema has a CAUSE schema, a TRY schema, and an OUTCOME as its immediate constituents. The TRY schema, in turn, has four major constituents: SELECTing a method, TRYing the preconditions of the method, DOing the method, and the CONSEQUENCE of DOing the method. We could, of course, continue the expansion of each schema at yet a lower level in the tree. Thus, for example, we could draw a branch from the TRY schema for TRYing to accomplish the preconditions of the method, and so forth. One other point should be made about the figure. I have illustrated schemata using polish notation. That is, I have written the schema name first, followed by a list of its immediate variables. Thus, EPISODES are about protagonists and require one variable on the surface. CAUSE requires two variables — the first is the causal event and the second is the result. Similarly, TRY involves two surface variables, a trier and that which is being attempted.

We can now illustrate the application of these schemata to the analysis of a simple story. Recall the story fragment (1) given at the beginning of the chapter:

(1) Mary heard the ice cream man coming down the street. She remembered her birthday money and rushed into the house. . . .

Now, consider how our theory of comprehension would apply to this fragment of a story. We would select, from memory, a set of schemata and attempt to see if they could account for the input information. Suppose, for purposes of illustration, that we have selected the EPISODE schema. We now want to determine whether it accounts for the given information. The process of verification is, in effect, the process of finding aspects of the input that we can associate with the variables of the EPISODE schema and its constituent schemata. In this case, for example, we need a protagonist, a goal, an initiating event, and so forth. We can associate the protagonist with Mary, the initiating event with Mary's hearing the ice cream man, and the goal with Mary's having ice cream. On having associated these variables in this way, we expect to find a case of Mary TRYing to get ice cream and some outcome of that attempt.

Now, TRYing involves first the selection of a method. Thus, we should find some evidence for Mary choosing some method that could lead to her getting the ice cream. Perhaps, *buying* is a plausible method here. This method has a precondition of having money. Thus, if buying is the method we might well expect to see Mary TRYing to get some money. She must choose an action that will result in her getting some money. In this case her remembering the birthday money seems a reasonable clue that she chose to get her birthday money. Finally, in order to get something you must be where the thing is located. Thus, when Mary rushes into the house we can interpret that as her fulfilling this precondition. In this way, we can interpret the story as Mary's hearing the ice cream man causing her to want ice cream, deciding to buy the ice cream from

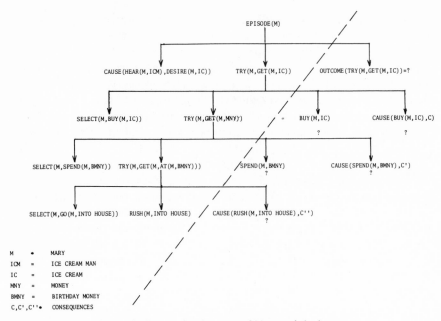

FIG. 2   Structure diagram for the story of Mary and the ice cream man.

the ice cream man, deciding to use her birthday money, and finally rushing into the house to get it.

Figure 2 shows, in graphic form, the way in which our schemata can account for the story. The top node of the tree indicates that it is an EPISODE about Mary. The major constituents of this EPISODE are shown as the highest branches of the tree, namely, Mary's hearing the ice cream man initiating her desire for ice cream, her attempting to get ice cream, and the outcome of her attempt. Similarly, lower levels of the tree show the expansion of the various instantiations of the TRY schema at the several different levels. The diagram nicely illustrates the various goals that presumably motivated Mary's going into the house. She was going into the house to get to the place where her birthday money was. She wanted to be there in order to get her birthday money. She decided to get her birthday money because she needed to get some money. She wanted to get some money because she wanted to have some ice cream.

It is interesting to note, also, from the figure that this is a story fragment and not an entire story. This is evident from the lower right-hand side of the tree. None of the consequences or outcomes are specified (I have indicated an unspecified constituent with a question mark), nor can they be readily inferred. (Will Mary be unable to find her birthday money? Will the ice cream man be gone when she returns? or Will Mary be able to have her ice cream and live happily ever after?) Thus, our system of schemata acts like a grammar for stories in two ways: (1) it assigns a constituent structure to the stories (i.e., it allows us to construct one of these trees for stories), and (2) it helps us discriminate between stories (of the problem-solving sort) and fragments of stories.

Essentially the same structure can be found in a remarkable number of brief stories. I will give two more examples before I address the role of our theory in the analysis of summaries of stories. The first example is a story I wrote based on the Old English folktale "The Old Woman and Her Pig." My story is entitled "The Old Farmer and His Stubborn Donkey." The text of the story is given in Table 1.

Evan a casual reading of the story should make clear the appropriateness of our problem-solving schemata. The main goal of the story is clearly for the farmer to get the donkey into the shed. The bulk of the story is a description of his attempt to attain this goal. This story is unusual in the amount of embedding, but as we shall see, substantial embedding occurs in most stories.

Figure 3 gives the tree structure underlying this story. Several aspects of this tree should be noted. First, note that the farmer actually makes three separate

TABLE 1
Text of "The Old Farmer and His Stubborn Donkey"

(1) There was once an old farmer who owned a very stubborn donkey.
(2) One evening the farmer wanted to put his donkey in its shed.
(3) First the farmer pulled the donkey,
(4) but the donkey wouldn't move.
(5) Then the farmer pushed the donkey,
(6) but still the donkey wouldn't move.
(7) Finally the farmer asked his dog to bark loudly at the donkey and thereby frighten him into the shed.
(8) But the dog refused.
(9) So then the farmer asked the cat to scratch the dog so the dog would bark loudly and thereby frighten the donkey into the shed.
(10) But the cat replied, 'I would gladly scratch the dog if only you would give me some milk'.
(11) So the farmer went to his cow
(12) and asked for some milk to give to the cat.
(13) But the cow replied, 'I would gladly give you some milk if only you would give me some hay'.
(14) Thus, the farmer went to the haystack
(15) and got some hay.
(16) As soon as he gave the hay to the cow,
(17) the cow gave the farmer some milk.
(18) Then the farmer went to the cat
(19) and gave the milk to the cat.
(20) As soon as the cat got the milk, it began to scratch the dog.
(21) As soon as the cat scratched the dog, the dog began to bark loudly.
(22) The braking so frightened the donkey that
(23) it jumped immediately into its shed.

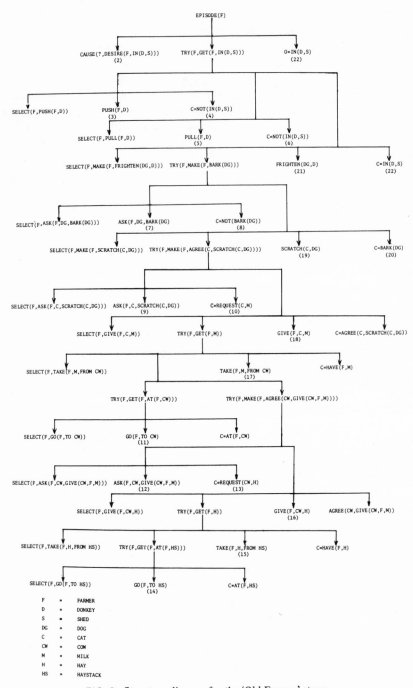

FIG. 3 Structure diagram for the 'Old Farmer' story.

attempts to get the donkey into the shed. This is illustrated in the diagram by three separate instantiations of the topmost TRY schema. In the first two cases, there is no elaboration (i.e., there are no preactions to be satisfied) and the attempts end in failure. The third attempt is finally successful, and it involves a good deal of elaboration. It should also be noted that sometimes multiple preconditions must be satisfied. Thus, when the farmer is TRYing to get milk from the cow we see two preconditions that must be satisfied. In the first place, the farmer must TRY to get to the place where the cow is located, and second, he must TRY to get the cow to agree to give him the milk. This story is fit very nicely by our schemata. In a sense it is a caricature for the sort of story I am talking about.

To show the relationship between the structure and the statements of the story, I have written the number of the statement that conveys the relevant information next to each node of the tree. Note that with the exception of statement number (1) each statement of the story is associated with a node on the tree. Thus, the tree gives us the structural relationships among the statements of the story.

Most stories have statements like number (1) that in effect introduce the characters and set the stage for the EPISODE. Such statements are outside the EPISODE schema presented earlier. This aspect of a story corresponds to what I have elsewhere called the SETTING of the story (Rumelhart, 1975). In most of the stories to be analyzed here, SETTINGS play a minor role and I shall ignore them.

TABLE 2
Text of "The Countryman and the Serpent"

(1)	A countryman's son, by accident, trod upon a serpent's tail.
(2)	The serpent turned
(3)	and bit him,
(4)	so that he died.
(5)	The father, in revenge,
(6)	got his axe,
(7)	pursued the serpent,
(8)	and cut off part of his tail.
(9)	So the serpent, in revenge,
(10)	began stinging several of the farmer's cattle.
(11)	This caused the farmer severe loss.
(12)	Well, the farmer thought it best to make it up with the serpent.
(13)	So he brought food and honey to the mouth of its lair
(14)	and said to it, 'Let's forget and forgive; perhaps you were right to punish my son and take vengeance on my cattle, but surely I was right in trying to revenge him; now that we are both satisfied, why should we not be friends again?'
(15)	'No, no', said the serpent, 'take away your gifts; you can never, never forget the death of you son, nor I the loss of my tail'.

(a)

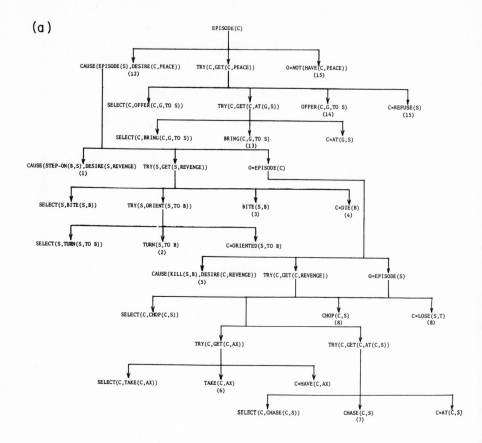

(b)

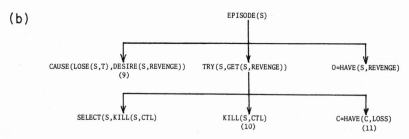

C	=	COUNTRYMAN
S	=	SERPENT
B	=	COUNTRYMAN'S SON
T	=	SERPENT'S TAIL
CTL	=	COUNTRYMAN'S CATTLE
G	=	GIFT OF FOOD AND HONEY

FIG. 4 Structure diagram for 'The Countryman and the Serpent'.

Thus far, I have said little about the structure of initiating events, outcomes, or consequences. As we shall see, these events are often elaborated beyond the simple statements of our previous examples. In particular, such events are often themselves EPISODES – perhaps even with a different protagonist. The fable entitled "The Countryman and the Serpent" offers an excellent example of such a case. The text of this story is given in Table 2; its structure is given in Fig. 4.

It will be observed from the figure that I have assumed that the main EPISODE is the countryman's attempt to make peace, which ends in failure. The initiating event for this EPISODE is itself an EPISODE with the serpent as protagonist. This initiating EPISODE was itself initiated by the boy stepping on the snake. The outcome of this embedded EPISODE is also assumed to be an EPISODE. This is another EPISODE with the countryman as protagonist, in which he seeks revenge for his son's death. The outcome of this EPISODE is yet another EPISODE, with the serpent again as protagonist. In this EPISODE the serpent seeks revenge for the loss of his tail. Thus, we see a case of quite another kind of embedding. In the previous story we found a series of embedded TRYs. In this story we have a series of embedded EPISODES – each EPISODE serving as either an initiation or an outcome of another.

I have again, in this diagram, given the statement numbers next to the nodes of the tree. Again, the tree gives an account for each of the statements of the story. It should be noted that in this case, as in the previous case, the order of the statements in the story corresponds exactly with the left-to-right order of the terminal nodes of the tree. Thus, not only does our tree provide a sort of deep structure for the stories, but it also determines the surface order of the various statements of the story.

Both this fable and the farmer story are somewhat extreme in the depth of embedding, but as we shall see in our analysis of other stories, embedding even in a simple story is substantial. I now turn to a discussion of summaries and show how our schemata can help account for the observed summaries of our stories.

SUMMARIES OF STORIES

As noted in the preceding section, an important function of a schema is to define the *constituent structure* of the situation to be understood. This constituent structure can be illustrated in the structure diagrams in the preceding section. The major constituents of a situation are those aspects of the situation that are represented directly in the highest level of the schema that accounts for the situation. Thus, in the case of a situation accounted for by the EPISODE schema the major constituents are the initiating event, the goal, the TRYing to attain the goal, and the outcome – in short, just those nodes in a structure diagram that are immediately dominated by the EPISODE node. Similarly, the major constituents of the TRY schema consist of the selection of a method, the fulfillment of the preconditions of the method, the carrying out of the method, and the consequence. The particular preconditions fulfilled and the methods by which they were satisfied are not directly constituents of the TRY schema. These are details that expand upon and explicate the schema of which they are a part. Thus, our representation of the structure of a story gives us a distinction between the *important* parts of a story and the details of the story. In general, the higher the information in the structure diagram, the more central to the story, and the lower the information, the more peripheral.

Suppose we took the structure diagram for a story and simply removed all nodes below Level *n*. If our analysis is correct, all of the information thus deleted would be less important than all of the information remaining. We have, in effect, produced a structure diagram of a *summary* of detail *n* of the story.

To produce the summary itself, we need rules for expressing the reduced structure diagram in the form of a sequence of statements. I have approached this problem by positing rules associated with each type of node (e.g., EPISODE, TRY, CAUSE, OUTCOME, etc.), with characteristic expressions for the content represented by that node. These expressions must state, as succinctly as possible, the central ideas of the schema named by that node. Thus, in the case of the EPISODE node, I assume that the attempt and its outcome are central and that the initiating event (since it can, in part, be inferred from the nature of the goal) is of secondary importance. Thus, I posit a summarization rule that involves two

TABLE 3
Summarization Formulas

Rule 1: Episode (P).
        Summary of Try (P,Get(P,G)).
        As a result, Summary of 0.
Rule 2: Try (P,Get(P,G))
        (a) IF Precondition, $-$delete
        (b) IF Successful, $-P$ got G by M.
        (c) IF Unsuccessful, $-P$ tried to get G by M, but summary of C.
Rule 3: Psychological Actions: Desire, Select, Feel
        Delete
Rule 4: Outcomes and consequences
        Delete if redundant with previous sentence.
Rule 5: Methods
        P did M to get G.
Rule 6: Cause (E_1, E_2)
        When Summary of E_1, Summary of E_2.
        (Note: If either E_1 or E_2 is a psychological action, then just summarize the
           remaining event.)
Rule 7: Any node for which no other rule exists is fully expressed by converting the predicate
        name to an English verb with the first argument as its subject.

---

statements. The first is a summarization of the TRY node, and the second is a summarization of the OUTCOME. The rule is given as Rule 1 in Table 3.

Similarly, there is a summarization rule for the expression of a TRY node. This is given as Rule 2 in the table. In the case of TRY I consider three contexts in which the TRY could occur:

1. The TRY could be an attempt to fulfill a precondition. In this case, the node may be deleted and not mentioned, since its outcome is inferrable from the subsequent action or consequence, which will be expressed.

2. The attempt may have been successful and not a precondition. In this case, it can be summarized simply by indicating that the goal was attained and the METHOD whereby this was accomplished.

3. The attempt may have been unsuccessful. In this case, the METHOD and the CONSEQUENCE both must be expressed since we must tell not only what was done, but what the result of that action was.

The entire summarization process, then, is to work in the following way. First, a level of summarization is chosen. Then the tree is "trimmed" to remove the nodes below the chosen level in the tree. This produces a structure diagram for the summary. Then the leftmost terminal node of this reduced tree is expressed according to the appropriate rule in Table 3. Then the next terminal to the right is expressed similarly. This procedure is repeated until the rightmost terminal node has been expressed. At that point the summary has been completed.

To illustrate this process, consider the story of "The Czar and His Daughters" given in Table 4. Figure 5 shows the structure diagram for the story. Now

TABLE 4
Text of "The Czar and His Three Daughters"

---

(1) There was once a Czar who had three lovely daughters.
(2) One day, the three daughters went walking in the woods.
(3) They were enjoying themselves so much that
(4) they forgot the time
(5) and stayed too long.
(6) A dragon kidnaped the three daughters.
(7) As they were being dragged off, they called for help.
(8) Three heroes heard the cries
(9) and set off to rescue the daughters.
(10) The heroes came and
(11) fought the dragon.
(12) They defeated the dragon and
(13) rescued the maidens.
(14) The heroes then returned the daughters safely to their palace.
(15) When the Czar heard of the rescue,
(16) he rewarded the heroes handsomely.

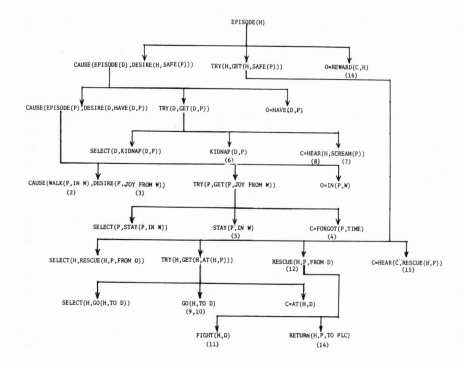

FIG. 5 Structure diagram for 'The Czar and His Three Daughters'.

suppose we wanted to produce a Level 0 summary of this story. This would involve deleting all but the root node of the (tree EPISODE(H)) and using our formula for summarizing an EPISODE. By Rule 1 we see that this involves summarizing first the attempt and then the outcome. Since the attempt was successful, the proper formula is given by (5):

(5) *P* got *G* by *M*. As a result, summary of *0*.

Now, the protagonists are 'three hoeroes,' the goal is for the three daughters to be safe, the method is rescue from the dragon, and the outcome is that the Czar rewarded the heroes. Thus, employing (5), we can write the following:

(6) Three heroes got three daughters of the Czar safe by rescuing them from a dragon. As a result, the Czar rewarded the heroes.

If we replace the awkward phrase "get safe by rescuing" with the verb *rescue,* we get a rather reasonable summary:

(7) Three heroes rescued three daughters of a Czar from a dragon. As a result, the Czar rewarded the heroes.

Now, consider how we can produce a Level 1 summary of this story. In this case we produce a Level 1 structure of the story by deleting all but the highest branches of the tree in Fig. 5. We begin with the leftmost terminal, which in this case is in the form $CAUSE(E_1,E_2)$, and by rule (6), since E_2 is a DESIRE, we express the whole as summary of E_1. Now, E_1 is an EPISODE, so it can be summarized by recursive application of Rule 1. Thus, we have the following:

(8) A dragon got three daughters of a Czar by kidnapping them.

The next terminal node we encounter is the TRY schema. I have already given the summary of this in (6). Finally, we get to the rightmost, or outcome, node of the reduced tree. The summary of the outcome is also just as it was for the Level 0 summary. Thus, putting the sentences together and replacing the awkward uses of *get* with more colloquial usage, we have the following Level 1 summary:

(9) A dragon kidnapped three daughters of a Czar. Three heroes rescued them from the dragon. As a result, the heroes were rewarded by the Czar.

By a similar procedure we can produce summaries at any level of detail. Thus, for example, a Level 2 summary would be as follows:

(10) Three daughters of a Czar were enjoying staying in the woods. A dragon kidnaped them. Three heroes heard their screams. The heroes rescued them from the dragon. The Czar heard of this. As a result, he rewarded the heroes.

This story contained only successful episodes. A fable entitled "The Dog and His Shadow" given in Table 5 and Fig. 6, illustrates summaries of unsuccessful attempts. The Level 0,1, and 2 summaries of this story are given in Examples (11)–(13):

(11) A dog tried to get the reflection of some meat he had in his mouth. The meat he had fell into the brook.

(12) A dog crossed a brook. As a result, he saw the reflection of some meat he had in his mouth and thought the reflected meat was real. He tried to get it by snapping at it. The meat he had fell into the brook.

(13) A dog encountered a brook. He crossed it and looked down at it. As a result, he saw the reflection of some meat he had in his mouth and thought that the reflected meat was real. He snapped at it to get it for himself. The meat he had fell into the brook.

TABLE 5
Text of "The Dog and His Shadow"

---

(1) It happened that a dog had got a piece of meat
(2) and was carrying it home in his mouth to eat.
(3) Now, on his way home he had to cross a plank lying across a running brook.
(4) As he crossed,
(5) he looked down
(6) and saw his own shadow reflected in the water beneath.
(7) Thinking it was another dog with another piece of meat,
(8) he made up his mind to have that also.
(9) So he made a snap at the shadow,
(10) but as he opened his mouth
(11) the piece of meat fell out,
(12) dropped into the water,
(13) and was never seen more.

Of course, one need not expand all parts of the tree to the same level. In general, any branch of the tree can be cut off at any level, resulting in summaries like (14):

(14) A dog crossed a brook. As a result, he saw the reflection of some meat he had in his mouth and thought it was real. He snapped at the reflected meat. The meat he had in his mouth fell into the brook.

What determines at what level any given branch will be cut off? As we shall see, it appears that the depth of the summary is determined jointly by the amount of detail required in the summary and the amount of information dominated by the node in question. Thus, all things being equal, the more information subsumed under a given node in the original story, the more likely it is to be expressed in the summary. This implies, for instance, that the more detail there is in the original story, the more detail we should observe in the summary of that story.

By the methods I have outlined, we can produce summaries of any story that can be analyzed by the schemata under discussion. In effect, then, upon giving an analysis of the structure of a story, we have also provided an ordering of importance of the story and thus provided a structure for producing summaries of the story. The question remains whether these summaries so produced bear a resemblance to summaries produced by subjects in simple experiments. The remainder of this section will be devoted to the analysis of such data.

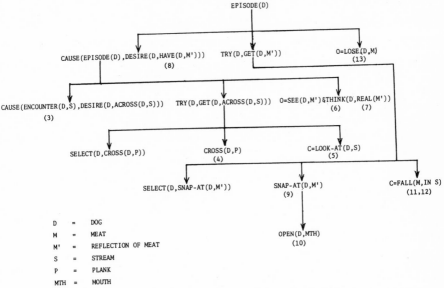

FIG. 6   Structure diagram for 'The dog and His shadow'.

The Summary Experiment

Ten subjects were asked to summarize a set of brief stories. Each subject was given a booklet containing a series of stories. They were instructed to write a summary for each of the stories in the book. Subjects were given unlimited time to complete their summaries and were allowed to refer to the texts of the stories while constructing their summaries. All subjects were graduate students in either psychology or linguistics. The set of stories included "The Dog and His Shadow," "The Czar and his Daughters," "The Countryman and the Serpent," and "The Wolf and the Crane" (a fable to be discussed later).

It is somewhat difficult to determine the quality of an account of data such as these. Our model determines a set of possible summaries; the data are our subjects' responses. Since traditional modes of analysis are difficult to apply, I will proceed by comparing the actual subject responses with the closest-fitting summaries for each subject for each story. I will discuss each story in turn.

The Dog and His Shadow. This was the shortest story among the set under discussion and produced the shortest summaries. Of the ten subjects in the experiment, five gave essentially Level 0 summaries and five gave Level 2 summaries. Table 6 compares our predicted responses with those of the five subjects classified as giving Level 0 summaries. The model predicts that there will

TABLE 6
Level 0 Summaries

A	D	Predicted: A dog tried to get the reflection of some meat he had in his mouth, but
	*	Observed:
*		S3: In attempting to increase his possessions, . . .
		S5: . . . he tried to grab its reflection in the water.
		S6: . . . [his] trying to get the meat held by his reflection.
		S7: . . . [his] trying to get more from his reflection.
		S8:
A	D	Predicted: . . . , the meat he had in his mouth fell into the brook.
	*	Observed:
*		S3: . . . , a dog lost what he had.
*		S5: A dog dropped a piece of meat he was carrying in his mouth when . . .
		S6: A dog accidentally dropped the piece of meat into a stream by . . .
	*	S7: A greedy dog lost his meat by . . .
		S8: A greedy dog lost his meat in a stream when . . .
		Unaccounted for:
		S8: . . . he confused his reflection for another dog with some meat.

be two major statements in the summary: one about the dog's unsuccessful attempt to get the phantom meat and one about the consequent loss of his real meat in the brook. Four of the five subjects give just this pattern of responses. One subject, S8, mentions the loss of the meat, but attributes it not to the attempt but to the dog's confusing his reflection for another dog with real meat.

Other subjects differ from the predicted summaries in more minor ways. The asterisks on the right in the table indicate statements that appear to deviate slightly, in meaning, from the predicted response. An asterisk in the column marked A (for addition) indicates an observation containing a slightly more specific statement than the predicted statement (i.e., a semantic component has been added to the predicted response). An asterisk in Column D (for deletion) indicates an observation that is missing some aspect of the meaning of the predicted statement. Statements without asterisks are judged to match the meaning of the predicted statement. Thus, an asterisk appears in Column D before S3's first response. This indicates the more general locution "attempting to increase his possessions" in place of "tried to get" the meat. Similarly, the asterisk in Column A indicates that "tried to grab" is more specific than "tried to get." The asterisks in Column D for the second statements of Subjects S3, S5, and S7 indicate that these subjects did not mention where the meat was lost as does the predicted statement. In most cases, I believe that these deviations are slight and the asterisks should be used to draw your attention to the worst fitting of the predictions.

The other five subjects gave more detailed summaries, which are compared to Level 2 predictions in Table 7. The fit of the model seems quite good here. There are five predicted statements in a Level 2 summary. Of the twenty-five

TABLE 7
Level 2 Summaries

Predicted: A dog got across a brook by crossing on a plank.

A   *D*   Observed:

    S1: As he crossed a plank over a brook, . . .

    S2: A dog was crossing a bridge with a piece of meat in its mouth.

    S4: He crossed on a plank across a bridge.

*   S9: . . . crossing the brook with a piece of meat in his mouth.

Predicted: As a result, he saw the reflection of some meat he had
                in his mouth, and . . .

Observed:

    S1: . . . he saw his shadow in the water.

    S2: Seeing his own reflection in the water, . . .

    S4: On the way, he saw his shadow reflected in the water.

    S9: A dog . . . saw his reflection.

    S10: Seeing his reflection in the water, . . .

Predicted: . . . thought the reflected meat was real.

Observed:

    S1:

    S2: . . . he thought it was another dog with another piece of meat.

    S4: He thought that the shadow was another dog carrying meat.

    S9: Thinking he saw a different dog with a different piece of meat, . . .

    S10: . . . and thinking it another dog with another piece of meat, . . .

Predicted: He snapped at the reflected meat to get it for himself.

A   *D*   Observed:

    S1: He tried to snap at the shadow to get its meat, . . .

    S2: He snapped at the shadow to get its meat, . . .

*   S4: He decided to take the other meat with him and made a grab for it.

*   S9: . . . to snap at it.

    S10: . . . he snapped at the reflected meat, trying to steal it
             from the 'other' dog.

Predicted: As a result, the meat he had fell into the water.

Observed:

    S1: . . . and while he did this his own meat fell into the water.

    S2: . . . and dropped his own piece of meat in the water.

    S4: As he did so, he dropped the meat into the brook.

*   S9: . . . thereby losing the real meat to the phantom.

*   S10: In his greed, he dropped his meat into the stream and it was
             lost forever.

Unaccounted for:

    S1: A greedy dog was on his way home with a piece of meat
          in his mouth.

setting   S4: A dog was carrying his meat home in his mouth.

    S10: While he was on his way home with a piece of meat, . . .

    S10: . . . a dog happened upon a stream.

    S9: . . . he opened his mouth . . .

predicted statements (five for each of five subjects) only two were missing. Subject S10 failed to mention the crossing of the stream, and Subject S1 failed to mention the dog's thinking that the reflected meat was real (although, of course, his summary clearly *presupposes* that the dog had this thought). In addition, five statements were added that were not predicted by the model. These five are listed at the bottom of Table 7 as "Unaccounted for." Of the five, three constitute setting information, which is ignored by the model, and two are more specific statements that should not have come into the summary until Level 3. Only the two deleted statements and these two more specific statements should be counted as deviations from the model. Thus, excluding setting statements, twenty-five statements were given by these five subjects. Of these, twenty-three were predicted by the model. In addition, two of the twenty-five predicted statements did not occur.

It should be kept in mind that we are not trying to predict the exact words a subject will use. Different subjects may have different ways of expressing essentially the same idea. All the model predicts is the *idea* of what will be said. A careful comparison of observed responses with those given will show that the predictions are rather good. There are, however, some deviations as indicated by the asterisks. Thus, for example, it is predicted that subjects will mention that the dog crossed the brook *on a plank.* One subject, S9, mentions that he crossed the brook, but does not mention the plank. Similarly, the same subject does not mention that the meat was lost *in the water* as predicted. He merely states that it was lost "to the phantom" (i.e., his [the dog's] reflection). These differences, although significant, are, I think, outweighed by the overall closeness of the fit.

Before leaving our discussion of these data, it should be emphasized that the subjects' *entire response protocols* are included in the data tables. Thus, the particular words a subject used can be pieced together by taking the various statements given under the observed rows for that subject. Thus, for example, S2's original response was as follows:

(15)   A dog was crossing a bridge with a piece of meat in its mouth. Seeing his own reflection in the water, he thought it was another dog with another piece of meat. He snapped at the shadow to get its meat and dropped his own piece of meat in the water.

This subject happened to give his sentences in exactly the predicted order. Sometimes for stylistic reasons subjects give a different order of output from that predicted. Nevertheless, the original protocol can always be pieced together from the data given. Thus, the model is attempting to predict the entire meaning of free written responses in a minimally structured task.

The Czar and His Three Daughters. This story also showed essentially two kinds of summaries: Level 1 summaries and what might be called Level 2.5 summaries. Seven of the ten subjects gave Level 1 responses. (It is interesting to note that all five of the subjects who gave Level 0 summaries to the previous

TABLE 8
Level 1 Summaries

		Predicted: A dragon got three daughters of a Czar by kidnapping them.
A	*D*	Observed:
	*	S3: Three daughters were kidnapped, . . .
		S5: . . . [three daughters] who had been captured by a dragon.
		S6: A dragon kidnapped the Czar's three daughters, but . . .
		S7: Three daughters of the Czar were kidnapped by a dragon . . .
*		S8: . . . [a dragon] who kidnapped them in the woods.
		S9: . . . [a dragon] who had kidnapped them.
		S10: Three princesses were kidnapped by a dragon.
		Predicted: Three heroes got the daughters safe by rescuing them from the dragon.
		Observed:
		S3: [Three daughters were] . . . then rescued.
		S5: Three heroes rescued the Czar's three daughters, . . .
		S6: . . . the daughters were saved by three heroes.
		S7: . . . and then rescued by three heroes.
		S8: . . . rescuing the Czar's three daughters from a dragon . . .
		S9: Three heroes rescued a Czar's three daughters from a dragon . . .
		S10: Three young knights came to their rescue . . .
		Predicted: The Czar rewarded the heroes.
A	*D*	Observed:
		S3: The rescuers were rewarded by the father of the three.
		S5:
		S6:
		S7:
		S8: Three heroes were rewarded for . . .
*		S9: The Czar rewarded them (the heroes) handsomely.
		S10:
		Unaccounted for:
		S10: . . . and killed the dragon.

story were among those giving the shorter summaries to this story. As we shall see these subjects tend to give the shorter summaries throughout.) The Level 1 predictions are compared with the subjects' responses in Table 8. Three basic statements are expected for a Level 1 summary: a statement about the kidnapping of the daughters by the dragon, a statement about the rescue, and a statement about the heroes being rewarded. Each of the subjects gave the first two statements. However, only three of the seven mentioned the reward. That is, all subjects summarized the initiating event and the attempt, but only three of the seven summarized the outcome. (As we shall see later, all three of the subjects giving longer summaries mentioned the reward. Thus, six out of ten subjects mentioned the reward.) In addition, there was only one statement that could not be accounted for by the model. Subject S10 responded that the heroes "killed the dragon." This was given in spite of the fact that the story does not say that the dragon was killed. It is not clear where this response came from.

For these seven subjects, then, of the eighteen statements included in the response protocols, seventeen were expected from the model. Of the twenty-one statements expected by the model seventeen were given.

The remaining three subjects (shown in Table 9) appeared to summarize the initiating event rather fully (down to Level 3), but gave only a Level 1 summary of the rescue itself. Six statements are expected for a summary of this sort. One subject, S2, gave all six statements. Each of the other two subjects gave five of

TABLE 9
Level 2.5 Summaries

		Predicted: Three daughters of a Czar were walking in some woods.
A	*D*	Observed:
		S1: ... who were walking in the woods.
		S2: ... one day they took a walk in the woods.
		S4: Three daughters of a Czar were taking a walk in the woods.
		Predicted: They got joy from the woods by staying in the woods.
		Observed:
		S1:
	*	S2: They stayed too long in the woods and ...
	*	S4: They enjoyed themselves so much that ...
		Predicted: A dragon kidnapped them.
		Observed:
		S1: ... suddenly a dragon kidnapped them.
		S2: ... were kidnapped by a dragon.
		S4: A dragon came and took the three daughters away.
		Predicted: Three heroes heard the daughters scream.
		S1: However, three heroes heard the girls' screaming, ...
		S2: Three heroes heard the cries of the daughters ...
		S4:
		Predicted: The heroes got the daughters safe by rescuing them from the dragon.
		Observed:
		S1: ... and saved them from the dragon.
		S2: ... and rescued them.
		S4: Three heroes ... rescued the daughters.
		Predicted: As a result, the Czar rewarded the heroes.
		Observed:
		S1: ... they were rewarded by the Czar.
		S2: The Czar rewarded the heroes.
		S4: The Czar ... rewarded the heroes.
		Unaccounted for:
		S1: Once there were three daughters of a Czar ... ⎫ setting
		S2: A Czar had three daughters and ... ⎬
		S1: It soon grew dark [in the woods] and ...
		S1: ... [the heroes] ran to them [the daughters] ...
		S1: When the heroes took the daughters to the palace, ...
		S4: ... they forgot the time.
		S4: ... [three heroes] fought the dragon and ...
		S4: [The Czar] upon hearing it ...

the six expected statements. One subject deleted the statement about the daughters enjoying themselves in the woods, and one deleted the statement about the heroes hearing the daughters' screams. (It should, of course, be noted that, as expected, all seven of the other subjects deleted both of these plus the one about the daughters walking in the woods.) Thus, of the eighteen statements expected by the model, sixteen appeared in these summaries. Eight statements appeared that were not expected by the model. Two of these were setting information and three each from S1 and S4. One of these did not appear in (nor was it implied by) the story, namely, 'It grew dark . . ..' The other five statements were all more detailed than would be expected from this level of summary. Thus, excluding setting statements, twenty-two statements were given. Of these, sixteen were expected. Four of the six remaining statements would be added if S4 were assumed to summarize the initiating event at one level lower and both S1 and S4 were assumed to summarize the rescue at one level lower.

Finally, it should be mentioned that the model gives a rather poor account of the part about the daughters enjoying the woods. The responses given are only very loose paraphrases of the statements actually given by the subjects. This may result from a somewhat superficial analysis of this aspect of the story in the first place.

Thus, excluding setting information, forty statements were given in response to this story. Of these, thirty-three were expected by the model, and the remaining seven were unaccounted for. Of the seven two were not even clear implications of the story. Of the thirty-nine statements expected, thirty-three were actually given.

The Countryman and the Serpent. Of the ten subjects, seven gave responses analyzable as Level 1 summaries and the remaining three gave Level 2 summaries. The Level 1 summaries are shown in Table 10. Five statements are expected for Level 1 summaries of this story. Of the thirty-five responses expected from the seven subjects, thirty-four actually occur. Subject S8 fails to mention the serpent's killing the countryman's cattle. Three responses are unaccounted for. All of these involve more than the expected amount of detail. Thus, of the thirty-seven observed statements, thirty-four are expected from the model. Most of the observed statements are pretty good paraphrases of the predicted statements. However, the predicted statement about the serpent biting the countryman's son is somewhat strained. All subjects mention that the serpent actually killed the son. The predicted version at best only implies that the son died. Only two subjects mention that it was a result of being bitten.

The eighteen statements given by the three remaining subjects can easily be matched with the eighteen statements expected from the Level 2 summary. Again, however, there may be some question as to how well some of the observed statements match the predicted ones. The observed statements about the son's being killed contain more detail than the predicted statement. Also, the statements about the countryman offering gifts to the serpent is somewhat less

TABLE 10
Level 1 Summaries

A	D	
		Predicted: A serpent got revenge on a countryman's son by biting him.
		Observed:
*		S1: ... [a serpent] who bit his son and killed him.
*	*	S3: A farmer lost his son to a serpent and ...
*	*	S6: ... it had killed his son.
*	*	S7: ... the serpent had killed the farmer's son.
*	*	S8: After a serpent killed his son, and ...
*		S9: ... his son's death at the mouth of a serpent ...
*	*	S10: A farmer's son was killed by a snake.
		Predicted: As a result, the countryman got revenge on the serpent by chopping off its tail.
		Observed:
		S1: A farmer sought revenge on a serpent ... and cut off its tail, ...
	*	S3: [The farmer] in turn retaliated.
	*	S6: A farmer cut the tail off of a snake after ...
	*	S7: A farmer cut off a serpent's tail after ...
		S8: ... he retaliated by cutting off its tail, ...
		S9: A countryman in revenge for ... cut off its tail.
		S10: The farmer chopped off the snake's tail in revenge.
		Predicted: As a result, the serpent got revenge on the countryman by killing his cattle.
A	D	Observed:
		S1: ... so the serpent in turn hurt the farmer by stinging several of his cattle.
	*	S3: The conflict escalated.
	*	S6: After the snake attacked the farmer's cattle, ...
		S7: The serpent killed many of the farmer's cattle in revenge, and ...
		S8:
		S9: The serpent in revenge began killing the farmer's cattle.
	*	S10: The snake took revenge for the loss of his tail by terrorizing the farmer's livestock.
		Predicted: The countryman tried to get peace with the serpent, ...
		Observed:
		S1: The farmer tried to make it up to the serpent ...
		S3: When the farmer asked the snake for peace, ...
		S6: the farmer asked for a truce, ...
		S7: ... peace offers from the farmer.
		S8: ..., a farmer tried to make peace.
		S9: The farmer attempted to make up, ...
		S10: The farmer tried to make peace with the snake ...
		Predicted: ... but the snake refused any peace offering.
		Observed:
*		S1: ... but the snake would not accept the gifts of truce, claiming the death of the farmer's son and the loss of his own tail could not be forgotten.
*		S3: ... the snake said that the die was cast and there could be no peace.
		S6: ..., but the snake refused.
		S7: ... and [the snake] refused [peace offers].
A	D	S8: But the serpent refused, saying that neither could forget their losses.

(continued)

TABLE 10 *(continued)*

*	S9: . . . but [the farmer] was rebuked by the serpent, who said gifts can never make up for losses.
*	S10: However, the snake told him to take back his gifts because each had lost too much to ever make peace.

Unaccounted for:

S1: The farmer soon reached the serpent, . . .

S1: . . . by bringing it food and honey, . . .

S10: . . . by bringing gifts.

TABLE 11
Level 2 Summaries

			Predicted: A countryman's son stepped on a serpent.
A	*D*		Observed:
*			S2: A boy accidentally stepped on a snake's tail, . . .
			S4: A son of a countryman stepped on a serpent's tail . . .
			S5: . . . a snake he stepped on . . .
			Predicted: The serpent got revenge on the boy by biting him.
			Observed:
*			S2: . . . and the snake bit the boy. The boy died.
*	*		S4: . . . and was killed.
*			S5: A man's son died when a snake . . . bit him.
			Predicted: As a result, the countryman got revenge on the serpent by chopping its tail off.
			Observed:
			S2: . . . and the father chopped off the snake's tail in revenge.
			S4: His father, in revenge, cut off its tail.
	*		S5: The man managed to cut off part of the snake's tail, . . .
			Predicted: As a result, the serpent got revenge on the countryman by killing his cattle.
			Observed:
*			S2: In return, the snake bit the farmer's cattle and killed them.
			S4: The serpent in retaliation killed off the countryman's cattle.
			S5: . . . and the snake got revenge by killing some of his cattle.
			Predicted: The countryman offered gifts to get peace with the serpent.
A	*D*		Observed:
	*		S2: The farmer tried to reason with the snake and bury the hatchet (but not in the snake).
			S4: The countryman decided to make peace and took food to the serpent.
			S5: The man tried to make peace by bringing the snake food, . . .
			Predicted: The serpent refused the peace offering.
A	*D*		Observed:
*			S2: But the snake would have none of it and said that neither one would ever forget his loss.
*			S4: The serpent refused, saying a loss of a son or of a tail could not be forgotten.
*			S5: . . . but the snake refused to end the feud, on the grounds that he couldn't forget the loss of his tail and the man would never forget about his son.

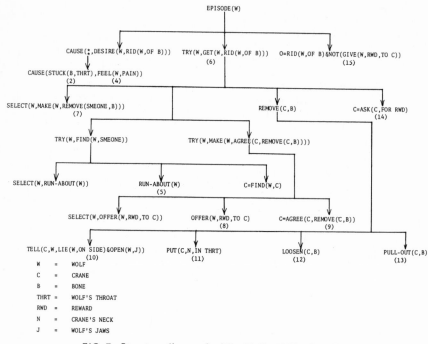

FIG. 7   Structure diagram for 'The Wolf and The Crane'.

TABLE 12
Text of "The Wolf and the Crane"

(1) A Wolf was gorging on an animal he had killed.
(2) Suddenly, a small bone in the meat stuck in his throat
(3) and he could not swallow it.
(4) He soon felt terrible pain in his throat
(5) and ran up and down groaning and groaning and
(6) seeking for something to relieve the pain.
(7) He tried to induce everyone he met to remove the bone.
(8) "I would give anything" he said, "if you would take it out."
(9) At last the Crane agreed to try
(10) and told the Wolf to lie on his side and open his jaws as wide as he could.
(11) Then the Crane put its long neck down the Wolf's throat and
(12) with its beak loosened the bone
(13) till at last it got it out.
(14) "Will you kindly give me the reward you promised?" said the Crane.
(15) The Wolf grinned and showed his teeth and said: "Be content. You have put your head inside a Wolf's mouth and taken it out again in safety; that ought to be reward enough for you."

well fit than most of the cases thus far discussed. Nevertheless, the overall account for these data seems rather good.

The Wolf and the Crane. The final story to be discussed in this section is the fable entitled "The Wolf and the Crane." This is the longest story and evokes the longest summary. The text of this story is given in Table 12; its structure diagram is given in Fig. 7.

As shown in Table 13, six of the ten subjects gave a Level 2 summary and four

TABLE 13

Level 2 Summaries

		Predicted: A bone stuck in a wolf's throat.	
A	D	Observed:	
	*	S3: [A wolf] in need . . .	
		S5: A wolf that got a bone stuck in his throat, . . .	
		S6: A wolf got a bone stuck in its throat, . . .	
	*	S7: . . . [a bone] from a wolf's throat, . . .	
		S8: . . . a bone stuck in his throat.	
		S9: A wolf with a bone stuck in his throat, . . .	
		Predicted: A crane removed it.	
		Observed:	
	*	S3: A wolf . . . was aided by a crane.	
*		S5: . . . got a crane to . . . get the bone out.	
*		S6: and a crane removed the bone with its head.	
		S7: A crane removed a bone [from a wolf's throat].	
		S8: A crane removed it . . .	
*		S9: [A wolf] was helped by a crane, who remov]ed] the bone.	
		Predicted: When the crane asked for his reward, . . .	
		Observed:	
	*	S3: When [the crane was] applying for his reward, . . .	
*		S5: When the crane asked the wolf for the reward it had promised, . . .	
*		S6:	
*		S7: . . . but when he asked for the promised reward, . . .	
		S8: . . . and asked for his reward.	
		S9: When the crane asked for a reward, . . .	
		Predicted: The wolf said, "Be satisfied with your life."	
A	D	Observed:	
		S3: The crane was told to be satisfied that he was still alive.	
		S5: . . . the wolf told the crane that it should be satisfied with having gotten its head out of the wolf's mouth alive.	
		S6: The wolf refused to give the crane a larger reward than the crane's life.	
		S7: . . . the wolf replied that to survive putting your head in a wolf's mouth should be reward enough.	
		S8: The wolf replied that going inside a wolf's mouth and living to tell the tale was reward enough.	
		S9. . . . the wolf replied: "Be content. You have put your head inside a wolf's mouth and out again in safety; that ought to be reward enough for you."	
		Unaccounted for:	
		S8: A wolf writhed in pain from . . .	
		S9: . . . [a crane who] stuck his head down the wolf's throat to . . .	

TABLE 14
Level 3 Summaries

		Predicted: A bone stuck in a wolf's throat.
A	*D*	Observed:

Predicted: A bone stuck in a wolf's throat.

A   *D*   Observed:

      S1: A wolf got a bone stuck in his throat . . .

      S2: . . . a small bone stuck in his throat.

      S4: A wolf had a bone stuck in his throat . . .

      S10: A wolf got a bone caught in its throat, . . .

Predicted: He found a crane to help him by running about.

Observed:

*   *   S1: He tried to get someone to help him get the bone out, . . .

     *   S2: He met a crane . . .

      S4: He sought help to get it out. A crane came along and . . .

      S10: The only one he could get to help was the crane, . . .

Predicted: He got the crane to agree to remove the bone by offering him a reward.

Observed:

     *   S1: . . . claiming he'd give anything to anyone who could take it out.

      S2: . . . and promised to give him anything he wanted if he would
           remove the bone.

*   *   S4: [A crane] offered his help.

      S10: [The only one he could get to help was the crane] to whom
           the wolf promised a great reward.

Predicted: The crane removed the bone.

Observed:

      S1: Finally a crane . . . got it out.

      S2: The crane . . . removed the bone.

      S4: The crane managed to get the bone out.

      S10: The crane . . . removed the bone.

Predicted: When the crane asked for his reward, . . .

Observed:

      S1: When the crane asked for his reward, . . .

      S2: When the crane asked for his reward, . . .

      S4: When he asked for the reward, . . .

      S10: When the crane asked for his reward, . . .

Predicted: . . . the wolf said, 'Be satisfied with your life'.

Observed:

      S1: . . . the wolf refused with a grin. 'The fact that I didn't bite
           your head off should be enough reward for you'.

      S2: . . . the wolf said he should be happy just to have put his
           head in the wolf's mouth and taken it out again.

      S4: . . . the wolf said it's reward enough to have had the opportunity to stick
           his head in the mouth of a wolf without having it close on him.

      S10: . . . the wolf replied, 'To have your head in the mouth of a wolf and to
           remove it safely should be reward enough for anybody'.

      Unaccounted for:

          S1: . . . while he was gorging on an animal. ⎫

          S2: A wolf was eating a dead animal when . . . ⎬ setting

          S4: . . . while eating an animal he caught. ⎭

          S2: He tried, but could not dislodge it.

(continued)

TABLE 14 *(continued)*

S10: . . . and he could not remove it by himself.
S4: The bone pained the wolf.
S1: . . . [a crane] put its long neck down the wolf's throat and . . .
S2: [The crane] put his neck in the wolf's mouth and . . .
S4: He told the wolf to lie on his side and open his mouth as wide as possible.
S10: The crane stuck his head down the wolf's throat and . . .

---

gave a Level 3 summary. All twenty-four of the expected Level 2 statements appear in these protocols. Two more specific unaccounted-for statements also occur. The fit to the individual statements also seems to be pretty good, with the exception of S3, who again gives very general responses. Instead of saying that the wolf got a bone stuck in his throat, S8 said that the wolf was "in need" and instead of telling how the crane helped the wolf, he simply wrote that "The wolf was aided" by the crane. All twenty-four of the statements expected from the four Level 3 subjects also occurred (see Table 14). However, ten statements occurred among these subjects that were unaccounted for. Of these, three were setting statements, two were implied, but not stated in the story, one was a psychological event, and four were further specifications on how the crane removed the bone. In addition, no one mentioned the method whereby the wolf found the crane (by running about). Otherwise, the model would appear to give a reasonable account for the statements in the summaries. In all (excluding the setting statements), fifty-seven statements were given to this story. Of these, forty-eight are expected from the model. Five of the remaining nine are further specifications on the method of removal of the bone, two are about the wolf's pain, and two are extensions on the story.

Overall Analysis of Summary Data

I have given a detailed accounting of the fit of the model to the individual response protocols of individual subjects, but it is rather difficult to get a general picture of how well the model accounts for our observations. It would seem that there are two relevant numbers: (1) 94% of the expected statements were actually observed; (2) 88% of the observed statements were expected. Not a perfect accounting — yet, considering that these are free verbal responses, perhaps as much as can be expected. The deviations are mainly idiosyncratic. If we were to use the responses of the most typical subject in each group of subjects for each story as the predicted summaries, the numbers would be 96 and 87%, respectively. This slight improvement represents the best account possible with just two groups of subjects per story.

It might be suggested that the fits are as close as they are because I determined the level of the summary independently for each subject for each story. To some

TABLE 15

	Summary levels					Best	Grouped
	0	1	2	3	4		
Pr observed ǀ expected =	94%	91%	74%	56%	46%	94%	91%
Pr expected ǀ observed =	40%	70%	84%	94%	98%	88%	87%

degree, of course, this is correct. However, if we assume Level 1 summaries for each subject for each story, our fit deteriorates only a little. In that case, 91% of the expected statements actually occur and 70% of the observed statements are expected. Table 15 compares these two statistics for Level 0, 1, 2, 3, and 4 summaries with the best-fitting summaries from the preceding section. The percentage of the expected statements actually observed ranges from 94% for Level 0 to 46% for Level 4. The percentage of observed statements that were predicted ranges from 40% at Level 0 to 98% at Level 4. The final column, labeled "Grouped," gives the observed values of these statistics when subjects are categorized into two groups, those that give long summaries and those that give short ones and are not recategorized for each story. I will discuss this later when I address the issue of individual differences.

Another way of cumulating the data is to look at those statements that would be introduced at each level of summarization and see what percentage of them appear in the summaries. These data are given in Table 16. For each level of summary, the table gives the observed percentage of statements that were predicted to first occur at that level of summary. There are 80 statements that are expected to occur in Level 0 summaries. Of these, 75 (or 94%) are observed in the response protocols. At Level 1, 60 additional statements would occur. Of these, 53 (or 88%) actually occur. Only 39% of the additional 70 statements that would be added in a Level 2 summary actually occurred in the data. Of the 110 additional statements to be expected for a Level 3 summary, only 23% occurred.

TABLE 16

	Summary level				
	0	1	2	3	4
Percentage of statements observed	94%	88%	39%	23%	6%
Total number of statements predicted to first occur at each level	80	60	70	110	90

Finally, only 6% of the 90 statements to be added at Level 4 occurred in the data. What we see, then, is that those statements that are predicted to occur in low-level summaries occur in nearly every summary. Those that are predicted to occur only with a detailed accounting of the story occur very rarely indeed. This is perhaps the least controversial evidence that the model is, in fact, differentiating between more and less important statements of the story.

A number of comments can be made about differences among subjects in this experiment. Some subjects, namely, Subjects S3, S6, S7, and S8, always gave very short summaries and were always included in the group giving low-level summaries. Two other subjects, namely, S5 and S9, were included in this group three out of four times. On the other hand, S2 and S4 always gave longer summaries and were always included in the groups giving more detailed summaries. Subject S1 appeared in this group three out of four times. Subject S10 was in each group half the time. If we analyze Subjects S3, S5, S6, S7, S8, and S9 as always giving more detailed summaries, the overall analysis of the data suffers only a little. In this case, we find that 91% of the expected statements occur and that 87% of the observed statements are predicted. To the degree that fewer individual level parameters must be determined, we can tolerate this slightly poorer fit. These are the data in Table 15 labeled "Grouped."

Before concluding my dicsussion of these data, a point should be made about the degree to which observed statements fitted the predictions. Of the 164 statements that were judged to be acceptable paraphrases, 102 were judged to be good paraphrases. Twenty-eight were judged to involve the addition of an element of meaning not in the predicted statements. Twenty-five of the statements were judged to involve the deletion of an element of meaning not in the original. In nine cases one element was added and another deleted. Thus, of the 186 statements given by the ten subjects, 102 (or 55%) were predicted almost exactly. An additional 33% of the responses were predicted acceptably and the remaining 12% unaccounted for.

With no well-articulated alternative models, it is difficult to evaluate the goodness of my account of this body of data. It is rare, however, that anyone has ever tried to account, in this much detail, for freely given prose responses. At the very least, the accounts given here must be considered promising and offer some hope that we can, in fact, deal with data of this complexity and account for processes of this importance.

SCHEMATA AND STORY RECALL

In the preceding section, I showed how a theory of summarization could be developed in terms of the schema theory of comprehension outlined in the first section of the chapter. How does that theory relate to the problem of story recall? In the first place, it should be noted that comprehensibility and recallability are invariably highly correlated in studies of memory for prose (cf. Bransford & Johnson, 1973; Thorndyke, 1975). Thus, to the degree that we have a theory of comprehensibility, we also have a theory of recallability.

Consider the following account of the story recollection process. When a story is first encountered, a configuration of schemata are discovered that will account for the story. If a single highest-level schema, such as the problem-solving schema, can be found that will organize the story, the story will be judged as highly comprehensible. The more different schemata required to make sense of the story in its entirety, the less comprehensible it will be.

Now, suppose a single schema can be found for some particular story. Upon finding this schema, we have, in effect, constructed a structure diagram for the story. Assume now that some transformation of the structure diagram constitutes the long-term representation of the story. Note that it need not be a complete representation. Some events of the story may never be encoded in long-term memory. In such a case, that node of the tree would simply be missing. In other cases, certain relationships among events may never have been stored. In this case, certain subtrees would be detached from the main body of information. Thus, *the stored representation of a story consists of a (possibly) fragmented copy of the interpretation of the original story.*

Now, the process of recall consists in locating, in memory, the stored traces and then, by use of the available schemata, attempting to reconstruct the original interpretation, and from there the original story. For simplicity, consider a case in which a subject has located the main body of the information and has determined correctly, let us say, that the information was encoded in terms of a problem-solving EPISODE. In this case, the recall consists simply of piecing the main body of fragments into the various slots of the problem-solving schema.

There are two phenomena that are expected on the basis of these assumptions: (1) Nodes higher in the tree are expected to be better remembered then those lower in the tree. (2) Stories are expected to be distorted during comprehension and/or reconstruction to fit into existing schemata. Thus new semantic elements are expected to be added and old ones deleted to make the story fit the available schemata. As we shall see, both of these phenomena are readily observed.

Thus, remembering the statements associated with the higher nodes is essentially equivalent to remembering the summary of a story. This prediction follows from two aspects of the account of the recollection process. First, if any bit of information is left out of the encoding of the story, it will tend to cut off lower branches of the tree leaving the higher, more general, information and fragmenting off the lower, more detailed, sections of the tree. Second, during the reconstruction phase of recall, to the degree that a subject uses a high-level schema to organize his memory, he will tend to build it from top to bottom. If at any point a relationship cannot be found, the result will again be the deletion of lower branches of the tree.

We have known, at least since Bartlett (1932), that we remember the gist of a story. What we have not been able to show is how this result related to an independent theory of what gist might be. However, with the postulation of models such as the one developed here, we can test explicitly the relationship between these structural variables and the probability of recall.

A simple experiment was carried out to compare summarizations and recalls. In this experiment, seventeen subjects were given aural presentations of "The Old Farmer and His Stubborn Donkey."[2] Then, following an approximately 30-minute intervening task, eight of the subjects were asked to summarize the story and the remaining nine were asked to recall the story. The recall subjects were asked to regenerate the story as nearly verbatim as possible, whereas the summary subjects were merely asked to tell what the story was about. All responses were written.

The major analysis involved measuring, for each statement of the original story, how many of the subjects from each group mentioned the statement in question. In this way, we got a direct comparison between subjects' responses to verbatim recall instructions and summary instructions.

According to the theory outlined earlier, we should expect that the higher a proposition is in the structure tree, the more likely it is to be represented in the recall or summary. Thus, the two statements at the top level in the diagram (Statements 2 and 23 in the text of Table 1) appeared in every recall protocol, whereas the bottom two statements (Statements 14 and 15) appeared in only half of the recalls. An average of 80% of the eleven statements at Level 3 or above appeared in the recall protocols. Only an average of 57% of the eleven statements below Level 3 appeared in the protocols. For the summaries, 67% of those above Level 3 were represented in the summary protocols, whereas only 32% of those below Level 3 were represented. Thus, for both recalls and summaries a preponderance of the statements appearing in the protocols are from the upper half of the structure diagram for the story.

Moreover, a direct comparison of the summary and recall data shows a strong correlation. Those statements that were included in all or nearly all of the recall protocols were also included in all or nearly all of the summary protocols. Those statements that appeared rarely in recall also appeared rarely in summarization. The correlation coefficient between the summary and recall data across the statements of the story was found to be $r = .87$.

Thus, attempted verbatim recall leads to responses that are very similar to the summary responses. They do, however, differ in some ways. The recalls are longer than the summaries. On the average, 68% of the statements of the stories are recalled, whereas only 49% of the statements of the story are represented in the summaries. Most of this difference comes from a reduced number of lower-level statements in the summaries as compared to the recalls. On the average, the lowest eleven statements appear 25% more often in recalls than summaries. Among the highest eleven statements, on the other hand, the

---

[2] As I will discuss later, some of the subjects received a slight variation on the story in Table 1. For purposes of this analysis, however, I have combined the two variations.

difference is only 13%. It thus appears that in terms of the statements given, recalls are like detailed summaries of the story. They contain all of the statements of the summary plus additional detail.

Before leaving this comparison, however, it should be noted that summaries and recalls differ in another way not reflected in our measure. Whereas recalls contain only about 40% more statements than summaries, they contain about 84% more words. That is, the statements included in the summaries are substantially briefer than those included in the recalls. This comes in part from a deletion of syntactic elements in summaries. Thus, for example, in one summary (Subject MB) we find the statement 'Farmer desired donkey in barn.' In another subject's (Subject SW) recall, we find an almost perfect paraphrase, 'He wanted the donkey to go into the shed.' The summary and recall statements have the same meaning, but a different number of words. Another example of the same thing can be seen from a comparison of Subject JC's summary "He pulled and pushed, but couldn't get him in" and Subject LO's recall "So he pulls the donkey, but the donkey doesn't move; he pushes the donkey but the donkey doesn't move."

Another area of difference between the summaries and the recalls comes in the area of indirect speech. The recalling subjects sometimes attributed direct quotations to the animals in the story (as in the original story). Such quotations never occurred in the summaries. It should be pointed out that differences such as these cannot be accounted for by the model presented here. This is an aspect of summarization that is taken up by Kintsch and Van Dijk (1975), but that I have ignored. I have attempted to deal with these data only at the level of roughly semantically equivalent statements.

The data presented here are based on only one story and using only a few subjects. However, a recent study by Thorndyke (1975) indicates that the pattern of results holds up for another story and for more subjects. In addition to the "Old Farmer" story discussed here, Thorndyke used the "Circle Island" story developed by Dawes (1966). Thorndyke analyzed both of these stories in terms of a variation on the problem-solving schema presented in Rumelhart (1975) and elaborated earlier. The variations introduced by Thorndyke are sufficiently mild to allow conclusions to be drawn in terms of the current formulation.

As in the experiment discussed here, Thorndyke found that higher-level statements are more readily recalled than lower-level statements for both stories. In the "Circle Island" story, he found that 88% of the top-level statements were recalled and only 45% of the statements from the lowest level were recalled. In the "Old Farmer" story, he found that 94% of the highest-level statements were recalled and only 73% of the statements from the lowest levels were recalled. Both results were statistically significant.

In one of his experiments, Thorndyke asked his subjects to both recall and summarize the stories. He was thus able to compare, within subjects, the similarities and differences between the two types of responses. The major results are entirely consistent with the findings reported earlier. Thorndyke found that the conditional probability of a statement being part of a summary, given that it was recalled, was a sharply decreasing function of the level of the statement. That is, if a particular high-level statement was included in the recall protocol of a particular subject, it would more often than not also be included in his summary. For low-level statements, this did not occur. Low-level statements rarely occurred in the summaries, whether or not they occurred in the recalls. This result held for both stories.

The evidence thus seems clear. Story recalls resemble summaries in that both give heavy emphasis to statements that appear at higher levels in the structure diagram for the story. However, during recall subjects generate more detail. Moreover, it is clear that the problem-solving schema plays an important role in the comprehension and recall of the brief stories we have studied thus far.

The fundamental assumption of schema theory is that situations can be understood only in terms of the schemata available to the comprehender. Thus, we expect that the aspects of stories that do not neatly fit the available schemata will be modified or deleted so that a good fit will be attained for the story as a whole. This distortion can occur in two basic ways: (1) new information may be added to make the story more congruent with the available schemata, or (b) presented information may be deleted to minimize the conflict with the available schemata.

Evidence on this point is also present in the literature. For example, Bartlett (1932) reports that stories are distorted to fit the conceptualizations of the subjects. Bransford and Johnson (1973) report that in an ambiguous story in which a particular sentence is interpretable only under one reading of the story, subjects remember that sentence much better when it is consistent with their reading of the remainder of the story than when it is not. Spiro (1977) has clearly shown that subjects distort stories with surprise endings (especially after long delays) to make the ending appear more probable. In his data, this distortion involved both the addition of congruent elements and the deletion of incongruent ones.

The virtue of the analysis presented here over those in the literature is that it allows the specification of the precise ways in which the stories do not fit and thus can offer predictions about the nature of the distortion that will occur.

In the previously mentioned experiment in which subjects were asked to summarize or recall the "Old Farmer" story, subjects were given one of two variations on the story of Table 1. Eight of the subjects were given the story as described in the table. The remaining nine subjects were given the same story with the following modification: line (21) "As soon as the cat scratched the dog, the dog began to bark loudly" was changed to read "The dog began to bark loudly," moved from its position, and inserted between Lines (15) and (16), which describe the farmer getting the hay. Thus, I moved the key element up from its climactic position to an earlier point in the story. The prediction, of course, is that subjects will be forced to distort the story by reintroducing this element into its proper place in the story. Of the nine subjects, five were asked to recall the story and four were asked to summarize it. Eight of the nine subjects reintroduced Sentence (21) of the story back to its proper conceptual location. One of the subjects (a recall subject) correctly kept the barking in its presented location. Three other subjects (all in the recall condition) put the sentence *both* in its place in the modified story they heard *and* in its 'appropriate' place. It is interesting that these three subjects each add elements to explain why the "second barking" was effective, as in the following examples:

(16) NS: "... the dog barked again – this time so frighteningly that ..."
SW: "... and the dog barked so loudly that ...."
KD: "... who barked so loudly he ...."

In each case, the addition of the *so* is a contrastive element to explain why the previous barking was ineffective. None of the subjects recalling or summarizing the unmodified story added the *so* or any other reference to a previous barking.

Unfortunately, this experiment is too limited to allow any firm conclusions. However, it is indicative of the kinds of distortions we can expect to find and illustrative of the kinds of systematic manipulations our analysis will allow.

GENERAL CONCLUSIONS

The purpose of this chapter has been to (1) develop a general theory of comprehension, (2) develop a special case of the theory to the point where it could be brought into contact with experimental data, (3) illustrate how the theory could be used in the study of summaries, and (4) illustrate the use of the theory in the study of memory for brief stories. It is clear that the development of the theory is in its infancy. However, it is, I think, promising that even at this early stage we can derive predictions and make rather detailed comparisons with experimental data of rather large complexity. I am hopeful that as the theory develops it will offer a methodology for the study of reading comprehension and memory that will allow us to sharpen our understanding of these phenomena.

ACKNOWLEDGMENTS

The research reported here was partially supported by Grant NS 07454 from the National Institutes of Health and Grant GB 32235X from the National Science Foundation, and by National Institute of Mental Health Grant MH 15828 to the Center for Human Information Processing.

REFERENCES

Bartlett, F. C. *Remembering*. Cambridge, Mass.: Cambridge University Press, 1932.
Bobrow, D. G., & Norman, D. A. some principles of memory schemata. In D. G. Bobrow & A. M. Collins (Eds.), *Representation and understanding*. New York: Academic Press, 1975.

Bransford, J. D., & Johnson, M. K. Considerations of some problems of comprehension. In W. G. Chase (Ed.), *Visual information processing*. New York: Academic Press, 1973.

Bransford, J. D., & McCarrell, N. S. A sketch of a cognitive approach to comprehension. In W. Weimer & D. Palermo (Eds.), *Cognition and the symbolic processes*. Hillsdale, N.J.: Lawrence Erlbaum Associates, 1974.

Collins, A. M., & Quillian, M. R. How to make a language user. In E. Tulving & W. Donaldson (Eds.), *Organization of memory*. New York: Academic Press, 1972.

Dawes, R. M. Memory and distortion of meaningful written material. *British Journal of Psychology*, 1966, 57, 77–86.

Hellman, L. *The little foxes*. New York: Random House, 1939.

Kintsch, W., & Van Dijk, T. A. Recalling and summarizing stories. *Mimeo*, University of Colorado, Boulder, 1975.

Minsky, M. A framework for representing knowledge. In P. Winston (Ed.), *The psychology of computer vision*. New York: McGraw-Hill, 1975.

Newell, A., & Simon, H. *Human problem solving*. Englewood Cliffs, N.J.: Prentice-Hall, 1972.

Norman, D. A., Rumelhart, D. E., & the LNR Research Group. *Explorations in cognition*. San Francisco: Freeman, 1975.

Rumelhart, D. E. Notes on a schema for stories. In D. G. Bobrow & A. M. Collins (Eds.), *Representation and understanding*. New York: Academic Press, 1975.

Rumelhart, D. E., & Levin, J. A. A language comprehension system. In D. A. Norman, D. E. Rumelhart, & the LNR Research Group, *Explorations in cognition*. San Francisco: Freeman, 1975.

Rumelhart, D. E., & Norman, D. A. The computer implementation. In D. A. Norman, D. E. Rumelhart, & the LNR Research Group, *Explorations in cognition*. San Francisco: Freeman, 1975.

Rumelhart, D. E., & Ortony, A. The representation of knowledge in memory. In R. C. Anderson, R. J. Spiro, & W. E. Montague (Eds.), *Schooling and the acquisition of knowledge*. Hillsdale, N.J.: Lawrence Erlbaum Associates, 1977.

Schank, R. C., & Abelson, R. P. Scripts, plans and knowledge. *Advance Papers of the Fourth International Joint Conference on Artificial Intelligence*. Tbilisi, Georgia, USSR, 1975, Pp. 151–157.

Spiro, R. J. Inferential reconstruction in memory for connected discourse. In R. C. Anderson, R. J. Spiro, & W. E. Montague (Eds.), *Schooling and the acquisition of knowledge*. Hillsdale, N.J.: Lawrence Erlbaum Associates, 1977.

Thorndyke, P. Cognitive structure in human story comprehension and memory. Unpublished doctoral dissertation, Stanford University, 1975.

10
Computer Simulation of a Language Acquisition System: A Second Report

John R. Anderson

Yale University

PURPOSE

The study of language acquisition is important for a number of reasons. There is a practical purpose in that such research might aid the development of competence in one's language. It is common to find remarks in the psycholinguistic literature (e.g., Chomsky & Miller, 1963) that full competence in a language comes to almost all humans despite their differing experiences and general intelligences. This would seem to deny that any practical benefits could arise from an understanding of language acquisition. However, competence in a language is not an all-or-none affair. Most members of our society suffer deficits in their language ability. The difficulty I have in writing this paper is witness to the fact that a Ph.D. is no guarantee of perfection in the use of language. If we understood how language is acquired and organized, it might be possible to improve the usefulness of language as a tool for all of us. Moreover, whatever ease we have with our first language, it is clear that second language acquisition is not an automatic matter. With respect to second language learning, an understanding of the mechanisms of language acquisition would be of enormous benefit.

The study of language acquisition also derives its significance from a point of view promoted in linguistics by Noam Chomsky. He often formulated problems of linguistic theory as questions about the construction of a language acquisition device. In his view, the deepest problems of linguistics were specifying what such a device would have to know in order to acquire a language. As Chomsky saw it, this would constitute specifying the defining (universal) features of natural languages.

From my point of view, the principle significance of language acquisition is that it is a paradigm case of the induction problem. The question of induction is central to my attempt to develop a general model for human intelligence. Other induction tasks studied by psychologists (e.g., concept formation, pattern formation, sequence learning, rule induction) are all much simpler (at least, in the laboratory experiments that study them) than language learning. The consequence is that the theories that evolve for these tasks tend not to be powerful enough to handle the induction problem in its full generality. An adequate set of induction mechanisms for language acquisition, however, will be much less vulnerable to such problems of logical adequacy.

A Mechanistic Explanation

My approach to the language acquisition problem is relatively unique within psychology because I am attempting to propose a concrete set of mechanisms that will explain how language acquisition is possible. The goal is to develop a computer simulation program that will be capable of learning languages. Part of that goal is to learn languages the way humans do. All attempts that I have observed in psychology to arrive at a set of mechanisms for language acquisition have been so vague, so incomplete, or both as to be totally useless. This is not to assert that there have not been important theoretical concepts developed in psychology. However, these concepts have been basically nonmechanistic. There is nothing wrong with a nonmechanistic theory, but I would prefer to have a mechanistic one.

There is ample reason to believe that it will be difficult to propose a successful mechanistic theory of language acquisition. One piece of evidence for this pessimistic forecast is that there exist no such well-specified mechanistic theories, successful or otherwise, in psychology today. In computer science and related disciplines there has been some concern with mechanisms of language induction (for reviews, see Anderson, 1974, 1975; Biermann & Feldman, 1972; Hunt, 1975). These efforts have typically, although not exclusively, been concerned with a wider class of languages than just the natural languages. While a good many interesting results have come out of these investigations, there have evolved no programs powerful enough that they will induce, in reasonable time, any interesting class of languages. Moreover, the mechanisms that have been proposed fail miserably as psychological models. This second remark should not be taken as a criticism of the computer science efforts since as a rule they made no claims as psychological models. Nonetheless, the fact suggests that it will be hard to develop a program that both is an adequate psychological model and can learn languages. Basically, natural language is quite complex, and it is not going to be easy to understand how it is acquired.

Therefore, it was clear to me from the outset that the first simulation program I developed for language acquisition would have to be woefully inadequate on many scores. That first program, dubbed LAS I, and some preliminary criticisms of it are reported in Anderson (1974, 1975). However, the program was relatively impressive given the current fare for computer models of language induction. It has served as a basis from which to develop additional ideas. The research plan is clearly incremental – to develop a series of models that are better and better approximations. Each succeeding model will attempt to build on the lessons learned in developing the earlier ones. From my perspective, this is the only way that scientific progress will occur on difficult questions like the mechanisms for language acquisition.

The purpose of this chapter is to report the successor to LAS I, appropriately dubbed LAS II. This program is quite similar in basic concept to the LAS I program. However, a few important additions have been made that greatly increase the program's power as a language user. The remainder of this chapter is devoted to description and evaluation of LAS II. The next section will describe LAS as a language user – how it uses its knowledge of the language, once acquired, to speak and understand sentences of the language. This will give a picture of what the end product of the language learning process will be. It will be easier to understand the learning program with this perspective. Then the third section will discuss the basic principles embodied in the language learning program and present evidence for these. The next section will consider some case studies of the LAS II program learning English and French. Finally, the fifth section will provide some summary evaluations of the LAS II program. It will also outline some of my ideas for a third-pass language learning program, which will be somewhat different from LAS I or II.

Before embarking on a description of LAS, I should make it clear what LAS is a theory of. It is not, as it is currently structured, a theory of child language acquisition. It makes certain assumptions about the cognitive development of the learner that are not properly satisfied in the case of a child learning his first language. It is also not a model of an adult learning a language in a classroom situation. It assumes that the learner must induce the rules of the language from examples; that is, the rules are not presented in textbook fashion. Rather, LAS is a model of an adult who must learn the language in a free learning situation from interactions in the language with speakers of the language. The fact that LAS is not properly a model of first language acquisition or classroom language acquisition does not mean that data will not be used from these sources, only that these data must be interpreted with some caution. It is also the case that I eventually aspire to have LAS say something about these other two forms of language acquisition. However, the LAS program that will direct itself to these matters is probably many years away.

LAS AS A LANGUAGE USER

The LAS Language System

The LAS language system is not very interesting as a serious attempt to model the complexities of language comprehension and production. It is clearly dwarfed by the very impressive programs of workers in artificial intelligence such as Winograd (1972) or Schank (1972). Its principal significance is that it provides a coherent, if simplified, framework in which to conceptualize the language acquisition problem.

The LAS program is written in Michigan LISP (Hafner & Wilcox, 1974). The program accepts as input lists of words, which it treats as sentences, and scene descriptions encoded in propositional language. It obeys commands to speak, understand, and learn. The logical structure of LAS is illustrated in Fig. 1. Central to LAS is an augmented transition network grammar similar to that of

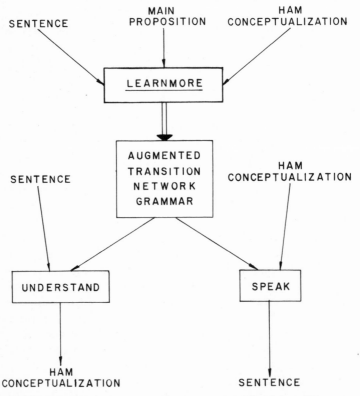

FIG. 1 A schematic representation giving the input and output of the major components of LAS – UNDERSTAND, SPEAK, and LEARNMORE.

Woods (1970). In response to the command, *Listen,* LAS evokes the program UNDERSTAND. The input to UNDERSTAND is a sentence. LAS uses the information in the network grammar to parse the sentence and obtain a representation of the sentence's meaning encoded as a propositional network in the HAM system – Anderson & Bower, (1973). (Note that propositional networks are different from augmented transition networks.) In response to the command, *Speak,* LAS evokes the program SPEAK. SPEAK receives a to-be-spoken HAM conceptualization and uses the information in the network grammar to generate a sentence to describe the conceptualization. Note that LAS is using the same network formalism both to speak and to understand. The third part of the program is LEARNMORE which induces these network grammars. This program takes as its inputs a sentence, a HAM representation of the meaning of the sentence, and an indication of the main proposition of the sentence. The outputs of the LEARNMORE program are changes to the augmented transition network. The HAM conceptualizations that are the input to LEARNMORE could arise from a number of sources. One possible source is pictures or other visual referents. In fact, later in this chapter we will consider experiments where subjects are given as input pictures plus sentences describing the pictures. With such information, subjects apparently can learn the language. I am assuming the existence of a perceptual parser that will transform these pictures into HAM conceptualizations.

The HAM Memory System

LAS uses a version of the HAM memory system (see Anderson & Bower, 1973) called HAM.2. HAM.2 provides LAS with two essential features. First, it provides a representational formalism. This is used for representing the semantic interpretations that are the output of the understanding program, the semantic intentions that are the input to the language generation program, and semantic and syntactic information in long-term memory that is used to guide a parse. Second, HAM.2 also contains a memory searching algorithm, MATCH1, which is used to evaluate various parsing conditions. For instance, the understanding program requires that certain features be true of a word for a parsing rule to apply. These are checked by the MATCH1 process. The same MATCH1 process is used by the generation program to determine whether the action associated with a parsing rule creates part of the to-be-spoken structure. This MATCH1 process is a variant of the one described in Anderson and Bower (1973, Chapters 9, 12), and its details will not be discussed here.

However, it would be useful to describe here the representational formalisms used by HAM.2. Figure 2 illustrates how the information in the sentence *The man who robbed the bank had a bloody nose* would be represented within the HAM.2 network formalisms. There is a distinct node in the memory structure for each object referenced in the sentence – a node X for man, a node Y for

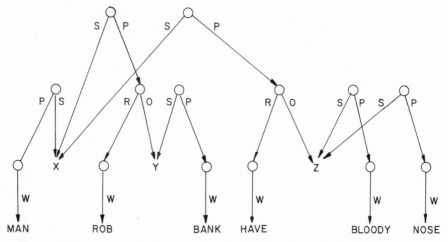

FIG. 2   An example of a propositional network representation in HAM.2.

bank, and a node Z for the nose. There are three propositions asserted about X — that X is a man, that X robbed Y, and that X has Z. Of Y it is also asserted that Y is a bank. Of Z it is also asserted that Z is bloody and that Z is a nose. Each proposition is represented by a distinct tree structure. Each tree structure consists of a root proposition node connected by an S link to a subject node and by a P link to a predicate node. The predicate nodes can be decomposed into an R link pointing to a relation node and into an O link pointing to an object node. The semantics of these representations are to be interpreted in terms of simple set theoretic notions. The subject is a subset of the predicate. Thus, the individual X is a subset of the men, the people that robbed Y, and the people that have Z.

One other point about this representation needs to be emphasized: There is a distinction made between words and the concepts that they reference. The words are connected to their corresponding concepts by links labeled W.

There are a number of motivations for the associative network representation. Anderson and Bower (1973) have combined this representation with a number of assumptions about the psychological processes that use them. Predictions derived from the Anderson and Bower model turn out to be generally true of human cognitive performances. (However, many of the specific details of HAM's representation have never been empirically tested.) The principal feature that recommends associative network representations as a computer formalism has to do with the facility with which they can be searched. Another advantage of this representation is particularly relevant to the LAS project. This has to do with the modularity of the representation. Each proposition is coded as a network structure that can be accessed and used, independent of other propositions.

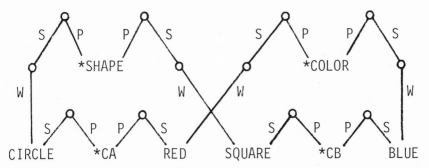

FIG. 3   An example of a HAM structure encoding both categorical and word class information.

So far, I have shown how the HAM.2 representation encodes the episodic information that might be the input to SPEAK and the output of UNDERSTAND. It can also be used to encode the semantic and syntactic information required by the parsing system. Figure 3 illustrates how HAM.2 would encode the facts that *circle* and *square* are both shapes, *red* and *blue* are both colors, and that *circle* and *red* belong to the word class *CA but *square* and *blue* belong to the word class *CB. Note that the word class information is predicated of the words while the categorical information is predicated of the concepts attached to these words. The categorical information would be used if some syntactic rule applied only to *shapes* or only to *colors*. The word class information might be evoked if a language arbitrarily applied one syntactic rule to one word class and another rule to a different word class. Inflections are a common example of syntactic rules that apply to arbitrarily defined word classes.

Augmented Transition Network Grammars

The other major representational formalism in LAS II concerns the Augmented Transition Network (ATN) grammars. The basic idea behind such network grammars is to have the units of language processing (the networks) correspond to the units that would be identified in a surface structure analysis of a sentence. For instance, consider again the sentence *The man who robbed the bank had a bloody nose.* A possible surface structure for this sentence is illustrated in Fig. 4.

The first noun phrase is analyzed as having an embedded relative clause *who robbed the bank*. That embedded relative clause contains an embedded noun phrase. There would be different networks set up to analyze each of these different types of phrases — sentences, noun phrases, and relative clauses. Suppose the network analyzing a sentence encounters a noun phrase. Then it will call upon the noun phrase network to process the embedded noun phrase. In fact, one network

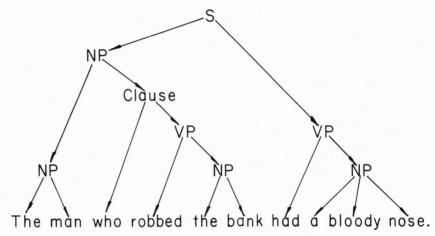

The man who robbed the bank had a bloody nose.

FIG. 4   A surface structure for a sentence. Compare with Fig. 2.

can call itself, giving the network grammar the power of a context-free grammar. The call to one network by another is known as a *push* — a term I will use. In Woods' formalism, there was the power to perform arbitrary computations in analyzing a sentence. As we will see, this is not the case in the LAS system. To permit the LAS system such powers would be unrealistic psychologically.

To illustrate LAS's network formalisms, I will present the grammar for a test language that has been used in the LAS project. It is defined by the rewrite rules in Table 1. This grammar describes a two-dimensional world of geometric shapes

TABLE 1

A Test Grammar

GRAMMAR2

S	→	NP is ADJ
	→	NP is RA NP
NP	→	(the, a) NP1 (CLAUSE)
NP1	→	SHAPE
	→	SHAPE CLAUSE
	→	ADJ NP1
CLAUSE	→	that is ADJ
	→	that is RA NP
SHAPE	→	square, circle, etc.
ADJ	→	red, big, blue, etc.
RA	→	above, right-of

Example
The red square that is small is above
the circle that is right of the triangle

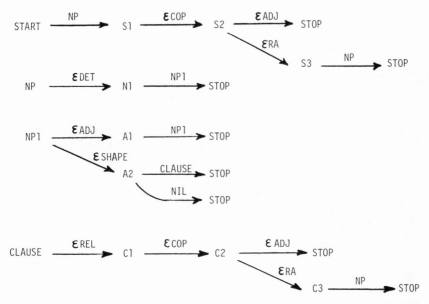

FIG. 5 The augmented transition networks encoding the grammar defined in Table 1.

that differ in color and size and spatial relations among each other. This has served as the domain for the language induction attempts.

Figure 5 illustrates the parsing networks for this grammar. There are a few conventions that need to be known in reading these networks. When a label like NP is alone on an arc, it indicates that a successful push is required to that network. When the label is prefixed by an $\in$ (e.g., $\in$ RA), this indicates that the next word must be in the word class referred to by the label (i.e., RA). If a NIL labels the arc, this means that the arc can be traversed without anything being processed about the sentence.

Such networks are modular in two senses. First, they are relatively independent of each other. Second, they are independent of the SPEAK and UNDERSTAND programs that use them. This modularity greatly simplifies LAS's task of induction. LAS only induces the network grammars; the interpretative SPEAK and UNDERSTAND programs represent innate linguistic competences for interpreting the networks. Finally, the networks themselves are very simple, with limited conditions and actions. Thus, LAS need consider only a small range of possibilities in inducing a network. The network formalism gains its expressive power by the embedding of networks. Because of network modularity, the induction task does not increase with the complexity of embedding.

The same network is used by the SPEAK program for sentence generation as by the UNDERSTAND program for sentence comprehension. As a consequence,

LAS has only to induce one set of grammatical rules to do both tasks. Thus, the LAS II program makes the prediction that acquisition of the ability to understand and the ability to generate go hand in hand. This seems to conflict with the conventionally accepted wisdom that comprehension precedes production. However, there may be reasons why child production does not mirror comprehension other than that different grammatical competences underlie the two. The learner may not yet have acquired the physical mastery to produce certain words. This clearly is the case, for instance, with Lenneberg's (1962) anarthric child who understood but was not able to speak. Also, the child may have the potential to use a certain grammatical construction, but instead uses other, preferred modes of production. The final possibility is that the child may be resorting to nonlinguistic strategies in language understanding. Bever (1970) has presented evidence that young children do not understand passives, but can still act out passives when they are not reversible. It seems that the child can take advantage of the conceptual constraints between subject, verb, and object. The child's grammatical deficit appears only when he is asked to act out reversible passives. Similarly, Clark (1974) has shown that young children understand relational terms like *in, on,* and *under* by resorting to heuristic strategies. It is clear that we also have the ability to understand speech without knowing the syntax. For instance, when Tarzan utters *food boy eat,* we know what he must mean. This is because we can take advantage of conceptual constraints among the words.

The study by Fraser, Bellugi, and Brown (1963) is often cited as showing that comprehension precedes production. They found that children had a higher probability of understanding a sentence (as manifested by pointing to an appropriate picture) than of producing the sentence. However, there were difficulties in equating the measures of production and comprehension. Fernald (1970), using different scoring procedures, found no difference. Interestingly, Fraser et al. did find a strong correlation between which sentence forms could be understood and which could be produced. That is, sentence forms that were relatively easy to understand were relatively easy to produce. This may indicate a common base for comprehension and production.

The SPEAK Program

The SPEAK program is simpler than the UNDERSTAND program because it does not require as elaborate a control mechanism for backup. A flow-chart giving a gross and approximate diagram of its information control is given in Fig. 6. SPEAK starts with a HAM network of propositions tagged as to-be-spoken and a topic of the sentence. The topic of the sentence will correspond to the first meaning-bearing element in a START network (e.g., see Fig. 5). SPEAK searches through its START network, looking for some path that will express a to-be-spoken proposition attached to the topic and that expresses the topic as

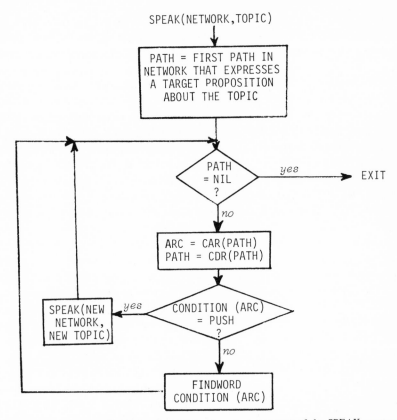

FIG. 6   A flow-chart illustrating the high-level control structure of the SPEAK program.

the first element. It determines whether a path accomplishes this by evaluating the action associated with a path and determining if they create a structure that appropriately matches the to-be-spoken structure. When it finds such a path, it uses it for generation.

The path retrieved is referred to as PATH in Fig. 6. It consists of a list of arcs. The SPEAK program will go through this list arc by arc. In Fig. 6 there is a test for when the list is exhausted (PATH = NIL?). There also appear in Fig. 6 some LISP terms for inspecting the list that need explanation. The function CAR applied to a list gives the first member of the list. The function CDR applied to a list gives a list of all members past the first.

Generation is accomplished by evaluating the conditions on each arc. If a condition involves a push to an embedded network, SPEAK is recursively called to speak some subphrase expressing a proposition attached to the main proposition. The arguments for a recursive call of SPEAK are the embedded network and the node that connects the main proposition and the embedded proposition.

This connecting node is what is common between the memory structure described by the embedded and embedding proposition. It is also the topic of the embedded network. In effect, the embedded network is elaborating on the semantic referent of that node.

If the condition does not involve a push it will contain a set of memory commands specifying that some features be true of a word. SPEAK will use these features to determine what the word is. The word so determined will be spoken. The subprogram FINDWORD is the one that uses a condition to retrieve a word.

As an example, consider how SPEAK would generate a sentence corresponding to the HAM structure in Fig. 7 using the English-like grammar in Fig. 5. Figure 7 contains a set of propositions about three objects denoted by the nodes G246, G195, and G182. Of node G246 it is asserted that it is a triangle, and that G195 is right of it. Of G195 it is also asserted that it is a square, and that it is above G182. Of G182 it is also asserted that it is square, small, and red. Figure 8 outlines the control structure of the generation of this sentence. LAS enters the START network intent on producing some utterance about the topic G195. The first path through the network involves predicating an adjective of G195, but there is nothing in the adjective class predicated of G195. The second path through the START network corresponds to something LAS can say about G195 – it is above G182. Therefore, LAS plans to say this as its main proposition. First, it must find some noun phrase to express G195. The substructure under G195 in Fig. 8 reflects the construction of this phrase. The NP network is called with its connecting node G195. It prints out *the* and calls NP1, which retrieves *square* and calls CLAUSE, which prints *that, is,* and *right-of* and recursively calls NP to print *the triangle* to express G246. Similarly, recursive calls are made on the NP1 network to express G182 as *the small red square.*

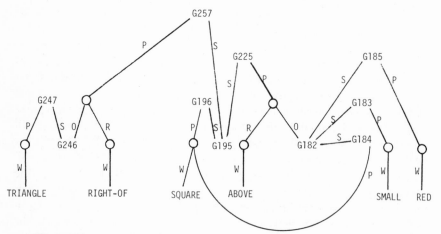

FIG. 7 This to-be-spoken HAM structure is given as input to the SPEAK program.

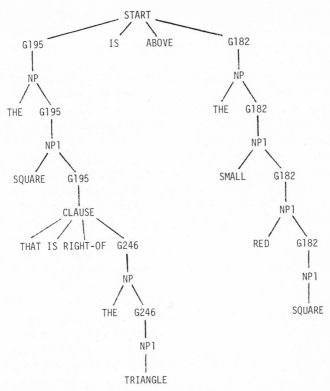

FIG. 8   A tree structure showing the network calls and words output in the generation of a sentence to express the information contained in Fig. 7.

A noun phrase is concluded once all the to-be-expressed information about the referent of the noun phrase has been expressed.

It is interesting to inquire what is the linguistic power of LAS as a speaker. Clearly it can generate any context-free language since its transition networks correspond, in structure, to a context-free grammar. However, it turns out that LAS has certain context-sensitive aspects because its productions are constrained by the requirement that they express some well-formed HAM conceptual structure. Consider two problems that Chomsky (1957) regarded as not handled well by context-free grammars. The first is agreement of number between a subject NP and a verb. This is hard to arrange in a context-free grammar because the NP is already built by the time the choice of verb number must be made. The solution is trivial in LAS — when both the NP and the verb are spoken, their number is determined by inspection of whatever concept in the to-be-spoken structure underlies the subject. The other Chomsky example involves the identity of selectional restrictions for active and passive sentences. This is also achieved automatically in LAS, since the restrictions in both cases are regarded simply as reflections of restrictions on the semantic structure from which both sentences are spoken.

While LAS can handle those features of natural language suggestive of context-sensitive rules, it cannot handle examples like languages of the form $a^n b^n c^n$ that require context-sensitive grammars. It is interesting, however, that it is hard to find natural language sentences of this structure. The best I can come up with are sentences using *respectively,* such as *John and Bill hit and kissed Jane and Mary, respectively.* This sentence is of questionable acceptability.

There are some linguistic constructions like number and active–passive that are more easily described by context-sensitive rules, but can be generated by context-free rules. Languages that contain such constructions are still called context-free. However, there are true context-sensitive languages like the $a^n b^n c^n$ example that, in principle, cannot be generated by a context-free grammar.

LAS could generate a language of the form $a^n b^n c^n$ if its HAM semantic structure contained to-be-spoken expressions of this form. The LAS networks really are *transducers.* That is, they translate one information representation, the HAM network, into another representation, the sentence. Thus, questions about the context-sensitive features of the languages generated by LAS can depend on context-sensitive features of the memory structure. Unfortunately, the context-sensitive features of the HAM representation are not well defined.

There is another way that LAS could gain context-sensitive powers from its memory structure. Suppose that in speaking a sentence it could write notes to itself in the memory structure and later read these notes. Given this general read-write capacity it could behave as a Turing machine. However, in speaking LAS can read only from its to-be-spoken memory structure. Its "writing" consists of outputing a sentence, and it is prevented from reading that sentence. These restrictions on reading and writing are probably too severe but it would be unrealistic psychologically to give LAS unlimited read–write capabilities.

Actually, LAS does have a certain very limited writing capability within its memory structure. It can tag memory structures as already spoken. This is to prevent it from generating expressions like *The blue blue square which is blue is blue,* in which the same proposition is expressed over and over again. This does give the grammar context-sensitive powers of a sort that cannot be obtained in a context-free grammar.

The UNDERSTAND Program

The search in SPEAK for a grammatical realization of the conceptual structure was limited to search through a single network at a time. Search terminated when a path was found that would express part of the to-be-spoken HAM structure. Because search is limited to a single parsing network, the control structure was simply required to execute a depth-first search through a finite network. In the UNDERSTAND program, it is necessary, when one path through a network fails, to consider the possibility that the failure may be in a parsing of a subnetwork called on that path. Therefore, it is possible to have to back into a network a second time to attempt a different parsing. For this reason the control structure of the UNDERSTAND program is more complicated.

Perhaps an English example would be useful to motivate the need for a complex control structure. Compare the two sentences *The Democratic party hopes to win in '76* with *The Democratic party hopes are high for '76.* A main parsing network would call a noun phrase network to identify the first noun phrase. Suppose UNDERSTAND identified *The Democratic party.* Later elements in the second sentence would indicate that this choice was wrong. Therefore, the main network would have to reenter the noun phrase network and attempt a different parsing to retrieve *The Democratic party hopes.* When UNDERSTAND reentered the noun phrase network to retrieve this parsing, it must remember which parsings it tried the first time so that it does not retrieve the same old parsing.

The control structure of the UNDERSTAND program is sufficiently complex so that space limitations prevent any attempt to describe it here (see, however, Anderson, 1974). It does perform a left-to-right parse of the sentence, building up HAM memory structure as it goes to represent the comprehended portion of the sentence. Backup facilities exist to enable the program to undo the work along a particular path and try another path through the network, should the first prove to be a "garden path." The control structure for backup basically permits a depth-first search through the space of possible parsings permitted by the ATN grammar. While the control structure is adequate to retrieve a parsing of a sentence should one exist, it is quite primitive compared to the scheduler mechanism developed by Kaplan (1973) for ATNs. The Kaplan control structure permits a more varied search of possible parsings than the simple depth-first option in LAS. It is unclear, as a psychological question, whether the greater flexibility is required to model human comprehension.

It is also of interest to consider the power of LAS as an acceptor of languages. LAS, as currently constituted, can accept exactly the context-free languages. This is because, unlike Woods' (1970) system, actions on arcs cannot influence the results of conditions on arcs, and, therefore, play no role in determining whether a string is accepted or not. However, what is interesting is that LAS's behavior as language understander is relatively little affected by these limitations on its grammatical powers. Consider the following example, where it might seem that LAS would need a context-sensitive grammar. In English noun phrases, it seems that we can have almost arbitrary numbers of adjectives. This led to the rule in Fig. 5 where NP1 could recursively call itself each time, accepting another adjective. There is nothing in this rule to prevent it from accepting phrases like *the small big square* or other unacceptable constructions. However, in practice this seldom leads LAS into any difficulties because LAS is unlikely to encounter such a construction due to the constraints on what a speaker may properly say to LAS.

It is useful to compare generation versus analysis in the LAS networks. The flow of control is somewhat different in the two circumstances. In sentence production LAS first finds a path through the START network to correspond to the main proposition that it wants to assert. Then it will proceed to generate the first phrase in the sentence. Thus with respect to the control structure of Fig. 8, SPEAK completely generates one level before it expands the leftmost substructure. In contrast, in UNDERSTAND the control structure is generated as the words come in. This means that before any further control structure is evoked at a particular level, the leftmost substructure will be completely generated. Network grammars are rather ideal in that they permit with equal facility the breadth expansion required by SPEAK to plan the production and the depth expansion required by UNDERSTAND to follow the spoken sentence.

BASIC PRINCIPLES FOR LANGUAGE INDUCTION

Before getting into a case history of the LEARNMORE program inducing a language, it would be useful to highlight and motivate the basic principles embodied in the LEARNMORE program. There are seven such principles. These principles are a rather mixed lot in that some are of the status of philosophy of approach and others are of the status of assumptions about the nature of natural language.

1. Use of Semantic Information

LEARNMORE takes as its basic input *pairs* consisting of sentences and representations of their meaning. The information about sentence meaning is critical to the successful performance of the program. This contrasts with an idea once popular in linguistics and psycholinguistics that syntactic information was sufficient for learning the syntactic structure of the language. That is, all one needed is information about the well-formed sentences of the language and not what they meant. At most, semantic information played the role of motivating the language learner. As Chomsky (1962) wrote,

> It might be maintained, not without plausibility, that semantic information of some sort is essential even if the formalized grammar that is the output of the device does not contain statements of direct semantic nature. Here, care is necessary. It may well be that a child given only the input of nonsense elements would not come to learn the principles of sentence formation. This is not necessarily a relevant observation, however, even if true. It may only indicate that meaningfulness and semantic function provide the motivation for language learning, while playing no necessary part in its mechanism, which is what concerns us here. [p. 531]

In the LAS program not only is semantic information critical to learning the grammar of the language, but it is also the case that there is not a clear distinction between the acquisition of syntax and that of semantics. The product of the acquisition process is an augmented transition network grammar. Such a grammar is a map between sentences and meaning. There is not a distinct semantic component versus a distinct syntactic component.

There are a number of reasons to believe that LAS is right in treating semantics as central to language acquisition. In the domain of child language acquisition, there is growing recognition that the acquisition of syntactic knowledge cannot be understood without also studying the semantic correlates of this syntactic knowledge (e.g., Bloom, 1970, 1973; Bowerman, 1973; Brown, 1973; Clark, 1975; McNeill, 1975; Nelson, 1974; Schlesinger, 1971; Sinclair-de Zwart, 1973). An interesting series of experiments, looking at older children and adults, has been performed by Moeser and Bregman (1972, 1973). They contrasted the learning of artificial (but natural-like) languages under two conditions. In the no-referent condition, their subjects saw only well-formed strings of the language. In the referent condition they saw well-formed strings plus pictures of the semantic referent of these strings. In either case, the criterion test was for the subject to be able to detect which strings of the language were well formed — without the aid of any referent pictures. After 3000 training trials in one experiment subjects in the no-referent condition were almost at chance in the criterion test, whereas subjects in the referent condition were essentially perfect.

Results from a formal analysis of the language learning problem argue for a similar conclusion. One can ask what kind of behavior is logically possible given only syntactic information. That is, suppose a learner is only given information about what are the well-formed strings of the language. Is it possible for him to learn the language? Gold (1967) has explored this situation, which he calls text presentation. He has shown that, provided that the class of possible languages is at least as large as the finite state languages,[1] it is not possible to learn the correct language.

Gold also identified a pure syntax situation in which language learning is possible. This he calls informant presentation. In this situation the learner is not only told what are the well-formed sentences of the language; he is also told what are not well-formed sentences. In this condition the language learner can learn any language in the primitive recursive class — a class of languages probably large enough to include all natural languages. However, this result should provide no comfort to those who hope to take a syntax approach to human language learning. Humans learn languages without negative information. This is particularly clear in the case of child language learning (Braine, 1971; Brown, 1973).

---

[1] Actually, Gold has shown this result for an even smaller class of languages, a class he calls the superfinite class. This includes all languages of finite cardinality plus just one infinite-cardinality language.

Children learning a language do not have access to information about all the possible nonsentences. The nonsentences they encounter or generate are very systematic. Second, children are seldom corrected when they utter a syntactically incorrect sentence. Third, in those experiments that have provided subjects with negative feedback, there is little evidence that the children can take advantage of this information.

I (Anderson, 1976) have explored the formal question of language learnability in a situation approximating the semantic condition of LAS. That is, the information to the learner consists of sentences and representations of their meaning. The task of the language learner is to induce a map between sentence and meaning, not to induce a syntactic characterization of the language. In this case any primitive recursive function relating sentence and meaning can be induced given only information about what are the correct pairings. It is not necessary to provide negative information about what are the incorrect pairings of sentence and meaning.

The use of semantic information makes a strong empirical assumption about the nature of the information that is available to the learner. That is, we are assuming that the language learner has available to him information about the meaning of sentences. I have already described one situation in which that seems a reasonable assumption – where the learner is presented simple pictures and sentences describing them. However, it is by no means obvious that this is always a reasonable assumption in the real world situations in which languages are learned. Visual referents can be very rich. Without knowledge of the language it may be ambiguous what aspect of the referent was described by the sentence. Also, many sentences would lack visual referents. This means that a prerequisite to language learning is that there be a teacher who is willing to disambiguate, by gesture, use of context, or whatever, the meaning of a sentence. There is evidence that children put in a situation where there is rich semantic information, but no one to disambiguate, do not learn. For instance, hearing children of deaf parents do not learn a language from watching and listening to television. Obviously, the meaning of sentences will not be obvious to a learner in all cases, but what is important is that it be obvious sometimes.

2.   Use of Heuristics versus Algorithms

A frequent distinction made in the discussion of intelligent programs is a distinction between a heuristic and an algorithm. An algorithm is a computational procedure that is guaranteed to provide a solution to a class of problems. A heuristic does not come with such guarantees, but often works. Heuristics are often preferred over algorithms because they can be faster. LAS's learning mechanisms embody a number of heuristics in that they clearly would not be able to learn all possible languages in all possible situations. However, the claim is that they will learn natural languages in the situations in which humans normally learn these languages.

There is at least one algorithm known to be successful for language induction. This is the enumeration algorithm introduced by Gold (1967). It is possible to enumerate all the primitive recursive grammars (if one is using the syntax approach) or the primitive recursive functions between sentence and meaning (if one is using the semantics approach). This enumeration is infinite but every grammar, including the correct one, has some finite position in the enumeration. The algorithm starts with the first grammar and makes that its first guess as to the correct grammar of the language. It sticks with this guess until some information comes in that contradicts the grammar. Then it searches through the enumeration until it finds the first grammar consistent with all the evidence to date. It sticks with this grammar until inconsistent evidence comes in, and so on. Provided that evidence will eventually come in to reject any inconsistent grammar, the correct grammar will eventually be selected because that grammar occupies some finite position in the enumeration.

This enumeration algorithm, as described, is clearly undesirable because of its extreme inefficiency. This inefficiency manifests itself in two ways. First, the algorithm must consider every grammar in the enumeration until a correct one and remember all the past information in order to evaluate each grammar. This imposes an enormous computational burden. It is unclear, however, whether other algorithms could not be proposed that avoid this difficulty. Biermann (1972) has shown that for the class of finite-state grammars it is possible to structure the induction problem so as to avoid explicitly considering grammars already disconfirmed by the available data.

The second problem is that, even avoiding already incorrect grammars, there are an infinite number of grammars compatible with any finite corpus. The position of the correct grammar among these compatible grammars is quite likely astronomical. Therefore, the enumeration algorithm will go through an astronomical number of guesses before considering the correct grammar. Gold has shown that there exists no algorithm uniformly faster than the enumeration technique in terms of the number of guesses it entertains before the correct grammar. That is, given any algorithm that is faster than the enumeration algorithm for some grammar given some information sequence, one can pick another grammar and information sequence for which the enumeration algorithm is faster. Gold's result can easily be extended to LAS's situation of trying to induce a function between sentence and meaning (see Anderson, 1976). That is, there is no procedure uniformly faster than enumerating all the possible functions. The significance of these results is that one cannot expect there to be an algorithm that can learn every possible language in a reasonable time.

Heuristics like those embodied in LAS are designed to learn certain languages rapidly. It is openly acknowledged that there are other languages for which LAS would be inordinately slow or that LAS would fail to learn at all. The claim will be that the languages on which LAS succeeds are natural languages and those on which it has trouble are not natural languages. That is, natural languages are a special subset of the possible languages in that they can be learned by human learning heuristics. This idea is not new. It was advanced by Chomsky (1965) to account for why children seem to have the success they do in language acquisition. However, Chomsky seems to have thought that there were purely syntactic constraints on the forms of natural language. In contrast, I am claiming that constraints concern the relationship between sentence and semantics.

3. Conceptual Development Is Somewhat Complete

A basic prerequisite to language learning for LAS is that it have already available a good subset of the concepts that are referenced in the language it is to learn. LAS does not have any mechanisms for concept induction. This prerequisite is clearly not satisfied in the case of child language acquisition. Indeed, much of the research on child language really seems to be the study of the acquisition of the concepts referred to in the language (e.g., Clark, 1973; Nelson, 1974). Many have now begun to argue (Clark, 1975; Slobin, 1973) that what underlies the timing of the acquisition of many grammatical structures is the acquisition of the requisite conceptual knowledge. That is, most linguistic structures signal conceptual distinctions, and the child does not develop these conceptual distinctions until he is well into the language learning process. For instance, Slobin (1973) argues that the reason plurality or past tense do not appear earlier in child language is that the child does not have these concepts. As soon as the child develops the concept, some manifestation of it will appear in the language. For instance, a child may initially mark plurality by *more* — for example, *more shoe*. Shortly thereafter he will acquire the adult grammatical mechanism, that is, the suffix *s*. Slobin proposes that the gap between the appearance of the conceptual distinction and the use of the adult marking for that distinction is the true indicator of the grammatical complexity involved in making that distinction in the language.

The assumption that conceptualization is somewhat complete seems reasonable for an adult immersing himself in another language community. One would expect a large overlap in concepts between the two communities. Of course, there need not be complete overlap in the concepts. There is no reason why LAS, having acquired the language using the subset of concepts that do overlap, cannot use the language to learn the concepts that are unique to the language community. Linguistic definition is one of the common ways of transmitting concepts.

4. Lexicalization Is Somewhat Complete

LAS, as currently developed, is a model of how one acquires a grammar that relates strings of words to meanings. It is not a model of how the meanings of individual words are acquired. Rather, it is assumed that the words are already attached to their meanings before grammar induction begins. In terms of a HAM representation like Fig. 2 (page 310), this means that the W links already exist. Of course, like the assumption that conceptual development is complete, this requirement that lexicalization be complete is not absolute. There is no reason why LAS, having once learned the language, cannot pick up the meaning of some words from context just as humans can. What is required for grammar induction is just that lexicalization be complete for a substantial subset of the language.

I think it is an accurate claim that in language learning there tends to be a preliminary phase in which word meanings are learned. One learns the grammar of the language only when one knows the meaning of the words that appear in the sentences. Initially, word meanings are acquired by simple pairing of words with ostensive referents or with definitions. Word meanings are not induced in the context of a complex sentence. Thus, there are two stages — a word learning stage and a sentence learning stage. These two stages overlap, but one does not learn grammatical information from a particular sentence unless he has finished the word learning stage for its particular words. I could have built into LAS a program that learned word meanings from pairings of single words and their meanings, but such a program seemed so trivial as to be silly.

It would also be possible to build a program that would learn word meanings by getting pairings of whole sentences and their complex meanings. Such a program would simply try to find pairings between words in the sentence and parts of the sentence's meaning representation. Such a program actually could learn faster (fewer pairings) than in the simple one-word-on-one-meaning situation (see Anderson, 1974). However, the amount of information processing required per pairing by the program is much larger and seemed beyond human capability. To test out my intuition on this issue I have looked at the learning of word meanings (see Anderson, 1974). Contrasted were the situations where subjects learned word meanings by pairing of single words with single meanings versus the situation where subjects learned by pairing three words with three meanings. In the latter case, it was not specified which of the three words corresponded to which of the three meanings. After 50 trials, they learned the meaning of 7.7 words in the one-on-one situation and 6.1 words in the three-on-three situation. This was a significant difference.

If we examine how languages are learned in real world situations, it also seems to be the case that lexicalization precedes grammar induction. This is certainly the case in classroom learning of languages. The typical textbook structure is to give the meaning of words on one page and then to give grammatical information about them on the next page. Children learning a language also seem to use words first in isolation and then use them in multiword strings. Also, children tend to learn words by hearing them in isolation paired with their referents. Or, if the words occur in sentences, they tend to occur in deictic frames with just a single content word, as in *There is a cat* (Ferguson, Peizer, & Weeks, 1973).

5. Induction of Syntactic Classes

In natural language there are word classes like nouns or verbs that tend to obey the same syntactic rules. A critical step in language acquisition is identifying these word classes. Then, instead of stating rules with respect to individual words, they can be stated more efficiently with respect to the word classes. It is important for the same reason to identify the existence of larger syntactic units like noun phrases. I have evolved a set of principles for identifying syntactic classes through the aid of semantic information. Similar ideas can be found in the programs of Klein (1973) and Siklóssy (1972). These principles seem to be reasonable assumptions about heuristics that a human language learner would bring to the language learning situation. I will discuss these principles embodied in the LAS program. In explaining these principles, I will work from simple examples to more complex examples of the types of generalizations LAS makes in forming syntactic classes.

Consider the following set of sentences:

> John kicked Mary.
> Fred kicked Mary.
> Fred amused Mary.
> Fred amused Jane.

Note that the first two sentences differ only in the first word. Thus, we have a minimal contrast. It seems reasonable to propose on the basis of this minimal contrast that there is a word class, call it *A*, that contains *John* and *Fred*. On the basis of these two sentences, one might propose that sentences of the language can consist of a member of the *A* word class followed by *kicked Mary*. The second and third sentences contain a minimal contrast in the second position. This would lead to the formation of a second word class, *V*, containing *kicked* and *amused*. The minimal contrast in the third position of the last two sentences would lead to the formation of a word class, *O*, containing *Mary* and *Jane*. The outcome of these word class constructions would be the following grammar:

$$S \rightarrow A \ V \ O$$
$$A \rightarrow \text{John, Fred}$$
$$V \rightarrow \text{kicked, amused}$$
$$O \rightarrow \text{Mary, Jane}$$

That is, sentences of the language can consist of an *A* word class, followed by *V*, followed by *O*, where these word classes have been defined by the minimal contrasts in the original sentences. Notice that this grammar generates more sentences than the original four that gave rise to it. Altogether it will generate eight sentences. Thus, the grammar has generalized from the original corpus to the acceptability of novel sentences. Such generalizations are obviously essential to language acquisition.

Note that in this example the grammar induced is specified only in terms of its syntax. These specifications are intended as an indication of the network grammars that LAS will induce. In these network grammars LAS would also have to store a specification of the semantic rules that went along with syntactic specifications. This information it would extract by comparison to the semantic referents that come along with the sentences. These semantic referents also play a role in the formation of syntactic rules, as we shall shortly see.

Overgeneralization

The preceding principle I have called the principle of minimal contrast. It is worth pointing out that the principle of minimal contrast, as stated so far, can lead to some rather silly overgeneralizations. Consider the following three sentences:

They are chasing dogs.
They are smart dogs.
Here are smart dogs.

The first two sentences contrast minimally in the third position and the last two sentences in the first position. If we were to blindly apply the principle of minimal contrast here, we would generate the following grammar:

$S \rightarrow A$ are P dogs
$A \rightarrow$ They, Here
$P \rightarrow$ chasing, smart

This grammar would then generate the unacceptable sentence *Here are chasing dogs.*

LAS can avoid this overgeneralization by making reference to the semantic information that comes with a sentence. Figure 9 shows the HAM network representations that would accompany the three sentences. Figure 9a encodes the fact that there are objects X chasing objects Y which are dogs. Figure 9b encodes the fact that there are objects X which are both smart and dogs. Finally, Fig. 9c encodes the fact that there are objects X which are smart — dogs — and at location Y. Note that, while each sentence is quite similar to the others, the graph structure of its semantic referent is quite different. In LAS generalizations suggested by minimal contrast are permitted only if they involve sentences whose semantic referents have isomorphic graph structure. By "isomorphic" it is meant that the graph structures are identical except for the identities of the nodes. This is one role semantics has in grammar induction — to edit out some of the overgeneralizations.

However, even using this semantic criterion to edit out generalizations, there still will occur overgeneralizations. Consider the following example:

The boys danced.
The girl danced.
The girl dances.

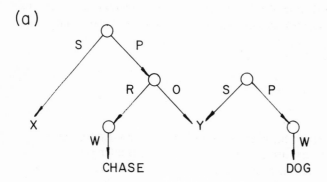

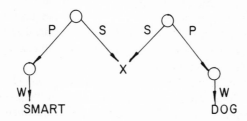

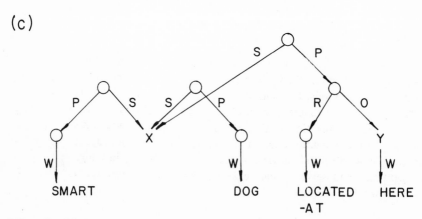

FIG. 9 Possible HAM structures for the following sentences:

(a) They are chasing dogs.
(b) They are smart dogs.
(c) Here are smart dogs.

These sentences all have basically the same HAM structure representing them. Therefore, the principal of minimal contrast would merge *boys* and *girl* into the same word class and *danced* and *dances* into the same word class. This would lead to the following grammar:

$S \rightarrow$ The A V
$A \rightarrow$ boys, girl
$V \rightarrow$ danced, dances

This grammar will generate the overgeneralization *The boys dances.* There is no way to avoid this particular overgeneralization in LAS. It is interesting, however, that such morphemic overgeneralizations are frequently found in child language (e.g., Ervin, 1964; Slobin, 1971). They occur in situations such as the preceding one, where there is a syntactic correlation (i.e., between subject number and verb inflection) without any semantic variation. There is just no semantic reason why the present tense inflection for the verb should vary with the number of the subject. So it is to LAS's credit that it makes such overgeneralizations. However, humans are able eventually to recover from such overgeneralizations, whereas there are not yet methods in LAS for error recovery. I will discuss what ideas I have on this issue in the last section.

So far, the source of suggestions for formation of word class have been syntactic. That is, we have looked for a single contrast in word order between two sentences. In LAS it is also possible to use semantic information to suggest generalization. Consider the following example:

John kicked Mary.
Fred amused Jane.

These two sentences do not display a minimal contrast in word order. Nonetheless, if LAS were given the semantic referent of each sentence and if it knew the meaning of the words, it could see that the first words, *John* and *Fred,* both served the semantic function of subject; the second words, *kicked* and *amused,* both served the semantic function of verb; and the third words, *Mary* and *Jane,* both served the semantic function of object. In LAS it is an adequate condition for merging words into a single word class that they occur in similar positions in the sentence and serve similar semantic functions. Therefore, the following grammar would be formed:

$S \rightarrow N$ V O
$N \rightarrow$ John, Fred
$V \rightarrow$ kicked, amused
$O \rightarrow$ Mary, Jane

Merging of Syntactic Classes

Note that the preceding grammar is missing one important generalization. There are two word classes, N and O, which really are the same. LAS has a process for merging word classes together. To explain this, I must specify one complication to the preceding generalization scheme. So far I have described the generalizations as if LAS kept a record of all the individual sentences that it had seen, and compared new sentences with this record. Actually, LAS's only record of past sentences is a network grammar adequate to generate all these sentences (and more if there are generalizations in the network). So, for instance, after the two sentences *John kicked Mary* and *Fred amused Jane,* LAS would have formed a network grammar equivalent to that specified by the rewrite rules given earlier. New sentences are compared to this existing network, and relevant contrasts are noted. Modifications are made to the network to incorporate new sentences. This is much more efficient than storing all the past sentences. It also has the advantage that one's record of past sentences, the grammar, can be used for speech and understanding.

Suppose LAS had the preceding grammar (in network form) and encountered the sentence, *Alice liked Fred.* It could accommodate this sentence by expanding the N word class to include *Alice,* the V word class to include *liked,* and the O word class to include *Fred.* However, note that LAS could also have parsed the sentence if N had been the third word class, that is, if its grammar had been $S \rightarrow N\ V\ N$. This is because N already includes *Fred.* LAS uses the fact that there is an overlap between what can be parsed in first position and in last position as a cue to merge the grammars for these two positions. Thus, it forms the following grammar:

$S \rightarrow N\ V\ N$
$N \rightarrow$ John, Mary, Fred, Jane, Alice
$V \rightarrow$ kicked, amused, liked

Note that LAS has generalized from three sentences to a grammar that will generate 75 sentences.

This principle for merging actually applies to phrases in the sentence and not to single words. In the example given these corresponded — there were single word noun phrases. LAS represents each phrase of a sentence by a network. Its principle for merging is to attempt to collapse two networks into one if it finds that they will redundantly handle the same phrase.

LAS derives much of its power because of its principles for merging phrase grammars together. This is what enables it to detect recursive rules, as we shall see in the next section. To be able to merge phrase structures it needs some principles for identifying what are the phrases of a sentence. These will be discussed next under the heading "The Graph Deformation Condition." However, I would like to give one example of how powerful these principles can be, assuming some mechanism for phrase segmentation. Consider the following pair of sentences:

The man praised John who is tall.
Fred thanked the man who liked the pizza.

First, the LAS will identify *Fred, John, the man,* and *the pizza* as examples of the same basic noun phrase structure. Second, it will identify *who is tall* and *who liked the pizza* as relative clauses that may optionally modify a noun. This leads to the formation of the following grammar:

$$S \rightarrow NP\ V\ NP$$
$$NP \rightarrow PN$$
$$\text{the } N$$
$$PN\ \text{CLAUSE}$$
$$\text{the } N\ \text{CLAUSE}$$
$$\text{CLAUSE} \rightarrow \text{who is } A$$
$$\rightarrow \text{who } V^*\ NP$$
$$V \rightarrow \text{praised, thanked}$$
$$PN \rightarrow \text{John, Fred}$$
$$N \rightarrow \text{man, pizza}$$
$$A \rightarrow \text{tall}$$
$$V^* \rightarrow \text{liked}$$

This grammar already has in it the capacity for unlimited right-embedding of relative clauses, since *NP* can rewrite into CLAUSE which can rewrite into NP.

6. The Graph Deformation Condition

As noted earlier augmented transition networks are constructed such that there is a network for every phrase in an immediate-constituent analysis of the sentence. Therefore, it is critical to be able to identify the phrase structure of a sentence. There exists a program, BRACKET, that takes a sentence and a representation of the sentence's meaning and outputs a bracketing of the sentence that indicates its surface structure. The functioning of BRACKET is possible because it assumes a constraint between the surface structure of the sentence and the graph structure of the sentence's network representation. I have called this constraint the graph deformation condition. This constraint is illustrated in Fig. 10. Fig. 10a gives the HAM network structure for the meaning of the sentence *The girl hit the boy who liked the cake.* Fig. 10b is the graph structure in Fig. 10a deformed to provide a surface structure for the content words in the sentence. Although the spatial locations of the links in Fig. 10b have been rearranged from Fig. 10a the links still maintain their interconnections. That is, *girl* is still connected to node *A* which is still connected to node *B*,

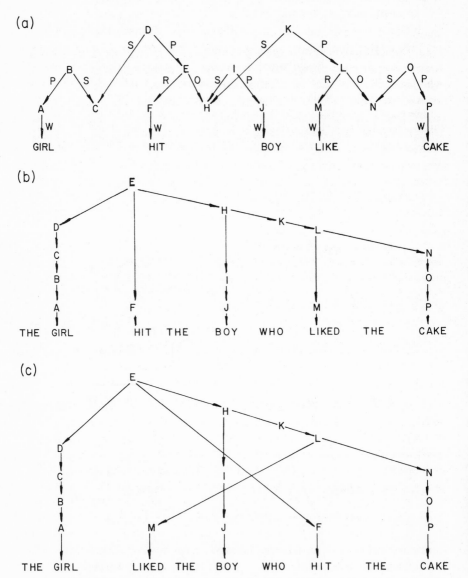

FIG. 10 The HAM structure in (a) can be deformed to provide a surface structure for the content words of the sentence in (b) but not for the sentence in (c).

and so on. Note that the graph deformation in Fig. 10b does capture some of the surface structure of the sentence: For instance, *girl, hit,* and *boy* are organized together under one unit, and *liked* and *cake* are organized together as a modifier of *boy.* The structure in Fig. 10b does not specify how nonmeaning-bearing morphemes like *the* and *who* fit into the surface structure. This is an issue to which we will return shortly.

The claim is that the surface structure interconnecting the content words of the sentence can always be represented as a graph deformation of the underlying semantic structure. This implies that certain word orders will be unacceptable ways to express certain semantic intentions. So suppose there were a language that attempted to express the referent in Fig. 10a by the word order in Fig. 10c. That is, the relative clause verb occurred within the main clause and the main clause verb within the relative clause. As Fig. 10c illustrates, there is no graph deformation of the semantic structure in Fig. 10a that will provide a surface structure for the sentence in Fig. 10c. No matter how this is attempted, some branches must cross. A surface structure is, by definition, a tree structure without crossing branches.

BRACKET's Computations

If the graph deformation condition is satisfied for a sentence, BRACKET can identify the surface structure interconnecting the content words. It would be useful to consider an example of how BRACKET performs this computation. The input required by BRACKET is a sentence, a semantic referent, and an indication of the main proposition. Figure 11 illustrates how this might be provided. A picture is given for the semantic referent along with a sentence. Note that the sentence is not grammatical in English although the words are English. This is an attempt to recreate for the reader the situation facing LAS as a language learner. That is, it knows the meaning of the words but not the grammar.

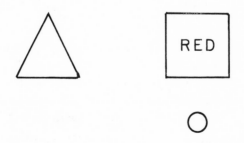

CIRCLE   SMALL   SQUARE   RED   BELOW

FIG. 11   BRACKET receives as input an encoding of this picture and the string of words.

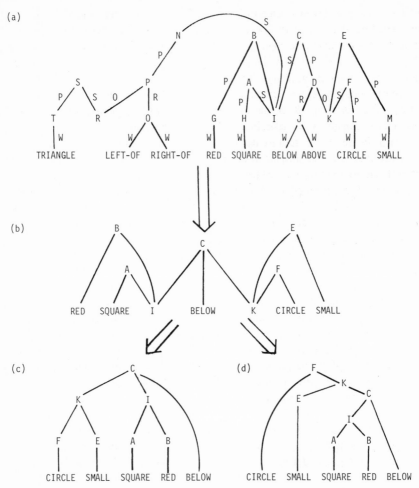

FIG. 12   The prototype structure in (b) is derived from the HAM structure in (a). From this prototype structure two surface structures, (c) and (d), can be imposed on the same string of words.

Figure 12a shows how HAM would represent this picture. There are three objects in the picture, represented by the memory nodes *I, K,* and *R.* Of *I* it is asserted that it is red, a square, above *K,* and to the right of *R.* Of *K* it is asserted that it is small, and a circle. Of *R* it is asserted that it is a triangle.

Note that the relational terms *J* and *O* are both connected to two words. This reflects an assumption that will be important in understanding the forthcoming induction history: LAS does not have distinct concepts corresponding to such symmetric relational terms as *above* and *below.* For instance, LAS will represent the picture in Fig. 11 to itself with the same relation concept independent of whether *above* or *below* is used in the sentence. From the viewpoint of LAS, the difference between these two words involves the rules for interpreting the noun phrases. *Above* takes the logical subject first whereas *below* takes the logical object first. This means that the program will learn to represent sentences with *above* and *below* identically. Thus, a learning program conveys upon the representational system a certain amount of invariance under paraphrase that many (e.g., Anderson & Bower, 1973; Norman & Rumelhart, 1975; Schank, 1972) have thought to be desirable.

From this semantic representation, BRACKET computes an intermediate structure that is much simpler than the semantic structure but preserves enough distinctions to permit the surface structure of the sentence to be calculated. I have called this intermediate structure the prototype structure. It is calculated by comparison between the semantic referent and the sentence. These comparisons determine what distinctions in semantic referent are needed. Only these will be preserved in the prototype structure. The prototype structure in Fig. 12b is derived by deleting from the HAM structure all nodes except proposition nodes (*A, B, C, E,* and *F*), the individual nodes (*I* and *K*), and the words (red, square, below, circle, small). Note that although *above* is part of the HAM structure, it is deleted in the prototype structure. Rather, *below* is the relation term used in the sentence. In addition, the structure encoding the proposition *I is right of the triangle* is deleted from the prototype. This was not mentioned in the to-be-bracketed sentence. This serves to illustrate an important product of the calculation of prototype structure. The calculation can disambiguate those aspects of a complex referent that are relevant to the sentence at hand.

Having the prototype structure, LAS attempts to find some graph deformation of it that will provide a tree structure connecting the content words of the sentence. Figure 12c indicates one such graph deformation of the prototype structure if the main proposition is *C*. If the main proposition is specified, there is at most one graph deformation of the prototype structure that will yield a surface structure for the sentence. Note that all the links in Fig. 12b are maintained but have been spatially rearranged to provide a tree structure for the sentence. Note that the prototype structure is not specific with respect to which links are above which others and which are right of which others. Although the prototype structure in Fig. 12b is set forth in a special spatial array, the choice is arbitrary. In contrast, the surface structure in Fig. 12c does specify the spatial relations of links. From Fig. 12c we may derive a bracketing of the sentence indicating its surface structure − ((circle small) (square red) below).

BRACKET needs to know more than just the prototype structure to infer the surface structure of the sentence. As parts (c) and (d) of Fig. 12 show, the same string of words can have the same prototype structure deformed into more than a single surface structure. The difference between (c) and (d) is the choice of which proposition is principal and which is subordinate. The structure in Fig. 12d might be translated into English as *Circular is the small thing that is below the red square.* Therefore, BRACKET also needs information as to what the main proposition is to be able to unambiguously retrieve the surface structure of the sentence. The assumption that BRACKET is given the main proposition amounts, psychologically, to the claim that the teacher can direct the learner's attention to what is being asserted in the sentence. Thus, in Fig. 12c the teacher would direct the learner to the picture of a red triangle above a small circle. He would have to assume both that the learner properly conceptualized the picture and that the learner realized that the aboveness relation was what was being asserted of the picture.

The assumption that the learner can be told what the main proposition is seems a bit strong. It is important to inquire, therefore, what the performance of the program would be like if it were not given information about the main proposition. The first thing to note is that the program could generally make a good guess as to what the main proposition is. For instance, of the five propositions in Fig. 12b, only two – C and F – could be main propositions given the ordering of the words in the main sentence. Second, C seems clearly to be the more natural choice. Usually, a few heuristics would do to identify the correct main proposition. Moreover, even if the incorrect main proposition is occasionally chosen, this will not do enormous harm to the network induced. This will just introduce an additional possibility in the network and not alter other parsing possibilities. This possibility will not be ungrammatical. Its "defect" will be detected only in that the speech of LAS will occasionally violate pragmatic rules about how to express presupposed versus asserted information. In conclusion, while the assumption about the availability of main-proposition information is convenient, it is very marginal to the successful performance of the LAS program.

The Details of BRACKET's Output

So far, for purposes of exposition I have simplified the specification of BRACKET's output. Also, the example in Fig. 12 was particularly simple because there were no nonmeaning-bearing words. Consider how BRACKET would handle the sentence *A triangle is left-of a square that is above a small red square,* given the HAM structure in Fig. 7 (page 316). (It is left as an exercise for the reader to derive the sentence's prototype structure.) BRACKET returned an expression of the form:

$$((A (\ ) \ triangle \ (\ )) \ is \ left-of \ (a \ (\ ) \ square \ (that \ is \ above \ (a \ (small \ (red) \ )$$
$$square \ (\ ))))).$$

The embedding of parentheses reflects the levels of the surface structure. The main proposition is given in the first level of bracketing. The first bracketed subexpression describes the subject noun phrase. The first two words of the sentence *A triangle* are placed in this bracketed subexpression. The next two words, *is left-of,* are in main bracketing. There are no embedded propositions corresponding to these two. The remainder of the output of BRACKET corresponds to a description of the object. It involves a relative clause and, embedded within that relative clause, another noun phrase. The rules for bracketing noun phrases will be explained later. Note that BRACKET induces a correspondence between a level of bracketing and a single proposition. Each level of bracketing will also correspond to a new network in LAS's grammar. Because of the modularity of HAM propositions, a modularity is achieved for the grammatical networks.

The insertion of nonfunction words into the bracketing is a troublesome problem because there are no semantic features to indicate where they belong. Consider the first word *A* in the example sentence. It could have been placed in the top level of bracketing or in the subexpression containing *triangle*. Currently, all the function words to the left of a content word are placed at the same level as the content word. The bracketing is closed immediately after this content word. Therefore, *is* is not placed in the noun phrase bracketing. This heuristic seems to work more often than not. However, there clearly are cases where it will not work. Consider the sentence *The boy who Jane spoke to was deaf.* The current BRACKET program would return this as

((*The* (   ) *boy* (*who Jane spoke*)) *to was deaf*).

That is, it would not identify *to* as in the relative clause. Similarly, nonmeaning-bearing suffixes like gender would not be retrieved as part of the noun by this heuristic. However, there may be a clue to make bracketing appropriate in these cases. There tends to be a pause after morphemes like *to*. Perhaps such pause structures could be called upon to help the BRACKET program decide how to insert the nonmeaning-bearing morphemes into the bracketing.

Discontinuous Elements

There is a class of sentences found in natural language that systematically violate the graph deformation condition. These are sentences with discontinuous elements. Figure 13 illustrates the clearest example of this in English, which is the *respectively* sentence. Figure 13a shows the HAM semantic structure for the sentence *John and Bill borrowed and returned, respectively, the lawnmower.* Figure 13b shows that there is no way to deform this semantic structure to achieve a surface structure for the sentence. Discontinuous elements are rare in English. Some of the few discontinuous elements like *up* in *John called the man up* do not strictly violate the graph deformation condition because they are not meaning bearing. However, in other languages with freer word order it is possible to find many instances of content words dislocated. Apparently, Latin is a good example of this. For instance, in vulgar Latin there is a possible construction that has the following word order *The girl who the boys best saw ran away,* where *best,* occurring within the relative clause, modifies *girl,* the subject of the main clause. LAS cannot learn any part of a natural language that involves such

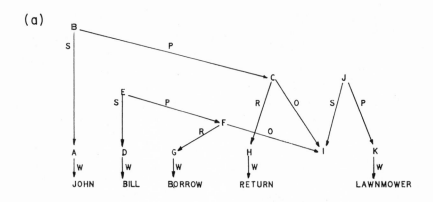

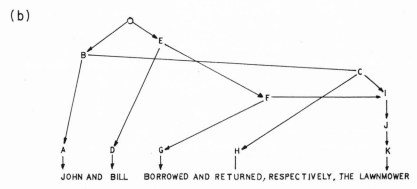

FIG. 13 There is no deformation of the HAM semantic structure in (a) that will provide a surface structure for the sentence in (b).

discontinuous elements. Fortunately, such constructions, while clearly present, are not dominant even in languages like Latin. I would want to claim that they are not the sort of constructions that are easy to comprehend or that are easily acquired. This certainly seems the case for the *respectively* transformation in English. While additional learning mechanisms must be brought to bear to learn discontinuous elements, the LAS mechanisms will go a long way toward learning a natural language. Moreover, if discontinuous elements are hard to learn, this would be a significant confirmation of LAS's reliance on the graph deformation condition.

An Experiment

We have performed an experiment to test LAS's predictions about the difficulty of learning languages with discontinuous elements. The experiment had English-speaking subjects attempt to learn a language with a syntactic structure as different from English as could be managed. Except for a relative pronoun (which was expressed as *te*), the words of this language were English. This is an easy way to guarantee that lexicalization is complete, which is a presupposition of the LAS program. The following rewrite rules define the grammar of the language:

$$S \rightarrow NP\ PRED$$
$$NP \rightarrow Shape\ (Size)\ (Pattern)\ (CLAUSE)$$
$$CLAUSE \rightarrow te\ PRED$$
$$PRED \rightarrow ADJ$$
$$\rightarrow NP\ Rel$$
$$Shape \rightarrow square, circle, diamond, triangle$$
$$Size \rightarrow large, small$$
$$Pattern \rightarrow Striped, dotted$$
$$Adj \rightarrow red, broken$$
$$Rel \rightarrow above, below, right\text{-}of, left\text{-}of$$

An example of a sentence in this language is *Square striped te triangle large te broken above circle small dotted right-of.* The experiment compares four conditions of learning for this language:

1. *No semantics.* Here subjects simply study strings of the language, trying to infer their grammatical structure.

2. *Bad semantics.* Here a picture of the sentence's referent is presented along with the sentence. However, the relationship between the sentence's semantic referent and the surface structure systematically violates the GDC. The adjective preceding with the ith shape will modify the $(n + 1 - i)$th shape in the sentence (where n is the number of noun phrases). For example, the adjective associated with the first noun phrase (striped) modifies the last shape (circle). Similarly, the ith relation term describes the relationship between the $(m + 1 - i)$th pair of shapes (where m is the number of relationships). So, for instance, the second relationship, *right-of,* describes the relationship between the first pair of shapes, *square* and *triangle.* The appropriate picture for the example sentence is given in Fig. 14a.

3. *Good semantics.* Here the adjective in each noun phrase modifies the noun in that phrase. Relations govern the appropriate nouns in the surface structure. The appropriate picture for the example sentence in this case is given in Fig. 14b.

4. *Good semantics plus highlighting.* The picture in this condition is the same as in (3) but the shapes in the main proposition are highlighted. It was explained to these subjects that the main proposition was being highlighted. The LAS program predicts better learning when the main proposition is indicated. The picture for this condition is given in Fig. 14c.

In some ways this experiment is like Moeser and Bregman's (1973 see discussion on p. 321). However, here English words are used so that the subjects do

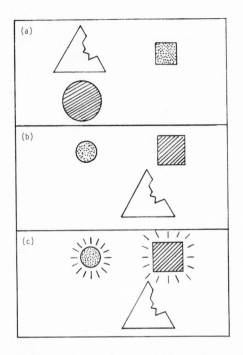

FIG. 14 Picture (a) was presented as a semantic referent in the bad-semantics condition; picture (b) in the good-semantics condition; and picture (c) in the good-semantics plus highlighting condition.

not need to induce the language's lexicalization as well as its grammar. Moeser and Bregman's language also differed from this language in that it only consisted of a finite number of sentences. Also they only contrasted conditions (1) and (3), finding condition (1) much worse. They did not have a condition like (2), where there was a semantics as elaborate as condition (3), but where the relationship between referent and sentence violated the graph-deformation condition. The graph deformation condition would predict no difference between conditions (1) and (2) and would predict that both would be much worse than (3).

The basic procedure in the experiment involved having all subjects pass through eight blocks of study–test. In each block the subject studied six sentences with the semantics appropriate to his condition (if any). The sentences were presented to the subjects on cards with pictures given below, depicting the appropriate semantic information. Subjects were given 30 seconds to study each sentence. After studying the six sentences the subjects were given a test booklet that contained on separate pages six pairs of sentences without picture referents. The subject's task was to indicate which sentence of each pair was grammatically well formed for the language studied. Subjects were given 30 seconds to make their decision for each sentence pair. Subjects in all conditions studied and were tested with the same set of sentences. The only variation between conditions was the information that accompanied the sentences on the study trials. The study and test sentences were randomly generated within the constraint that they mention at least two objects and no more than four objects. The test pairs were of two sorts. There were pairs that tested for some minimal syntactic contrast. So a subject might have to choose between a pair like the following:

A. Square striped large triangle te red above.
B. Square large striped triangle te red above.

which tests for knowledge of adjective order. The second sort of test presented a correct sentence with some unrelated sentence that had a gross semantic defect. So a subject might see the following:

C. Circle large te triangle small below above.
D. Square striped large triangle te red above.

In this example C is wrong semantically because *above* requires two noun phrase arguments and only one is given (*triangle* is an argument for *below*). Subjects found the two types of tests to be of approximately equal difficulty. Therefore, I will present data pooled over the two test types.

Figure 15 provides a summary of the main results of the experiment. It is based on data collected from 12 subjects in each condition. In Fig. 15, the data are classified by whether they came from the first or second half of the experiment, and by the condition. The percentage of correct choices on the test pairs is plotted. In all conditions subjects were able to pick up on some regularities and perform better than chance (50%). However, subjects performed less well in the bad-semantics and no-semantics conditions than in the two good-semantics conditions. Also subjects in the bad- and no-semantics conditions showed little improvement from the first to the second half of the experiment, whereas subjects in the good-semantics conditions showed considerable improvement.

Subjects with good semantics plus highlighting of main propositions performed nonsignificantly less well than subjects without highlighting. The difference is due entirely to the two subjects in the highlighting condition who performed very poorly. It seems that these two subjects did not understand the intention of the highlighting information. However, there is clearly no evidence that highlighting information helped.

There are three significant conclusions from this experiment. First, it has reinforced the Moeser and Bregman demonstration about the importance of a semantic referent. Second, it has shown that this semantic referent is useful only if it satisfies the graph deformation condition. A language with discontinuous elements that violates the graph deformation condition is much harder to learn. Third, there is no evidence that information about main propositions helps. Apparently, subjects in the good-semantics condition, without highlighting, were able to disambiguate the main proposition through use of heuristics.

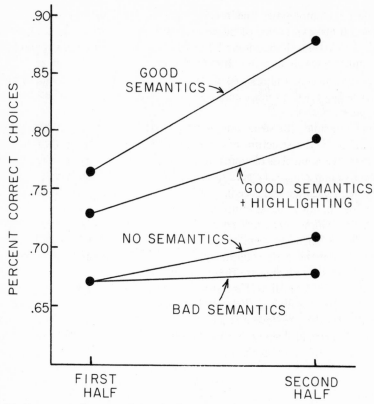

FIG. 15 Percentage of correct choices in the grammaticality task as a function of semantic condition and block of the experiment.

7. Assumptions about Noun Phrase Structure

One of the important ways in which LAS II differs from LAS I is in its assumptions about the structure of noun phrases. As discussed in Anderson (1974, 1975) LAS I would have fundamental difficulty in identifying the structure of noun phrases in certain languages. Built into LAS II are certain assumptions about the structure of noun phrases that seem to be universal. Basically, LAS II assumes that noun phrases have a structure given by the following rewrite rules:

NP → morphemes (MOD) *noun* morphemes (MOD)
MOD → *proposition* (MOD)

The obligatory elements in these rewrite rules are italicized. These rules indicate that noun phrases consist, optionally, of some initial nonmeaning-bearing morphemes, followed by an optional embedded list of prepositional modifiers, followed by an *obligatory* noun, followed by an optional embedded list of postpositional modifiers. The rewrite rule for MOD indicates that modifiers consist of the expression of some proposition modifying the topic, plus an optional right-embedding of another MOD. This information about noun phrase structure is incorporated into BRACKET and is reflected by the embedding it imposes on the noun phrase. As an example, Fig. 16 shows the bracketing that the preceding rewrite rules would impose on the expression *the tall blond man with one black shoe.*

These principles for structuring noun phrases may not appear to impose any restrictions on the structure of language. However, they do in that they assert that there is a noun class of words from which it is obligatory to select a member for every noun phrase. Logically, there need not be this obligatory word class. One could imagine a language in which one could refer to a small red pillow by any subset of these three terms, including *the small, the red, the small red,* as well as *the pillow, the small pillow, the red pillow,* and *the small red pillow.* However, all languages seem to have an obligatory noun class for referring to objects. The items in this obligatory class tend to be the functionally significant terms for classifying objects. Thus, little can be predicted about an object from the fact that it is small or that it is red, but much follows from the fact that it is a pillow. What serves as a noun is not hard and fast, but will change with context. Thus, while *square* is an adjective when referring to picture frames it becomes a noun in a geometry class. Similarly, while *red* is usually an adjective it can serve as a noun in Las Vegas.

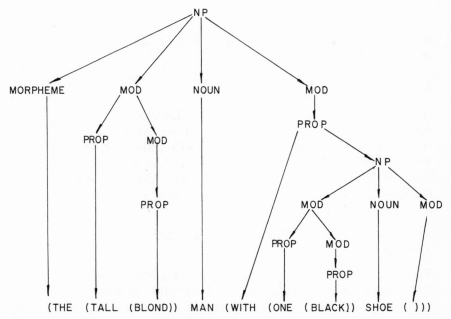

FIG. 16 An example of the bracketing imposed on a noun phrase.

Note that the noun phrase grammar is built around this obligatory noun. Morphemes and modifiers that occur before the noun do not occur after the noun and vice versa. For this reason, identifying the noun becomes the key to unlocking the structure of noun phrases. LAS is given information as to what are the functionally significant classifications in its environment, that is, what concepts will serve as nouns. In LAS's semantic domain, this turns out to be shape. This is supposed to reflect the outcome of cognitive predevelopment, which we do not pretend to model. However, these cognitive prerequisites are critical because with this information about the noun class LAS can appropriately structure its noun phrase grammar. This is another contribution of semantics to language acquisition.

CASE HISTORY OF LANGUAGE INDUCTION

In the preceding section a number of principles have been identified for language induction. I would now like to illustrate how they will work in combination to induce a language. We will observe the program as it induces the subset of English defined in Table 2. This is a subset of English adequate to describe all the spatial relations that exist in a rather circumscribed semantic domain. This is a two-dimensional world of geometric objects that vary in the properties of size and color and may bear various spatial relations one to another. LAS has learned a number of natural and artificial languages, but they all concern this specific semantic domain. I think it important to have a well-defined subset of language to learn. It is impossible to take as one's task the learning of an entire natural language. However, one can set as a goal the learning of a subset of a natural language adequate to completely describe a circumscribed semantic domain. The problem with some of the other language learning efforts (e.g., Klein, Siklóssy) is that they have taken on the learning of ill-defined chunks of the language. They present a history of the program learning a sequence of sentences and making some generalizations, and then the program quits. It is very difficult on the basis of such histories to assess what aspects of the language the program can handle, let alone what aspects it cannot.

LAS was presented with the 11 sentences given at the bottom of Table 2 in that order. I will go through these sentences one by one and discuss how LAS evolves an augmented transition network grammar to parse these sentences.

Sentence 1

Figure 17 illustrates LAS's processing of the first sentence. LAS is presented with the sentence *The red square is above the red circle* along with a picture of a red square above a red circle, which is analyzed into the HAM structure shown in

TABLE 2
The English Subset to Be Learned

Grammar

S	→ NP PRED
NP	→ DET (ADJP) Shape (CLAUSE)
ADJP	→ (Size) (Color)
PRED	→ is ADJ
	→ is Relation NP
CLAUSE	→ which PRED
ADJ	→ Size
	→ Color
DET	→ a, the
Shape	→ square, circle
Relation	→ above, below, left-of, right-of
Size	→ large, small
Color	→ red, blue

Sentences Studied

1. The red square is above the red circle.
2. The square is below the circle.
3. A large blue square is left-of the small red square.
4. A small square is right-of a large square.
5. The square which is above the red circle is red.
6. The circle which is red is small.
7. The circle which is right-of the circle is blue.
8. The circle which is blue is large.
9. The square is above the circle which is left-of the blue circle.
10. The blue square is right-of the square which is below the circle.
11. The circle which is small is right-of the circle which is large.

Fig. 17. (Actually, the program is presented with the HAM structure directly.) Comparing the sentence to the HAM structure, the BRACKET program produces the bracketing of the sentence illustrated in Fig. 17. The LEARN-MORE program will build a level of network to reflect every level of bracketing in the sentence. The START network, illustrated in Fig. 17, was set up to encode the top level of the sentence. The first expression in the sentence is a bracketed subexpression, and therefore the first arc in the START network consists of a push to an NP network to parse the subexpression.[2] On this arc is

[2] Actually, the program did not generate labels like NP in building up the network. Rather, it generated nonsense labels. However, I have taken the liberty of replacing the program's nonsense labels with labels I thought were more mnemonic.

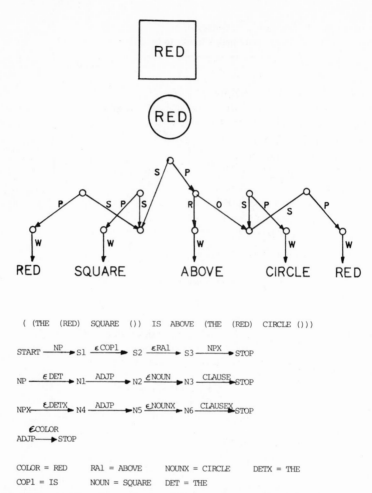

FIG. 17 Upon receiving the semantic referent at the top of the page paired with the sentence, LAS constructed the ATN illustrated at the bottom of the page.

stored the fact that the referent of NP serves the semantic role of subject of the sentence.

The next item in the main level of bracketing is *is*. A word class, COP1, is set up to hold this item. On the arc is placed the condition that the word be a member of the COP1 word class. There is no semantic action put on this arc. The third item in the bracketing is *above*. Another word class, RA1, is set up to contain this word. On the arc is put a condition that tests if the word is in the RA1 word class and a semantic action that builds the meaning of this word as the relation in the main proposition. The fourth and final item is a bracketed subexpression. A push to network NPX is put on this arc to parse this bracketed subexpression. The semantic action put on the arc makes the referent of NPX the object of the main proposition.

The network NP is set up to parse the first bracketed subexpression (THE (RED) SQUARE (   )). For the first item, *the,* a word class, DET, is set up. The condition on the first arc is that the word be out of the DET word class. There is no semantic action associated with this arc. On the second arc, a push is made to the ADJP network to handle the bracketed pre-positional modifier. On the third arc, a word class, NOUN, is set up to handle the next item, *square.* This word class is made the condition of the third arc, and the semantic action is to predicate of the topic of the NP network that it is an instance of this NOUN concept. Note that the last expression in the noun phrase subexpression is a bracketing of the null element. BRACKET automatically imposes the bracketing for post-positional modifiers even when there are none. Thus, a final arc is built with an optional push to a CLAUSE network to parse postpositional modifiers. The CLAUSE network will not be built until the fifth sentence, which contains the first relative clause.

The NPX network for the object position is built up much in the manner of the NP network. Note that LAS has built up two redundant networks for noun phrases. However, it has no way to know this yet. It is possible that the grammar for object noun phrases will be different than the grammar for subject noun phrases. Note, however, that both networks push to the same adjective phrase network, ADJP. This is because in building NPX, LAS detected that the ADJP network that it had built for NP could parse the expression (RED), which occurred in the expression that NPX was built to parse.

Figure 17 illustrates all the network structure and word class information built up after the first sentence. This would be adequate for the program to comprehend that sentence or for the SPEAK program to generate it. However, the grammar after this first sentence can handle virtually nothing else. This is not surprising, since one sentence offers little basis for comparison and generalization. The one generalization contained in the grammar of Fig. 17 is based on LAS's knowledge that pre-positional modifiers are optional. Thus, the grammar in Fig. 17 would successfully parse *The square is above the circle.*

Sentence 2

Figure 18 summarizes the processing of the next four sentences. The second sentence, after comparison with its semantic referent, was returned in the bracketed form shown in Fig. 18a. This sentence involves use of the relation *below.* Recall that *above* and *below* are attached to the same concept in memory (see discussion on page 334). Therefore, LAS will regard the first noun phrase of this example as semantic object and the second noun phrase as semantic subject. A second path, illustrated in Fig. 18a, is built through the START network to accommodate this possibility. Note that the first arc in that path involves a push

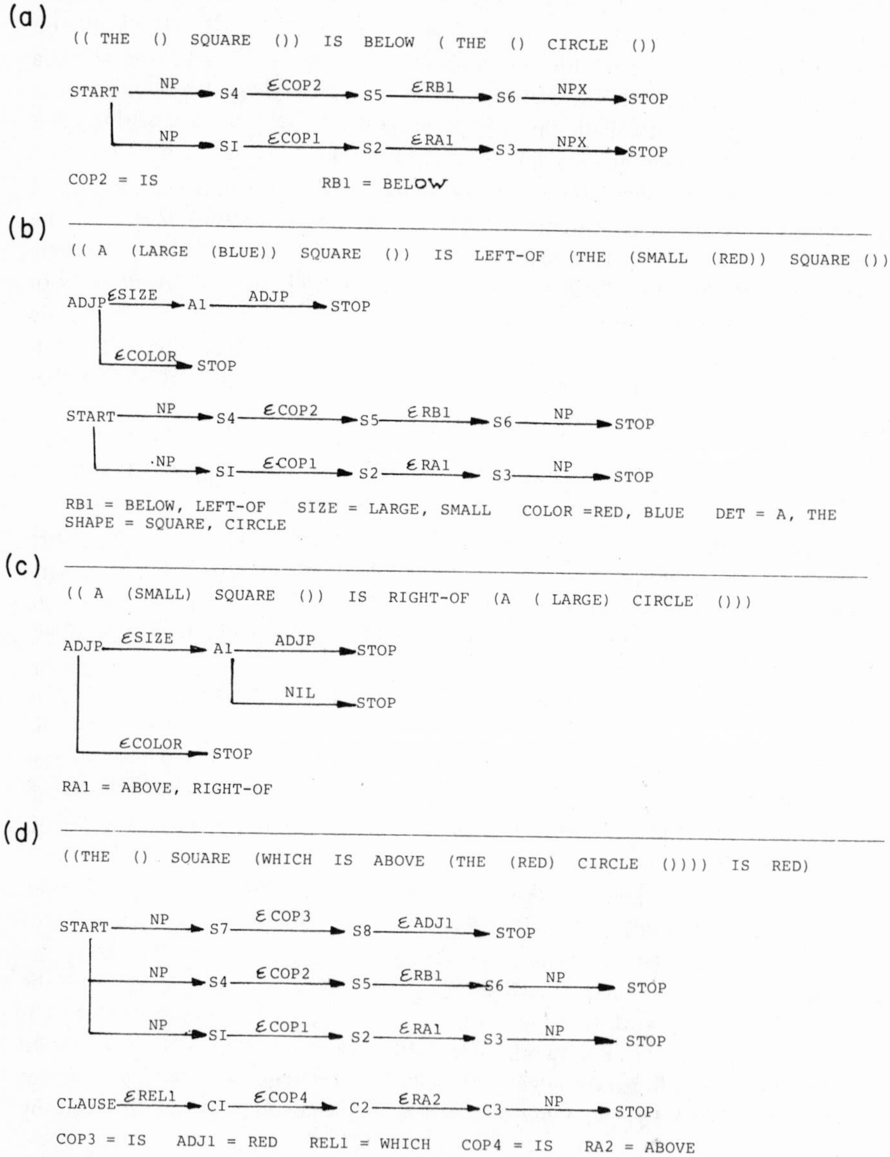

(a)

((THE () SQUARE ())) IS BELOW (THE () CIRCLE ())

START —NP→ S4 —εCOP2→ S5 —εRB1→ S6 —NPX→ STOP

—NP→ SI —εCOP1→ S2 —εRA1→ S3 —NPX→ STOP

COP2 = IS   RB1 = BELOW

(b)

((A (LARGE (BLUE)) SQUARE ()) IS LEFT-OF (THE (SMALL (RED)) SQUARE ())

ADJP —εSIZE→ A1 —ADJP→ STOP

—εCOLOR→ STOP

START —NP→ S4 —εCOP2→ S5 —εRB1→ S6 —NP→ STOP

—·NP→ SI —εCOP1→ S2 —εRA1→ S3 —NP→ STOP

RB1 = BELOW, LEFT-OF   SIZE = LARGE, SMALL   COLOR =RED, BLUE   DET = A, THE
SHAPE = SQUARE, CIRCLE

(c)

((A (SMALL) SQUARE ()) IS RIGHT-OF (A (LARGE) CIRCLE ())))

ADJP —εSIZE→ A1 —ADJP→ STOP

—NIL→ STOP

—εCOLOR→ STOP

RA1 = ABOVE, RIGHT-OF

(d)

((THE () SQUARE (WHICH IS ABOVE (THE (RED) CIRCLE ())))) IS RED)

START —NP→ S7 —εCOP3→ S8 —εADJ1→ STOP

—NP→ S4 —εCOP2→ S5 —εRB1→ S6 —NP→ STOP

—NP→ SI —εCOP1→ S2 —εRA1→ S3 —NP→ STOP

CLAUSE —εREL1→ CI —εCOP4→ C2 —εRA2→ C3 —NP→ STOP

COP3 = IS   ADJ1 = RED   REL1 = WHICH   COP4 = IS   RA2 = ABOVE

FIG. 18 Parts (a) through (d) illustrate the changes to the ATN as a consequence of the processing of Sentences 2 through 5 from Table 2.

348

to the NP network set up to handle the first sentence. The old NP network is referenced, rather than a new one built, because that network can already parse the expression ((THE ( ) SQUARE ( )). The second arc in the new START network path references a word class, COP2, that contains IS. The word class on the third arc, RB1, is set up to hold *below*. Finally, the fourth arc contains a push to a network, NPX. Network NPX was set up for Sentence 1. It is referenced in the new path through the network because LAS has determined that NPX will handle the second noun phrase.

The examples involving the networks NP and NPX illustrate the mechanism of LAS for merging phrase structure grammars that occur in multiple locations. The principles behind this were discussed earlier under the induction of syntactic classes (page 330). In LAS II, every time there is a need to add a new network or modify an existing network to accommodate a new phrase, a check is made whether any existing network will handle the new phrase. Detection of this fact is the stimulus for attempting to merge networks. We shall shortly see further examples of network merging.

Sentence 3

Figure 18b illustrates some significant aspects of the processing of the third sentence. This sentence involves use of the relational term, *left-of*, which assigns the first noun phrase to the semantic role of object — just as *below* does. Note that the top level of the bracketed sentence consists of (a) a bracketed subexpression serving the semantic role of object; (b) a nonmeaning-bearing morpheme; (c) a word indicating relation; and (d) a bracketed subexpression serving the semantic role of subject. This is just the sequence of items on the upper path of the START network. Therefore, according to the principles articulated earlier for induction of syntactic classes, it attempts to parse this sentence by this path already existing through the network. This requires that it expand the RB1 word class to include *left-of.*

The first noun phrase, (A (LARGE(BLUE)) square ( )), can be parsed by the existing NP network (see Fig. 17), except that the DET word class (first arc of NP) must be expanded to include *a*. This noun phrase requires a push to the ADJP network to parse (LARGE (BLUE)). This cannot be parsed by the existing ADJP network (see Fig. 17). As indicated in Fig. 18b a second path is built through the ADJP network. The first arc on this path references the word class SIZE, which parses *large*. The second arc contains a push to another network, ADJPX, to parse *blue*. As we will see shortly, ADJPX is replaced by ADJP.

The second noun phrase should be parsed by NPX (see Fig. 17). However, it cannot do this without enlarging the NOUNX word class to include *square*. In contrast, the NP network will already successfully parse a noun phrase with *square*. This state of affairs is a stimulus for LAS to attempt to merge the NP and NPX networks. This it does, and it replaces NPX wherever it occurs in the grammar by NP. Another outcome of this merging is that the SHAPE word class is expanded to contain *circle* (from word class NOUNX in network NPX) as well as *square*. LAS has made a significant generalization here, namely, that the grammar that will handle first position noun phrases will also handle second position noun phrases.

The subexpression (SMALL (RED)) in the second noun phrase is to be handled by the ADJP network. The upper path through this network will handle this expression, except that the SIZE word class must be expanded to include *small*. The ADJP network will push to the ADJPX network (set up in parsing the first noun phrase of this sentence) to parse (RED). This will require expanding the word class in the ADJPX network, which so far includes only *blue*. In contrast, the second path through the ADJP network will parse this expression with no changes. This is the stimulus to merge the ADJPX and ADJP networks. Thus, as can be seen in Fig. 18b, the ADJP network involves a push to itself. Another consequence of the merging is that the COLOR word class is expanded to include *blue* as well as *red*.

Sentence 4

The effects of processing the fourth sentence are shown in Fig. 18c. This involves the relational term *right-of*, which takes subject noun phrase first. This can be handled by the lower path through the START network by expanding the RA1 word class to include *right-of*. Note that both noun phrases in this sentence contain adjectives of size. The first arc in the upper path through the ADJP network can parse these size adjectives, but that path expects a bracketed subexpression following the size terms. Therefore, a NIL arc is added to the ADJP network in Fig. 18c to allow size adjectives without subsequent color adjectives.

It is worth emphasizing how much generalization has occurred in the formation of the grammar after just four sentences. LAS has generalized to a grammar that will handle 5,184 sentences. Such generalizations are clearly required if LAS is going to go from a finite corpus to a grammar that covers many more sentences than it studied. Of course, just how rapid these generalizations are will depend on the exact sentences presented.

Sentence 5

The processing of the fifth sentence is illustrated in Fig. 18d. The highest level of bracketing consists of a bracketed subexpression, a nonmeaning-bearing morpheme, and an adjective. This is a new type of top-level structure. Therefore, an additional path is introduced through the START network. It is determined that the NP network can parse the first bracketed subexpression. Therefore, a push is made to the NP network on the first arc in this new path.

The noun phrase contains a relative clause — (WHICH IS ABOVE (THE (RED) CIRCLE ( )))). This is the first time there has been a nonnull expression to parse in the postpositional CLAUSE. Figure 18d shows the path grown through the CLAUSE network to accommodate this possibility. Note that in the CLAUSE network a push has been made to NP to parse (THE (RED) CIRCLE ( )). Thus, we have the first recursive structure in the network with NP calling CLAUSE, which calls NP. On the basis of one right-embedding, LAS has made the assumption that infinitely many right-embeddings are possible. As a consequence, the grammar has been generalized to the point where it will handle infinitely many sentences.

Sentences 6—11

The remaining sentences use further additions and generalizations of the same sort that have been discussed with respect to the first five sentences. Figure 19 shows the final network grammar induced, which is sufficient to handle all the sentences that can be generated by the grammar in Table 2. So LAS has achieved its goal. The arcs in Fig. 19 are labeled with the number of the sentence that caused them to be created.

The Paraphrase Test

As a test of the grammar induced in Fig. 19, I wrote a simple program, PARAPHRASE. It received a sentence and passed it to UNDERSTAND to build up a conceptualization of it. Then it selected a different topic for the paraphrase sentence. SPEAK was then called with this new topic. Here are a couple of examples of the paraphrases generated:

Original: The square is left-of the circle.
Paraphrase: A circle is right-of a square.

Original: The large square which is above the small circle is red.
Paraphrase: A circle which is below a large red square is small.

The French Example

Another language LAS II learned was the French subset defined in Table 3. I cannot personally vouch for the correctness of the grammar in Table 3. (My French informant assured me that the sentences were grammatical, but she giggled a lot at them.) The final grammar induced is given in Fig. 20. It follows the same conventions used in Fig. 19, where the parenthesized digit indicated the sentence that caused the formation of that rule. The induction history has little

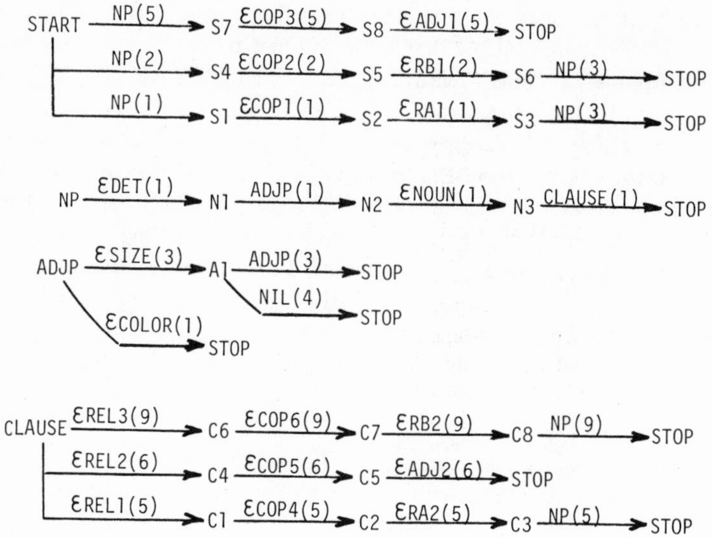

START $\xrightarrow{\text{NP(5)}}$ S7 $\xrightarrow{\mathcal{E}\text{COP3(5)}}$ S8 $\xrightarrow{\mathcal{E}\text{ADJ1(5)}}$ STOP

$\xrightarrow{\text{NP(2)}}$ S4 $\xrightarrow{\mathcal{E}\text{COP2(2)}}$ S5 $\xrightarrow{\mathcal{E}\text{RB1(2)}}$ S6 $\xrightarrow{\text{NP(3)}}$ STOP

$\xrightarrow{\text{NP(1)}}$ S1 $\xrightarrow{\mathcal{E}\text{COP1(1)}}$ S2 $\xrightarrow{\mathcal{E}\text{RA1(1)}}$ S3 $\xrightarrow{\text{NP(3)}}$ STOP

NP $\xrightarrow{\mathcal{E}\text{DET(1)}}$ N1 $\xrightarrow{\text{ADJP(1)}}$ N2 $\xrightarrow{\mathcal{E}\text{NOUN(1)}}$ N3 $\xrightarrow{\text{CLAUSE(1)}}$ STOP

ADJP $\xrightarrow{\mathcal{E}\text{SIZE(3)}}$ A1 $\xrightarrow{\text{ADJP(3)}}$ STOP
$\xrightarrow{\text{NIL(4)}}$ STOP
$\xrightarrow{\mathcal{E}\text{COLOR(1)}}$ STOP

CLAUSE $\xrightarrow{\mathcal{E}\text{REL3(9)}}$ C6 $\xrightarrow{\mathcal{E}\text{COP6(9)}}$ C7 $\xrightarrow{\mathcal{E}\text{RB2(9)}}$ C8 $\xrightarrow{\text{NP(9)}}$ STOP

$\xrightarrow{\mathcal{E}\text{REL2(6)}}$ C4 $\xrightarrow{\mathcal{E}\text{COP5(6)}}$ C5 $\xrightarrow{\mathcal{E}\text{ADJ2(6)}}$ STOP

$\xrightarrow{\mathcal{E}\text{REL1(5)}}$ C1 $\xrightarrow{\mathcal{E}\text{COP4(5)}}$ C2 $\xrightarrow{\mathcal{E}\text{RA2(5)}}$ C3 $\xrightarrow{\text{NP(5)}}$ STOP

```
COP1,COP2,COP3,COP4,COP5,COP6 = IS
ADJ1,ADJ2 = SMALL,LARGE,RED,BLUE
RA1,RA2 = ABOVE,RIGHT-OF
RB1,RB2 = BELOW,LEFT-OF
DET = A,THE
NOUN = SQUARE,CIRCLE
SIZE = LARGE,SMALL
COLOR = RED,BLUE
REL1,REL2,REL3 = WHICH
```

FIG. 19 The network induced by LAS II after studying the 11 English sentences in Table 2.

to reveal that was not already observed with respect to the English example. Therefore, I will not discuss it in detail.

Note that separate noun phrase grammars are induced for subject, NPS, and for object, NPO. These are not merged because they begin with different morphemes. The subject noun phrases begin with *le* and *un* while the object noun phrases begin with *du* and *d'un*. Actually, these object morphemes are contractions of the subject morphemes with the French *de*. However, LAS does not have the facility to detect these morphemic contractions. Nonetheless, an adequate, if less efficient, grammar is induced.

TABLE 3
The French Subset to Be Learned

Grammar

S	→ DET_s NP est Relation DET_o NP
S	→ DET_s NP est ADJ
NP	→ (Size) Shape (Color) (CLAUSE)
CLAUSE	→ qui est ADJ
	→ Relation DET_o NP
ADJ	→ Size
	→ Color
DET_s	→ le, un
DET_o	→ du, d'un
Relation	→ au-dessus, au-dessous, à-gauche, à-droit
Size	→ grand, petit
Color	→ bleu, rouge
Shape	→ carré, cercle

Sentences Studied

1. Le carré rouge est au-dessus du cercle rouge.
2. Le grand carré est au-dessous du petit cercle qui est rouge.
3. Le petit carré est à-droit du grand carré qui est bleu.
4. Un cercle qui est grand est à-gauche d'un cercle rouge.
5. Le carré est au-dessous d'un cercle qui est petit.
6. Le carré rouge est au-dessous d'un cercle rouge qui est petit.
7. Le cercle rouge à-gauche du cercle bleu est grand.
8. Le carré à-droit du carré est bleu.
9. Le cercle au-dessous du carré rouge est rouge.
10. Le cercle au-dessus du carré est petit.

The Translation Test

LAS, having learned the two languages, is now in a position to translate between the two. Translation is possible because synonymous words in the two languages are connected to the same idea node. So in the program TRANSLATE the French grammar might be used with the UNDERSTAND program to analyze a French sentence. UNDERSTAND creates a representation of the sentence in the HAM memory network. Then SPEAK is called with the English grammar to generate an English equivalent. The following are examples of translations from French to English and English to French:

(1)   Original: The red square is below the blue circle.
      Translation: Un carré au-dessous d'un cercle bleu est rouge.

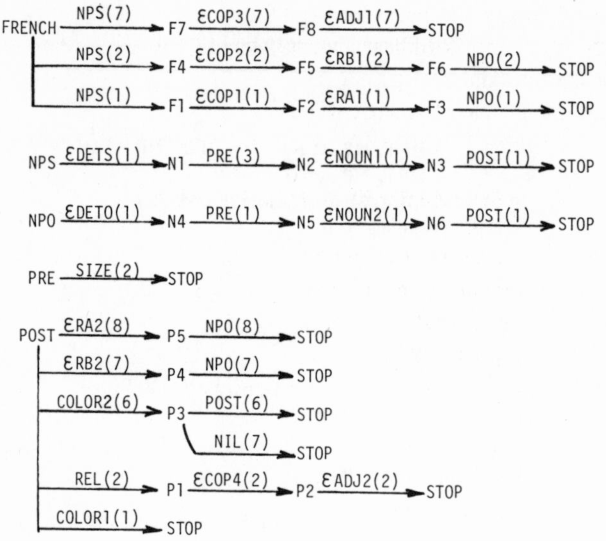

FRENCH $\xrightarrow{\text{NPS(7)}}$ F7 $\xrightarrow{\text{ECOP3(7)}}$ F8 $\xrightarrow{\text{EADJ1(7)}}$ STOP

$\xrightarrow{\text{NPS(2)}}$ F4 $\xrightarrow{\text{ECOP2(2)}}$ F5 $\xrightarrow{\text{ERB1(2)}}$ F6 $\xrightarrow{\text{NPO(2)}}$ STOP

$\xrightarrow{\text{NPS(1)}}$ F1 $\xrightarrow{\text{ECOP1(1)}}$ F2 $\xrightarrow{\text{ERA1(1)}}$ F3 $\xrightarrow{\text{NPO(1)}}$ STOP

NPS $\xrightarrow{\text{EDETS(1)}}$ N1 $\xrightarrow{\text{PRE(3)}}$ N2 $\xrightarrow{\text{ENOUN1(1)}}$ N3 $\xrightarrow{\text{POST(1)}}$ STOP

NPO $\xrightarrow{\text{EDETO(1)}}$ N4 $\xrightarrow{\text{PRE(1)}}$ N5 $\xrightarrow{\text{ENOUN2(1)}}$ N6 $\xrightarrow{\text{POST(1)}}$ STOP

PRE $\xrightarrow{\text{SIZE(2)}}$ STOP

POST $\xrightarrow{\text{ERA2(8)}}$ P5 $\xrightarrow{\text{NPO(8)}}$ STOP

$\xrightarrow{\text{ERB2(7)}}$ P4 $\xrightarrow{\text{NPO(7)}}$ STOP

$\xrightarrow{\text{COLOR2(6)}}$ P3 $\xrightarrow{\text{POST(6)}}$ STOP

$\xrightarrow{\text{NIL(7)}}$ STOP

$\xrightarrow{\text{REL(2)}}$ P1 $\xrightarrow{\text{ECOP4(2)}}$ P2 $\xrightarrow{\text{EADJ2(2)}}$ STOP

$\xrightarrow{\text{COLOR1(1)}}$ STOP

```
COP1,COP2,COP3,COP4 = EST
ADJ1,ADJ2 = ROUGE,BLEU,GRAND,PETIT
RB1,RB2 = A-GAUCHE,AU-DESSOUS
RA1,RA2 = A-DROIT,AU-DESSUS
DETS = LE,UN
DETO = DU,D'UN
NOUN1,NOUN2 = CARRE,CERCLE
SIZE = PETIT,GRAND
COLOR1,COLOR2 = BLEU,ROUGE
REL = QUI
```

FIG. 20 The network induced by LAS II after studying the 10 French sentences in Table 3.

(2)   Original: Le cercle rouge à-gauche du petit carré bleu est grand.
       Translation: A red circle which is left-of a small blue square is large.

(3)   Original: A square which is above a large blue square is below a small blue square.
       Translation: Un carré au-dessus d'un grand carré bleu est au-dessous d'un petit carré bleu.

Note that the translations are rather liberal. For instance, *red* is a modifier in (1) whereas *rouge* is a predicate. This is because SPEAK is only given the topic of the to-be-translated memory structure. It is not told which proposition is the main assertion and which propositions are subordinate. It would be easy to remedy this translation program. However, the point of the program was only to illustrate the adequacy of the induced grammars. One would hardly want to claim that these examples indicate that LAS has any immediate promise for language translation. The real problems in language translation arise when one must deal with much richer semantic domains.

SUMMARY EVALUATION OF LAS

The preceding examples serve to show that LAS can learn significant portions of natural language. It remains to be defined what is the class of languages that LAS can learn. I will argue that it can, in fact, learn at least the class of all context-free languages. However, this answer will prove to be less than satisfactory for two reasons. First, the learning program is sufficiently complex so that it is not possible to provide anything like a formal proof of the conjecture. Second, this characterization is purely syntactic, whereas we want some characterization that also takes semantics into account. That is, we would like to know what relations the program can learn between sentence and semantic referent.

My conjecture is that given any context-free language one could design a presentation sequence and semantics such that LAS could learn that language. I will describe the characteristics needed of the presentation sequence and semantics to achieve language learnability.

The presentation sequence must, obviously, consist of sentences and their semantic referents. There must be no grammatical mistakes in this sequence, and the sequence must give examples of all the grammatical structure in the language. It would be easy enough to construct such a presentation sequence. Also the semantics must satisfy the various constraints assumed by the heuristics for inducing surface structure and for making generalizations about syntactic classes (see discussion on pp. 326–344). I think it is possible to construct for any context-free language a semantics that satisfies these requirements. As noted many times these requirements are largely but not completely satisfied by the semantics associated with natural languages. This is one way that LAS is an incorrect model of natural language learning — it assumes more of the semantics of natural language than they provide. Second, LAS is inadequate because there are a few aspects of natural language (such as the *respectively* construction) that cannot be captured with a context-free grammar. The weaknesses of LAS on both these scores are sufficiently minor so that I am of the opinion that LAS-like learning mechanisms could serve as the basis for language learning with the addition of a few correcting procedures.

Criticisms of LAS

There are a number of other criticisms that can be made of LAS besides the fact that its mechanisms are not adequate for all of natural language. It is worth summarizing these.

Missing generalizations. As it stands now, the LAS program misses a number of important generalizations that one might think it should make. These can be seen by inspecting the grammar in Figure 19 that arose after learning the English subset. Note the redundancy within the START and CLAUSE networks. For instance, in the START network all the sentences begin in the form NP *is*. Therefore, it would seem more efficient if the different branches in the START network were merged to obtain a network of the following form:

$$
\text{START} \xrightarrow{\text{NP}} \text{S1} \xrightarrow{\in \text{COP1}} \text{S2}
\begin{array}{l}
\xrightarrow{\in \text{ADJ1}} \text{STOP} \\
\xrightarrow{\in \text{RB1}} \text{S3} \xrightarrow{\quad \text{NP} \quad} \text{STOP} \\
\xrightarrow{\in \text{RA1}} \text{S4} \xrightarrow{\quad \text{NP} \quad} \text{STOP}
\end{array}
$$

One of the reasons this generalization did not occur is that the first noun phrase corresponds to either logical object or subject in the underlying construction dependent on the subsequent relation word. LAS currently assigns a semantic interpretation corresponding to a noun phrase as soon as it parses it. Therefore, different branches are required so that the noun phrase may be assigned the different subject and object interpretation. A structure like the one just presented would be possible only if semantic interpretation were delayed until the relational word.

Another point of potential generalization is that the network START for the main clause and the network CLAUSE for the relative clause have marked similarities that are not being capitalized upon. LAS will not merge two networks unless one is completely a subset of another. START begins with an NP while CLAUSE has the initial element *which*. To detect partial overlap, the program that performs network merging would have to note the similarity in the networks after the first element. In general, every time LAS tried to parse an element by one arc, it would have to consider whether other arcs could also parse the element.

Another missed generalization has to do with the fact that the same words that are occurring as predicate adjectives are occurring as prenominal adjectives. However, different word classes have been set up for the word occurring in the two positions. There is also reduplication of the COP word class, the RA word class, and the RB word class. Both detection of common word classes and partial network overlap are projected goals for later versions of the LAS program.

Augmented transition networks are too powerful. Augmented transition networks (ATNs) come with a control structure for recursion, backtracking, and other such operations that are much more powerful in their information-processing capabilities than the human system is. I have elaborated on this problem at length in Anderson (1976). The consequence is that ATNs make unreasonable predictions such as that center-embedded sentences will be as easy to process as right-embedded sentences. Another problem with ATNs is that they are too strongly designed to take advantage of phrase structure grammar. As a consequence, it is very difficult, although not impossible, to deal with discontinuous elements. One would like a processing formalism that shares with ATNs the advantages of modularity, but does not make unrealistic assumptions about human information-processing capacity and is not irretrievably committed to phrase structure analysis. I think I have found such a processing formalism in a production system that is remarkably like ATNs. This production system formalism is described in Anderson (1976). My current work on language acquisition is using that formalism.

Impoverished semantics. The semantics of LAS's two-dimensional geometric world is too simple in a number of important ways. The relational terms are all binary. It is important to show that LAS can deal with multiargument terms like *buy*. Also one would want to see LAS deal with sentence types other than simple declaratives. The interesting feature about sentence types like questions and imperatives is that the semantic intentions that lead to the production of such sentences seem quite different from the semantic intentions that result from comprehending the sentences. The intention behind uttering "Please pass the salt" involves a desire for the salt, while the intentions resulting from comprehending the sentence may be a procedure to pass the salt. It does not seem that LAS's reversible networks for production and comprehension will be adequate for these aspects of natural language, which are more concerned with *procedural* semantics.

No mechanisms for error recovery. As LAS stands, it has no mechanisms for recovering from incorrect rules it might form owing to overgeneralizations or incorrect input sentences. The production system learning program currently deals with this problem by associating a strength with each rule in the system. All rules initially enter the system in a very weak state and become strong only after repeated use. This prevents the occasional incorrect sentence from setting up permanent incorrect rules. Rules resulting from overgeneralization could be overcome by accruing strength to the correct, more particular rule. Brown (1973) notes that the acquisition of certain grammatical morphemes (e.g., 's for pluralization) appears to have a gradual course. Over a period of time the child comes more and more to use the morpheme in the correct context. There is not a sudden all-or-none appearance of the morpheme. This suggests that the grammatical rule is acquired by a gradual strengthening process.

Information-processing limitations. The current LAS system is not affected by sentence length. In fact, the longer the sentence, the more constructions LAS can learn from studying it. This conflicts sharply with human performance. LAS has been given too powerful an information-processing capacity in the interest of getting the program to work. For one thing, the program should show limitations of immediate memory.

A clear manifestation of LAS's excessive information-processing capacity is the fact that it initially produces and comprehends complete sentences. Its grammar will at first handle only a rather narrow range of sentences, but all these sentences are complete. In contrast, children learning the language initially speak in short, incomplete utterances. There is no evidence available as to how adults will perform in free learning situations, but there is every reason to suspect that they would show the same truncated speech style.

Left-to-right processing. Another aspect of the LAS system that is unrealistic psychologically is that it processes sentences during learning in a top-down fashion, rather than a left-to-right fashion. First, it takes in the whole sentence; then it performs a bracketing of the whole sentence; then it checks the top level of the bracketing for compatibility with the main network; then it will check the leftmost noun phrase network for compatibility; and so forth. Thus, it will have processed the whole sentence at the top level many times before it comes to deciding whether the first word in the sentence can be processed by the noun phrase grammar. The reason LAS was given this top-down structure is that it is easier to make local decisions after more global decisions have been made. However, a psychologically realistic learning algorithm will have to work in a more left-to-right manner.

CONCLUSION

As claimed in the introduction to this chapter, the LAS II system has taken us closer to the goal of a mechanistic model for language acquisition. There remains much to be done before this goal will be achieved.

ACKNOWLEDGMENTS

This research is supported by Grants GB-40298 from NSF and MH26383 from NIMH. I would like to thank Clayton Lewis for much advice and suggestion about the conceptual issues involved in this research. Rebecca Paulson performed the experiments and data analyses reported.

REFERENCES

Anderson, J. R. *Language acquisition by computer and child.* Human Performance Center Technical Report No. 55, Ann Arbor, Michigan, 1974.
Anderson, J. R. Computer simulation of a language-acquisition system. In R. L. Solso (Ed.), *Information processing and cognition: The Loyola Symposium.* Hillsdale, N.J.: Lawrence Erlbaum Associates, 1975.

Anderson, J. R. *Language, memory, and thought.* Hillsdale, N.J.: Lawrence Erlbaum Associates, 1976.

Anderson, J. R., & Bower, G. H. *Human associative memory.* Washington, D.C.: Winston, 1973.

Bever, T. G. The cognitive bases for linguistic structures. In J. R. Hayes (Ed.), *Cognition and the development of language.* New York: Wiley, 1970.

Biermann, A. W. An interactive finite-state language learner. Paper presented at First USA–Japan Computer Conference, 1972.

Biermann, A. W., & Feldman, J. A. A survey of results in grammatical inference. In S. Watanabe (Ed.), *Frontiers of pattern recognition.* New York: Academic Press, 1972.

Bloom, L. M. *Language development: Form and function in emerging grammars.* Cambridge, Mass.: MIT Press, 1970.

Bloom, L. M. *One word at a time.* The Hague: Mouton, 1973.

Bowerman, M. Structural relationships in children's utterances: Syntactic or semantic? In T. E. Moore (Ed.), *Cognitive development and the acquisition of language.* New York: Academic Press, 1973.

Braine, M. D. S. On two types of models of the internalization of grammars. In D. I. Slobin (Ed.), *The ontogenesis of grammar.* New York: Academic Press, 1971.

Brown, R. *A first language.* Cambridge, Mass.: Harvard University Press, 1973.

Chomsky, N. *Syntactic structures.* The Hague: Mouton, 1957.

Chomsky, N. Explanatory models in linguistics. In E. Nagel, P. Suppes, & A. Tarski (Eds.), *Logic, methodology and philosophy of science: Proceedings of the 1960 International Congress.* Stanford, Calif.: Stanford University Press, 1962.

Chomsky, N. *Aspects of the theory of syntax.* Cambridge, Mass.: MIT Press, 1965.

Chomsky, N., & Miller, G. A. Introduction to the formal analysis of natural languages. In R. D. Luce, R. R. Bush, & E. Galanter (Eds.), *Handbook of mathematical psychology,* Vol. II. New York: Wiley, 1963.

Clark, E. V. What's in a word? On the child's acquisition of semantics in his first language. In T. E. Moore (Ed.), *Cognitive development and the acquisition of language.* New York: Academic Press, 1973.

Clark, E. V. Non-linguistic strategies and the acquisition of word meanings. *Cognition: International Journal of Cognitive Psychology,* 1973, **2**, 161–182.

Clark, E. V. First language acquisition. To appear in J. Morton and J. C. Marshall (Eds.), *Psycholinguistics Series.* London: Paul Elek (Scientific Books), 1975.

Ervin, S. M. Imitation and structural change in children's language. In E. H. Lennenberg (Ed.), *New Directions in the Study of Language.* Cambridge, Mass.: MIT Press, 1964, 163–189.

Ferguson, C. A., Peizer, D. B., & Weeks, T. E. Model-and-replica phonological grammar of a child's first words. *Lingua,* 1973, **31**, 35–65.

Fernald, C. Children's active and passive knowledge of syntax. Paper presented to the Midwestern Psychological Association, 1970.

Fraser, C., Bellugi, U., & Brown, R. Control of grammar in imitation, comprehension, and production. *Journal of Verbal Learning and Verbal Behavior,* 1963, **2**, 121–135.

Gold, E. M. Language identification in the limit. *Information and Control,* 1967, **10**, 447–474.

Hafner, C., & Wilcox, B. *LISP: MTS programmer's manual.* Mental Health Research Communication 302 and Information Processing Paper 21, University of Michigan, 1974.

Hunt, E. B. *Artificial intelligence.* New York: Academic Press, 1975.

Kaplan, R. A general syntactic processor. In R. Rustin (Ed.), *Natural language processing.* Englewood Cliffs, N.J.: Prentice-Hall, 1973.

Klein, S. *Automatic inference of semantic deep structure rules in generative semantic grammars* Technical Report #180, Computer Sciences Department, University of Wisconsin, Madison: May, 1973.

Lenneberg, E. H. Understanding language without ability to speak: A case report. *Journal of Abnormal and Social Psychology,* 1962, 65, 419–425.

McNeill, D. Semiotic extension. In R. L. Solso (Ed.), *Information processing and cognition: The Loyola Symposium.* Hillsdale, N.J.: Lawrence Erlbaum Associates, 1975.

Moeser, S. D., & Bregman, A. S. The role of reference in the acquisition of a miniature artificial language. *Journal of Verbal Learning and Verbal Behavior,* 1972, 11, 759–769.

Moeser, S. D., & Bregman, A. S. Imagery and language acquisition. *Journal of Verbal Learning and Verbal Behavior,* 1973, 12, 91–98.

Nelson, K. Concept, word, and sentence: Interrelations in acquisition and development. *Psychological Review,* 1974, 81, 267–285.

Norman, D. A., Rumelhart, D. E., & the LNR Research Group. *Explorations in cognition.* San Francisco: Freeman, 1975.

Schank, R. C. Conceptual dependency: A theory of natural language understanding. *Cognitive Psychology,* 1972, 3, 552–631.

Schlesinger, I. M. Production of utterances and language acquisition. In D. I. Slobin (Ed.), *The ontogenesis of grammar.* New York: Academic Press, 1971.

Siklóssy, L. Natural language learning by computer. In H. A. Simon & L. Siklóssy (Eds.), *Representation and meaning: Experiments with information processing systems.* Englewood Cliffs, N.J.: Prentice-Hall, 1972.

Sinclair-de Zwart, H. Language acquisition and cognitive development. In T. E. Moore (Ed.), *Cognitive development and the acquisition of language.* New York: Academic Press, 1973.

Slobin, D. I. *The ontogenesis of grammar.* New York: Academic Press, 1971.

Slobin, D. I. Cognitive prerequisites for the development of grammar. In C. A. Ferguson & D. I. Slobin (Eds.), *Studies of child language development.* New York: Holt, Rinehart, and Winston, 1973. Pp. 175–208.

Winograd, T. Understanding natural language. *Cognitive Psychology,* 1972, 3, 1–191.

Woods, W. A. Transition network grammars for natural language analysis. *Communications of the ACM,* 1970, 13, 591–606.

Author Index

Numbers in *italics* refer to the pages on which the complete references are listed.

Subject Index